Philosophy and Its History

SUNY Series in
PHILOSOPHY

George R. Lucas, Jr., Editor

Philosophy and Its History

Issues in Philosophical Historiography

Jorge J. E. Gracia

STATE UNIVERSITY OF NEW YORK PRESS

Production by Ruth East
Marketing by Theresa A. Swierzowski

Published by
State University of New York Press, Albany

Printed in the United States of America

For information, address State University of New York Press, State University Plaza, Albany, N.Y. 12246

Library of Congress Cataloging-in-Publication Data

Gracia, Jorge J. E.
Philosophy and its history : issues in philosophical historiography / Jorge J. E. Gracia.
p. cm. — (SUNY series in philosophy)
Includes bibliographical references and indexes.
ISBN 0–7914–0817–5 (alk. paper) . — ISBN 0–7914–0818–3 (pbk. : alk. paper)
1. Philosophy—Historiography. I. Title. II. Series.
B51.4.G72 1992
109—dc20

90–24213
CIP

10 9 8 7 6 5 4 3 2 1

The earliest philosophy is, on all subjects, like one who lisps, since it is young and in its beginnings.

Aristotle, *Metaphysics* A, ch. 9, 993a15

The historical sense involves a perception, not only of the pastness of the past, but of its presence.

T. S. Eliot, "Tradition and the Individual Talent"

The history of philosophy is the *lingua franca* which makes communication between philosophers, at least of different points of view, possible. Philosophy without the history of philosophy, if not empty or blind, is at least dumb.

Wilfrid Sellars, Ch. 1, *Science and Metaphysics*

Brief Contents

Long Contents

Preface

My longstanding interest in the relation of philosophy to its history came to a head as a result of the NEH-sponsored conference, Doing Philosophy Historically, organized by Peter H. Hare in Buffalo in 1987. Having been asked to write a paper relevant to the conference theme, I began to pull together my thoughts systematically about the relationship between philosophy and its history. Some of the resulting ideas were published in the conference's proceedings, but I felt dissatisfied with the amount of ground I had been able to cover; just too many questions and unresolved issues seemed pressing. After the conference I continued to think about those issues and found that, in the best of cases, I had only partial answers to them and, in the worst, I had been functioning under inconsistent assumptions. I realized that, after nearly a quarter of a century of writing and thinking about philosophy and the history of philosophy, I was in the position of what Aristotle described as an "experienced" person. That is, my situation was similar to that of a cook who is successful in producing tasty dishes and thus can be said to have the skill of cooking but at the same time cannot tell us how he does it or why he is successful at it. As a philosopher and historian of philosophy, I was accustomed to dealing with philosophical issues more or less effectively, and likewise with matters related to the history of philosophy, but I could neither describe the procedure I followed nor give the reasons why it worked. More shocking still, I had no clear view of the exact nature of the relation between philosophy and its history, or of the value that my historical work had for the advancement of philosophy, even though I constantly mixed philosophy and its history in my writing, thinking, and teaching. In short, Aristotle would have said, had he been able to judge my predicament, that I had knowledge of neither the art nor the science of the subject matter in question: I was no better, as a practitioner of philosophy and the history of philosophy, than a cook unschooled in the art of cooking, let alone the science of culinary taste.

But this was not all. I realized also that my problem was not unique. The vast majority of philosophers use the history of philosophy not only for teaching purposes, but also as a point of departure of their own philosophical reflection. Indeed, some may want to argue that all philosophers deal with the history of philosophy from the moment they reflect on some past thought or idea. And, since once a thought or an idea has been proposed or even entertained its recollection implies that it is part of the past, it turns out that philosophical reflection is inextricably tied to the reflection on the history of philosophy. Accordingly, no philosopher can escape the history of philosophy.

Of course, this position is somewhat extreme. It is not clear that, once a thought or an idea has been proposed, let alone just entertained, it automatically becomes part of what is considered the history of philosophy. But one need not hold this extreme position to see how most philosophers use the history of philosophy in their philosophical activity. They do so in at least two cases: First, when they deal with problems and their solutions they frequently attribute the formulations of and solutions to those problems, at least in part, to historical figures. Second, when they teach philosophy, the texts they use are usually historical texts, often regarded as masterpieces of philosophical writing. In either case, philosophers use the history of philosophy when they practice their profession.

Yet, many philosophers appear unaware of the philosophical issues raised by the uses and practices in which they engage when they deal with the history of philosophy. Their position in that respect is very similar to the one in which I found myself before I began to reflect on the historiographical issues raised by the relationship between philosophy and its history.

Through these considerations I arrived at the conclusion that I needed, mostly for my own benefit and peace of mind, but also out of a sense of professional honesty, to address the issues raised by the relation between philosophy and its history. It was just not possible to continue practicing and claiming to practice both, as I wished and continued to do, without a considered examination of those issues. The result of my attempt to address those issues is this book.

Before I proceed to give a brief synopsis of the contents of the book, I would like to clarify a couple of methodological points in order that its readers may be able to understand better what I set out to do in it and how I set out to do it. The first point is that I did not intend to write a history of philosophical historiography. Although I discuss in this book various views that can be attributed to historical authors, I have not concerned myself with the historical dimension of those views. The discussions contained in the text are philosophical insofar as they deal with problems and issues that I take to be philosophically important or at least interesting and with the solutions to those problems that I consider best articulated from a philosophical standpoint. Consequently, it would be a mistake to try to apply to this book or the methodology it employs the kind of criteria that should be applied to historical studies.

I do not mean to imply in any way, however, that a history of philosophical historiography is useless or that it has nothing to do with the subject matter treated here. Indeed, I believe that the history of philosophical historiography is as useful to philosophical historiography as the history of philosophy is to philosophy. And for that reason I frequently refer both to the history of philosophy and the history of philosophical historiography throughout the book. But my main concern has not been historical, a fact that has allowed me to take certain liberties with the sources I use that I would otherwise not have felt free to take.

The second point I would like to make clear at the outset is that the intent of this book is both descriptive and normative. It is descriptive insofar as the point of departure of the book is the historiographical practices in which I have been engaged for many years. The book is rooted, then, in my practice as a historian, in those habits, procedures, and uses into which I have been immersed for over a quarter of a century. This is the reason why the book uses examples that refer back to that practice. I have proceeded in this way because it seemed to me that historiography, like science, is very much a matter of procedure and, therefore, just as the philosopher of science ought to be in close touch with the practice of science, so ought the philosophical historiographer keep in close touch with the practices involved in doing history of philosophy.

But the book does not stop at description. It moves away from description in order to establish what I believe are the norms that should guide philosophical historiography. I am perfectly aware that normative programs are quite unfashionable these days. Descriptivism rather than prescriptivism has been in the air for many years and for many valid and important reasons. There is a salutary and general tendency toward tolerance and a suspicion among intellectuals in particular of anything that smacks of ideology, absolutism, dogmatism, and intransigence. This tendency to reject absolutes of any sorts is evident both in Anglo-American and Continental philosophy. Nonetheless, I have found that in order to deal with the various problems that come up in philosophical historiography one must begin by formulating views, examining their value, and moving on to those that seem more acceptable. As a result I have found myself adopting and defending normative principles concerning not only the understanding of the history of philosophy but also its practice. I do not claim, however, to have any undeniable proofs for them. Nor am I dogmatically attached to them in spite of the strong language I sometimes use in their support. On the contrary, I regard the views I defend here as tentative proposals and the chapters of this book should be seen as probing essays rather than scientific reports on the results of exhaustive investigations.

The book contains two main theses. One belongs to philosophical historiography, for it concerns the methodology of doing history of philosophy. The other is closer to the philosophy of history and involves both an interpretation of the reasons behind the current state of philosophy and a suggestion as to how to influence the future historical development of the discipline. The first and primary thesis is that the history of philosophy must be done philosophically. The second thesis is secondary. It claims, first, that Kant's influence is largely responsible for initiating the process that would eventually result in the current estrangement between the Anglo-American and Continental philosophical traditions; and, second, that one way to bring about a rapprochement between these traditions is through the study of the history of philosophy and its historiography. The first thesis is presented and defended in Chapters One to Six. The second functions as a fold within which the historiographical investigations contained in those chapters are enclosed, providing a philosophical locus and justification for them. It is presented in the Introduction, and Chapters One to Six constitute an indirect argument for it whose significance I try to bring into focus in the Conclusion.

In the Introduction I present my claim that we are at a very important juncture in the history of Western philosophy, in which the study of the history of philosophy and the historiographical issues that its relation to philosophy pose may help to overcome the impasse that has developed between the Anglo-American and the Continental philosophical traditions. This is the most personal and unsubstantiated part of the book. It involves a very individual and intuitive view concerning the overall historical development of philosophy and the current state of the discipline, as well as a prescription for what must be done in order to move philosophy forward. I do not claim to provide any definitive arguments for this position in the Introduction. As already noted, the historiographical chapters of the book provide such justification, albeit indirect, for it. Those readers who find the Introduction too loose and personal for their taste should move quickly to the first chapter, where the more careful and argumentative style that characterizes the rest of the text begins.

The six chapters that follow the Introduction constitute the body of the book proper. They address six issues in the historiography of philosophy that stand out most sharply when one begins to think about the relation of philosophy to its history: (1) the nature of the history of philosophy, (2) the relation of philosophy to its history, (3) the justification and value of the history of philosophy, (4) the nature of texts and their interpretation, (5) the methodology of doing history of philosophy, and (6) the way in which philosophy develops and progresses. The function of these chapters is to present and defend the overall historiographical thesis of this book, namely, that the history of philosophy must be done philosophically. By 'must' I mean not only that it is inevitable, but also that it is desirable. The defense of this thesis entails the following: (1) explaining what it means in detail, (2) showing that contrary views are unacceptable, (3) presenting arguments in its favor, and (4) providing a blueprint of how the history of philosophy is to be done. I carry out the first three tasks directly in Chapters One and Two, and indirectly in Chapters Three, Four, and Six. Chapter Five takes up a different task: It shows how the history of philosophy can be objective in spite of its philosophical character.

The first chapter proceeds by exploring the natures of history, philosophy, and the history of philosophy. It discusses also the thorny issues concerned with the translation of the past into the present, the matter of its interpretation, and the legitimacy of making evaluative judgments, particularly truth value judgments, in the history of philosophy. In it I try to show how interpretation and evaluation are essential to the history of philosophy, and therefore that the history of philosophy must be done philosophically.

The second chapter completes the argument begun in the first chapter in favor of a philosophical understanding of the history of philosophy. In contrast with views supported by substantial numbers of historiographers, it proposes that, although philosophy does not require the study of its history, philosophy is indispensable for doing history of philosophy.

Having established that philosophy is essential to the history of philosophy, although the history of philosophy is not essential to philosophy, it is necessary to address the question of the usefulness of the history of philosophy for philosophy. This is carried out in the third chapter, where I examine the various justifications for the use of the history of philosophy in philosophy, that is, for "doing philosophy historically." My thesis in it is not only that there are pragmatic, pedagogical, and therapeutic reasons for doing philosophy historically, but that there are important theoretical reasons as well, related to the cultural nature and aims of the discipline. This chapter provides indirect support for the philosophical nature of the history of philosophy by showing that the value of the history of philosophy lies precisely in its philosophical character.

The fourth chapter goes back to a difficult issue raised in the first chapter but left unresolved there. It concerns the immediate object of study of the historian of philosophy, namely, philosophical texts, and their interpretation, and the role that the author and the audience play in that interpretation. This area has received considerable attention in Continental philosophical literature and raises important historiographical issues. The overall thesis of the chapter is that texts are collections of signs arranged in various ways in order to convey certain meanings to an audience and that textual interpretations are texts meant to produce acts of understanding similar to those that both the author and the contemporaneous audience of the text were supposed to have. The need for interpretation in order to recover the meaning of historical texts again adds support, although indirectly, to the general thesis of the book that the history of philosophy must be done philosophically.

Having examined the difficulties related to the interpretation of texts and other factors that play a role in the production of the historical account of the philosophical past, I need to turn to the question of how to do the history of philosophy philosophically, that is, the methodology in the investigation of the history of philosophy. This is done in the fifth chapter, where several historiographical approaches are examined and evaluated on the way to the formulation of what I argue is the most effective approach, which I call the *framework approach.* This long, taxonomic chapter is meant to be of use in particular for those who have a strong interest in methodology.

The sixth chapter addresses what I believe is an important source of error in historical accounts, namely, the lack of understanding of the various historical stages of development of philosophical ideas. It is intended as a concrete illustration of the role philosophy plays and should play in the study of the history of philosophy. By presenting a philosophy of the development of philosophical ideas and of progress and showing how the understanding of such development and progress is essential for the production of accurate historical accounts of the philosophical past, this chapter gives added support to the thesis that the history of philosophy must be done philosophically. For, if a philosophy of the development of philosophical ideas is indispensible in order to account for them, it is obvious that philosophy must play a role in such an account. I should add that, like the Introduction, this chapter is highly speculative and should not be taken as an indispensible building block of the main argument developed in the book.

Finally, in the concluding remarks I return to the thesis presented in the Introduction, pulling together the conclusions at which I have arrived in the course of previous chapters and indicating how the analyses I have provided should serve as bases for the establishment of dialogue between Anglo-American and Continental philosophers. Whether they in fact do, remains to be seen. As noted earlier, I do not attempt to demonstrate explicitly how the study of the history of philosophy and philosophical historiography are instrumental in building a bridge between Continentalists and analysts. That would require much more than I can do in a book where the primary focus is something else, namely, the defense of a philosophical conception of doing history of philosophy. But, if the historiographical issues I raise and discuss here prove of interest to both analytic and Continental philosophers, I will have achieved my secondary aim, for I will have shown in practical terms that philosophical historiography can serve as a common ground of operation and as a basis for communication for philosophers of both traditions. Still remaining would be the task of showing how the study of the history of philosophy itself could bring about a similar result. But that task would involve much more than I can or should do here. For it would require not only doing some history of philosophy, but also some history and philosophy of what both analytic and Continental historians of philosophy have done with it.

In closing, I would like to thank all those who have helped me in the preparation of this book. Peter Hare is entirely to blame for having organized the event that prompted me to begin thinking systematically about the issues contained in this book and, therefore, should be held at least indirectly responsible for its existence. Moreover, once a draft of the manuscript was produced and he saw it, he encouraged me to proceed with the project, providing advice about various aspects of the manuscript that have substantially improved it. I must also thank him and Prometheus Books for allowing me to use parts of the article "Philosophy and Its History: Veatch's *Aristotle*," which originally appeared in Hare, ed., *Doing Philosophy Historically* (New York, 1988), pp. 92–116. A Spanish version of part of the article was published by *Revista Latinoamericana de Filosofía* 13 (1987), pp. 259–278 and I also thank the editor, Ezequiel de Olaso, for his permission. I have used materials from that article in Chapters One and Two of this book, although most of the borrowed materials have been modified substantially. I am also indebted to Jude Dougherty for allowing me to use parts of "Texts and Their Interpretation," *The Review of Metaphysics* 49 (1990): 495–542, in Chapter Four. I also should add that some of the ideas contained in Chapter Six were first presented in "The Centrality of the Individual in the Philosophy of the Fourteenth Century," *History of Philosophy Quarterly* 8 (1991).

I am also grateful to many others. Kenneth Barber and George Allan read the manuscript with gusto and raised fundamental issues that forced me to rethink many parts of the text and introduce substantial changes in it. Ky Herreid, Derek Heyman, John Kronen, Timothy Madigan, Jane Miller, and Hyuryun Park took my seminar in philosophical historiography in the spring semester of 1989 and gave me no rest during the term, making the seminar the kind of pleasurable experience that I have seldom encountered in my twenty-odd years of teaching. Parts of the book reflect in many ways the discussions that were carried on in class as well as the questions the students raised concerning the draft of the book I circulated among them. Ky Herreid is responsible for compiling much of the bibliography that appears at the end of the volume, and, as my research assistant for part of the period when I was preparing the manuscript, he proved invaluable for scanning some of the literature, for discussing with me various ideas before I set them down in writing, and for offering suggestions and criticisms of various drafts of the manuscript. He also helped to get the notes in proper format. Timothy Madigan was quite industrious. He read the complete manuscript carefully and made many useful suggestions. I am especially indebted to him in the part of the Introduction where I discuss various objections to my view. Derek Heyman brought to my attention the second sense of 'dialectical' discussed in Chapter Five; and Kronen, Miller, and Park came up with many useful examples throughout the semester. In addition Michael Gorman helped with proofreading the manuscript and made several substantive suggestions.

I also profited from discussions with Carlos Bazán, Yvon Lafrance, and David Raynor during a visit to Ottawa; with R. M. Hare, Robert D'Amico, and Ofelia Schutte during a visit to Florida; with Eduardo Rabossi and Alejandro Tomasini during a visit to Mexico; and from comments on the Introduction by Barry Smith and on Chapter Four by Carolyn Korsmeyer and Joseph Margolis. I had several conversations that were beneficial with John Corcoran concerning ontogeny and phylogeny and with John Kearns concerning parts of Chapter Four. Moreover, Dominick LaCapra had some useful criticisms concerning the overall theses and approach of the book. To Georg Iggers and Kah Kyung Cho I am indebted for their presentations at my seminar, which sparked some ideas and helped with the research. Newton Garver and Robert Bertholf brought to my attention various pertinent bibliographical items. Finally, Marie Fleischauer, with her usual patience, good humor, unbounded diligence, and unrivaled expertise, is ultimately responsible for the preparation of most of the manuscript. To all those mentioned, and many others who have helped me think about the issues discussed in this book, I will be forever indebted.

Jorge J. E. Gracia

Introduction: The History of Philosophy and the Future of Philosophy

A look at the history of philosophy from Thales to the present reveals three fundamental traditions. I call them *mainstream, poetic,* and *critical.* These traditions have dominated the philosophical development of the West throughout its history. What distinguishes them is not so much the substantive ideas they hold concerning the world, although indeed there are some such differences among them. Rather, the most fundamental differences that set them apart have to do with the way the philosophers who belong to them approach their task as philosophers and with the views and assumptions they hold concerning the very nature of that task. The differences, therefore, have more to do with goals and to a certain extent with methodology, the more formal aspects of philosophy, than with its substance. Yet, these differences are so profound and affect philosophers so drastically that they determine in many ways, if not the details, at least the sorts of views that philosophers hold.

In this Introduction I propose to examine these three traditions briefly, uncovering their fundamental assumptions about philosophy and its methodology. My most general claim is that the mainstream tradition held sway over philosophy until Kant, but that Kant's attack on its presuppositions launched in the *Critique of Pure Reason* (1781) pushed the mainstream tradition to the sidelines and opened the way for the dominance of the poetic tradition in Continental Europe and of the critical tradition in the Anglo-Saxon world. Note that I do not claim that every country in Continental Europe experiences the uncontested dominance of the poetic tradition. Nor do I wish to maintain that there are no exponents of that tradition in the Anglo-Saxon world. My claim is that in general the poetic tradition takes center stage in Europe and the critical tradition does so in English-speaking countries.[1] Moreover, I also claim that this division of the philosophical world into two opposing traditions is responsible for the kind of impasse that philosophy has reached today. My second, and more specific, thesis is both a prescription for a remedy and a justification for this book: a return to the serious study of the history of philosophy and the historiographical problems that such a study raises. Let me begin, then, with the first tradition mentioned.

I. THE MAINSTREAM TRADITION

The *mainstream tradition,* as its name suggests, counted with the largest number of adherents as well as the most influential philosophers in the history of Western philosophy until Kant. This is the tradition within which Parmenides, Plato, Aristotle, Augustine, Averroes, Aquinas, Suárez, Descartes, Leibniz, and Locke, among many others, worked. In general, these philosophers held the view that the primary function of philosophy is to know and describe what there is, and they believed that for the most part the natural faculties possessed by human beings, namely reason and perception, were effective for the accomplishment of their task.

This attitude is eminently displayed in Aristotle's *Metaphysics,* where he begins with the well-known saying: "All men by nature desire to know." This is quickly followed by a schematic description of how knowledge develops, beginning with sensation and memory and ending with wisdom. Then he proceeds to identify the marks of the wise man:

> We suppose first, then, that the wise man knows all things, as far as possible...; secondly, that he who can learn things that are difficult, and not easy for man to know, is wise...; again, that he who is more exact and more capable of teaching the causes is wiser, in every branch of knowledge; and that of the sciences, also, that which is desirable on its own account and for the sake of knowing it is more of the nature of Wisdom than that which is desirable on account of its results....[2]

Scientific knowledge for Aristotle is not only possible, but is also a natural aim of human beings; and it is knowledge, conceived in rigorous and nonutilitarian terms, that occupies the highest position.

The marks of rigor are supplied in detail in the *Posterior Analytics*, where Aristotle discusses the different types of knowledge and specifies the requirements of scientific, that is, demonstrative, knowledge. Given this view, it comes as no surprise that metaphysics occupies the highest position in the hierarchy of the sciences.

Neither Aristotle nor other members of the mainstream saw their function *qua* philosophers as fundamentally different from that of those involved in the pursuit of science. Indeed, until the eighteenth century the word 'science' (*scientia*, from *scio*, to know) was commonly used to refer to philosophy as well as to what today we refer to as the *natural sciences*, and the word 'philosophy' was used to refer to the natural sciences as well as to philosophy. The uses of 'science' and 'philosophy' in these rather broad, if measured by contemporary usage, senses go back to the Middle Ages, although their ultimate bases are to be found in ancient Greek thought.[3] These uses can be easily illustrated in the philosophical and scientific literature of various times before Kant. Newton, for example, thought that he was doing philosophy in his *Philosophiae naturalis principia mathematica* (1687) and Descartes thought he was doing science in *Le discours de la méthode* (1637).

Many mainstream pre-Kantians held also that there are some limitations to the human natural capacity to know, but they did not believe that such limitations necessitated fundamental changes in the mode of philosophical inquiry or invalidated all the conclusions reached in philosophical discourse. Because of their emphasis on trying to know and describe what there is, the central core of these individuals' philosophical thought, as we saw with Aristotle, usually was taken up by metaphysics. They did discuss issues related to other branches of philosophy, of course. And many of them in fact were led to metaphysics as a way of solving ethical and other problems, as is clear in the case of Plato. Most of them had also methodological and epistemic concerns that led them to deal with logical matters and with the nature of language. This was quite evident in modern philosophy. Descartes, in particular, dramatized the importance of epistemic and methodological issues and set out explicitly to devise a method that would yield truth and certainty. But at no time did he put into question that the primary function of philosophy is to know what there is or the human capacity to know and to do so with certainty. His program was meant only to correct what he considered to be the inadequate philosophical methodology of the scholastics. His well-known "doubt" was instrumental rather than final and its primary function was to ensure that the piece of knowledge that survives it is established with absolute certainty. The human capacity to know and the effectiveness of human faculties in knowing the real world, then, were not put into question; questions were raised only about the method we must use to make the best of the powers we have. As he put it at the beginning of the *Discourse:*

> Good sense is, of all things among men, the most equally distributed; for everyone thinks himself so abundantly provided with it, that those even who are the most difficult to satisfy in everything else, do not usually desire a larger measure of this quality than they already possess. And in this it is not likely that all are mistaken: the conviction is rather to be held as testifying that the power of judging aright and of distinguishing truth from error, which is properly what is called good sense or reason, is by nature equal in all men; and that the diversity of our opinions, consequently, does not arise from some being endowed with a larger share of reason than others, but solely from this, that we conduct our thoughts along different ways, and do not fix our attention on the same objects.[4]

What has been said about Descartes can also be said about most other mainstream modern philosophers, let alone Greek and medieval philosophy. Although epistemic questions did not occupy as central a place in ancient Greek and medieval thought as they did in the modern period, it is undeniable that nonetheless they were discussed and taken seriously. Aristotle's *Organon* and many of Plato's dialogues, such as the *Theaetetus* and the *Meno*, were devoted to questions of knowledge and certainty, and the Middle Ages did not fall far behind. Augustine's *De magistro* and *Contra academicos* stand out in the early Christian period, but after the thirteenth century discussions of epistemological issues were never too far behind other philosophical issues popular at the time. After Henry of Ghent began his *Summae questionum ordinariarum* with a question concerning the possibility of knowledge, it became customary for subsequent thinkers to raise epistemological questions of various sorts.[5]

Note also that not all mainstream pre-Kantians believed that our natural powers are adequate to know *all* of what there is. Indeed, some of them held that there are aspects of reality that do not fall into the province of our natural faculties. A central area of concern for scholastics, for example, was the role of faith in the acquisition of knowledge. Indeed, the dominant epistemic concerns of the Middle Ages centered on the nature of faith, its relation to reason, and the respective realms of effective operation of each. Faith was understood as a supernatural gift freely given by God to those he chose, whereas reason was generally identified as the natural capacity of human beings to make sense of the world around them, and thus included perception. There were medieval authors who rejected reason altogether, of course, but in general mainstream authors sought to find a place for both faith and reason in such a way that they complemented each other and neither was undermined by the other. This was the thrust of the thought of Augustine, Anselm, and Aquinas, for example. In spite of their overriding theological concerns, these authors considered metaphysical questions of central importance, and, when dealing with logical and epistemological issues, these issues were understood to be propaedeutic and subordinate to the main business of philosophy, which was taken to be the understanding of reality, that is, metaphysics, even if philosophy were not competent to yield knowledge of all of reality.

The trust that mainstream pre-Kantians put in our natural faculties of knowledge led them to adopt a mode of philosophical discourse in which argumentation played an essential part. They saw the job of the philosopher not just as the exposition of a view, but as providing grounds and arguments for it. Claims were not to be based on authority or go unsubstantiated; they had to be backed up by reasons and arguments. This led over the years to some excesses, examples of which were quite evident in the later Middle Ages. Thus, we find thirteenth and fourteenth century scholastics listing dozens of positions, with corresponding supporting arguments, objections, and counter-objections, on every issue, regardless of how minor it was. The lean *quaestio* of Thomas Aquinas, where two or three authorities and arguments were given against the view he wanted to support, was turned by some of his contemporaries and later writers into a veritable maze of opinions and counteropinions, arguments and counterarguments, that often seem to create more confusion than enlightenment. Indeed, it was in part this scholastic argumentative method, often based on mere speculation, that drew the pained cries of Renaissance humanists. Be that as it may, what is important to note is the argumentative character of philosophy in the scholastics' view. And, of course, we find the same emphasis, without perhaps the scholastic extremes, in the Greeks and the moderns. Aristotle is to be held largely responsible for the deductive conception of science, where knowledge is understood to be achieved through demonstration and demonstration to consist of a sound deductive argument with two self-evident or demonstrated premises. The examples of Descartes, Spinoza, and Locke should be sufficent to illustrate the point that argument is a central element of modern mainstream philosophy.

Finally, the emphasis on argumentation led mainstream pre-Kantians to avoid, sometimes consciously, sometimes otherwise, the use of metaphorical language and of rhetorical tricks aimed at persuasion rather than understanding. Averroes, for example, pointed to the use of objective—that is nonsymbolic and nonmetaphorical—language as one of the necessary conditions of scientific discourse.[6] And likewise we find in Aquinas, Suárez, and Leibniz, to mention just three mainstream authors, the kind of nonmetaphorical discourse that Averroes would have approved.

II. THE POETIC TRADITION

The *poetic tradition* also has a long history but, although it was favored by many thinkers and influenced many of the authors that I would classify as belonging to the mainstream, it never became a philosophically dominant force in the West before Kant. Among its supporters we find such figures as Pythagoras, Plotinus, the Pseudo-Dionysius, Tertullian, Master Eckhart, Bruno, and many others. Most of those who worked within this tradition accepted, as the members of the mainstream did, that the fundamental task of the philosopher is to achieve an understanding of what there is, but they differed from them on some important points. In the first place, they did not think that the human natural powers of knowledge are effective in reaching an understanding of reality, for what we perceive through the senses or grasp through reason is only a poor mirror of reality. The way to reach an understanding of reality, which they identified precisely with that entity or entities that transcend the world with which we are acquainted through perception or reason, is through a mystical or quasi-mystical experience in which our inner self somehow is given direct access to it. This means that, like the members of the mainstream, this group of thinkers stressed metaphysics as a fundamental area of philosophical inquiry, but they disagreed with them as to the means that should be used in philosophy in general and in metaphysics in particular. They thought that the way to know reality is not through cognitive categories, but, like poets, we must approach it in a noncognitive way. I have chosen the term 'poetic' to refer to this tradition to emphasize the aesthetic, mystical, and intuitive approach of those who belong to this group. Other terms, such as 'romantic,' for example, also might be applicable, but their close identification with particular historical periods or movements and their technical meaning makes them less useful for my purpose.[7]

The view just described has important implications for philosophical methodology. Since neither perception nor reason can reveal to us the ultimate nature of reality, the course to be followed in the pursuit of understanding it must be different. Argument, whether based on reason or empirical evidence, the means we use normally to establish truths about the world, has no import in this process. What is needed, according to some supporters of this position, is to develop a way of life that will lead to the achievement of the mystical insight revelatory of reality. Accordingly, the writings of individuals who belong to this tradition contain little or no argumentation. They are primarily expository, describing the results of the experience that needs to be achieved (and that some of them claim to have had) or the steps that lead to it. Since this sort of writing is not meant to appeal to reason or to empirical evidence, it is full of metaphor, and suggestive and mysterious connotations abound in it. Its aim is to appeal to those aspects of the human mind that are outside the realm of reason and perception. Philosophical discourse in this context becomes primarily expressive and directive. The descriptive character of philosophical discourse prevalent in the mainstream tradition is missing for the most part. Logical categories and pigeonholes, like contradiction, are dismissed because they apply only to the realm of reason, not to what is beyond reason, with the consequence that supporters of the poetic tradition believe that no effective criticisms based on logical categories or empirical evidence can be brought against their point of view.

One of the best examples of this way of thinking about philosophy is Plotinus. In the *Enneads* he describes for us the way we need to approach the ultimate ground of reality, The One:

> Awareness of The One comes to us neither by knowing nor by the pure thought that discovers the other intelligible things, but by a presence transcending knowledge. When the soul knows something, it loses its unity; it cannot remain simply one because knowledge implies discursive reason and discursive reason implies multiplicity. The soul then misses The One and falls into number and multiplicity. Therefore we must go beyond knowledge and hold to unity. We must renounce knowing and knowable, every object of thought....[8]

Awareness of The One transcends knowledge and discursive reasoning. Indeed, the aim of discourse about The One is not to understand, but to lead us in the right direction so that we may experience a vision:

> If nevertheless we speak of The One and write about it, we do so only to give direction, to urge towards that vision beyond dis-

> course, to point out the road to one desirous of seeing. Instruction goes only as far as showing the road and the direction. To obtain the vision is solely the work of him who desires to obtain it. If he does not arrive at contemplation, if his soul does not achieve awareness of that life that is beyond, if the soul does not feel a rapture within it like that of the lover come to rest in his love, if, because of his closeness to The One, he receives its true light—his whole soul made luminous—but is still weighted down and his vision frustrated...he has no one to blame but himself and should try to become pure by detaching himself from everything.[9]

The vision of which Plotinus speaks in this passage is noncognitive, a matter of love and rapture, whose achievement has more to do with morality and attitude than methodological precision. We are, indeed, in a world quite different from the world of Aristotle, where knowledge was possible and depended on procedure. Knowledge for Plotinus is a kind of mystical union, a fusion of knower and known in experience.[10] Naturally, Plotinus is aware that the procedure he describes and its results must look foreign and odd to those who are not appropriately prepared for it:

> If, before beginning serious investigation, we were jestingly to say that all beings are striving after contemplation...who would listen to such nonsense? But we are here by ourselves and run no risk in treating our own doctrine jestingly.[11]

These words sound very much like those of St. Paul, when he notes that Christian wisdom appears to be foolishness to those who are not Christian.[12] What Plotinus and other members of the poetic tradition are telling us is that in order to understand their position we must not look at it from the outside but rather that we must approach it from within. The conceptual edifice they present to us is very much like a Christian basilica seen from the outside. A Christian basilica makes no architectural sense when observed externally because we do not see or understand how it is put together, how it can stand up, and why the roof does not collapse. It is only when we walk through the door, when we are allowed to enter a space reserved for a small group of initiated faithful, that we can see how the structure is supported: The columns on which the roof rests are inside, its symbolic plan as a cross becomes evident, the focus of attention is the altar, and the stories that reveal God's nature and his plan for us are depicted on the walls. The basilica is a good symbol of the poetic philosophical tradition, where the way to know requires commitment and is achieved through inner experience rather than through objectively detached rational or empirical consideration. The result of the inner experience is a private view that can be understood only by those who have had similar experiences. We must enter the basilica to understand, and we are allowed to enter only when we have accepted a set of beliefs required of those who "belong."

The Christian basilica differs in important ways from a Greek temple. In the Greek temple, the support and plan of the building and the stories about the gods are evident when one looks at it from the outside. The Greek temple is a public structure, a public statement, open for everyone to consider and evaluate, and it therefore is a good symbol of the mainstream tradition—it is a building whose structure and significance should be evident to everyone who cares to look at it. There are no hidden requirements for its understanding, no prerequisites or commitments needed to grasp its meaning. The Greek temple is a structure open to public inspection and understanding, like the mainstream tradition.

III. THE CRITICAL TRADITION

The third tradition that has played an important role in Western philosophy I call *critical*. Often the critical approach appears as a reaction to the excesses of the poetic tradition. Among those who might be cited in its ranks before Kant are sophists like Protagoras; skeptics like Carneades, Montaigne, and Bayle; and positivists like Francis Bacon. Note that all of these authors are influential in the history of philosophy. My argument is not that the critical and poetic traditions had no major adherents or that they did not influence the mainstream; the point I wish to defend is only that most philosophically influential authors before Kant did not belong to either of them. The tone of the times, then, was not dominated by either the poets or the critics.

The critical tradition is characterized by the belief that philosophy cannot yield knowledge of reality and therefore that metaphysics is impossible. This separates it from both the pre-Kantian mainstream and from the poetic tradition. This stance, in comparison to those of the other two traditions, is fundamentally critical, precluding any progress toward the establishment of metaphysical knowledge. Now, when it comes to the reasons why philosophy cannot yield knowledge of reality, the critical tradition breaks up into two subgroups: the skeptics and the positivists. Skeptics reject the possibility of knowledge not only in philosophy but in any area of human cognition. They hold that the faculties at the disposal of human beings, reason and perception, are equally flawed and thus ineffective in yielding knowledge of reality. This is where the Greek sophists and skeptics fall. Perhaps the most radical of these philosophers from antiquity is Gorgias, who is reputed by Sextus Empiricus to have written a work entitled *On Not-Being* or *On Nature*. This work was written against the Eleatic rationalists, who had an unbounded trust in human reason. Sextus describes Gorgias's position as follows:

> Gorgias sets out to prove three successive points: first, that nothing exists; second, that even if it does it is incomprehensible by men; and third, that even if it is comprehensible it is certainly not expressible and cannot be communicated to another.[13]

This text is followed by an intricate piece of argumentation that supports each of the theses proposed. We need not dwell in the details of the arguments given by Gorgias. What is of interest for our present purposes are three points: First is the very argumentative way of supporting the skeptical theses and its reliance on reason. In the case of Gorgias this is particularly compelling and understandable, for he is using against the Eleatics the very tools they used to support their views. Second, we must note that both reported titles of the work suggest that it deals with very basic objects of understanding—being, its negation, and nature. Gorgias's views, then, undermine not only metaphysics, but every discipline that aims to give us knowledge of reality. Finally, the second and third theses attack the epistemic bases of all knowledge by noting that, contrary to what is generally assumed by those involved in inquiries of any sort, human beings are capable of neither understanding nor communicating.

It would be difficult to conceive a more radical statement of skepticism or a better example of what I have called here the *skeptical branch* of the critical tradition. In method, intention, and result, Gorgias falls with the skeptics. The motives and outcome of his skepticism are still debated by scholars, but it is beyond doubt that he meant to undermine the very foundations of rigorous inquiry.

The second group of critical philosophers, the *positivists*, question only the use of human epistemic powers for the knowledge of non-physical entities. Thus, although they reject metaphysics, they are willing to accept knowledge of the physical world based on empirically backed evidence. Philosophy, conceived as metaphysics, therefore, must be abandoned both because it cannot possibly achieve its aim and because it lacks a proper method of inquiry. Indeed, as Francis Bacon points out, the method traditionally used in the sciences, including philosophy, namely that dictated by Aristotelian logic, is at the heart of its mistakes: "the art of logic...has had the effect of fixing errors rather than disclosing truth."[14] For the sciences to work and yield knowledge, they must abandon the old aprioristic scholastic method characteristic of metaphysical thinking in favor of an inductive one: "What the sciences stand in need of is a form of induction which shall analyze experience and take it to pieces, and by a due process of exclusion and rejection lead to an inevitable conclusion."[15] The key to knowledge is observation: "Man...can do and understand so much and so much only as he has observed in fact or in thought of the course of nature. Beyond this he neither knows anything nor can do anything."[16]

Since metaphysics, as understood traditionally within the mainstream, is not based on observation, it could not yield knowledge. Knowledge is the business of the empirical sciences; that is the inevitable conclusion to which Bacon's views lead.

Note that those who favor the critical approach share with the poetic tradition their distrust of achieving metaphysical knowledge through the exercise of our natural powers. Human faculties are effective in the prosaic, everyday world of experience, but they do not give us information about ultimate reality.

The critical tradition has some features in common with the mainstream tradition that distinguish both traditions from the poetic tradition. Critics share with members of the mainstream a methodological emphasis on argumentation, and they favor the use of clear and objective language in philosophical discourse, even if they do not always achieve clarity or objectivity in practice. These emphases are quite evident in the work of both skeptics and post-Kantian positivists, who go to great lengths in the use of arguments against the view, held by both members of the mainstream and poets, that metaphysics is possible.

The emphasis on empirical evidence that characterizes most positivists, however, leads them to the exaggerated use of what they consider to be "scientific" techniques in their discourse. This feature is not as evident among pre-Kantians since the positivist point of view was not fully developed before Kant and, as mentioned earlier, the distinction between what we now call "sciences" and philosophy was not drawn precisely. Indeed, the *Novum organon*, the major work of Francis Bacon, who was perhaps the most clear advocate of a positivistic point of view before Kant, contains little in the way of the methodology and rigor generally advocated by post-Kantian positivists. But that did not deter him from making extravagant claims about the vacuity of metaphysics and the need to borrow empirical techniques and apply them in philosophy.[17]

IV. THE KANTIAN REVOLUTION

It should not be concluded from what I have said so far that every Western philosophical figure between Thales and Kant unequivocally belonged to one and only one of these three traditions and that they had nothing in common with the other two. The conceptual categories I have identified as traditions, like all historical classifications, do not impose rigid boundaries on history. There are no such boundaries in history in fact. What we have is a flowing complex reality where emphases, rather than boundaries, determine the group into which a particular figure may be placed. Accordingly, we must keep in mind that most individuals who practiced philosophy in the period about which we are speaking in most cases shared ideas and views from the three traditions. The point I would like to make is not that there were pure exponents of either one of the traditions, although some authors indeed write as if they were. No, my point rather is that in most figures one can discern an emphasis that would place the author primarily in one of these traditions: some with the assumptions I have identified with the mainstream tradition governing their philosophizing, others with stronger poetic or critical attitudes and concerns. No one is exclusively one to the exclusion of the others, but most authors tend to fall more into one than into the others. I do claim, however, that, on the whole, more authors can be classified as members of the mainstream tradition than as members of either of the other two and that this tradition claims as its members more historically influential figures from Thales to Kant than either of the others. These facts, of course, gave character and continuity to philosophy in the period mentioned and allowed it to function as the arbiter of philosophical discourse. Moreover, the elements it had in common with the other two traditions made possible for it to communicate with them and also to serve as an indirect source of communication between the clearly opposed poetic and critical traditions. Of course, there were repeated challenges to the mainstream from the fringe groups, the poets and the critics, in the history of philosophy before Kant, but with rare exceptions philosophy moved along the lines chartered by the mainstream.

This situation underwent a drastic change with Kant, for he questioned the very foundations on which the mainstream tradition rested. By doubting the power of what he called *pure reason* to establish the metaphysical truths that are its natural province, such as the existence of God and the immortality of the soul, Kant gave what was widely taken as a historically mortal blow to the epistemic assumptions on which the mainstream philosophical tradition had relied. It should be kept in mind, however, that Kant's explicit purpose was not to do away with metaphysics and thus undermine the mainstream tradition. On the contrary, he saw himself as answering the attacks on metaphysics made by some of his predecessors. His aim in fact was to rescue metaphysics and establish it on firmer ground, where it could not be assailed by empiricist and skeptical objections. Nevertheless, the way he went about this, by putting into question the power of natural reason to reach metaphysical knowledge, contributed more than any other challenge before him to the undermining of the mainstream. Indeed, it was precisely because of Kant's aim to save the philosophical program which had engaged the members of the mainstream that his blows to the very bases of that program were so devastating. For nothing is more damaging than a devotee's acknowledgment of faults in the object of devotion. Thus with Kant we have the paradoxical situation of someone who considered himself a member of what I have called the mainstream and yet functioned most effectively as its critic.

It is important to understand, moreover, the differences between the Kantian challenge and those that had been put forth at other times in the history of philosophy prior to Kant. For I do not claim by any means that Kant was the first to attack the enterprise carried out by mainstream philosophy. On the contrary, as already pointed out, there were many challenges to it from the poets and the critics, but, in contrast with Kant's attack, none of them had been successful in dislodging the mainstream from its place of prominence. The reason for their lack of success was that, unlike Kant, they did not effectively attack the epistemic foundations of the philosophical mainstream, concentrating rather on nonfundamental aspects of it, which was not sufficient to bring down the whole mainstream edifice. Let me refer to a couple of examples to illustrate the point.

One of the most important steps in the Kantian argument, as we shall see later, was his antinomies. Now, paradoxes, to which genus the antinomies belong, were by no means new to philosophy. Perhaps the most famous of them before Kant were those formulated by Zeno in the fifth century B.C. But there is a fundamental difference between Zeno's paradoxes and Kant's antinomies. The logical puzzles that Zeno devised were not meant to undermine the natural capacity of human beings to know, but actually to confirm it by showing how reason was effective vis-à-vis the suspect power of perception. For his point was that sense perception, according to which there is motion in the world, is inaccurate, and reason, understood in contrast with perception and according to which motion is impossible, gives us an accurate picture of reality. True, it has been argued that Zeno's paradoxes contributed to foster the distrust in the human capacity to know and the subsequent rise of sophism and skepticism in ancient Greece. And that may very well be correct. However, this does not seem to have been Zeno's intention, and his paradoxes cannot be considered as necessarily leading to a skeptical point of view. Nor do they seem to have shaken the philosophical community to such an extent that all subsequent philosophical speculation and discourse ceased or shifted gears so that the human natural faculties were replaced by other means of knowing. Indeed, after Zeno, Socrates, Plato, and Aristotle follow, and all of them seem to have been quite aware of Zeno's paradoxes, their thrust and weaknesses.

The reasons why Zeno's paradoxes did not lead to a skeptical point of view are two: First, he was in fact defending the metaphysical position of his teacher Parmenides, and this position presumably justifies the conclusions to which his paradoxes led, namely, that change is impossible. And, second, he fervently believed that reason gives us knowledge of reality even if that knowledge is contradicted by the information supplied by the senses.

The purpose of Zeno's paradoxes is explained by Plato in the *Parmenides,* where he has Socrates ask Zeno: "And do you regard each of your arguments as proof of this, so that in your view the arguments put forward in your treatise are just so many proofs that there is not a many? Is that right, or have I misunderstood?"[18] To which Zeno dutifully answers that Socrates is completely right. And later on in the same dialogue Zeno adds: "The truth is that these writings were meant as a kind of support to the arguments of Parmenides against those who try to ridicule him by saying that if the whole is one, many absurdities and contradictions follow."[19] The absurdities and contradictions to which the Zeno of Plato's dialogue refers are not the result of shortcomings in the human epistemic equipment, but rather of the position that Parmenides' critics held, namely, that motion is possible.[20] Indeed, reason, which for Parmenides was the only reliable natural instrument of knowledge, brings out those absurdities and points the way in the direction of the right view. Moreover, nothing in the paradoxes themselves indicates that their purpose is to undermine the human capacity to know. Take, for example, the paradox of Achilles:

> The second argument is the so-called Achilles. This is, that the slowest runner will never be overtaken by the swiftest. For the pursuer must first reach the point from which the pursued started; so that the slower must always be some distance ahead.[21]

In a more elaborate rendition this argument is reported as follows:

> This argument too is based on infinite divisibility, but is set up differently. It would run as follows. If there is motion, the slowest will never be overtaken by the swiftest. But this is impossible, therefore there is no motion. The argument is called the "Achilles" because of the introduction into it of Achilles who, the argument says, cannot overtake the tortoise he is chasing. For the pursuer, before he overtakes the pursued, must first arrive at the point from which the latter started. But during the time which it takes the pursuer to get to this point, the pursued has advanced some distance. Even though the pursued, being the slower of the two, covers less ground, he still advances, for he is not at rest. Thus, assuming the distances to be successively less without limit, on the principle of the infinite divisibility of magnitudes, it turns out that Achilles will fail not only to overtake Hektor but even the tortoise.[22]

What does this argument prove or try to prove? That motion is not possible because we cannot explain how it happens without falling into contradiction. But does it argue against the human capacity to know? On the contrary, Zeno, like his master Parmenides, whom he was trying to defend, was a committed rationalist; and rationalists accept that we can know reality, although such knowledge is accomplished only by means of reason and not the senses. Parmenides expressed the point well when he said: "Thought and being are the same."[23] What can be thought exists, what cannot be thought cannot exist.

I believe it is possible to provide similar analyses of other pieces of reasoning that may be thought to have tried to accomplish something similar to what Kant did. This is the case of the well-known arguments by Hume and others that challenge many of the metaphysical doctrines held by previous philosophers. In most of these cases, the aim is not to question the effectiveness of the natural powers used by human beings to know the world, but to do away with views about the world that seem unsupported or to supplant what are considered outdated and flawed methods of inquiry with more accurate ones.

This seems well exemplified in the case of Hume, whose overall aim, like that of other empiricists who preceded him, was to provide a new basis for knowledge, namely experience, and to move away from the empty speculations and excesses of rationalism. His criticisms were directed not to the human capacity to know and achieve a certain degree of certainty; they were aimed rather at the sort of pure speculation whose effect is precisely confusion and uncertainty.

> Nor is there required such profound knowledge to discover the present imperfect condition of the sciences.... Disputes are multiplied, as if every thing was uncertain.... Amidst all this bustle it is not reason, which carries the prize, but eloquence....[24]

The solution to this cacophony of claims is "to leave the tedious lingering method, which we have hitherto followed, and...to march up directly to the capital or center of the sciences, to human nature itself."[25] This new foundation can serve to make scientific knowledge secure:

> In pretending therefore to explain the principles of human nature, we in effect propose a complete system of the sciences, built on a foundation almost entirely new, and the only one upon which they can stand with any security.... And as the science of man is the only solid foundation for the other sciences, so the only solid foundation we can give to this science itself must be laid on experience and observation.[26]

Hume's aim was not to undermine the human capacity to know. On the contrary, he was trying to ground philosophy and the sciences on a more secure basis than the one on which they had rested before. He put limits to what reason can do by itself—it cannot go beyond experience[27]—but he was not willing to discard reason altogether or to substitute for it a poetic and mystical intuition. Indeed, one of his stated aims in *A Treatise on Human Nature* was to prove what he regarded as a new system of ethics based on sympathy.[28] Thus, although Hume may have prepared the way for Kant's attack on the human capacity to know reality, he cannot be held historically responsible for the dislocation of mainstream philosophy into the sidelines.

A different and more direct challenge to our natural epistemic powers was frequently found in the Middle Ages among those who wished to emphasize the reliability of faith when its doctrines are in conflict with views accepted on the basis of reason, which, as mentioned earlier, they understood to include perception. A typical statement of this attitude was put forward by Bonaventure in the thirteenth century:

> the recognition of truth is not for the Egyptians [namely, unbelievers], but rather, for the sons of Israel, [namely, believers].... It is patently obvious...that there is no sure passage to wisdom through science...faith is above reason and is proved only by the authority of Scripture and the divine power, which is manifested in miracles.[29]

Obviously this passage contains a serious indictment of the human capacity to know independently of faith. But such an indictment is presented from a religious perspective and concerns primarily religious truths. Bonaventure, like most Christian writers who have assailed the human power to know, did so in the context of theological truths, not usually in the context of purely scientific or philosophical truths. Of course, there are exceptions. Peter Damian attacked even grammar, holding that the Devil was the first teacher of the discipline because he was the first to decline the word *deus* in the plural.[30] But most religious thinkers objected to the use of our natural epistemic powers only when those powers were used to go beyond the natural world in order to say something about the supernatural world, where, according to them, the only arbiter of truth is faith. So, there were no widespread or profound criticisms of the human capacity to know as such in the Middle Ages as long as the powers in question stayed within the field of their competence. Most medieval writers trusted the human natural powers of knowledge as appropriate means to deal with the natural realm. And that included, of course, not only what we would consider today to be the realm of the natural sciences, but also some truths such as the existence of God and the immortality of the soul, which many of them thought could be proven independently of faith.

This epistemic structure is well exemplified in Dante's *Divine Comedy,* where Virgil, who represents reason unaided by faith, cannot lead Dante into Heaven. Only Beatrice, who represents faith, can help to bring Dante's soul into God's presence and thus into a deeper knowledge of reality.

The contrast between the approaches we have examined and that of Kant are dramatic, for what Kant claimed was precisely that reason was simply not competent to carry out one of the tasks for which it was naturally meant. The opening paragraph of the Preface to the first edition of the *Critique of Pure Reason* makes explicit Kant's main thesis in the work:

> Human reason has this peculiar fate that in one species of its knowledge it is burdened by questions which, as prescribed by the very nature of reason itself, it is not able to ignore, but which, as transcending all its powers, it is also not able to answer.[31]

Human reason, then, is in a terrible bind. By its very nature it is unable to avoid asking certain questions, metaphysical questions, but it is also unable to answer them, falling in its attempts to do so into confusions and contradictions from which it cannot liberate itself. These confusions and contradictions result from the fact that reason begins with principles that are implicit in human experience and, therefore, cannot be avoided but lead reason beyond experience to the realm of pure speculation. Once there, according to Kant, reason cannot detect the errors into which it falls because it has no means of verifying them empirically.[32]

The *Critique of Pure Reason* is nothing but a long and detailed argument to substantiate these claims. In this argument, the antinomies of pure reason play an important role, for they aim to show how reason cannot resolve certain basic questions of metaphysics, arriving at contradictory answers through perfectly rational procedures.

It is not pertinent here to discuss in detail the four antinomies that Kant presents nor to examine their possible solutions. For my purposes it is sufficient to understand their overall purpose. I shall content myself, then, with presenting two of them as examples.[33]

Antinomy I

Thesis: The world has a beginning in time, and is also limited as regards space.

Antithesis: The world has no beginning, and no limits in space; it is infinite as regards both time and space.

Antinomy II

Thesis: Every composite substance in the world is made up of simple parts, and nothing anywhere exists save the simple or what is composed of the simple.

Antithesis: No composite thing in the world is made up of simple parts, and there nowhere exists in the world anything simple.

If reason can equally justify contradictory theses, what use is it, and how are we to establish knowledge and certainty? Up until Kant, as already mentioned, there had been attacks on various uses of reason and various types of methodologies, but no mainstream author had mounted an attack on a Kantian scale on reason itself and its capacity to know reality as it is. Some authors had given arguments against certain uses of reason, as some scholastics did. And there had been criticisms about reason's application and its ignoring empirical data, as we find early modern empiricists doing. Even Hume, who is regarded by some as having undermined reason more than most before Kant, showed only that reason needs the constant monitoring of experience to deal adequately with certain issues and not that it has to be abandoned. Kant began where Hume left off, trying to show that reason is inadequate in certain areas. But he went much further, for he tried to demonstrate with the antinomies how reason itself cannot avoid contradictory conclusions when it is dealing with the most basic metaphysical questions about the world that it is designed to answer. The very instrument of inquiry, then, is intrinsically flawed. Moreover, because reason is inadequate to deal with questions that it cannot avoid, it cannot be considered illegitimate for reason to deal with those questions. Thus, for Kant the problem with reason is not that it overextends itself, as scholastics charged when reason meddled in the province of revelation, or that it needs careful watching and the input of experience, as empiricists argued. The problem with reason is that it cannot answer the most fundamental questions that it *naturally* seeks to answer and therefore is entitled to ask.

This was an extraordinary historical development, a veritable Copernican revolution. Prior to Kant, the view that faculties and powers were effective in reaching the results for which they were naturally designed was commonplace. But Kant's *Critique* went contrary to that view. Indeed, his criticism of reason undermined the very bases and assumptions on which the mainstream tradition had always relied in a way in which it had not been done before. The only road open to philosophers who were persuaded by Kant's criticism of reason was either to continue believing that philosophy yields knowledge of reality but through means other than our natural powers (poets) or to reject the knowledge of reality as a legitimate function of philosophy (critics), either because such is the province of science only (positivists) or because such knowledge is impossible (skeptics). In short, the result of Kant's criticism was the replacement of the mainstream tradition from the position of dominance it had held for 2,000 years by the two other traditions that until Kant had played only marginal roles in the history of Western philosophy.

The first reaction to the Kantian criticism was the progressive rise of the poetic tradition to a place of prominence. German philosophy in the nineteenth century abounds with examples of philosophers who share the poetic attitude. One need mention only Schiller, Schopenhauer, and, with some qualifications, Hegel, to see the turn toward the expository, the mystical, and the literary. The absence of argument and the practice of philosophy as an expression of the self, the spirit, or the culture becomes pervasive, reaching extraordinary proportions during that century. Because of the fondness for metaphor and other literary means to reveal a glimpse of hidden truths, this tradition reached excesses unheard of in the whole prior history of Western philosophy.

Having dispensed with the requirement of clarity necessary if one is pressed to defend one's views with arguments, the poetic tradition fell into a quagmire from which it has not yet been able to break loose. A large portion of the work of the post-nineteenth century philosophers who fall within this category appears incomprehensible to almost everyone except a small group of devotees who claim to understand it, but generally fail to explain what it is they understand to anyone who is not a member of the group. Like members of a cult, where communication is carried out by secret signs, they take no account of the external philosophical community, let alone the human family at large. A good proportion of what has been written by phenomenologists, existentialists, structuralists, deconstructionists, and post-modernists in general is expressed in an abstruse jargon highly inaccessible to anyone but themselves.

On the other hand, the excesses of the poetic tradition were partly responsible for a counterreaction to the movement in the direction of criticism. The reaction began in the nineteenth century itself with various forms of positivism. We find it first in Saint-Simon and other socialists, but it quickly spread beyond the initial socialist group. Among its main figures at the time were Comte, Bentham, James and John Stuart Mill, Spencer, Mach, Haeckel, and Wundt.[34] It is in the twentieth century, however, that the movement flourished and became a dominant force in parts of the German world, the English-speaking countries, and Scandinavia. The scientistic attitude reached its climax with the rise of logical positivism among the members of the Vienna Circle, but its influence was not restricted to that group. It extends also to most branches of the rather amorphous tradition known as *philosophical analysis*.

The originating actors in the analytic movement were Bertrand Russell and G. E. Moore in England and the already mentioned members of the Vienna Circle.[35] All of them were reacting against the extraordinary excesses into which Hegelian philosophy and its followers had fallen. The views of the founding fathers of the analytic movement as well as of their many and diverse disciples differ considerably, but most of them share some basic assumptions that give some unity to the tradition: the concern with language and the clarification of its meaning, a strong interest in and use of logic and logical symbolism in philosophical discourse, an almost reverential attitude toward science, and the belief that nonempirical claims of a nonsyntactical sort are suspect and should be subjected to stringent tests.

The analytic movement became a great success particularly in English-speaking countries, because these countries were inheritors of a philosophical perspective that, since medieval times, had included an underlying empirical bent. The assumptions of analysis seemed to fit well the tradition started by Roger Bacon and emphasized later by William of Ockham, Francis Bacon, and David Hume, among others. As a result, analysis in various forms (linguistic, ordinary language, and others, as well as under the garb of logical positivism) became the dominant philosophical current in English-speaking countries and Scandinavia, displacing the poetic tradition from a position of leadership in those countries and preventing the pre-Kantian mainstream tradition from regaining the place it had held in the prior history of Western thought. Instead of dealing with the metaphysical questions that had dominated philosophy before Kant, analysts concentrated their efforts on matters of language and usage. Metaphysical claims were regarded as illegitimate since they could not be verified by empirical evidence. Spiritual realities, such as the soul and God, had to be eliminated from the field of investigation of philosophy; for philosophy as a rigorous enterprise could not deal with what was unverifiable in terms of sense perception. Traditional normative issues in ethics were transformed into issues concerning linguistic usage. Questions such as, What is the good? became, How is the term 'good' used in ordinary language? Thus, prescription was eradicated from ethics in favor of a descriptive procedure that tried to clarify how we think and talk about morality but offered no guidance as to what is right or wrong.

Nowhere else can we find a better example of the spirit of philosophical analysis than in Strawson's notorious distinction between descriptive and revisionary metaphysics. The key distinction between the two, according to him, is that descriptive metaphysics "is content to describe the actual structure of our thought about the world, revisionary metaphysics is concerned to produce a better structure."[36] And, of course, for Strawson it is descriptive metaphysics that ought to be pursued. If we are going to make of philosophy a rigorous pursuit, we must content ourselves with the description of our thought, and this is better achieved, as most analysts would want to argue, by analyzing the tool with which we think, namely, language. Consequently, philosophy becomes a study of thought through language and ultimately of language, since thought itself is considered to be known empirically only through language. This study is to be pursued rigorously, applying the most exacting methods available and the latest advances in logic, and, as any scientific study open to question, the value of the conclusions reached would depend on the validity and soundness of the arguments that support them. There is no surrender to intuition and the mystical insight in philosophical analysis, therefore. Argument and counterargument, proof and counter-proof are of the essence of this procedure and set it apart from that used by the members of the poetic tradition. But philosophical analysis differs from the pre-Kantian mainstream in its rejection of philosophy as a discipline that inquires into what there is—philosophy can deal only with the way we think or speak about reality, not with reality. It is science that yields knowledge of reality and only physical reality at that. So, although knowledge of reality, that is, of physical reality, is possible, it is not through philosophy that we can achieve it.

V. THE CURRENT SITUATION

The rise of the poetic and the critical traditions and the displacement of the pre-Kantian mainstream have produced a kind of schizophrenic split in the philosophical world of the twentieth century, with critics largely dominating the English-speaking countries and poets dominating for the most part the European continent. The critics usually go by the name of *analysts* and the poets have come to be called *Continental* philosophers. This split, with which we have lived now for the better part of this century, has been pervasive and destructive. It has been pervasive because it has affected practically every nucleus of philosophical activity in the West. And it has been destructive because it has stopped the communication between analysts and Continentalists to a degree that the very languages they speak, let alone the procedures they follow, seem completely foreign to each other. This lack of communication would be no great problem if it were easily seen that one of the two groups is in the right and the other completely mistaken. But the fact is that neither seems to be going in an unambiguously right course and both have clearly produced excesses. On the one hand, the poets, divorced as they are from argumentation, have moved farther and farther from common sense and rigor, building conceptual structures seemingly supported only by the whims and personalities of those who put them forth. On the other hand, analysts appear to be less and less concerned with substantive issues, producing ever-increasing sets of arguments and counterarguments, and criticisms of criticisms of criticisms, that seem to go on forever and appear to be completely irrelevant to anything that has to do with ordinary human experience and intellectual needs. This is the point at which we found ourselves in the third quarter of this century, in a schizophrenic philosophical world in which what had been fringe philosophical attitudes before Kant had become dominant. This unwelcome split was lamented by Walter Kaufman as early as 1956:

> It is one of the saddest features of our age that we are faced with an entirely unnecessary dichotomy: on the one hand there are those whose devotion to intellectual cleanliness and rigor is exemplary but who refuse to deal with anything but small, and often downright trivial, questions; in the other camp are men like Toynbee and some of the existentialists who deal with the big and interesting questions, but in such a manner that the positivists point to them as living proofs that any effort of this kind is doomed to failure. Aware of their opponents' errors, both sides go to ever greater extremes; the split widens; and the intelligent layman who is left in the middle will soon lose sight of both.[37]

By the mid-1980s these traditions had become so estranged from each other that each regarded the other as engaged in illegitimate tasks and procedures. Each party thought the other had left the philosophical flock as it were and therefore could be ignored. There was no sense in trying to communicate with each other, for all common ground between them had disappeared. Indeed, even the appearance of professional civility was shattered when the struggle between the two traditions abandoned any pretense of being a matter of philosophical disagreement that could be settled by philosophical reasoning and became "political."[38] In 1987, a group of poets, fed up with what they regarded as their marginalization in the American Philosophical Association as a result of actions taken by "analysts," formed a political organization to dislodge them from their seat of power. Since then they have succeeded in getting some members of the Continental group elected to positions of authority in the association, and a kind of uneasy truce has ensued. But the acrimony has not really left us. Most analysts still think that members of the poetic tradition are not really philosophers. And many Continentalists are convinced that the analysts are wasting their time on trivial matters of language and logic.[39]

This situation contrasts sharply with that which prevailed before Kant. Prior to Kant, mainstream philosophers had several things in common, so that even though they might disagree with respect to the positions they adopted, nonetheless they shared enough common ground to have a basis for communication and argument. This ground involved, as we saw, a common conception of the aim of philosophy, an object of investigation, and certain assumptions concerning philosophical methodology. So, even though they might disagree as to the answer or even the formulation of the questions they were trying to answer, there was a sufficient common foundation to maintain open communication. Philosophers shared a common object because most assumed there is a reality that has some kind of existence independent of any reflection about it and that one goal of philosophy is to know that reality. In the post-Kantian philosophical climate, it is frequent to find philosophers who put reality in suspension—indeed, some reject it altogether—leaving us with substitutes such as "consciousness" and "language," which lack the objectivity and resilience of the reality widely accepted before Kant. Of course, the process of erosion of reality had begun long before Kant. Kant is not solely responsible for its removal as object of philosophical reflection. Some British empiricists and some Continental rationalists had prepared the way. But even in authors like Berkeley, who surely can be counted among those who prepared the way, we find a substantial emphasis on the objectivity and independence of reality, even if one needs God to preserve them.

Likewise with certain assumptions concerning philosophical methodology. The pre-Kantian mainstream, as pointed out earlier, generally accepted that the human natural powers of reason and perception are effective in yielding knowledge of the world. But, after Kant's successful attack on reason, the very epistemic bases of philosophy were pulled from under it, leaving the discipline no alternative but either to look elsewhere for the means to fulfill its goal or to abandon the goal altogether.

Finally, most pre-Kantians shared a concern for common questions that arose from their shared understanding of the aims of philosophy. Since the trust in the human capacity to know had not been eliminated, they also thought that they could come up with answers to those questions. And because human epistemic powers could be trusted, it was on the bases of argument that these answers were to be reached and disagreements concerning them settled.

Today, however, we find ourselves in a situation where the two leading philosophical traditions share no such common grounds. Their objects of reflection are different; their methodological assumptions and procedures seem sometimes to be diametrically opposed; and they appear to be interested in no common questions.[40] Analysts study language, whereas Continental philosophers speak of "consciousness." The first, at least for a while, channeled their efforts into the dissolution of philosophical problems, which they regarded as mere conceptual confusions brought about by the tricks that language plays on us, whereas Continental thinkers have never accepted this diagnosis or remedy. Finally, the sorts of questions raised by Continental philosophers are frequently dismissed by analysts as illegitimate, and the questions they regard as legitimate are dismissed by Continental philosophers as trivial, as we saw earlier. This technique of dismissal is a serious matter, for it clearly points to a kind of antiphilosophical, dogmatic attitude that runs contrary to the very nature of the discipline as traditionally conceived. Note that this is not a case of simple philosophical *hubris*, a common philosophical vice even before Kant. This goes beyond the mere pride of a particular philosopher and permeates not one but both dominant traditions in contemporary philosophy. To reject at the outset any attempt and possibility of communication with those who oppose us is something that always has been criticized by philosophers and that, nonetheless, is generally accepted in the profession today. The curiosity to understand those who don't think as we do is gone from philosophical circles to the detriment of the discipline. The situation, therefore, is intolerable not only from a practical standpoint, but, more important, because it threatens to transform the discipline into one more of the many ideologies that permeate our times, where differences of opinion are settled not through argument but through political action or force.

VI. THE ROLE OF THE HISTORY OF PHILOSOPHY IN THE FUTURE OF PHILOSOPHY

As stated at the beginning of this Introduction, one of the theses of this book is that the history of philosophy can help us to bridge the gap between Continentalists and analysts and hopefully take us back to a situation similar to that which prevailed before Kant, when common grounds ensured philosophical dialogue and communication, if not necessarily agreement. The question that we need to answer, then, is how the study of the history of philosophy can help resolve the impasse in contemporary philosophy between Continentalists and analysts, bringing back these two groups into a situation that will establish the foundation that would lay the groundwork for and encourage fruitful communication. My thesis is that the history of philosophy can do so by providing the object, the method, and the questions to bridge the chasm between our contemporary critics and poets. The object consists of the historical texts we have, the writings of Plato, Aristotle, Hegel, and all other philosophers from whom works or parts of works have been preserved. The methodological principles are the result of the requirements that the very nature of historical philosophical texts imposes on anyone who wishes to deal with them. And the common questions are both those that past philosophers have raised and the historiographical questions that surface when one wishes to explore the past.

The object to which I refer, the texts that we have from the past, in many ways has the characteristics of the "reality" pre-Kantian philosophers generally accepted. It is an object *given*, not created.[41] It is independent of us, not dependent on our art. We *come to* the text, which is as it were *presented to us*. The text, therefore, has the status of a fundamental object of experience, just as the pre-Kantian "reality" had. Moreover, although it is presented to us in *a* language, it is not necessarily presented to us in *our* language, so that we cannot confuse it with a part of our linguistic experience and usage. Nor can the text be seen as a product of our mental organizing powers. True, it is given in our consciousness, but it appears in it as coming from without it, as a foreign object whose presence we have to reckon with.

Now let us look for a moment at what happens when we are presented with a historical text in order that we may understand how it imposes on us certain methodological requirements if we wish to understand it. The text with which historians are confronted is either written in a language that they know or one that they do not know.[42] In either case certain methodological conditions are required of historians for a text to reveal its content to them. However, because this is more obvious in cases where the text is written in a foreign language, I shall use that case as an illustration to facilitate the understanding of the point I wish to get across.

When we confront a text not written in a language we know, the meaning of the text has the status of a mystery. We see some paper with marks on it, but we do not know what those marks mean. We could capriciously assign meaning to the marks, but we do not do it because we know that the text is the product of some other human being's attempt at communicating a message, and we want to find out what that message is, not to project our ideas into the text. We are conscious that to assign meanings capriciously to the marks would not help us uncover the meaning of the text. So what do we do? We go to a dictionary where the meanings of the marks in question are identified. And we consult grammar books of the language in question to find out how the language works. This is a time consuming and difficult process in which we have very little latitude. But if we want to know what the text says, we must go through these and other procedures. Note, of course, that it is not necessarily the case that we will understand what the text means in the end. It may be that it contains words and symbols no one has yet been able to identify, for example. But that is not so important for my present purposes. What is important is to realize the character of the text and how it imposes itself on us, to be aware of its independence from and, I am tempted to say, its "power" over us. It is also important to see how the text reveals itself to us only if we follow certain procedures. In the case of a foreign text we need to go to dictionaries and grammars, for example. Methodological requirements and constraints, therefore, are imposed by the text on *all* those who wish to understand it.[43]

Just as a foreign text imposes certain conditions on those who wish to unravel its meaning, so there are methodological preconditions that the very character of the history of philosophy imposes on its students. These preconditions can serve as common ground and bases for communication among adherents to different philosophical traditions. For those who wish to understand the text, whether poets or critics, must accept these fundamental methodological preconditions in order to understand it. For example, they must assume that the object before them is a text, that someone produced it, that it has some meaning, that its meaning is understandable to some extent, that there are right and wrong ways of getting at that meaning, and so on. And all these serve as bridges among those who are dealing with the history of philosophy.

Finally, the third common ground that the history of philosophy can provide consists of the questions that occur in it as well as those that surface in the attempt to understand it. From the very beginning, it is quite evident that philosophers were trying to answer certain questions. Plato's question in the *Republic,* What is justice? Aquinas's question in the *Summa theologiae,* Does God exist? and so on, are just two examples of questions that philosophers have tried to answer. Now, it is essential to the attempt of historians of philosophy to understand the history of philosophy that they see why and how those questions came about and that they understand their full import. But the attempt at understanding can also serve as a common ground of communication between Continentalists and analysts, for they cannot simply dismiss the questions at the outset by saying that they are meaningless or trivial. In the first place, both Continentalists and analysts regard the history of philosophy as their common ancestry—indeed, each group seems to think that it is the rightful heir of that history and the other group is some kind of interloper upstart. But if the members of each group claim the history of philosophy as their own, they would find it difficult to ignore it, reject it as meaningless, or dismiss the issues and questions found in it as "trivial" or "illegitimate." Moreover, as students of history, their job is to understand what went on and, therefore, they must be willing to take that history at face value, trying to make sense of it by discovering what philosophers from the past had in mind. To dismiss the questions raised by past philosophers as meaningless or trivial at the outset would preclude any understanding of the past. So both Continentalists and analysts are forced to do with history what they refuse to do with each other, namely, listen with an open mind and engage in an honest attempt to understand it. Not that they will not conclude eventually that Plato and Aquinas were wrong in asking the questions they asked. Contemporary philosophers may even conclude that the questions with which Plato and Aquinas were concerned are after all meaningless and trivial. But if they do, they will have done so *after* they have engaged the texts and established a bridge to them that could also serve as a bridge to other current philosophical traditions. So much, then, for the issues found in the history of philosophy.

Other elements could also serve to establish bridges among those who study the history of philosophy. These are the historiographical issues that arise out of the historian's desire to understand the past. These issues have to do, for example, with the interpretation of past philosophical texts, the inclusion of truth value judgments in historical accounts, the value of the study of the history of philosophy, the proper methodology to be followed in the exploration of the history of philosophy, the question of philosophical progress, and many others. These issues constitute a kind of kernel of problems that can unite those who study the history of philosophy in a way that the philosophical problems we find in the history of philosophy itself may not be able to do. The history of philosophy is too vast and one can easily be lost in one period or author and thus not have to deal with issues that historians exploring other periods and authors deal with. There may be no overlap between what different philosophers study in the history of philosophy, or the overlap may be so minimal that it does not effectively establish the common ground necessary to bring about communication among philosophers working within different traditions. But no philosopher concerned with the history of philosophy can ignore the very philosophical issues that arise out of his or her attempt to understand and use it. Those historiographical issues, then, can form a basis of communication among philosophical traditions; indeed, they could be the foundation of a new beginning in philosophy.

It goes without saying, of course, that this book is a first modest attempt in that direction. In the chapters that follow I try to begin the reconstruction of a set of issues and problems that should be accessible and of concern to both Continentalists and analysts with the hope that philosophical dialogue may extend beyond the rigid parameters that developed after Kant. I do not mean to suggest that we need to return to the pre-Kantian mainstream. It may be that we will never go back to metaphysics as it was understood before Kant. But perhaps that will not be necessary in order to reestablish a philosophical climate where communication is considered important in philosophy. Indeed, it is my claim that we can find in the history of philosophy and in philosophical historiography the common object, the common methodological principles, and the common issues that the Kantian revolution relegated to the margins.

It may not be easy to convince everyone, and least of all Continentalists and analysts, that my argument is sound. They might regard it as far from convincing. In the first place is the question of whether there is a history of philosophy at all. Some philosophers have argued in fact that there is no such thing; and if there is no history of philosophy, the whole argumentative edifice I have presented would seem to collapse.

Second, even if one were to grant that there is such a thing as the history of philosophy, there is the question of its value. After all, have we not superseded it? Why should we go back to old and outmoded formulations and solutions from former ages, when what we need to do is face the problems and challenges of the present and future? What can we find in the past that may be of use to us today?

But suppose that one accepts that the history of philosophy is of some use, we may still ask, third, which part of the history of philosophy should we use? The history of philosophy is a very vast field, and no one can master the whole of it—indeed, some argue, not even big sections of it—in a single lifetime. Historians are specializing more and more on particular ages and within them on particular problems and authors in order to be able to understand fully the object they wish to master. Moreover, there is the question of the canon. Which authors and problems should be considered canonical and therefore the object of study of the historian of philosophy? There seems to be no agreement on this and, if there is none, how can we argue that we will find a common basis of communication by studying the history of philosophy?

Still, as if this were not bad enough, we could point out, fourth, that, even if a canon were to be accepted and that canon became the common object of study of all historians of philosophy, Continentalists and analysts would approach its study from such radically different points of view and with such conflicting methodological assumptions that having a common object of study would be ineffective in bringing about the kind of communication that I have argued should result from the study of the history of philosophy.

Finally, even if one were to grant that the history of philosophy and the historiographical issues that it raises could form the basis of some communication and dialogue between analysts and Continentalists, why should such communication and dialogue be expected to extend beyond those boundaries? One can imagine the two groups conversing about the history of philosophy and the historiographical issues it raises but drifting apart again when it comes to other philosophical questions.

These, indeed, are serious objections that go to the heart of my argument. They mean to point out that the study of the history of philosophy does not provide Continentalists and analysts with a common object, and, even if the object were conceded to be common, it would not provide the methodological basis and the core of issues that I have argued it would. Indeed, there is no point in denying the premises on which these objections are based. Continentalists and analysts are far apart in their views about the history of philosophy, its task, and the way to go about that task. But this does not mean that the study of the history of philosophy cannot provide a common ground to establish communication between them. For one thing, even if some philosophers adopt the extreme position of rejecting the independent status of the history of philosophy, that does not mean that all do.[44] Most in fact, do not. But, what is more important, even those that do reject it, in fact do *use* the history of philosophy in their work. This points to an important fact, namely, that their denial of the independent status of the history of philosophy is a theoretical posture. Now, for my argument I do not need to claim that Continentalists and analysts theoretically agree on the independent status of the history of philosophy at the outset; what I need to claim is merely that in practice they use the history of philosophy in their philosophizing, and investigating that history is part of what they do. My argument concerns practice, not theory. Indeed, mainstream philosophers before Kant frequently disagreed as to the ultimate status of so-called reality and the elements within it, but that did not mean that they did not have a common object of study. Descartes and Berkeley, for example, disagreed as to the status and nature of physical reality, but that does not mean that they did not discuss it and argue about its status and nature. Likewise, to disagree theoretically as to the ultimate status of the history of philosophy does not preclude an agreement in practice with respect to it as an object of study; that is, it does not preclude philosophers from actually going about its discussion and interpretation.

To the second objection, which points to the uselessness of dealing with superseded ideas, my response is that even if one were to grant that past ideas are worthless and outmoded, something that only few extremists would claim, what is important for my argument is not that those historical ideas and positions be useful, but that the investigation of the past raise philosophical questions both in general and of a historiographical nature. Moreover, history imposes itself on its students in a way that leads also to the adoption, either in practice or theory or both, of some methodological principles whose acceptance and discussion creates bridges among those engaged in the study of the history of philosophy. This I think should be clear from what was said earlier.

With respect to the questions raised concerning the canon, my answer is that they are largely irrelevant.[45] Doubtlessly, there will be more common ground among philosophers who study the same historical period or author than among those who do not. Such a study would provide not only a common basis of ideas but even a language that would have to be shared, namely, the terminology of the period or author under study. But none of this is necessary insofar as, regardless of the historical period or author under scrutiny, the student of the history of philosophy is confronted with certain historiographical issues common to all those students. Indeed, the very question concerning which is or should be the canon or works and authors of a particular period poses a historiographical issue that students of the history of philosophy need to address at some point, regardless of their ideological leanings. So, even to raise this objection to a certain extent is to be on the right track, that is, to be talking about a problem that should concern most philosophers and could bridge the gap between Continentalists and analysts.

As for the fourth objection, the answer would follow suit. The very differences in approach that Continentalists and analysts might employ concerning the study of the history of philosophy raise the kind of methodological questions that can bring together the two groups. Besides, I do want to emphasize the point I made earlier and that I illustrated with reference to the understanding of a historical text written in another language: Historical texts impose on those who wish to understand them certain conditions that are not negotiable and therefore must be accepted by those who wish to deal with them. These texts are like bacteria, visible only through a microscope. Regardless of what we may think of them, we can observe them *only through microscopes* and we can handle them *only with certain instruments.* In order to see them we must conform to certain procedures. Likewise, to study and understand the history of philosophy we must conform to the methodological parameters under which such study and understanding are possible.

In order to answer the last objection I must bring up two points. First, we must keep in mind that part of the chasm that separates analysts and Continentalists is practical, involving behavior and custom. Indeed, the strategy of dismissal so widespread in contemporary philosophy is a symptom of the practical, I am tempted to say "moral," dimension of the problem. And practical and moral problems are not solved with theoretical proposals. Let me explain. Contemporary philosophers, whether analysts or Continentalists, for the most part have been trained under the rigid parameters of their traditions. They have studied in ideologically onesided programs; they have been taught certain rules about philosophical method and style; they associate only with members of their own tradition; they read materials that conform to the rules they have been taught; and so on. All this has created certain habits that have become ingrained and prompt the reaction of dismissal when they are confronted with philosophers who do not write and behave as they do. Now, if it were possible to establish some area of philosophy where members of both traditions could communicate, we would go a long way toward overcoming the habits that have prevented communication in other areas. The establishment of at least one area of common activity could break the habitual insularity of both traditions and open the doors to communication and dialogue in other areas. And my proposal is that the best candidate for such an area is the history of philosophy and its historiography.

The second point that I must bring up is that, as I hope to illustrate in this book, the study of the history of philosophy is tied to philosophical issues of a nonhistorical nature. This is so in part because the historian of philosophy deals with the philosophical views of past philosophers and in part because the history of philosophy must be done philosophically. But also, as important as these, the historiographical issues posed by the study of the history of philosophy are closely related to fundamental issues in the philosophy of language, hermeneutics, and even metaphysics. Thus, the study of the history of philosophy and its historiography should plant the seeds of dialogue concerning other areas of philosophy among those who engage in it.

I should point out in closing that my hope that the study of the history of philosophy will bring together Continentalists and analysts, or at least some of them, is not purely speculative. There are indications that the philosophical climate is changing, at least in certain quarters. A few years back all signs pointed to the ever-increasing bifurcation of the Western philosophical tradition and the continued schizophrenia between analysts and Continentalists. Recent developments indicate, however, that some portions of the philosophical community are tired of this situation and are looking for ways to move beyond the impasse created by these two groups. There are many signs of these efforts. In the first place, there is an explicit awareness of both the philosophical bifurcation that has occurred and its pernicious effects.[46] These constitute a necessary first step in the search for a solution. As with any disease, the first step toward a cure is the realization that something is wrong with the organism. But, second, there have also been diagnoses of the origin of the problem and prescriptions for solution. Richard Rorty's widely known book, *Philosophy and the Mirror of Nature,* is an example of an analysis that aims at a diagnosis and prescription of sorts.[47] Third, there is a renewed interest among analysts in metaphysical questions and among Continentalists in language. Indeed, metaphysics once again is a reputable subject in Anglo-American philosophy, even if what is meant by that may not be exactly the same sort of thing in which Aristotle and Suárez were engaged. Fourth, even the term 'analyst' is being rejected by some members of the group, who insist that they are part of the philosophical mainstream that goes back to Descartes and Aristotle.[48]

All these are significant indications that the time is ripe for a rapprochement between Continentalists and analysts. The greatest sign of this change of attitude, however, is the renewed interest in the history of philosophy by both groups. Indeed, most other signs are somehow connected with a fresh interest in the history of philosophy. Among both analysts and Continentalists there is a growing concern with the philosophical past and an acknowledgment of its importance for the philosophical community.[49] This is evident among analysts in the work of P. F. Strawson, R. M. Hare, and Jonathan Bennett, for example, and among Continentalists in the work of post-Heideggerians, such as Gadamer and Foucault, whose interest in the history of philosophy in general has increased with time, although the seeds of it had already been planted by Heidegger himself. This in turn has fueled interest in historiographical questions related to the history of philosophy and has generated polemics concerning the interpretation and understanding of the past. Indeed, the word 'hermeneutics' has become fashionable in philosophical circles, and, although originally connected with the Continental tradition, it is now frequently found in discussions by Anglo-American philosophers. Hardly a month goes by in which one does not find items in the periodical literature that deal explicitly with historiographical issues.

The movement toward the history of philosophy is not misguided for the Western mainstream before Kant has elements common to both the critical and the poetic traditions. With the critical tradition it shares the emphasis on argumentation and the use of objective language; and with the poetic tradition it shares its interest in substantive metaphysical issues rather than purely formal or linguistic ones. The history of philosophy, therefore, may serve as a bridge between contemporary critics and poets. But we still do not know the details of how it may carry out such rapprochement and how it can be used to bring it about. In order to find an answer to those questions we need to know something about the history of philosophy, what it is, and how it is related to philosophy. To investigate such issues is precisely the task of this book. I shall begin, then, with a discussion of history, philosophy, and the history of philosophy.

NOTES

1. In Austria, for example, as Barry Smith has pointed out to me, the poetic tradition has not been able to establish dominance thanks to the strong Aristotelian-scholastic influence on Brentano, Meinong, and others.

2. Aristotle, *Metaphysics*, ch. 2 (982a5–18), trans. W. D. Ross, in Richard McKeon, ed., *The Basic Works of Aristotle* (New York: Random House, 1941), p. 691.

3. I am quite aware that in European languages other than English terms equivalent to 'science' are used to this day to refer to any rigorous procedure even in cases when they involve what we refer to as "the humanities." Thus much editorial and philological work is frequently described as "scientific." Note, however, that even in these cases, it is the procedure that is called "scientific," because it follows strict rules, and not the discipline itself. Thus philology is seldom called a science, whereas philological procedures are described as scientific if they fit certain models of rigor.

4. René Descartes, *A Discourse on Method*, trans. John Veitch (New York and London: Everyman's Library, 1951), p. 3.

5. Henry of Ghent, *Summae questionum ordinariarum* I, a. 1, q. 1.

6. Averroes, *On the Harmony of Religion and Philosophy*, ch. 2, trans. G. F. Hourani (London: Luzac & Company, 1961).

7. Richard Rorty has used the term 'poetic' to refer to the Heideggerian tradition. My use of the term is both wider and different. For his position, see "Philosophy as Science, as Metaphor, and as Politics," in A. Cohen and M. Dascal, eds., *The Institution of Philosophy: A Discipline in Crisis* (La Salle, Ill.: Open Court, 1989), pp. 13–33.

8. Plotinus, *Enneads* VI, 9, [9], 4, in Elmer O'Brien, ed. and trans., *The Essential Plotinus* (Indianapolis: Hackett Publishing, 1975), p. 78.

9. Ibid.

10. Ibid., III, 8, [30], 6, p. 168.

11. Ibid., III, 8, [30], 1, p. 163.

12. I Corinthians 1:20 ff.

13. Appendix B, in John Mansley Robinson, *An Introduction to Early*

Greek Philosophy: The Chief Fragments and Ancient Testimony, with Connecting Commentary (Boston: Houghton-Mifflin, 1968), p. 295.

14. Francis Bacon, *The New Organon,* Preface, in Fulton H. Anderson, ed., *The New Organon and Related Writings* (New York: Liberal Arts Press, 1960), p. 34.

15. Francis Bacon, *The Great Instauration,* The Plan, in *The New Organon and Related Writings,* p. 20.

16. *The New Organon,* Aphorisms 1, in *The New Organon and Related Writings,* p. 39.

17. Ibid., Preface and *statim.*

18. John Mansley Robinson, *An Introduction to Early Greek Philosophy,* p. 127.

19. Ibid., p. 128.

20. These critics were the pluralists. See ibid., p. 129.

21. Ibid., p. 133.

22. Ibid.

23. Ibid., p. 110.

24. David Hume, Introduction, *A Treatise of Human Nature,* ed. L. A. Selby-Bigge (Oxford: The Clarendon Press, 1965), pp. xvii–xviii.

25. Ibid., p. xx.

26. Ibid.

27. Ibid., p. xxii.

28. Ibid., p. 618.

29. Bonaventure, Introduction to fourth vision, *Collationes in Hexaëmeron,* III, VII, ed. R. Delorme (Florence: Ad Claras Aquas, 1934).

30. Étienne Gilson, *History of Christian Philosophy in the Middle Ages* (New York: Random House, 1955), p. 616.

31. Immanuel Kant, Preface to First Edition, *Critique of Pure Reason,* trans. Norman Kemp Smith (London: Macmillan, 1963), p. 7.

32. Ibid.

33. Ibid., pp. 396–408.

34. For some of the reasons why positivism and exact, scientific philosophy developed in Continental Europe, see Barry Smith, "Austrian Origins of

Logical Positivism," in B. Gower, ed., *Logical Positivism in Perspective* (London and Sydney: Croom, 1987; and Totowa, N.J.: Barnes and Noble, 1988), pp. 35–68.

35. Brentano also seems to have played an earlier role on these developments in Austria. See Barry Smith, "On the Origins of Analytic Philosophy," *Grazer Philosophische Studien* 35 (1989): 153–173.

36. P. F. Strawson, Introduction, *Individuals,* (Garden City, N.Y.: Doubleday and Company, 1963), p. xiii.

37. Walter Kaufman, *Existentialism from Dostoevsky to Sartre* (Cleveland and New York: World Publishing, 1966), p. 51.

38. See A. J. Mandt, "The Inevitability of Pluralism: Philosophical Practice and Philosophical Excellence," in Cohen and Dascal, *The Institution of Philosophy,* pp. 77–101.

39. See Richard Bernstein, "Philosophical Rift: A Tale of Two Approaches," *New York Times* (December 29, 1987), p. A1. Also Roy Edley, who states that "English-speaking philosophy [i.e., linguistic analysis] in particular has submissively dwindled into a humble academic specialism, on its own understanding isolated from the practical problems facing society, and from contemporary Continental thought." See his short editorial foreword to Jonathan Rée, Michael Ayers, and Adam Westoby, *Philosophy and Its Past* (Hassocks, Sussex: Harvester Press, 1978).

40. Indeed, it has become commonplace to hold that there are no common problems even in the history of philosophy. See Rorty's Preface in *Philosophy and the Mirror of Nature* (Princeton, N.J.: Princeton University Press, 1979), p. xiii; and Jonathan Rée, "Philosophy and the History of Philosophy," in Rée et al., *Philosophy and Its Past.* The notion that there are no fundamental and perennial questions in philosophy goes back at least to Hegel's view that history is never quite the same, resulting as it does from a dialectical process. See his *Logic* (Encyclopedia), ch. 1, par. 13 and ch. 7, par. 83, trans. William Wallace (Oxford: University Press, 2nd. ed. 1892), pp. 22 and 159–160.

41. Not all philosophers agree with this point. For some arguments against it, see Richard A. Watson, "Method in the History of Philosophy," in *The Breakdown of Cartesian Metaphysics* (Atlantic Highlands, N.J.: Humanities Press International, Inc., 1987), pp. 13–15.

42. Texts, as we shall see in Chapter 4, also can be composed of sounds; they need not be written. However, for present purposes I shall assume we are dealing with written texts.

43. Cf. Michael L. Morgan, "The Goals and Methods of the History of Philosophy," *Review of Metaphysics* 40 (1987): 720; and Oskar Kristeller, "Philosophy and Its Historiography," *Journal of Philosophy* 82, no. 11 (1985): 623.

44. My answer to this position here is obviously pragmatic. In the sec-

tion on History of Chapter 1, I return to it, but deal with it in a different way. For another approach, see Jack W. Meiland, *Scepticism and Historical Knowledge* (New York: Random House, 1965).

45. The questions are important for other reasons, however, as Bruce Kuklick has shown in "Seven Thinkers and How They Grew: Descartes, Spinoza, Leibniz; Locke, Berkeley, Hume; Kant," in Richard Rorty, J. B. Schneewind and Quentin Skinner, eds., *Philosophy in History: Essays on the Historiography of Philosophy* (Cambridge: Cambridge University Press, 1984), pp. 125–139.

46. Cf. articles by O'Connor, Dreyfus, and Haugeland in *APA Newsletter on Teaching Philosophy* 2, no. 3 (1981). Many philosophers think that philosophy is in crisis, although some deny it. For an analysis of the situation, see the various papers in Cohen and Dascal, *The Institution of Philosophy*. Héctor-Neri Castañeda is one of those who disagrees with the view that philosophy is in crisis. See his "Philosophy as a Science and as a Worldview," in ibid., pp. 35–59.

47. See also Kenneth Baynes, James Bohman, and Thomas McCarthy, eds., *After Philosophy: End or Transformation?* (Cambridge: MIT Press, 1988). For another diagnosis and prescription, see Hilary Putnam's "Why Is a Philosopher?" in Cohen and Dascal, *The Institution of Philosophy*, pp. 61–75. He argues for a return to common sense. Mandt's solution to the analytic-Continental split is to understand analysis as a "community of discourse" rather than as an "ideological system," thus allowing the breakup of *prima* facie barriers to communication. See paper cited in note 28. Both of these suggestions are helpful but, if my analysis is correct, we need much more; we need the restoration of a common object and method, and this cannot be achieved through these suggestions alone.

48. This is a popular stand these days. See the articles cited in note 30.

49. The Editor's Page of a recent issue of *The American Philosophical Quarterly* 26 (1989), includes the following statement: "it is our shared exposure to salient developments in the history of philosophy that binds us philosophers...into a single community.... It is our common training in the history of the subject that binds us into a community sharing a common culture and prevents philosophy from splitting into a set of disparate enterprises unified in name only for the sake of administrative convenience."

Chapter One

History, Philosophy, and the History of Philosophy

Any inquiry into philosophical historiography must say something about the nature of the history of philosophy, and, since the history of philosophy involves the notions of history and philosophy, it must begin by saying something about them as well. In the remarks that follow my primary purpose is to set some limits to the notions in question, distinguishing them from each other and from other notions frequently confused with them. I begin by discussing a difficulty often raised when trying to pinpoint the nature of the history of philosophy. The rest of the chapter is divided into three parts, dealing respectively with history, philosophy, and the history of philosophy. In this context I take the opportunity to raise the thorny question concerning the translation of past ideas into the conceptual frameworks of the present and the controversial issue concerning whether the history of philosophy can include truth value judgments about ideas from the past. The main thesis I defend is that the history of philosophy includes descriptive, interpretative, and evaluative propositions and therefore can avoid neither interpretation nor evaluation. I also defend in passing the position that it is possible to translate past ideas into present conceptual frameworks without substantially distorting them; that is, indeed, the role of interpretation in the history of philosophy. Let me begin, then, with some remarks about the initial difficulty concerning the nature of the history of philosophy to which reference was made.

To investigate the nature of something entails coming up with an appropriate definition of the thing in question. The job of the definition is to specify a set of necessary and sufficient conditions. Thus the traditional definition of *human being* as "rational animal" is supposed to identify those conditions (i.e., rationality, animality, and whatever is entailed by them) that make a human being human and without which he or she could not exist as human. Linguistically one can say that a definition is an expression that identifies the necessary and sufficient conditions for something to be called such and such.

The task of finding definitions has been challenged in contemporary philosophy, in particular by the disciples of Wittgenstein. They argue that it is not always possible to identify necessary and sufficient conditions that apply to all members of a class of things to which we refer with the same term other than the fact that we refer to them with that term.[1] Thus, it is not possible to find a feature common to all cats, tigers, or human beings beyond the fact that they are called cats, tigers, and human beings. The reason is that they seem to be related not in the way in which things that share a feature are related, but rather in the way families are related by resemblance: Each member of the family resembles at least one member of the family in some way, but no member of the family resembles every member of the family even in one way. No tiger is like every tiger even though it is like at least one other tiger in some respect. This is a standard objection against the attempt to find definitions, and one that is certainly sufficiently serious to merit special attention. Because it is such a blanket indictment against the entire procedure of determining definitions and also because I have already dealt in some way with it elsewhere, I shall not consider it further here.[2] Its discussion should be part of a more specific treatise on epistemology. I mention this objection only to make clear that at some point it has to be met.

The second objection is much more pointed. Unlike the previous one, it is not based on the rejection of any search for definitions. It merely attacks the possibility of establishing a definition of the history of philosophy by arguing that the history of philosophy is not a natural kind and as such is not definable.[3] This leaves open, of course, the question of the posssibility of the definition of natural kinds, but that is of no concern to us at present.

That the history of philosophy is not a natural kind seems to me rather obvious. Natural kinds include only entities that are naturally produced, that is, entities that are not the product of human art. A fig tree is an instance of a natural kind and so are Paul and my cat Medea. Neither Paul, nor Medea, nor the tree is the result of human creation. Paul's parents had something to do with his conception and fig trees may be planted and cared for, but the processes responsible for their production are not the product of human invention and design. The case is quite different with the chair on which I am sitting or the signs I use to write these thoughts. Neither the chair nor the signs are instances of natural kinds, for both are the products of human design. The history of philosophy, too, does not seem to me to be in any way like Paul or Medea, but more like the chair and the signs. So I am willing to accept, at least provisionally and for the sake of argument, that the history of philosophy is not a natural kind. This means, of course, that it must be an artificial kind, since the categories of natural and artificial are both exclusive and mutually exhaustive. The history of philosophy, then, must be considered to be the product of human art.

Still, although not natural, the history of philosophy is a kind and as such should be able to be defined in the same way that other artificial kinds are defined. For there is nothing strange, let alone impossible, about defining artificial kinds. The definition in that case will not be the sort of definition that one provides for natural kinds, but it will be a definition nonetheless insofar as it specifies the necessary and sufficient conditions for something to qualify as history of philosophy or to be called "history of philosophy." The fact that these conditions may be conventional or even stipulative does not mean that it is impossible to specify them clearly and with precision nor that they are useless. For example, we will all agree, I am sure, that the letter 'A' is a conventional sign and not a natural kind. Thus the conditions that are necessary and sufficient for something to qualify as A are subject entirely to an agreement among users of A. Yet it is clear also that those conditions are quite effective in determining a good from a bad A, a well written from a badly written A, and in distinguishing an A from, say, a B.

An even more dramatic example and one that both resembles the cases of philosophy and the history of philosophy more than the one just given and also pinpoints the source of at least some definitions of artificial kinds is the case of an artifact such as a chair. Clearly chairs are artificial kinds, invented by human beings. There was a time at which there were no chairs and some bright ancestor of ours came up with the idea of making one. Presumably human beings sat down from the very beginning, so that there have been objects used as chairs from the moment humans made their appearance on Earth. But that does not mean that there were chairs at the time. Chairs have existed only from the moment in which someone made one. Now, it is also clear that there are comfortable and uncomfortable chairs, chairs that serve their purpose well—we might call them "good" chairs—and chairs that do not serve their purpose well—we might call them "bad" chairs—as well as beautiful and ugly chairs, and so forth. One may want to argue that, once we get into the area of beauty, things get too complicated to draw any conclusions from the example. But if we restrict ourselves to whether a chair does or does not serve the purpose for which it was intended, we then must accept that we have some kind of idea of what a chair should be. That idea, of course, is a definition of sorts that arises from the function for which the chair was made. Likewise, then, with the history of philosophy: The history of philosophy, as a product of human art, was invented for a certain purpose and that purpose should provide us with criteria whereby we can distinguish between the history of philosophy and other things as well as between good and bad histories of philosophy. That we in fact use such criteria, by the way, is clear from among other things the very distinction we draw between the history of philosophy and chairs.

Thus, to say that the history of philosophy is not a natural kind should not be an obstacle to reaching a definition of it that will distinguish it from other things and allow us to separate good from bad history of philosophy. Having said that, I should point out that in what follows I do not provide a precise and well-formed definition of the history of philosophy. Indeed, I identify only some features associated with it that distinguish it from history and philosophy. The reason is that, given the purpose of this and subsequent chapters, such a definition is not required. There is no need for us, then, to engage in the complicated and controversial process of actually trying to formulate one. Let me begin with history.

I. HISTORY

The term 'history' is ambiguous in the sense that it is used in the language to mean a number of different things. In one sense the term is used to refer to a series of events or happenings.[4] Thus, for example, we speak of the history of Ancient Greece when we want to refer to a series of events that took place during a certain period of time in Greece. And we also talk about the history of our lives as comprising such events as birth, marriage, education, accidents, and so on. In this sense any event is part of history as long as it is not presently taking place. Indeed, to take place is in a sense to become part of history, since the present consists of a fleeting moment constantly turning into the past.

But the term 'history' has also a second meaning derived from the etymology of the original Greek word, which meant information, inquiry, and narrative. In this sense the term is used to refer to an account of past events rather than to the events themselves.[5] Insofar as it is an *account* it goes beyond a simple narrative, chronicle, or annal, for it contains or should contain references to their causes, to the relations among the events in question, and to the consequences they brought about.[6] Narratives, chronicles, and annals simply record past events dispensing with any attempt to account for them by providing explanations of why they happened and of their relations and results.[7] Moreover, insofar as history refers to past, rather than future, events, it has to be distinguished from prophecy. Prophecy, like history, is an account of events, but the events in question have yet to occur. History, understood in this second sense, is a product of human enterprise. Although events themselves may or may not be the result of human action, history as an account of such events is necessarily the result of human action. An earthquake is without a doubt a historical happening that must be recorded in the history books of the particular place where it happened, even though it is also a natural event in whose origin human beings play no role. And Caesar's murder by Brutus is also a historical occurrence, although in this case the event is not natural, but rather the result of human will and action. Still, an account of either event is necessarily the product of human will and action. So, history in the second sense, that is, understood as an account of events, is necessarily the result of human enterprise.

There is still a third meaning of the term 'history' that should not be overlooked and that results precisely from the human effort to provide an account of past events. In this sense, 'history' refers to the procedure followed in the production of the account of events. By 'history' is meant, then, a certain discipline of learning whose function is both to produce appropriate accounts of past events and to devise the rules that, when applied, would yield such appropriate accounts.

From what has been said it would appear that there are important ontological differences among history considered as a series of events, history as an account of those events, and history as a discipline of learning. The first may be composed of linguistic or nonlinguistic elements. Demosthenes's speeches are historical events and composed of language, but Caesar's death is not, regardless of what one might wish to call it, a linguistic fact. On the other hand, the description of historical events generally yields linguistic facts, namely, propositions such as: 'Demosthenes gave a speech on such and such a date,' 'Caesar died,' or 'Caesar was killed by Brutus.'

Moreover, history considered as a discipline of learning may involve either an activity, a set of linguistic facts, or both. The activity occurs when someone is in the process of producing an account of certain events. Clearly the process is neither the linguistic account of events nor the events themselves, but rather the activity whereby the events are described and explained. On the other hand, history as a discipline may also include a set of linguistic facts or propositions, but those facts and propositions have to be distinguished from the facts and propositions that propose to give an account of nonlinguistic events. They are quite different, indeed, for they formulate, explain, and justify the rules that need to be followed to produce a historical account of events. For example, one such rule might stipulate that "eyewitness accounts of events should be given more weight in the establishment of facts than noneyewitness accounts of events." And another rule might establish that "contemporaneous documentary evidence is generally more reliable than noncontemporaneous verbal evidence." The formulation, explanation, and justification of those rules is what has come to be called "historiography" in order to distinguish it from history considered as a series of events, as an account of those events, and as the activity whereby an account of events is produced. I should add at this point that historiography itself is both a set of rules concerning the procedure to be followed by historians in their production of an account of past events and also the activity, that is, the procedure followed in a historiographical investigation. I omit further immediate reference to this last wrinkle in order to avoid unnecessary complications.

History may be interpreted, therefore, in the following different ways:

I. History as a series of past events.
II. History as an account of past events.
III. History as a discipline of learning
   A. Activity whereby an account of past events is produced.
   B. Formulation, explanation, and justification of rules to which the production of an account of past events must adhere (historiography).

Before I go on let me add at this point that the notions of history as a series of past events, an account of past events, and a discipline of learning have all been challenged at one time or another. Some argue, for example, that there are no such things as past events to which we can have access and for which we can provide an account. Past events, they argue, are constructs "created" by the historian, so the whole notion of being able "to account" for them is absurd. Past events are not independent from what we say and think about them. Indeed, the very notion of "a series" of past events points to the kind of ordering that the mind brings into history. The ontological distinction made above between a series of events and the account of it breaks down. Moreover, under these conditions, the whole idea of a discipline of learning with rules and regulations to guide the procedure whereby an account of past events is produced becomes meaningless and/or useless.

There are many ways of answering this objection, but for our purposes I believe we could dispose of it in the following way. One could point out that this objection is part of a more fundamental epistemic view in which the object of knowledge is seen as dependent on the knower insofar as all the categories through which the knower approaches it are part of the knower and not categories that apply to the object of knowledge independently of the knower. Because this objection is based on a general epistemic assumption, the place to deal with it is not in a specific historiographical context, but rather in a general discussion of epistemology. For our purposes it is sufficient to point out three things: First, the distinction between a series of events and the account of those events is one substantiated by our ordinary ways of looking at the world and therefore can serve for our present limited purpose. Second, this distinction is generally operative in the work of historians and it is only historiographers who challenge it. In that sense it is more appropriate for us to take it for granted than to reject it at the outset. Finally, the very notions of a series of past events and an account of those events are easily distinguishable and seem to reflect the intent of the historical enterprise. For these reasons, then, I believe we can dispense with this objection here, although I do not believe by any means that it need not be addressed or that my answer to it has been completely satisfactory. It is for epistemologists, however, to deal with it in greater detail.[8]

Now, apart from the objection just discussed, the understandings of history as a series of past events or as a discipline of learning seem quite uncontroversial. But the conception of history as an account of past events needs further clarification and analysis. I shall, therefore, turn my attention to this notion before we proceed further.

Let me begin by pointing out that history interpreted as an account of past events does not necessarily have to be linguistic; for example, there are pictorial accounts of events. Moreover, it is logically possible that there may be nonlinguistic, nonpictorial accounts of events as well. For example, it is altogether possible that there are beings who communicate with each other telepathically without the use of linguistic—whether written, oral, or mental—signs, although I have a hard time imagining how that could happen.[9] On the other hand, it is obvious that most human accounts of events use linguistic signs of one sort or another, and in fact we are restricted to written or oral signs owing to the requirements imposed on the transmission of information over long spans of time. So, for all intents and purposes, our discussion may be restricted to linguistic accounts. And since linguistic accounts are composed of propositions, my discussion of history as an account of past events will concern the propositions used to provide such an account.[10]

A general survey of historical propositions, that is, of propositions that form part of linguistic accounts of past events, yields three basic categories. I use the terms 'descriptive,' 'interpretative,' and 'evaluative' to refer to them. The primary function of descriptive propositions is to present accurately those events and their relations for which there can be direct empirical evidence. Therefore, they involve descriptions of events and their relations, descriptions of contemporaneous statements concerning those events and their relations, and descriptions of what later historians said or wrote concerning those events and their relations as well as descriptions of the relations of the statements of various historians concerning their own views. As examples of these propositions consider the following:[11]

1^h. X killed Y.

2^h. X died.

3^h. X's death followed X's killing of Y.

4^h. M, a contemporary of X, stated that X had not killed Y.

5^h. N, another of X's contemporaries, disagreed with M concerning M's view that X had not killed Y.

6^h. R, a later historian, stated that M was right in holding that X had not killed Y.

7^h. S, another later historian, disagreed with R's view concerning M.

Note that in all cases the function of propositions 1^h–7^h is descriptive in the sense specified earlier, although in some cases the description is of events (1^h, 2^h) and their relations (3^h) whereas in other cases it concerns what historians and other persons have said or written about those events and their relations (4^h–7^h). Note also that for a proposition to be descriptive it is not necessary that the historians who put it forth themselves have direct empirical evidence of the event the proposition is supposed to describe. Historians can rely on eyewitness accounts of an event, for example. The point I wish to stress, then, is that the primary function of these propositions is to describe an event for which somewhere along the line historians believe there is or could be direct empirical evidence, even if no historian witnessed the event, as most likely they did not. Thus, for example, the proposition 'Brutus killed Caesar' is descriptive even though no historian witnessed the event. The reason is that historians believe there were or could have been eyewitness accounts of it. Indeed, it is quite common to have events for which there are no surviving eyewitnesses, but which nonetheless are the subject of descriptive propositions. For example, let us suppose that when Brutus killed Caesar no one but the two of them were present and that in the scuffle between Caesar and Brutus, Brutus also was mortally wounded and died before anyone entered the room where the event took place. In that case the proposition 'Brutus killed Caesar' would still be descriptive according to the given criteria because, although living eyewitnesses of the event could not have testified to it, there was at least one (perhaps two, if Caesar was aware of what was happening) eyewitness of the event and he could have testified about it. The point, of course, is not whether there are or are not eyewitnesses, or whether they testified or not, or even whether there is any empirical evidence for it or not, but rather whether or not the propositions' function is to describe events of the sort that can yield direct empirical evidence.

The use of the expression 'empirical evidence' is meant to rule out evidence of a nonperceptual nature, such as reports concerning mental states and events even when the reporter is the person who is experiencing them. Thus propositions such as 'I thought X had killed Y' (when 'thought' is used descriptively and not as standing for something like "I believe"), 'I intended to kill Y,' or 'I am mentally distressed when I think that I intended to kill Y,' do not meet the criteria I have established for descriptive historical propositions. One could point out, of course, that the subjects who propose such propositions and are not lying when they do so are describing states of affairs for which they have direct evidence—they are reporting their thoughts, intentions, and mental states. And that seems reasonable to me. But the evidence in question is not "empirical"; it is rather the peculiar type of evidence to which one has access in one's mind. This poses interesting and difficult questions related to the philosophy of mind, but since they are related only marginally to our subject matter and our purposes are limited, they will not be discussed here. Let it suffice to point out that the description of one's mental states is a tricky business for at least two reasons: First, the reporter is an interested party, and interested parties do not make the best witnesses; and second, one's memory of one's mental states is unreliable even in cases where the mental event in question is fairly recent.

It is important to recognize as well that descriptive propositions may be false. That is, even though historians may think the empirical evidence they have verifies those propositions, they may be wrong. Whether a proposition is descriptive or not, then, does not depend on whether it actually describes accurately the event it purports to describe, but whether it purports primarily to do so on the basis of direct empirical evidence. Most historians' work, by its very nature, is far removed from the events that it studies and thus has to rely on second- and thirdhand sources. But that does not change the descriptive character of certain propositions they use in their accounts.

In contrast with the primary function of descriptive propositions, the primary function of interpretative propositions is not to describe events for which there can be direct empirical evidence, but rather to go beyond them and reconstruct the fabric of unstated motives, intangible factors, and implicit circumstances within which events take place and for which there can be no direct empirical evidence. In addition, some of these interpretations contain broad generalizations based on limited evidence but backed up by more or less accepted historiographical interpretative principles; and others include inferences concerning events for which there is no direct empirical evidence but which it makes sense to suppose happened. This indicates that there is some descriptive import and intent in interpretative propositions, but the historian is well aware that the description is based only on a reconstruction of elements that fails to adhere to strict evidential empirical criteria. Therefore, we find in histories interpretative propositions such as the following:

a^h. X must have killed Y in order to inherit Y's fortune.

b^h. That X killed Y meant that X had an intense hatred for Y's mother.

c^h. The killing of Y gave rise to a series of events that led to the collapse of monarchy.

d^h. N, a contemporary of X, thought that X had killed Y in order to inherit Y's fortune.

The use of terms such as 'must have,' 'meant,' and 'thought' in the first two (a^h and b^h) and the last (d^h) propositions and the general and causal character of the third proposition indicate that these propositions go beyond the facts for which there can be direct empirical evidence in various ways. The first proposition (a^h) presents a conjecture concerning the reasons why X killed Y. The second (b^h) interprets the import and meaning of what X did. The third (c^h) draws a causal connection for which there can be no direct empirical evidence. Finally, the fourth (d^h) attributes a view to a person which that person may not in fact have held despite what she actually said or wrote and for which there is no direct empirical evidence. The last case may be illustrated with the example of Galileo, who according to the records of his trial is supposed to have recanted his view that the Earth moves around the Sun. The documented evidence we have indicates that he recanted, and thus on that basis we could infer that he actually thought that the Earth does not move around the Sun. But that would be a conjecture that in fact subsequent history has rejected, going to the extreme of giving credance to an unsubstantiated story according to which Galileo actually said to himself at the end of his trial: "But it moves."

To the type of propositions listed under the interpretative category must be added also propositions that report the mental states of those who report them. For example, take the three mentioned earlier:

e^h. I thought X had killed Y.

f^h. I intended to kill Y.

g^h. I feel distressed when I think that I intended to kill Y.

In these cases, as already pointed out, the evidence for the propositions is not only private and available only to the reporter, it also is not the kind of empirical evidence used to back up what I have classified as descriptive historical propositions. The evidence is direct but it is not empirical, since thoughts, intentions, and feelings are not subject to perception. One thinks thoughts, has intentions, and feels or has feelings, but one does not perceive them as I perceived, for example, that X killed Y.

None of the propositions a^h–g^h, then, restricts itself to the description of events for which there can be direct empirical evidence. The first two propositions refer to motives that may very well have been the causes of the events in question, but that certainly cannot be regarded as facts for which there could be observable evidence. And the third and fourth go well beyond the facts. These propositions, then, describe an edifice of reconstructed circumstances that in turn is used to interpret and make sense of particular historical events within a larger context.

Finally, we come to a third category of historical propositions, the evaluative. These propositions are characterized by the fact that they contain evaluations both of historical events and of the views of historians concerning those events. In this case there is generally no attempt at description. Moreover, the evaluations in question are based on principles and criteria that are part of neither descriptive nor interpretative historical propositions and, therefore, are derived from sources other than history as we have understood it here; they are either part of historiography, which sets the rules for generating historical accounts, or are derived from some other disciplines. As examples of evaluative propositions consider the following:

A^h. X was a bad ruler.

B^h. X's death was advantageous for country C.

C^h. M, a contemporary of X, was wrong in thinking that X had not killed Y.

D^h. R, a later historian, who stated that M was right, was wrong.

E^h. From year y^1 to year y^{1+n} there was considerable progress.

F^h. Developments d and d' meant a step backward in cultural development.

This third category of propositions clearly is the most controversial, for the terms 'bad,' 'advantageous,' 'wrong,' 'right,' 'progress,' and 'backward' indicate value judgments. Some historians will want to argue that it is not the business of the historian to issue evaluations of any kind, but simply to describe historical events in an objective and intelligible fashion. Others agree that description is not enough and interpretation is required, but reject the view that evaluation has a place in historical accounts. And the case becomes more controversial in the context of the history of philosophy, as we shall see later. At this point, however, I would like to argue that history involves both *de facto* and *de jure* evaluation. It is evident, *de facto,* that most histories and certainly all good histories make judgments as to the value of historical characters and events. What history of Portugal, for example, would not characterize the eighteenth century Lisbon earthquake as disastrous? And what historian of the Roman empire would refrain from commenting on the lack of moral restraint of Nero and Caligula? Certainly Suetonius was not shy about making such comments. Indeed, I do not think that we can find any history so value-sanitized that it does not have any propositions of the type represented by A^h–F^h.

Not only *de facto,* however, but also *de jure* it makes sense to argue that history without evaluation is not history or at least not good history, for values themselves, though intangible, play important roles in historical development. Therefore, only if historians understand those values *qua* values, by judging their appropriateness and validity, can they truly understand historical processes (more on this when I get to the history of philosophy). Moreover, what would be the use of studying history if we cannot learn anything from it?

And to learn implies judgments concerning what is right and wrong, good and bad, worthy and unworthy, and whether progress or regress has occurred. It should indeed be no surprise that the overriding moralistic concerns of the Greeks and Romans are responsible for their concern with history. We must accept, then, that evaluation and evaluative propositions are an integral part of historical accounts. Since my main concern in this book is with the history of philosophy and not just with history, I will let the case for the inclusion of value judgments in history rest on these grounds. When we come to the history of philosophy, however, I shall provide a more elaborate and, I hope, convincing set of arguments.

From all of this we may conclude, on the one hand, that history comprises a wide range of propositions and that it is a mistake to think, as some philosophers of history have thought, that history is exclusively descriptive, or interpretative, or evaluative. Nor should it be thought, on the other hand, that these categories are meant to be mutually exclusive and exhaustive. They are not mutually exclusive because there may be cases in which a particular proposition does not fit clearly into any one of the three categories and there are cases where a proposition would seem to fall into more than one category. Indeed, some of the examples of propositions that we saw earlier reveal on analysis that they contain elements of description, interpretation, and evaluation. Certainly it is quite evident that most evaluative propositions contain descriptive and interpretative elements even though their primary function may be to evaluate. Take the first example given of evaluative propositions, A^h: "X was a bad ruler." In saying the X was a bad ruler one is also asserting that X was a ruler and thus giving a description. When we come to proposition C^h ("M, a contemporary of X, was wrong in thinking that X had not killed Y"), the use of the term 'thinking' to talk about M clearly indicates an interpretation, since there cannot be direct empirical evidence of what someone else thinks or even of the fact that he or she is thinking. And similar points could be made about most of the other examples of propositions. In short, I am quite aware that the dividing line between these categories of propositions is tenuous, but I do want to insist that with respect to *their primary function* in a large number of cases propositions will clearly fall into one of these categories and only into one; and that most of those propositions that seem to defy this classification can be brought in line with it through analysis.

Again, the categories are not meant to be exhaustive, because it may turn out on further reflection that one or more of these categories need to be subdivided into further categories or that there may be categories not included in the three mentioned. For example, the category of evaluative propositions may be subdivided according to various evaluative criteria: one may want to separate those propositions that involve truth value judgments from those that express aesthetic and moral judgments. And interpretative propositions could be subdivided into those that involve psychological elements, social aspects, and so on. Moreover, there seem to be interpretative and evaluative factors that do not fit the categorical analysis as given. For example, clearly the historian "selects" materials and such selection determines in important ways the nature of the resulting historical account. But where do we put selection? Certainly not in the categories that have been specified, since selection is an act and not a proposition. Indeed, I would classify it as an act based, in the best of cases, on some historiographical principle itself expressed by a proposition and, in the worst, on idiosyncratic consciously or unconsciously operating principles. As such, however, selection influences historical accounts and, since it is not based on direct empirical evidence, involves interpretation or evaluation.[12] But selection is not a proposition that is part of the historical account itself. All this should indicate that the analysis of historical propositions into the three categories I have introduced here has its advantages but also its limitations. Those limitations, however, do not undermine the conclusions to which we shall arrive.

Before I finish the discussion of history, I must note a very important feature of historical propositions that seems to characterize all of them regardless of their primarily descriptive, interpretative, or evaluative import: All of them have a reference to temporality, provenance, and individuals. This should come as no surprise, for the aim of history is to give an account of the past, and although that aim is variously carried out through description, interpretation, and evaluation, the descriptions, interpretations, and evaluations that result always carry a reference, either direct or indirect, to time, to a source or origin, and to individuals. This should be evident in the examples of historical propositions we have provided. In all of them there is an explicit temporal element that characterizes all historical propositions. Indeed, even when historians use the historical present tense, it is always evident at some point that the historical account refers to the past.

Now, the case for provenance should be as easy to make. Although there may not be explicit references to a particular place in every historical proposition, even in those cases where there is not, we can always find some indirect reference that indicates that the proposition involves events that took place in a certain location. Temporal reference and provenance, then, are of the essence of history and no account can claim to be historical that lacks reference to time and provenance. The necessary reference to time and provenance gives history a unique character and separates it from all other disciplines of learning. There are, of course, other disciplines of learning, such as archeology and natural history, that also deal with the past, but a closer look at these disciplines indicates that they are in fact historical. The case of natural history should require little argument, since its historical character is displayed in its very name. And with archeology, it should suffice to point to its concern with the understanding of and accounting for the existence and character of artifacts from the past.

The comparison between history and other disciplines of learning brings me to the third characteristic of historical propositions: the reference to individuals. This raises an interesting issue, namely, the question of whether history can be considered a science, when science is generally understood, as Aristotle postulated more than 2,000 years ago, to deal with the universal. After all, so the argument could go, the aim of science is to discover principles and relations that apply to all cases and which scientists formulate as laws that allow them to understand the way the world functions and to predict the future. Scientists are not interested in what is idiosyncratic of, say, this particular rock or that particular heart; they examine the particular only to learn some general principle that may be applicable to all instances of a type. By contrast, historians seem to do just the reverse; they are interested in particular events rather than in universal laws or principles that govern events.

Of course, if by history one means historiography, then it is clear that it deals with universals, for the aim of historiography is to formulate the universal rules of procedure to be used in all historical investigations. Those rules are meant to apply to the investigation of particular events, but they are not themselves individual or concerned with individual procedures. If they were, they would be useless, since they would apply to an individual case (or cases) and not to any others, whereas it is precisely the latter that the historiographer seeks to understand. But, as mentioned earlier, it is useful to keep history separate from historiography, for the historian and the historiographer are involved in enterprises that have different aims and follow different procedures.

Nor should history be confused with the philosophy of history.[13] The philosophy of history, unlike history, deals with the way in which historical events in general, not particular events, unfold, how they are related, and the forces that bring about change and development. Philosophers of history refer to individuals, as other philosophers and scientists do, in order to gather data that may help them draw generalizations or as examples to illustrate their views. But their main concern is with the formulation and discovery of the laws and principles that govern history, and those are necessarily universal. The philosophy of history, then, deals with universals, and this is something quite different from history when history is considered as an account of past events.[14]

Now, since we do not understand history here as either historiography or the philosophy of history, can we still say that it is a science in spite of its primary concern with the individual rather than the universal? Aristotle answered this question affirmatively but relegated history to a lower scientific level than those disciplines of learning that deal exclusively with the universal. I am not going to defend or attack Aristotle on this point, nor am I going to argue that history is or is not a science. To do that I would have to get involved in an extended discussion of what constitutes scientific knowledge that would take us far from our present concerns and would require more time and space than I have at my disposal. What I am prepared to defend is that the argument against the scientific nature of history based on the fact that history deals with individuals rather than universals is not convincing. I have two reasons to support my claim. The first reason is that, contrary to what Aristotle thought, not all science deals primarily with the universal. We already saw the cases of natural history and archeology, for example. Of course, someone might wish to say that those disciplines themselves, insofar as they do not deal with universals, cannot be considered sciences. But even if we were to grant that natural history and archeology are not really sciences, what do we make of natural theology and astronomy? I mention natural theology both because it is supposed to deal with only one individual, namely God, and because most of those who follow the Aristotelian model accept theology as a science. But even if we were to discard natural theology, we still have astronomy, for an integral component of astronomy is the investigation of individual celestial bodies.

The second reason for affirming that history could be a science in spite of its concern with the individual is, first, that history is not concerned exclusively with the individual, and that the other sciences, even those whose primary concern is the universal, are not concerned exclusively with the universal. It is true that the primary aim of history, as already stated, is the understanding of the past, but such an understanding, because it requires interpretation and evaluation, involves the use of universal concepts and principles. Moreover, part of the aim of history is to learn from the past and as such it does not shy away from the formulation of principles that can be applied to other circumstances. These always will be found in a context whose overall concern will be with the past, but they themselves may not be restricted to the past. Second, even the sciences that are supposed to be concerned with the universal deal in some ways with the individual. For one, all empirical sciences gather the data on the basis of which they draw generalizations from the observation of individual phenomena. And, once they have reached the formulation of generalizations, those generalizations are applied to individual cases.

In short, it is not the case that all sciences deal exclusively with the universal. Some deal primarily with the universal and secondarily with the individual, whereas others deal primarily with the individual and only secondarily with the universal.[15] Therefore, it makes no sense to argue that history is not a science because it deals primarily with individuals and only secondarily with universals. Hence, it is not the case that, for that reason, history should be considered less scientific than any of the sciences. But that does not mean, of course, that history is a science. To establish that would require much more than I have done here.

II. PHILOSOPHY

The first thing that needs to be noted when discussing philosophy is that the term 'philosophy,' like the term 'history,' presents us with a certain ambiguity. We found that 'history' had at least the following important meanings: (I) a series of past events, (II) an account of past events, and (III) a discipline of learning that could in turn be interpreted as (A) the activity whereby the account of past events is produced or (B) a set of rules to which the production of the account of past events must adhere. The last, (B), was called "historiography."

The ranges of meanings of the term 'philosophy' coincide with some of the categories that apply to 'history' but not with all. No meaning of 'philosophy' corresponds to the meaning of 'history' as series of past events. True, philosophy deals with the world and human experience, but neither the world nor human experience can be called philosophy. On the other hand, there is a sense in which philosophy can be understood as a set of ideas or beliefs concerning something or other that a particular person may hold. Thus we speak, for example, of "Wolfgang's philosophy" as the set of ideas he holds about life, or of "Brunhilda's philosophy of love" as the ideas she has concerning how to go about her work, and so on. Philosophy, understood in this way, is not to be identified with the set of ideas philosophers in particular hold. It is not a worked-out point of view nor does it involve only certain ideas. It is, in short, the point of view that any ordinary person may have.

Moreover, there is some correspondence among the other categories of meanings for 'history' and those that apply to 'philosophy.' In the first place, philosophy is a discipline of learning that entails both an activity and a set of rules that govern such an activity. These meanings correspond to the meanings of 'history' as activity and historiography, respectively, although the philosophical counterpart of historiography is called philosophical methodology instead. Finally, the resulting product of philosophy understood as a discipline consists in a view of the world that seeks to be consistent, accurate, and comprehensive, and this product is the counterpart of the view of history as an account of a series of past events. Philosophy may be interpreted, therefore, in the following different ways:

I. Philosophy as a set of ideas or beliefs, concerning anything, that an ordinary person may hold.
II. Philosophy as view of the world, or any of its parts, that seeks to be accurate, consistent, and comprehensive.
III. Philosophy as a discipline of learning.
   A. Activity whereby a view of the world, or any of its parts, that seeks to be accurate, consistent, and comprehensive, is produced.
   B. Formulation, explanation, and justification of rules to which the production of a view of the world, or any of its parts, that seeks to be accurate, consistent, and comprehensive, is produced (philosophical methodology).

Let me add before I proceed that the understandings of philosophy which have been indicated are by no means exhaustive. One of the most frequent areas where philosophers disagree is precisely in what they interpret philosophy to be. I hope, however, that the classification I have provided would be acceptable to most philosophers. At any rate, for present purposes I shall work with the view of philosophy that sees it at least as a view of the world that seeks to be accurate, consistent, and comprehensive. Those who disagree with such a view will find, I trust, that those disagreements about the nature of philosophy will not alter the validity of my arguments or the soundness of the conclusions I draw from them. I should also add that the reference to "the world" in this working definition of philosophy should not be taken to imply either a realistic metaphysics or a realistic epistemology. I leave open the interpretation of the referent of 'world' in this context.

In order to facilitate matters I shall treat philosophy understood in the stated sense as a set of propositions, in the manner I treated history considered as an account of past events. Note also that philosophical methodology, just like historiography, can be both a set of rules meant to govern philosophical investigation and the activity whereby that set of rules is produced. But, as in the case of historiography, I shall ignore this complication. I shall also bypass the issues that can be raised concerning the relation between philosophy considered as philosophical methodology and epistemology. Let it suffice to say in passing that if epistemology is understood to be concerned with the nature of knowledge and the means of its acquisition, philosophical methodology must be a branch of epistemology, dealing as it does with the means of acquiring a specific kind of knowledge.

Now, then, philosophy as a view of the world should consist of propositions that, like historical propositions, describe, interpret, and evaluate. Regardless of whether one accepts the meaning, objectivity, and truth of philosophical propositions, one would expect that at least most of those authors who have proposed them have intended them to describe, interpret, or evaluate. But the threefold distinction among propositions with which we have been working in the case of history does not seem to work as well in the case of philosophy. Let me explain.

At first it would seem that philosophy does contain purely descriptive propositions. Indeed, the following examples seem to substantiate that claim:

1P. P (where, for example, P = God is omnipotent, omniscient, and benevolent).

2P. Q (where, for example, Q = God is not the cause of evil).

3P. P, therefore, Q.

Still, if we go back to the initial presentation of descriptive and interpretative propositions, we find that the primary function of descriptive propositions is to present events and ideas *for which there can be direct empirical evidence*, whereas the function of interpretative propositions is to go beyond empirical facts in order to reconstruct the fabric of unstated motives, intangible factors, and implicit circumstances within which events and ideas occur and for which there can be no direct empirical evidence. But, of course, if the distinction is presented in these terms, then clearly none of the examples of philosophical propositions that have been given and that *prima facie* appeared to be descriptive can be regarded as such, since there can be no direct empirical evidence to support them. What direct empirical evidence can be brought to bear on the question of God's omnipotence and omniscience, for example? And the same applies to the statement that God is not the cause of evil. Such propositions must be classified, consequently, as interpretative. And, indeed, a survey of philosophical propositions will show that philosophy as such contains no purely descriptive propositions in the sense we have understood here.

Of course, philosophical accounts do contain propositions taken from our everyday discourse that appear to refer to facts for which there is direct empirical evidence. Descartes's famous claim, "I think, therefore I am" contains the proposition 'I am,' which is obviously descriptive. And we also find propositions such as 'Descartes wrote "Cogito, ergo sum"' or 'Peter killed Mary because he hated her.' But upon inspection it turns out that these propositions (1) are used only as examples that illustrate a type of action or event or a particular point of view (the case of 'Peter killed Mary because he hated her.'), or (2) are mentioned and not used (the case of 'Cogito, ergo sum.'), or (3) are part, as in the case of Descartes's 'I am,' of a larger claim for which there cannot be direct empirical evidence, or, finally (4), are historical reports (as is the case of 'Descartes wrote "Cogito, ergo sum."'). So, the first difference we may note between philosophy and history is that in philosophy there are no purely descriptive propositions in the sense that we have understood them, and those that *prima facie* appear to be descriptive turn out, on analysis, to be interpretative.

Since we have concluded that all philosophical propositions are interpretative, there is no need to provide further examples of this category of propositions. The three propositions that appeared to be descriptive but turned out to be interpretative can serve just as well as examples of the interpretative category.

On the other hand, philosophy, like history, does contain evaluative propositions. The following should serve as examples:

AP. P is true (where, for example, P = God is omnipotent, omniscient, and benevolent).

BP. Argument 3P is invalid.

CP. P lacks proof.

DP. Doctrine 1P is incoherent.

I do not believe that many philosophers would dispute that the propositions of the types exemplified in AP–DP are typical of philosophical discourse. After all, the aim of philosophy is to determine truth value and validity. Indeed, even if we were going to argue, as some do, that the aim of philosophy is purely clarificatory, clarification entails evaluations of various sorts, as is clear in propositions such as: '"P" means Q rather than M,' 'X confuses P with Q,' '"P" truly expresses Q rather than M,' and the like.

A second important difference between history and philosophy needs to be noted. In philosophy there is a third category of propositions that does not appear in history. The function of these propositions is to describe the relations among ideas or, to put it more exactly, the logical relations among propositions that express those ideas. Examples of such propositions would be

I. $P \rightarrow Q$.

II. $(P \cdot Q) \rightarrow P$.

In the first place, these propositions are different from strictly descriptive propositions in that they do not describe events or ideas for which there is direct empirical evidence. Nor do they describe relations among events or relations among the ideas of this and that author. They describe relations among ideas themselves. Second, they differ from evaluative propositions in that they do not make claims about the value of events or ideas. And third, they stand apart from interpretative propositions in that they do not deal with hidden reasons, broad generalizations, and so on, but resemble them in that they make explicit the implicit logical connections among ideas.

There is a third important difference between philosophy and history. As we saw earlier, two essential characteristics of propositions belonging to history were their references to time and provenance. But no such references are necessary for philosophical propositions. References to provenance and time occur in philosophical discourse, but when such is the case, the references are immaterial to the main task of that discourse. For this task, unlike that of history, is the establishment of philosophical knowledge, and this knowledge, unlike historical knowledge, has nothing to do with occurrences happening at a particular time or place. The most frequent references to time and place found in philosophical propositions occur precisely in philosophical discussions of time and place. When philosophers discuss the nature of time, for example, they will both mention time and give examples of propositions in which temporal terms are used. But in neither case are temporal terms used as part of the philosophical discourse. And something similar can be said about spatial or locational circumstances. Time and place are of the essence of history but are not necessary to do philosophy. This gives us, then, a point of distinction between philosophy and its history. For reference to time and place is essential to the history of philosophy, but is only accidental in philosophy.

Finally, philosophy, unlike history but like some other disciplines of learning, deals primarily with the universal, whereas history deals primarily with the individual. The aim of philosophy is to account for the world and our experience of it, whereas history seeks to account for individual events. In its account of the world, philosophy may refer to individuals as examples, it may begin with the examination of individuals in order to discover some universal truth, and in some cases it may even aim to discover the nature and role of such individuals, as happens with God. But its general thrust is not with individuals but with universals. History, by contrast, centers primarily on individuals and only secondarily, except as historiography or when understood as the philosophy of history, seeks to reach universal conclusions.

In conclusion, what sets philosophy apart from history is that (1) it does not contain propositions merely descriptive of events or ideas for which there can be direct empirical evidence, (2) it contains propositions whose function is to describe logical relations among ideas, (3) its propositions may lack reference to time and provenance, and (4) its propositions deal primarily with universals rather than individuals. I return to points (3) and (4) in Chapters Two and Three.

III. THE HISTORY OF PHILOSOPHY

As with 'history' and 'philosophy,' the term 'history of philosophy' presents us with a certain ambiguity. In one sense the term simply refers to a series of past philosophical ideas. Thus when we speak about the history of philosophy of a period, say the Middle Ages, we refer to the philosophical ideas current during the period. In another sense, however, 'history of philosophy' is used to refer to an account given of past philosophical ideas. For example, we might refer to Gilson's account of medieval philosophy in his *History of Christian Philosophy in the Middle Ages* as a history of philosophy of the period. A historical account, just like any account, is as much a product of human art as are the ideas it studies, but it is a reflection on those ideas, their sources, relations, and consequences, rather than those ideas themselves. This is an important distinction to which I shall come back later. That history in the first sense is as much a product of human art as history in the second sense is an interesting fact that merits further reflection but that I merely note in the present context.

Finally, as with history, the history of philosophy can be taken as a discipline of learning, namely, the discipline whose object is the history of philosophy understood in the first sense just identified. In this third sense, however, we may also subdivide it into an activity whereby the study mentioned is carried out and the account of past philosophical ideas is produced, or as a reflection on the rules and regulations that should guide such a study. The last sense points to a branch of historiography that I call *philosophical historiography* and of which this book is meant to be an example. Note that philosophical historiography, like historiography and philosophical methodology, can itself be subdivided into an activity and a set of propositions. The activity points to the process that yields historiographical rules, and the propositions express those rules. But this complication need not concern us at the moment.

From all this it should be clear that the history of philosophy has common elements with both history and philosophy but also that it differs in important ways from both. I shall return to these similarities and differences in a moment. At present let me summarize the various meanings of 'history of philosophy' as follows:

I. History of philosophy as a series of past philosophical ideas.
II. History of philosophy as an account of past philosophical ideas.
III. History of philosophy as a discipline of learning.
   A. Activity whereby an account of past philosophical ideas is produced.
   B. Formulation, explanation, and justification of rules whereby the production of an account of past philosophical ideas is carried out (philosophical historiography).

For our present purposes, and following a procedure adopted in the discussion of history and philosophy, I frame the discussion in terms of meaning II: The history of philosophy is identified with an account of past philosophical ideas and thus with a set of propositions that express that account. Now, insofar as the history of philosophy is history and, therefore, an account of the past, it should contain descriptive, interpretative, and evaluative propositions. And, indeed, many of the propositions that form part of histories of philosophy are not significantly different from the propositions that form part of ordinary histories, and in some cases the same propositions appear in both. For example, the proposition 'Marcus Aurelius was a Roman emperor' will necessarily appear in a good history of the Roman empire as well as in a good history of Roman philosophy. Therefore, as far as both history and the history of philosophy describe, interpret, and evaluate events they do not differ.

And yet, from experience we know that there are differences between history and the history of philosophy. It suffices to pick up a history of the Roman empire and a history of Roman philosophy to realize where some of those differences lie. Indeed, although the information that both histories might contain will overlap on occasion, as we saw in the case of the just-mentioned proposition, most of the information contained in the history will not be duplicated in the history of philosophy. The reason for the difference is that history of philosophy is concerned primarily with philosophy, that is, about a particular set of "facts." I placed the term 'facts' in double quotation marks because the history of philosophy deals with a very peculiar set of facts. Indeed, its primary aim is to describe, interpret, and evaluate the beliefs, doctrines, and arguments of past philosophers together with their internal relations as well as their external relations to and influences on the beliefs, doctrines, and arguments of other philosophers. In short, as stated earlier, historians of philosophy are concerned with the history of philosophical ideas and their relations. Naturally, since these ideas do not occur in a vacuum, a history of philosophy will contain references to those events and circumstances that seem to shed light on those ideas. As in the example given earlier, it is pertinent to the historian of philosophy that Marcus Aurelius was a Roman emperor. For even though the primary aim of the historian of philosophy is to understand Marcus Aurelius's philosophical ideas rather than the political events or positions that affected his life, his office and the travails and responsibilities that it entailed may give us a deeper understanding of some of his philosophical views. On the other hand, the exact color of Marcus Aurelius's hair or his preferences for breakfast would seem to be irrelevant for the reconstruction of his philosophical ideas, even though they are certainly relevant for the reconstruction of the complete history of Marcus Aurelius. (I address the issue of what is important for historico-philosophical accounts in Chapter Five.)

In general, therefore, the kind of propositions contained in a history are different from those contained in a history of philosophy simply because the object of study of the historian of philosophy is only a part of the more encompassing object of the historian. The history of philosophy of a period, then, is part of the general history of that period, whereas only some of the events of the period are relevant for a history of philosophy of the period.

Of course, the history of philosophy does not deal with every sort of idea. For example, although a history of nineteenth-century German philosophy might contain some reference to the development of scientific ideas in physics, astronomy, and psychology in Germany during the nineteenth century, its main concern is not with those ideas, but with philosophical ideas. The distinction between those ideas and philosophical ideas might be a matter of dispute, but that debate is irrelevant to our present task and I do not intend to deal with it here. In the present context it is sufficient for us to note in passing that the history of philosophy is not the history of all ideas, but only of those that are philosophical or that have a bearing on philosophical ideas.[16] I shall return to this point at the end of the chapter.

As was the case with history, then, the history of philosophy would seem to be composed of three types of propositions: descriptive, interpretative, and evaluative. Moreover, as in the case with all history, those propositions should have a reference to time and provenance and be concerned primarily with individuals rather than universals. Let me begin with descriptive propositions.

A. Description

The purpose of descriptive propositions contained in histories of philosophy is simply to present accurately what particular philosophers said or recorded they thought, as well as to recount contemporaneous and later statements concerning the views of historical figures. In all cases it is assumed that there is or can be direct empirical evidence of the material in question, such as written statements to that effect or credible reports of verbal pronouncements. Typical examples of descriptive propositions occurring in any history of philosophy are the following:

1^{hp}. X stated that P (where, for example, P = God is omnipotent, omniscient, and benevolent).

2^{hp}. X stated that Q (where, for example, Q = God is not the cause of evil).

3^{hp}. X's stating that P is the reason that X gave for holding that Q.

4^{hp}. M, a contemporary of X, stated that X did not hold that P.

5^{hp}. N, another of X's contemporaries, stated that he disagreed with M concerning M's view that X did not hold that P.

6^{hp}. R, a later historian of philosophy, stated that M was right in holding that X did not hold that P.

7^{hp}. S, another later historian of philosophy, stated that he disagreed with R's view concerning M.

These propositions illustrate how historians of philosophy in their descriptive role are concerned primarily with the presentation of information concerning historical views for which there is direct empirical evidence. But that information must be understood broadly to include not only statements and reports of beliefs and doctrines, but also of arguments. Moreover, the descriptive task of the historian of philosophy is not just to describe those statements and reports of beliefs and arguments, but also to present their relations insofar as there is direct empirical evidence for them. That is, if Y says that he borrowed P from X, then clearly historians in their descriptive role must record that fact. And if X states that he holds that P because he holds that Q, this must also be recorded, even if in fact it turns out that P and Q have no discernible relation. In short, in their descriptive capacity historians of philosophy should go as far as the direct empirical evidence at their disposal allows and not beyond it.

B. Interpretation

On the other hand, as interpreters, historians of philosophy can, should, and do go beyond explicit evidence furnished by philosophers and other sources concerning past ideas. Their purpose in that capacity is to suggest, as already noted in the case of history, unobservable facts, such as the views of historical authors, and hidden relations that may hold among ideas themselves, among the various ideas of a single philosopher, and among the ideas of several philosophers. In addition, historians of philosophy will draw broad generalizations that seek to characterize a philosopher's global approach as well as the overall philosophical perspective of a period. Finally, historians of philosophy will also try to translate the ideas of earlier philosophers into the language and conceptual framework of their own times in order to determine their meaning and import. In this third task they go beyond the limits within which some historians work.

Historians who are concerned primarily with events rather than ideas do not have to worry too much about the problem of translating past ideas into contemporary conceptual frameworks. They deal primarily with events, physical actions, objects, and the like. Moreover, the terminology used in many historical accounts has generally developed fairly clear terms, as well as unambiguous concepts corresponding to those terms, that can be easily exchanged. This is quite evident in how easily purely descriptive relations of events can be translated from language to language without losing accuracy or creating ambiguity. For example, the word *currere* in Latin is accurately translated by the English 'to run' and the Spanish *'correr.'* Likewise *'Hic feles niger est'* can be rendered by the English 'This cat is black' and the Spanish *'Este gato es negro.'* There are no serious problems here because the meanings of the words in each of the languages in question correspond to the same concepts (*hic*-this-*este; feles*-cat-*gato; est*-is-*es*).

Of course, when users of a language are not acquainted with the objects described in another language, then difficulties arise. These difficulties often are surmounted by describing the new objects in terms of other objects known. For example, when Cortez reached the coast of Mexico, Montezuma's advanced observers described Cortez's ships as mountains resting on water. So, even in historical accounts that describe events problems may surface, but in general the problems are easily solved through the use of analogies, circumlocutions, and illustrations. This is why interpretation in history consists primarily in *filling in* the picture with conjectures, speculations, and surmises about facts for which there is no direct empirical evidence and about the interrelation among the known facts themselves and between those facts and those other ones accepted on the basis of speculation.

On the other hand, interpretation in the history of philosophy goes beyond the task of filling in the picture with conjectures, speculations, and surmises. For philosophy deals with ideas, and ideas are very different from the events, actions, and objects of which ordinary history presents an account. In the first place, ideas, unlike physical objects, physical actions, and most events, are not perceivable. It is possible to point to an object of vision and say "cat" in order to teach English to a Spanish speaker, or to teach an English speaker the meaning of the Spanish *correr* by engaging in the action of running. But it is not at all clear what one could point to in order to teach someone the meaning of 'good' or 'justice'. Of course, even teaching the meaning of the names of physical objects is not as simple as it appears. I am perfectly aware of the questions that have been raised concerning ostensive definitions from time *in memoriam* to the present.[17] My point is not that straightforward history involves no difficulties in its interpretative task, but rather that whatever difficulties it may involve are compounded enormously when we move away from accounts of observable events to the account of nonobservable entities such as ideas. Indeed, this sort of difficulty led Plato and Augustine to conclude that teaching is not possible and Averroes to hold that all humans have one and the same intellect.[18]

There are two extreme positions with respect to the role of conceptual translation in the history of philosophy, which I call the *antiquarian* and the *anachronist* views. Antiquarians hold that conceptual translation has no role to play in history. The job of the historian is to present whatever concepts past philosophers held without trying to translate them into contemporary concepts. To do otherwise is to fall into anachronism, precluding an accurate understanding of the past, since any attempt at translating the past into contemporary ideas could only result in more or less clever distortions of it. To translate the past into the present has the actual effect of keeping the past hidden from us. The task of the historian of philosophy, then, is to understand a past philosopher "on his own terms" rather than in terms of our own conceptual categories.[19]

Note the strong descriptive emphasis of the antiquarian point of view. Some of those who defend it will go so far as to argue that historians are wrong in trying to figure out what past philosophers "thought"; their job is only to describe what they "said," since no one can have direct empirical evidence of someone else's thoughts. This point of view is behind a number of well-known books about historical figures and is illustrated in the title of Paul Shorey's *What Plato Said*.[20]

At the opposite extreme are the anachronists, who hold that translation is not just unavoidable but that it permeates the historians' task to such an extent that there is no possibility of avoiding the anachronism it necessarily carries with it.[21] According to this point of view, there is no way in which the philosophical past can be recovered as it was. Our view of it is vitiated by our contemporary categories of thought to such an extent that, just as with the Kantian *noumenon*, which is known only insofar as it is structured according to the fundamental categories of thought, so with the historical past we can become conscious of it only within the conceptually interpretative framework within which we think at present.[22] Thus, although anachronism is unavoidable, we need not worry about it because it cannot be helped or escaped. For the present there is in fact no past, but only "interpretations" of it.

These two extreme positions seem equally unacceptable. If we were to adopt the first position strictly, it is clear that the task of the historian of philosophy would be restricted to the role of reporting what so and so said at such and such a time. Anything more than that would involve the kind of interpretation that would require contemporary concepts and ideas and thus would not be acceptable. We could certainly not say that Aristotle, say, "thought" this or that, for such a claim would involve a leap for which we have no direct empirical evidence. Aristotle indeed may have thought this or that, but the historian can claim only that he said it, not that he thought it. Aristotle in fact may have said something mechanically without thinking about what he was saying. Or he may have said what he said while adding mental terms to it that changed its meaning but that he did not bother or wish to say. (This is essential to casuistry, for example.) However, if one accepts this point of view, it is even questionable whether texts written in one language could or should be translated into another, since languages imply in many ways different ways of looking at things and map the world in conceptually different ways. How can we be sure that Aristotle and we are speaking about the same thing when Aristotle used the term *ousia* and we use 'substance'? Indeed, this example makes the point quite dramatically, for as any historian of Greek thought knows, it simply would not do to substitute 'substance' for *ousia* every time *ousia* occurs in the Greek text.

Unfortunately for those who reject all conceptual translation for fear of anachronism, it is not at all clear that they succeed in saving the past, which after all is their explicit aim. Indeed, it looks as if in their attempt to save it they lose it, for if none of our concepts can be safely used to explore the past for fear of contamination, we have no way of approaching it, since we are not blank slates on which the past can be written. Of course, if the past were not a spatio-temporal dimension but just another place, we could move there, try to learn its language as children do, forget everything we know, and through a total immersion in the culture and its practices become members of it. But that course of action is not open to us. We cannot move into or live in the past and, therefore, if antiquarians are correct the inescapable consequence is that we could never understand or recover it.

Moreover, even if, by some fluke, we were able to recover the past as it was, what use would it be for us as persons living in the present? If the past cannot be somehow translated into the present, if bridges cannot be established between the past and the present, if what we find about the past cannot be compared with what we have and think in the present, why would we want to recover it at all and what use would it be? To recover it would be like owning some artifact whose purpose has been forgotten and cannot be recalled. Or alternatively, if one understood what it was for, one could not find any use for it today. Most sensible people presented with that situation would throw the artifact away rather than have it occupy valuable space.

On the other hand, those who hold the opposite extreme view, the anachronists, are no less misguided. Their assumption, that all we have are "interpretations" and that we can never hope to transcend them and reach or understand any dimension of the past as it actually was, is not supported by our experience. For, although it is true that we approach the past through a contemporary conceptual grid, there are aspects of the past that are not broken or restructured in passing the grid.[23] The grid has holes that allow complete phases of past history and ideas to come through fairly intact. This seems quite evident in our understanding of dead languages and ancient texts. Even students with little historical knowledge, when confronted with some past texts, are able to make some sense of them. And the reasons are simple: First, human beings do not seem to have changed much in the more than 5,000 years of recorded human history and certainly not in the 2,500 years of the history of philosophy. The epistemic and ethical concerns of Plato and Aristotle do not seem foreign to us because they arise from basic problems common to all thinking beings. Plato was concerned about injustice, about the status of women in society, and about the best form of government, among other issues, and so are we. And many of his views seem to have nothing so odd and foreign to us that we cannot understand what they are, what they entail, and the reasons why he held them even when we disagree with them.[24] The fact is that we share with other members of the human community certain needs, passions, tendencies, and ways of thinking that establish bridges among us and help us communicate across time and cultures.[25] As Vico noted, the foundations of history are the institutions that we all hold in common:

> Now since this world of nations has been made by men, let us see in what institutions all men agree and always have agreed. For these institutions will be able to give us the universal and eternal principles (such as every science must have) on which all nations were founded and still preserve themselves. We observe that all nations, barbarous as well as civilized, though separately founded because remote from each other in time and space, keep these three human customs: all have some religion, all contract solemn marriages, all bury their dead. And in no nation, however savage and crude, are any human actions performed with more elaborate ceremonies and more sacred solemnity than the rites of religion, marriage and burial. For, by the axiom that "uniform ideas, born among peoples unknown to each other, must have a common ground of truth," it must have been dictated to all nations that from these three institutions humanity began among them all, and therefore they must be most devoutly guarded by them all, so that the world should not again become a bestial wilderness. For this reason we have taken these three eternal and universal customs as three first principles of this Science [of History].[26]

But I would go beyond that and argue that it is not only what Vico calls the institutions of religion, marriage, and death that unite humankind. A core of human nature binds us all and forms the basis for the variegated customs and ideas that we develop. How this core is interpreted is not my concern at present. What is important for us is to realize that there is a foundation to our similarities and that foundation makes possible intercultural communication.

But the commonality of human nature is not the only reason why the understanding of the past is possible. There is even a more obvious reason in the case of Western philosophy: We are part of a tradition of which the past is a part. Our philosophical past is not like some artifact that we found on Venus, completely alien and new to us. Our philosophical past is causally related to what we are and think at present. We are the product of a long tradition in which past ideas often have been modified but as often have been preserved. And even where those ideas have been modified, the causal links that tie them to us, with effort and good historical methodology, can be followed up and reconstructed. For just as a dinosaur's footprint can tell scientists much about the animal that made it, so can we reconstruct the history of our ideas based on the traces that remain of them in the present.

The very word 'tradition' comes from the Latin *traditio*, which refers to a saying handed down from former times, a passing on from one to another. Indeed, it brings home the point that we are linked to the past not only causally, as already stated, but that repeated attempts have been made throughout history to go back and recapture the past as it was. Each of these attempts discovers something new that becomes available and passed on the future generations. These scholarly and pedagogical links are as important as the causal ones and help us bridge the apparent chasm that separates us from the distant past.

Our situation is not that of first-time visitors to Venus who find an object with certain marks on it and are at a loss as to how to interpret it. Our situation is rather like that of the archeologist of pre-Columbian artifacts who finds an object with marks on it. Its interpretation would be no doubt difficult. Are the marks meant as linguistic signs or are they simply decorative? But they have something to go on: previous discoveries, reports by the *conquistadores*, cultural (linguistic and otherwise) traces of past customs in contemporary Mexican society, other attempts to interpret those signs, and so on. We are not totally unrelated to the past, and those relations can help us in its recovery. We are linked to the past through the practices that are at the core of human society and are preserved through generations.

These practices, linguistic, conceptual, and so on, are fundamental to social survival and, therefore, are never completely obliterated. Although human societies may modify their customs, something always remains, and such remains are the threads through which we can return to the past.

Besides, with respect to ideas, there seem to be some whose character is such that they do not seem to be affected, or at least not substantially affected, by their cultural location. Take for example, the notion of "four" or the notion that "two plus two make four." Can we sensibly argue that those two notions are so culturally permeated that what they meant for the Assyrians and what they mean for North Americans today is different? No doubt the signs through which those ideas are communicated are different in the two cultures, but the very ideas and their use do not seem to be affected by the cultural circumstances that surround them. Of course, there may not be many ideas like the ones mentioned. In particular, most philosophical ideas seem to be entangled quite badly in their cultural locus. But it would be dogmatic to hold that to disentangle them is impossible and that none of them have the purity of the idea of four. Some ideas at least are like coins that can pass from hand to hand with relatively little alteration, serving at the time those who hold them.

Perhaps an example taken from the history of philosophy will illustrate how some philosophical ideas can be passed from culture to culture and language to language without undergoing substantial changes. The ancient Greek texts that were translated into Latin in the twelfth century in Spain, and that constituted the basis for the thirteenth century revival of learning and the development of scholasticism, were not translated directly from Greek. Some of the original Greek texts were translated first, around the seventh century, into Syriac, and later from Syriac into Arabic. Then in Spain they were finally translated with the help of Spanish Jews. The Jewish translator, who knew Arabic and Romance (medieval Spanish), would translate verbally the text from Arabic into Romance. Then the Christian translator, who knew Romance and Latin, would translate what he heard into Latin. This means that the Latin translation of some texts were separated from the original Greek by three different languages. Moreover, each of the languages involved in the translation reflected substantially different cultures—Syriac, Muslim, Jewish, and Spanish. One would expect that under these circumstances the resulting Latin text would be totally unintelligible, and if at all intelligible would yield a very different meaning from that of the original Greek. Yet, the fact is that nothing is further from the truth. Indeed, the Latin text of many of these works is not only intelligible and quite reliable, but some of the Latin translations of the sort mentioned are as good as and sometimes even better than, the translations done later directly into Latin from Greek. Moreover, the interpretations of some ancient authors, like those provided by Averroes of Aristotle, who had access only to translations of translations (in the case of Averroes's, Arabic ones), are still regarded by many scholars as viable ones. Now, this phenomenon can only be explained by accepting that some ideas are not substantially affected by their cultural location. They can move from culture to culture, language to language, and individual to individual without undergoing drastic changes.

Finally, it is clear that if the anachronist position were right, then the past and its study would have no value for us. For the value of the past depends to a great extent on how different and independent of our interpretation it is. It is its different character that forces us to contemplate a different picture, to entertain and understand a different perspective, and thus to raise questions about our own views, their viability and truth. But that confrontation and reexamination is not possible if we are imprisoned in our interpretations and can never go beyond them. We need access to the past to learn from it.

This brings me to an important point, namely, that both those who reject all interpretation of the past, the antiquarians, and those who believe we cannot transcend our current conceptual prejudices about it, the anachronists, make the past inaccessible to us: The first because we cannot translate the past into our current ideas; and the second because we can never escape the present. Translation requires an original and a derived version of the past. Antiquarians, who fear anachronism, are left with the original without the derived version, and anachronists, who believe we cannot escape our interpretations, eliminate the original and are left only with derived versions of it. Moreover, both views undermine the value of the past and its study, since on neither view can any contemporary use be derived from it. For the first because whatever is valuable in the past cannot be separated from it; and for the second because the past can never be brought into the present. The first are imprisoned in the past, and the second are imprisoned in the present.

Obviously neither of these two alternatives is sound and most historians of philosophy are quite aware that the truth of the matter lies somewhere in between them: The recovery and translation of past conceptual frameworks into contemporary frameworks is possible, even if it is difficult. The problem, then, is not whether it is possible or not, but to what extent and in what way it is so. The issue has to do with the approach that should be used to translate the past into the present. This situation parallels in some ways the divide in epistemology between those who conceive of their task as proving that knowledge is possible and those who conceive of it as showing how it takes place. The first take Descartes's doubt at face value and try to establish an absolute point of certainty on which knowledge could be based. The others take the evidence provided by the sciences as proof that knowledge is possible and worry rather about how that knowledge occurs and is justified. The first approach leads to paralysis and skepticism; the second results in progress and methodological discoveries. It is of course the second that I advocate with respect to the history of philosophy. We should accept the witness of experience that tells us that the present can have access to the past. What should concern us (and I explore it further in Chapter Five) is the formulation of an approach and method appropriate to the understanding of the philosophical past.

Having concluded that an understanding of the philosophical past is possible and that interpretation is an intrinsic element in the history of philosophy, we may provide some examples of the sorts of interpretative propositions found in histories of philosophy:

a^{hp}. X held that Q.

b^{hp}. X held that Q because X held that P.

c^{hp}. X held that P because Y held that P.

d^{hp}. X's holding that P led to the abandonment of ~Q by subsequent philosophers.

e^{hp}. What X meant by C was D.

Interpretative propositions present in the history of philosophy, then, go beyond statements of ideas for which there is direct empirical evidence to posit hidden facts (a^{hp}), hidden relations (b^{hp}), unstated reasons (c^{hp}), and broad causal generalizations (d^{hp}). Moreover, they aim to render the language and conceptual framework of historical figures intelligible by translating it into a language and conceptual framework easily understood at present (e^{hp}), although taking care not to distort the original intent and content of that language and conceptual framework.

C. Evaluation

Interpretative propositions should not be confused with those that contain evaluations of philosophical ideas or their impact on future history. Such evaluations are accomplished in a separate category of propositions, which I call *evaluative*. Consider the following examples:

A^{hp}. X's view, that P, is true.

B^{hp}. X's argument A is valid.

C^{hp}. X's argument A' is unsound.

D^{hp}. X was perspicacious when he asked question Q.

E^{hp}. X was right in formulating problem N in the way he did.

F^{hp}. X was unclear on issue I.

G^{hp}. X is an excellent philosopher.

H^{hp}. X contradicted himself.

I^{hp}. X's view, that P, was useful in the development of Y's view, that Q.

J^{hp}. M, a contemporary of X, was wrong in thinking that X's view, that P, was false.

K^{hp}. R, a later historian, who thought that M was right, was wrong.

L^{hp}. X's view about S shows that Western thought had undergone substantial progress.

M^{hp}. Y's view indicates a step backward in the development of philosophy.

N^{hp}. R was right in thinking that X held that P.

All these propositions have in common that in some way they evaluate a philosopher, an idea, an argument, or an age. In general, I believe few historians of philosophy would quarrel with propositions such as D^{hp}, G^{hp}, I^{hp}, or N^{hp}. Some would go beyond this and also accept propositions such as E^{hp} or F^{hp}. But many would find difficulty in accepting as part of the history of philosophy propositions such as A^{hp}, B^{hp}, C^{hp}, H^{hp}, J^{hp}, K^{hp}, L^{hp}, or M^{hp}.[27] The reason that they would object to the second and third sets of propositions is that they contain judgments about the truth and value of philosophical ideas, arguments and so on, and these historians are under the impression that history, let alone the history of philosophy, is not supposed to make such judgments. The historian of philosophy, according to them, at most can interpret but never judge.

The various examples of evaluative propositions just provided indicate a wide range and different types of evaluative judgments. But the core of the controversy surrounding this issue concerns truth value judgments. It is with them that most historians draw the line, excluding them from any account that they consider truly historical. They particularly object to propositions such as A^{hp} and to judgments of falsehood, such as "X's view, that P, is false." As historians, they argue, their job is not to judge the truth or falsity of views expressed in the past. They are concerned with what Guérolt has called "historical truth" rather than with *philosophical truth*.[28] Historical truth refers to the truth value of propositions that describe the past, such as 'Plato held that P.' Philosophical truth refers to the truth value of propositions that are not historical, such as 'Human beings have immortal souls.' Philosophers are concerned with the latter, whereas historians are concerned exclusively with the former. Historians, then, are not allowed to judge whether Plato was right or wrong in holding that P; they are allowed to judge only whether Plato did or did not hold that P. Now, some supporters of this view are willing to accept some evaluation, particularly "historical" evaluations such as those represented by propositions D^{hp} and F^{hp}, because those evaluations help to understand, for example, the impact of the philosopher in question on other philosophers. And a few others are sometimes willing to do the same with some of the other types of evaluative propositions mentioned. They refuse, however, to have anything to do with straightforward truth value judgments about the claims made by historical figures.

This position is well established among historians of philosophy and has been ably defended by Daniel Garber in a recently published paper, where he calls it *disinterested history*,[29] and by Yvon Lafrance, who calls it *positivist history of philosophy*.[30] Many arguments are brought up in support of this position but I believe the strongest are the following three.

The first argues that the value of the history of philosophy lies in the fact that it confronts us with different views and perspectives that have been taken seriously in the past and, therefore, makes us aware of issues and questions that may have escaped us. The history of philosophy opens up new areas of inquiry and challenges our views, helping to uncover some of the assumptions and presuppositions implicit in our conceptual framework of which we are not consciously aware. This function cannot be rendered by our contemporaries because they are immersed in the same conceptual and cultural framework as we are, but it can be performed exceedingly well by the history of philosophy. Now, if this is the source of the value of the history of philosophy, so the argument goes, the truth value of historical views has nothing to contribute to it. As Garber has put it:

> If it is a historical *perspective* on our beliefs and assumptions we are interested in, then the truth *or* the falsity of past views is *simply irrelevant*. It matters not at all whether Descartes's or Aristotle's or Kant's views are true or false for this use of history.[31]

The second argument appears in a variety of forms in the literature, but its main thrust is to point out that any history of philosophy concerned with truth and falsity introduces in the historical inquiry an element of interest that distorts the resulting account of the past.[32] When we look at the past not just with the aim to know it, but with the wish to assess what of value and truth it has to contribute, we are necessarily led to emphasize those aspects of it that seem to us to be most valuable and truthful, while neglecting those that seem to us less valuable. This procedure not only distorts the account of what truly happened, but leads to further manipulation and distortion. It is as if we looked to the past through a pair of glasses that would allow us to see only certain parts of it and to see them as we wish to do. Thus the past as it was remains distant and unknown.

The third also appears under various garbs in the literature and has been recently revived by Michael Frede. It makes a distinction between a historical and nonhistorical approach to the history of philosophy and argues that evaluation has a place only in the nonhistorical approach. The nonhistorical approach is that of the philosopher whose main interest is to learn something about truth from the history of philosophy. It approaches the history of philosophy with its own views, interests, and standards because the purpose of the enterprise is philosophical, not historical; indeed, it is for this reason that it judges the value of the views it studies. The other approach, however, the historical, studies the history of philosophy in its own right, seeking to understand it on its own terms, apart from any views, standards, and interests to which the historian might subscribe. As Frede has put it:

> the philosopher will be interested in the view and the reasons given for it as such. He will ask questions like: Is the view true, reasonable, plausible, possible, or not? Are the reasons offered for it adequate or even conclusive? Which other reasons could one advance in favor of the view, which ones do speak against it? The historian, on the other hand, is interested, not in the view and the reasons as such, but in the historical fact that a certain person in a certain historical context held this view and gave these reasons for it. The questions he will ask are not whether the view is true or the reasons are adequate, but rather whether the view would have seemed to be true or plausible at the time,

whether at that point in the past the reasons offered would have been taken to be adequate or conclusive.[33]

In short, there is a radical difference between a philosophical interest in history and a historical one, and the historical study of the history of philosophy requires a purely historical interest. Philosophical disinterest, according to this view, is a necessary condition of the historical interest in the history of philosophy, but the aim of the historian of philosophy as such is not to be confused with that of the philosopher.[34]

These are no doubt strong arguments in favor of a disinterested view of the history of philosophy that leaves out any consideration of truth. But they miss some fundamental aspects of the question. I shall develop three arguments based on them.[35]

My first argument in defense of an interested history of philosophy consists in pointing out that many of the value judgments that do not seem to involve truth value and are, therefore, accepted by those who favor a disinterested history of philosophy, do in fact involve judgments of truth. Take two of the propositions mentioned earlier, examples of which are frequently found even in histories of philosophy that claim to be disinterested.

D^{hp}. X was perspicacious when he asked question Q.
G^{hp}. X is an excellent philosopher.

In the first proposition (D^{hp}) we have a judgment of perspicacity and in the other (G^{hp}) of excellence. But, we may ask, don't perspicacity and excellence, when applied to philosophers, refer to their ability to get at the truth? After all, philosophers are after truth, so when they say that other philosophers are excellent or perspicacious, they usually mean that those philosophers did better in their quest for the truth than others and that they saw something more than others.[36] To call artists or automobile mechanics excellent or perspicacious does not have anything to do with truth. For artists it may mean that they have rendered accurately a certain feeling, or that they have presented us with a beautiful piece of art, or whatever it is that artists are supposed to do. And automobile mechanics are excellent if they fix our automobiles efficiently and inexpensively. So in neither case is truth at issue. But in the case of philosophy a reference to truth cannot be avoided, for the search for truth is the very essence of philosophy.

In short, evaluative judgments made by historians of philosophy, even those that do not explicitly mention truth and seem therefore disinterested in that respect, often implicitly refer to or entail a judgment about it. To have a purely disinterested history of philosophy we would need to purge historical accounts not only of explicit truth value judgments but of all evaluative judgments in order to make sure that the discipline has been properly sanitized. I do not believe, however, that even the most recalcitrant supporters of disinterested history would want to take such a drastic step.

Indeed, it is practically impossible for historians of philosophy to be completely neutral in their task, and, therefore, the complete neutrality for which those who support a disinterested approach to the history of philosophy argue cannot be a requirement of carrying out that task. Complete neutrality may be logically possible, of course, and we all understand that a certain degree of neutrality and objectivity are essential to historical work. But no person can send all his or her beliefs and values into limbo while engaged in doing history of philosophy. What often happens is that we get the impression of objectivity and value-free discussion, while hidden values and principles lurk in the dark. The result is the worst kind of history of philosophy, one with the pretense of neutrality that in fact pursues a hidden agenda. Nowhere is this more evident than in the very process of selection that historians follow and to which we referred earlier. The time and space they have is limited whereas the matter seems limitless, so historians are forced to choose and in choosing they are already presenting a partial view of the past and necessarily making decisions as to what is more or less important. Intellectual honesty on the part of historians, then, would seem to require that they hang out to air as many of their assumptions and values as they can—of some, of course, they are unaware—making explicit value judgments and thus reaching a higher level of objectivity than if those assumptions and values were to remain unidentified.[37] Unfortunately, we live in a world where even philosophers, who ostensibly pride themselves in the search for truth, often value appearance more than reality, and where a biased but consistent account often is favored over an honest but less consistent one.

But this is not all I wish to argue. I would like to go further and argue, second, in favor of an interested history of philosophy, that in order to make past ideas and philosophical positions intelligible we must understand both what we take to be their truth value and the validity and soundness of the arguments on which they are based. The reasons for this are three. The first (a) is that the understanding of the ideas of a past author entails rethinking them and that in turn involves both working through the problem that prompted them and following the thought processes of the author in question. This is precisely the point that Collingwood made so clearly. According to him, the job of the historian who is trying to understand a text from the past is

> to discover what the person who wrote these words meant by them. This means discovering the thought...which he expressed by them. To discover what his thought was, the historian must think it again for himself...he must see what the philosophical problem was, of which his author is here stating his solution. He must think that problem out for himself, see what possible solutions of it might be offered, and see why this particular philosopher chose that solution instead of another. This means rethinking for himself the thought of his author, and nothing short of that will make him the historian of that author's philosophy.[38]

This brings me to the second reason (b), namely, that philosophy, as we saw earlier, is not a purely descriptive discipline, and as such the understanding of philosophical ideas does not entail only working though them, but also interpreting and evaluating them. Indeed, the most important task of the philosopher is to judge what is true and best. As we mentioned earlier, no philosophical claim is purely descriptive; all of them involve at least an element of interpretation and many of them also involve value judgments. Propositions such as 'P is true' (AP) and 'P → Q' (I) clearly involve more than description and interpretation, and the understanding of the meaning of those propositions requires historians to make judgments, for in order to reach such an understanding they have to place themselves in the shoes of those who held them and see and judge what they were trying to do and its value. The point I wish to make is that in order to understand truth value judgments we have to appropriate them, as it were, for the meaning of evaluative judgments cannot be separated easily, if at all, from their truth value. As Rorty has pointed out: "Just as determining meaning is a matter of placing an assertion in a context of actual and possible behavior, so determining truth is a matter of placing it in the context of assertions which we ourselves should be willing to make. Since what counts for us as an intelligible pattern of behavior is a function of what we believe to be true, truth and meaning are not to be ascertained independently of one another."[39]

One cannot understand the full import of Aristotle's assertion that a human being is composed of matter and form until one understands why he held it, and if one does that, one has in fact, directly or indirectly, and explicitly or implicitly, assessed the degree of truth and adequacy of the claim. And one cannot provide an adequate account of a claim unless one understands it in this sense. Indeed, as

Schneewind has stated: "The most satisfying account possible of why someone believes something is one which shows that what is believed either is true or is the proper outcome of a compelling argument from premises the person accepts, and that the person was in a good position to notice this."[40] This does not mean that historians cannot disagree with past judgments. It means rather that they have to function as evaluators, just as past authors did, otherwise they cannot fully understand the authors they study and account for their views. A proper understanding and account of history entails in a sense becoming part of it, becoming a contemporary, and that involves judgment, since contemporaries engaged in the philosophical enterprise are in the business of judging truth value. The case would be different, of course, if the enterprise in which past and present philosophers are engaged were different. But it is not so. The view that their tasks and aims must be different is a historiographical assumption that goes contrary to what most philosophers have claimed. The fundamental aim and standards of the discipline seem to run through the history of philosophy without so much change that they become unrecognizable. And, precisely because past philosophers were fundamentally after the same thing we are, it is essential for our understanding of them to apply to their views those very general standards of the discipline that run through its history.

Of course, some might object that I am assuming too much, for my claim boils down to saying that all past philosophers have adhered to the same standards in the discipline.[41] And it is by no means clear that most, let alone all, philosophers have done so. Indeed, rationalists seem to be applying standards that are vastly different from those applied by empiricists. Even the most commonly adhered-to principles, such as the principle of noncontradiction, have been rejected by some philosophers at one time or another. Some of the poets described in the Introduction, for example, see contradiction as a principle applying only to what one might call "the surface of our thought." A deep understanding of reality goes beyond this superficial level and reaches more profound levels of awareness. The extant writings of the Chinese philosopher Lao Tzu, for instance, contain many cases of what appear to be contradictions, where something is said to be both itself and its opposite. But we need not go to the Orient to find such statements. In the Western tradition there have always been those who have rejected the laws of logic as inoperative in some deeper realm of understanding. Some of the pre-Socratics seem to have believed so and in the Christian era there were many authors who spoke in this way. Tertullian's famous saying, "I believe because it is absurd" (*"Credo quia ineptum"*), and Peter Damian's position that God could bring it about that what happened has not happened are examples of this attitude.

Are there standards, then, that are applicable throughout the history of philosophy? I have already argued in the context of interpretation that the understanding of the past is possible for reasons that I specified there and apply to the present case as well, although I shall not repeat them. Here I would like to add, however, that certain standards and requirements are necessary conditions of cognitive communication and they are the bases for the understanding not only of what others say and think in the present but of what others said and thought in the past. This does not mean that we cannot communicate in other ways and do so effectively. Emotions can be communicated through signs to which the laws of logic do not apply. Tears on a face, for example, are generally regarded as signs of strong emotion (sadness or gladness). Indeed, the communication may be so strong that it may arouse sympathy in others, who themselves might shed tears. But logic does not apply to tears or to sympathy. Again, one may communicate feelings and emotions through art objects, and so on, and logic does not apply to them either. But logic does apply to the communication of cognitive thought processes; it is a kind of grid that filters only what fits it. Cognitive communication is impossible, for example, if the signs (words) used for that purpose always are employed equivocally, so that they do not stand for the same thing twice in the discourse in question. And like the requirement of univocity, noncontradiction, and other logical prerequisites of cognitive thought, there are other standards and rules that most philosophers would have to observe. True, some have rejected and argued against them, as we saw in the cases mentioned, but in doing so, they must adhere to them for the purposes of effective communication.

In short, then, the objection based on the relativity of standards does not seem to me to undermine the argument that evaluation must be included in the understanding of the philosophical past and that such evaluation does not distort it. The bases of philosophical evaluation may vary in diverse ways from philosopher to philosopher and from philosophical school to philosophical school, but there is a sufficiently solid core of standards, based on the most fundamental requirements for communication and the overall aims of the discipline, to ensure that such evaluations can take place. Those who argue against this seem to me to be so out of line with what philosophers generally do that they deserve no attention.

But what are we to do with the apparent contradictions in Lao Tzu and others? Are they to be given a special status? Should they be ignored? Or are we to dismiss them as senseless? The answer to this hermeneutical question is not difficult. What needs to be done to answer it is to establish, assuming that the contradictions are not merely apparent but real, whether Lao Tzu (or other philosophers who fall in the same category) was involved in the communication of cognitive material or not. If he was, then we must apply to what he said, or is reported to have said, the logical and epistemic standards to which we have referred, just as to understand what he wrote we need to apply to it the grammatical rules to which he adhered. If according to those standards he made mistakes, they must be recognized. On the other hand, if he was not involved in the communication of cognitive material, then there is no sense in applying those standards to his discourse, just as there is no sense in applying grammar to painting.

The third reason (c) why, in order to make past ideas and philosophical positions intelligible, we must understand both what we take to be their truth value and the validity and soundness of the arguments on which they are based has to do with texts. Texts are the main means of access we have to philosophical ideas from the past. But texts, as we shall see in Chapter Four, are artifacts conventionally endowed with meaning so they can function to help in the communication of ideas. Now, for historians to get at the meanings of texts they must approach them with certain assumptions as to what their authors were trying to do and how they were trying to do it. For the job of historians is to recreate the intangible meaning of the text and to do that they must recreate the past. But to do so entails using evaluative criteria and principles that will allow them to choose this rather than that meaning, because this makes sense or is true whereas that does not make sense or is false. Value judgments have an important role to play in choosing among various possible interpretations of the views of historical figures. It is a common occurrence that historians are faced with situations where there are at least two, and sometimes more, possible interpretations of the views of a particular author. What does one do when evidence is inconclusive and several interpretations are compatible with the textual evidence and the general philosophical principles that guide an author's thought? If to this are added various interpretative traditions of the author in question that are incompatible among themselves, what can one do? On what basis should one decide what the author held or, if one has qualms about doing that, at least deciding what the author most likely held? Of course, in those situations one can go outside philosophy and try to find some historical determining factor of a psychological, sociological, or cultural nature. But there are cases where no such factor can be found and then the question is left undecided. Here is where truth value and sense are important; for under those circumstances it makes perfectly good sense to favor one interpretation over the other because it makes better philosophical sense or because it is the truth or closer to the truth. In short, to repeat the point made earlier, since truth is the ultimate aim of the philosopher, its consideration should play a role in the study of the history of philosophy. To say, then, that Aristotle or Plato must have held this rather than that view, other things being equal, because the first makes sense or is true and the second does not make sense or is false, is perfectly within the province of the historian of philosophy.[42]

The best interpretation, of course, is the one that makes more sense both historically and philosophically because the historian must assume that the past philosopher was in search precisely of what makes more sense. Indeed, what allows historians of philosophy to be good historians of philosophy is not only their familiarity with the period they study, but their familiarity and understanding of philosophy itself. Other things being equal, I would say that the better the philosopher the better the historian.

Historians of philosophy in many ways resemble historians of music. Historians who wish to account for the musical past do not need to rewrite compositions from the past, but they must understand the notation in which those compositions were written and they must be able to interpret them. They have to be critics and thus able to judge what those marks on the page must mean, and to do that they use not only what they know about the past, but the musical sense they have developed throughout their lives.[43] Because of that they are at risk. They may make mistakes. But they have no choice but to judge what makes sense musically and what does not and to assume, based on that, that certain interpretations of a historical composition are not acceptable. The act of re-creation, then, entails both for the historian of music and for the historian of philosophy, the kind of value judgments that those in favor of disinterested history reject.

A third argument in favor of an interested view of the history of philosophy is based on its ultimate meaning to us. The study of history answers two needs: the human curiosity to know the past and the human desire to learn from it in order to guide future behavior. I have already argued that even understanding the philosophical past involves evaluation, and now I would like to add that learning from it does so even more clearly. Learning from the past involves judging its mistakes and successes so that we can avoid the former and imitate the latter. That is why it is so important to determine what has worked and to what extent, where past philosophers have gone astray and where they have reached the truth. It is particularly useful to see how a philosopher came to hold a view that seems to us patently false today, for in doing so, although we might not change our position after all, we may discover patterns of thinking and argumentation that are new to us and beneficial in deepening our philosophical understanding. Descartes's lucubrations in the *Discourse* that end with the startling description of the motion of the heart are certainly instructive, for they help us see patterns of thinking that may lead us astray and should be avoided. And Bacon's celebrated method that led him to conclude that "heat is a motion" certainly illustrates the blatant limitations of his method.

In this sense, I tend to agree with the view that what we regard as past mistakes are sometimes more philosophically useful to the present than what we regard as successes.[44] The reason is that mistakes shock us, they move us away from complacency and force us to reexamine and rethink our views, helping us to prune away dead matter. When we find that a first rate mind from the past, devoted to the pursuit of truth, has made what looks to us like a mistake, we are thrown back into the dialectic of the problem for which we thought we had an answer. We are perplexed, and this perplexity, as Socrates argues in the Platonic dialogues, is the beginning of true wisdom. But the history of philosophy cannot fulfill this instructive role if it excludes evaluation. A faithful value-neutral description of the past, then, would be totally useless.

Note that I am not advocating through these three arguments the obliteration of the distinction between what are frequently called "judgments of value" and "judgments of fact" and which I have recast as *evaluative* and *descriptive propositions*.[45] My point is not that there is no distinction between these, although I have pointed out that some disguised evaluative propositions are taken as descriptive by historians and historiographers and I have granted that many evaluative propositions include description as well. My point is rather that a historical account of the philosophical past necessarily includes evaluative judgments, and the historical task involves evaluation. My position is not, then, that of those who argue that objectivity in historical knowledge is impossible. I believe the objective and accurate account of the past is possible both in principle and in practice, if understood correctly, although I am quite aware of the difficulties involved in it. My point is rather that the objective and accurate account of the past entails certain value judgments in all history and truth value judgments in the history of philosophy. My view, then, is contrary to that of the objectivists who, in order to preserve objectivity and accuracy in historical accounts, reject value judgments in those accounts. But it is also contrary to the view of subjectivists who admit value judgments in historical accounts but argue that because of it historical objectivity and accuracy are impossible.[46]

Now let me go back to the three arguments in favor of disinterested history we saw earlier and try to identify the specific ways in which they seem to me to be misguided. Those arguments rest on three misunderstandings. The first is a confusion between what I call *ideological interest* and *philosophical interest*.[47] Ideological interest is the kind of interest that someone has when he or she turns to the history of philosophy with the purpose of justifying a particular point of view. Unfortunately, as we shall see in Chapter Five, there are many historians of philosophy whose approach displays precisely this kind of interest. Naturally an ideological interest tends to distort the historical account, and thus the criticisms that historiographers who favor a disinterested approach to the history of philosophy bring against it are entirely justified. For historians of this sort see only what they want to see in the past, and their selectivity is quite pernicious.[48] Moreover, some go so far as to modify the originally stated views of historical authors, correcting them so that they may more appropriately express the truth while at the same time not acknowledging that the result is not historically accurate.[49]

On the other hand, one can also approach the history of philosophy with a nonpernicious interest. Philosophical interest in the history of philosophy does not necessarily result in a distortion of the past. By philosophical interest I mean the kind of interest had by someone who is after truth. One can be interested in enlightenment and still preserve a considerable degree of objectivity. Indeed, the interest in truth leads to extraordinary efforts to achieve objectivity. This contrasts with those whose interest lies in defending and promoting a particular point of view and who as a result have lost all objectivity. That the history of philosophy contain value judgments and is guided by an interest in truth does not entail its distortion. For it is one thing to judge and another to modify. One can understand a view to be wrong and still preserve its historical integrity. It is only when historical integrity is tampered with for ideological or other reasons that interest becomes pernicious. There are dangers to be faced by those who approach the history of philosophy in the search for truth, no doubt, but falling prey to them is not necessary, and, therefore, they do not justify the accusations of those in favor of disinterested history. The problem with authors who identify the history of philosophy with disinterested history is that they confuse these two types of interests, thinking that all interest, including philosophical interest, is ideological and therefore pernicious.

The second source of misunderstanding is the attempt to draw a sharp distinction between philosophy and the history of philosophy on the basis of the role that evaluation plays in them. Such a distinction is nothing short of artificial and does not take into account that, since philosophy is what its history studies, the standards of philosophy must play a role when one studies its history, as I have argued earlier.

Finally, those who insist on disinterested history seem to think that value judgments necessarily entail an unhistorical interest in history. But nothing could be further from the truth. The concern of historians of philosophy can be the understanding of the philosophical past and still they can make value judgments concerning that past. There is no logical incompatibility between the two. Indeed, the earlier arguments show that those value judgments are not only an integral part of any historical inquiry but also highly desirable.

I believe these considerations should be sufficient to answer the arguments of those who wish to insulate the history of philosophy from value judgments and particularly from judgments of truth and falsity. As Rorty has put it:

> We should treat the history of philosophy as we treat the history of science. In the latter field, we have no reluctance in saying that we know better than our ancestors what they were talking about. We do not think it anachronistic to say that Aristotle had a false model of the heavens, or that Galen did not understand how the circulatory system worked. We take the pardonable ignorance of great dead scientists for granted. We should be equally willing to say that Aristotle was unfortunately ignorant that there are no such things as real essences, or Leibniz that God does not exist, or Descartes that the mind is just the central nervous system under an alternative description.[50]

Rorty may be wrong in his opinion of Aristotle, Leibniz, Descartes, and even Galen in the points he brings up, but he is right in saying that to do history of philosophy involves being willing to say that we know better. Moreover, just as we should be willing to judge where the past went wrong, we should also be willing to judge where it went right. We can and should agree with Suárez, for example, when he distinguishes between incommunicability and difference, or with Aristotle when he says that the good is the object of desire. To include value judgments in the history of philosophy does not mean that those judgments should be negative; they can and should be positive when appropriate.

In conclusion, then, the history of philosophy contains a wide range of propositions, including descriptive, interpretative, and evaluative propositions. These propositions reflect a concern with the past and its origin. In the case of history past events are the subject of concern, whereas in the history of philosophy only past ideas and the events related to them are pertinent. In either case, however, time, provenance, and the concern with the individual are of the essence, although they may not always be explicit in all propositions that are part of a history of philosophy. Note that, although the ideas with which historians of philosophy deal may be universal, historians deal with them as belonging to an individual or set of individuals. So, although historians may speak, for example, of the view that monads are psychic entities, and as such deal with universals, their aim is to describe Leibniz's view. Universals thus become individuated by their historical occurrence in philosophical accounts.

It should be clear from what has been said, moreover, that the introduction of value judgments in the history of philosophy carries with it the introduction of philosophical propositions that one would not normally expect to find in historical accounts. I am referring to propositions such as those that establish logical relations among ideas that do not involve reference to provenance, time, or individuals. The reason for this is that value judgments concerning historical views entail conceptual analyses of the sort found in philosophy. Thus in order to judge, for example, if X's view that P is correct, I might need to know whether P implies Q. The difference between these propositions when found in philosophy and when found in the history of philosophy is purely contextual. In one case they are part of an account of the world that has nothing to do with history. In the other case, they are part of a historical account where the overall aim is to understand particular events in the past. Thus, although the propositions in themselves are the same and lack historical character, their context when they are used in history is historical.

D. An Illustration: Thomas's Theory of Individuation

The descriptive, interpretative, and evaluative character of the history of philosophy can be illustrated easily in various ways. Since it would be redundant to dwell on several examples or even to provide a very lengthy illustration of that character, I shall content myself with providing a brief, concrete example of the kind of problems historians of philosophy face and how their solutions lead them to engage in descriptions, interpretations, and evaluations.

I have chosen as an example the rather notorious Thomistic doctrine concerning the principle of individuation of material substances. As a preliminary clarification I should point out, first, that for Thomas material substances are things such as a man, a cat, and a tree, that is, what Aristotle called "primary substances" in the *Categories*. Second, it should also be clear that the principle of individuation of material substances is that in virtue of which an individual material substance is individual. Third, it should also be noted that to be individual for Thomas means that a thing is (1) not divisible into entities specifically similar to itself, and (2) distinct from everything else. Thus, Minina, my cat, is an individual because (1) she cannot be divided into other beings that are also cats (Minina's species), and (2) she is distinct from all other substances. We will take all of this for granted and merely as propaedeutic to the issue for the historian, namely, Thomas's view concerning the principle of individuation of material substances. The question for the historian concerns the identification of that principle and its understanding.

The question of the identification of the Thomistic principle of individuation seems easy, at first sight, because Thomas was quite explicit about it. He repeatedly stated that the principle of individuation was *materia signata*. The problem arises when the historian tries to translate that term into other languages and to understand what the term means. Since the term is technical, we could decide not to bother much about its translation, choosing a term that could be easily identified as the standard translation of *materia signata*, say 'designated matter' or simply leaving it untranslated. But not all historians agree with this assessment and as a result we find quite a variety of translations of the term. The point of those who disagree with the suggested translation is that the translation of a technical term should not be just a transliteration that means nothing to the user of the language, but should suggest as much of the meaning of the original term as possible without leading to confusions. Of course, if that is the case, then we cannot even offer a translation of *materia signata* without providing an understanding of Thomas's doctrine. Moreover, since there is no exact equivalent in English of the term used by Thomas, every English translation of it will necessarily involve an interpretation of it. So we can see quite clearly that at least in this particular case, the very description of what Thomas said in a language other than the one he used involves already an interpretation.

But, how should *materia signata* be interpreted? The problems faced by the historian who wishes to answer this question are two: First, Thomas himself does not seem to have held a single view on this issue. In his *Commentary on Boethius' "On the Trinity"*, he explicitly states that *materia signata* is to be understood as matter under indeterminate dimensions rather than matter under determinate dimensions.[51] And he even provides an argument why it should be so. According to him, the dimensions in question cannot be determinate because if they were, then an individual would not remain as the same individual when it changes its dimensions through time, whereas in fact we know that individuals do so. In other words, if what individuates Minina are her determinate dimensions (such and such a weight, and such and such a volume, etc.), then she could not be the same individual when those dimensions change (when she eats, grows, puts on winter fat, breathes, etc).

All this seems to be quite clear. The problem for the historian is that elsewhere Thomas says quite unambiguously that the dimensions in question are determinate.[52] So, what is the historian to do? Did Thomas think one or the other, or perhaps both? Did he think one first and then change his mind? Which is the proper and more consistent view? In short, which is the more Thomistic view?

In answering these questions the experienced historian will turn to Thomas's commentators and disciples, first his contemporaries who were closer to the source and second to those who came later but who have been traditionally identified by scholars as orthodox interpreters of Thomas. Unfortunately, what we get from those sources is a cacophony of views.[53] On the one hand, there are many interpretations of how to understand Thomas's doctrine and, on the other hand, even single authors change their views from time to time. So we get very little help from either Thomas or his commentators on Thomas's view concerning the principle of individuation.

What should the historian do, then? Give up? Conclude that Thomas had no definite view on the principle of individuation, or conclude that he had a view but that we can never know what it was? Good historians, I believe, will not give up so easily. First of all, they will make sure they have on hand all the pertinent primary and secondary sources; and second, they will turn to their own philosophical understanding of the problem Thomas was trying to solve and apply that understanding to the evidence they have before them. In sum, they will, *qua* philosophers, try to put themselves in Thomas's shoes and attempt to decide what is the best solution that Thomas could have devised within the parameters within which he was working. This, of course, involves evaluation. Thus we see how in this case evaluation is not only necessary for interpretation but is indirectly necessary for description and even translation. Other cases that can serve as illustrations of these points can be found easily in the history of philosophy, but there should be no need to belabor the point further.

IV. HISTORY, PHILOSOPHY, AND THE HISTORY OF PHILOSOPHY

Having provided a general characterization of history, philosophy, and the history of philosophy, it would be useful to draw a comparison among the three. On the one hand, from what has been said earlier, it should be clear that history and the history of philosophy share their concern with the past and the location where the individual events that constitute that past took place, as well as with the identity of the players who took part in it. On the other hand, it should also be clear that this concern with the past and its origin is completely missing from philosophy. Provenance and time are of no importance to philosophers. Philosophy shares with the history of philosophy its concern with ideas, although for philosophers those ideas are considered apart from their spatio-temporal location, while for historians of philosophy it is essential to deal with them in that contextual matrix. Now, insofar as the history of philosophy is part of general history, we cannot deny that general historians also deal with philosophical ideas. The difference between general historians and historians of philosophy is that for the former philosophical ideas are only a small part of the object they study in their attempt to produce a complete history of the past, whereas for the latter philosophical ideas constitute the major part of their object of study. Note that historians of philosophy do pay attention to factors other than philosophical ideas. Other ideas—social, cultural, scientific, and the like—are of interest to them in providing an account of the origin and development of philosophical ideas. And the same is true with respect to events and other historical phenomena. The context of philosophical ideas is important for historians of philosophy, for it helps in the understanding of those ideas, their origins, and their development. But historians of philosophy take those other factors into account only insofar as they help in the understanding of those ideas, their origins, and development. Consequently, their study is subservient to the main task, which is the account of philosophical ideas. (I shall return to this issue in Chapter Five.)

This brings me back to the question of the main tasks of historians, philosophers, and historians of philosophy, and how they compare. In all three cases the task involves the production of an account. For the general historian the account is of the past and whatever was part of it. The historian, *qua* historian, aims to provide us with an understanding of what happened, how it happened, why it happened, and the consequences that ensued. The philosopher also has to provide an account, but that account does not consist of an explanation of a particular happening in the past. A philosophical account involves the development of an adequate, consistent, and comprehensive view that explains why the world is what it is and clarifies the way we should think about it. The product of philosophical activity is, therefore, of necessity interpretative and evaluative and involves the analysis of logical relations among ideas and judgments of truth. Now, the task of historians of philosophy involves elements from both history and philosophy. As *historians* of philosophy, they are concerned with the past, its origin, and consequences. But as historians *of philosophy* they cannot avoid being concerned with the logical relations among ideas and with their truth. It is incumbent upon them, therefore, as *historians of philosophy* to observe the logical relations among past ideas and to judge their adequacy and truth value.

I discuss the relation between philosophy and its history in more detail in Chapter Two and, therefore, will not go into it here, but something must be said about the relationship between history in general and the history of philosophy at this point. This is necessary because so far we have been dealing with history and the history of philosophy as sets of propositions that provide an account of the past, and the relation between history and the history of philosophy has thus been considered in those terms. But history, as we saw earlier, could also be a series of past events, an activity whereby an account of past events is produced, and a set of rules and procedures that guide the production of an account of past events. And we also saw that the history of philosophy could be interpreted as a series of past philosophical ideas, an account of those ideas, the activity whereby the account is produced, or the rules and regulations that govern the production of such an account. Each of those interpretations of the history of philosophy corresponds to the various interpretations of history mentioned. Now the question that arises is: How are they related?

The relation is one of inclusion, where history considered generally functions as the larger, more encompassing partner. The history of philosophy interpreted as a series of past philosophical ideas is included in history considered as a series of past events. Indeed, past philosophical ideas can be understood as events of a certain type that make their appearance at a certain time and place. The global historical account of past events, that is, the set of all propositions about them, if we revert to speaking linguistically, encompasses the set of propositions that the historian of philosophy produces as an account of the philosophical ideas that have been entertained by philosophers. The history of philosophy considered as the activity that produces the account of past philosophical ideas is again part of the activity that goes into the production of the global historical account. And, finally, the history of philosophy understood as philosophical historiography is simply a branch of general historiography, namely, that concerned with the particular issues and problems raised in the development of an account of past ideas. In all cases, then, the history of philosophy is part of history and should encounter no conflict with it.

All this would probably seem to those unacquainted with historiographical literature as rather obvious and even trivial. The view that the history of philosophy is a branch of history, however, is by no means universally accepted. The argument in support of the view that it is not is based on the conviction that there are important distinctions between the nature of history in general and special histories. These distinctions are believed to be based on the way historians of special histories handle their subject matter. So that, even though the materials used in various special histories do "belong to the province to which the general historian devotes his attention," nevertheless these materials are handled so differently that it does not warrant the conclusion that special histories are part of general history, according to those historiographers who wish to maintain this distinction.[54] These materials, so the argument goes, are handled differently for at least three reasons: (1) The focus of interest is different; (2) special histories concern events that are not necessarily continuous whereas general history presupposes the continuity of the events for which it provides an account; and (3) special histories introduce a notion of development into the historical account that is missing in general history. Let me try to illustrate these reasons in terms of history and the history of philosophy.

First is the focus of interest: Those who try to draw a sharp distinction between history and the history of philosophy might point out, for example, that the interest of the historian rests in providing an account of past events, describing what in fact occurred, pointing out the causes, both evident and hidden, of what occurred, and the consequences of those events. The task of general historians, then, is to provide an understanding of the past. On the other hand, historians of philosophy are not concerned with events but with ideas, and their interest extends to the value of those ideas. In short, historians of philosophy are interested in finding what is of value in the past and not just understanding past ideas and their interrelations.

Second, history concerns events that are continuous. Indeed, it is the task of history to fill in the gaps among events that seem discontinuous, for its aim is to present a complete picture of the past and that past is presupposed to have no breaks within it. But special histories, and particularly the history of philosophy, feel free to jump from one author to another and even from one age to another, neither assuming nor requiring continuity in the subject matter they study. Thus, for example, an account of the development of the problem of individuation in the early Middle Ages might jump from Boethius (sixth century) to John Eriugena (ninth century) without any qualms, but the general historian would feel constrained to deal with all the intervening centuries.

Finally, the general historian aims to describe and explain change, whereas special historians, and particularly historians of philosophy, are concerned with development. Now, change and development are quite different. Change is the introduction of difference. Thus we say that something has changed or has undergone change if it is in some sense different than it was. But the change does not presuppose a direction or an end. Any introduction of a difference is a change. Development, on the other hand, is change in a certain direction, toward a certain end. The historian, then, is concerned simply with providing an account of the past and the changes in it. But the historian of philosophy is concerned with seeing a pattern of development in the past, that is, of change in a certain direction. Note, incidentally, that development and progress are also different. Progress is development for the better, whereas development can actually involve regress. I shall leave the discussion of progress, however, for Chapter Six.

These three arguments do not seem to me to be very compelling. To the first, one can easily respond that general history, as much as the history of philosophy, involves evaluations and not just description. Indeed, as stated earlier, one of the fundamental motives for the production of an account of past events is precisely to learn from the past in order to avoid making the same mistakes in the future, and that learning involves judging. But enough was said earlier about evaluation in history to answer this argument.

To the second argument one may wish to answer that the cleavage between continuous and discontinuous objects of study does not seem to be so fundamental to merit a radical distinction between history and the history of philosophy. The difference can be illustrated as follows. Suppose that we have a picture of differently colored pebbles scattered on a white surface. Special historians would be like observers who concentrate their attention on, say, the blue pebbles, and the patterns that they form. Some of those blue pebbles might be next to other blue pebbles, but others might not. Nonetheless, the blue pebble historian would consider all of them regardless of whether they are next to each other or not, looking for patterns they may make. General historians, by contrast, would be like observers who take in all the pebbles, not just the blue ones, looking for overall patterns. But in doing that general historians do not neglect the blue pebbles. Indeed, it is essential to their task to take those into account and use the conclusions of the blue pebble historian in the overall description of the pebbles. It makes no sense, then, to separate the general historian from the special historian because one looks at only certain types of events, whether continuous or discontinuous, and the other looks at all events, which for that very reason are continuous.

The answer to the third argument is that it is a mistake to assume that the business of the historian is to account for change, whereas the business of special historians is to show development. Indeed, no good special historian will grant that. It is true that special historians look for development, a direction, an end. But they try not to impose it on their object and often record regression rather than progression. In that sense they are not different from the general historian, for the latter also sees development when it occurs. The very notion of an account of change, of its causes and consequences, involves judgments concerning directions and ends. Or is the general historian not to say that after the enormous development in the Roman empire, for example, a period of economic and cultural stagnation and regression followed in the early Middle Ages?

Let me finish by pointing out that the whole notion that general history is something entirely other than special histories and that those histories are somehow not part of it seems absurd to me. If history is an account of the past and special histories are accounts of some aspects of that past, they must be part of general history. Not that general history is reducible to special histories. The task of the general historian is to integrate into a general account the partial accounts provided by special histories and, therefore, the overall account will contain much more than those partial accounts contained. But the more it contains is not the result of having a special province or object of study which is not covered by any special historian. The elements it adds to special histories constitute the integrating intellectual glue that binds them together into an overall enlightening picture of the past.

Nor does it matter that the special historian may need to apply and use certain idiosyncratic methods not applicable to histories of events other than his special kind of history. For those methods would indeed be part of the general methodology employed by the general historian, except that, as stated, they would pertain only to that branch of the methodology dealing with the object of study of the special historian.

V. THE HISTORY OF IDEAS, THE HISTORY OF CULTURE, THE HISTORY OF SCIENCE, AND THE GENRES OF THE HISTORY OF PHILOSOPHY

Having established some of the fundamental characteristics of the history of philosophy, it is appropriate at least briefly to distinguish it from other enterprises closely related to it and sometimes even confused with it before we establish its relation to philosophy in Chapter Two. Among these enterprises the most frequently discussed are the history of ideas, the history of culture, and the history of science.

That there are clear distinctions between the history of philosophy and the history of science should be quite obvious, as long as one is prepared to accept a distinction between philosophical and scientific ideas. The notion of phlogiston used in the past to explain various physical phenomena is clearly scientific and belongs in the history of science, but it does not necessarily belong in a history of philosophy.[55] Of course, there may be a philosophical truth that one could learn from the theory of phlogiston and how it was developed, and so forth, but in that case the theory of phlogiston would be mentioned in a philosophical account rather than used. We might say, for example, that the theory of phlogiston led such and such a philosopher to conclude something or other about the ultimate nature of reality. But that is not the same as giving an account of the philosophical ideas of a period or an author, only to refer to the nonphilosophical factors that may have influenced those ideas and that author.

The case with the history of ideas is similar to but not quite like the case of the history of science. For here what we have is that the history of philosophical ideas is a part of the whole history of ideas since philosophical ideas are merely a type of idea. And something similar is the case with the history of culture. The history of culture includes not only the history of ideas but the history of all products of human enterprise, including science, technology, art, and of course philosophy. Philosophical ideas are only a small part of culture.

This does not mean, of course, that there are no differences between the methodology used when developing a general history of ideas or a history of culture on the one hand and a history of philosophical ideas on the other. As we shall see in Chapter Five, the history of philosophy entails certain methodological procedures that are peculiarly its own. But such methodological differences do not prevent the incorporation of the conclusions reached by the history of philosophy into the history of ideas or the history of culture.

Now, questions sometimes arise concerning the task of the historian of philosophy. There have been doubts raised as to what exactly the historian of philosophy is supposed to do. We all know that writing historical novels, even good ones, is not the same as doing history of philosophy. But what about writing intellectual biographies of philosophical authors, editing philosophical texts, producing translations of philosophical works, and determining the authorship of disputed philosophical materials? Are these legitimate tasks of the historian of philosophy?

It seems to be undeniable that most of these tasks require not only a superficial but actually a profound knowledge of philosophy. Indeed, anyone who has edited Greek and Latin philosophical texts, for example, knows how much knowledge of the thought of the author of the text is required to accomplish the task. And the same could be said concerning translations and the determination of authorship. Even the production of intellectual biographies of philosophers requires knowledge of philosophy and philosophical acumen, since an intellectual biography of a philosopher must necessarily include discussion of the philosophical ideas of the figure in question.

Moreover, it is not just that these tasks require a knowledge of philosophy, but that they are essential prerequisites to the task of providing an account of past philosophical ideas, which is after all the task of the historian of philosophy. Indeed, they are not prerequisites in the sense that they predate in a temporal or even logical sense the work of the historian of philosophy; they are very much part and parcel of the work of that historian. Not that every historian of philosophy need be an editor, translator, or biographer, of course. What I mean is that the production of good translations, biographies, and editions are an essential part of the history of philosophy.

Those philosophers who easily dismiss historians who work primarily in the production of editions and translations as "textmen" are only displaying their ignorance of the nature of the history of philosophy and what it takes to do it. The work of editors and translators of philosophical texts as well as of biographers is an important component of the history of philosophy. That does not mean that the work of historians of philosophy is to be confined to the edition and translation of texts and the production of biographies, as some historians seem to think. The work of the historian should go beyond that and provide studies that enlighten us concerning the philosophical ideas of the past and their interrelationships. But it does mean that the work of editors, translators, and biographers, when concerned with philosophical texts and authors, is to be included as part and parcel of the work for which the historian of philosophy is responsible.

This brings me to a question that has been discussed seldom, if at all, in the historiography of philosophy, namely, the genres of the history of philosophy. As already mentioned, it seems appropriate to include as part of the historian of philosophy's task the production of critical editions and translations of philosophical texts. Critical editions are particularly important when the work in question is extant only in various manuscript versions that present differences among themselves. The historian has to produce a text that approaches as much as possible the original autograph produced by the author (or the secretary) in question. It is also important in situations where the original is available in manuscripts where idiosyncratic abbreviations are common and the reader must supply expansions of those abbreviations. For example, the works of most medieval authors survive in manuscripts that display important variants, and the words in the manuscripts are often abbreviated to save space. (Parchment was very expensive at the time, and it was the only readily available material medievals had on which to write.) The task of the historian of philosophy who is trying to provide an account of the ideas of the author of a medieval text, then, must begin by providing an accurate reading of those abbreviations and a version of the text that is as close as possible to the one first produced by the author.[56] All this, of course, requires a thorough knowledge of the language in which the text was written, of the system of abbreviation used by scribes, of the philosophical and cultural context of the times, and most important of all, of the ideas and style of the author in question.

The work of the translator begins where the work of the editor ends. Translators do not have to come up with a text; their job is to change the text from one language into another. As such their task requires all the knowledge needed by the editor except for the palaeographical knowledge that allows the editor to read various scripts and expand abbreviations. Moreover, they have the additional burden of presenting the ideas expressed by the text in a new linguistic garb, without changing them. This task is very difficult because it involves transcultural communication, something not required of the editor, who works, as it were, within the cultural domain of the author who produced the text in the first place. But the translator must bridge the gap between two languages and at the same time maintain the integrity of the ideas to be transferred from one language and culture into another. This is the reason why good translations are usually accompanied by substantial commentary either in the form of introductory remarks or notes to the text. This critical apparatus is necessary to explain nuances of thought, difficult turns of expression, obscure passages, and so on.

Biographers come in diverse types. Most biographers, even those who write about philosophers, are interested primarily in the nonphilosophical events of an author's life. Nowadays what seem most important for them are sexual idiosyncracies. But, of course, not all biographers are interested in that subject matter. Biographers of saints, for example, usually concentrate on the moral character and good deeds of the individuals they discuss. Now, biographies that are not concerned primarily with philosophical ideas cannot be considered part of the history of philosophy, even if they may provide valuable information for the philosophical biography of an author. The aim of a philosophical biography must be to present an account of the events of the life of an author and their relation to his or her philosophical ideas. As such it has to contain detailed reference to those ideas, including the main positions the author took and the reasons why he or she did so. Thus, a philosophical biography involves an exposition of the views of the historical figure in question, whence its philosophical content and character.

The genres discussed so far are usually considered less philosophical than others by historians of philosophy and, as already mentioned, some go so far as to deny that they are legitimate genres of the history of philosophy. The reason, of course, is that the overall aim of these genres is often perceived to be different from the aim the historian of philosophy is supposed to have. The aim of the historian of philosophy is the understanding of past philosophical ideas, but the aim of the editor is the production of a text, of the translator a translation, and of the biographer a description of a life and the events in it. And none of these aims seems to be the same as that of the historian of philosophy.

What this objection misses is that the aim of the historian of philosophy is not just understanding, but also the production of an account that will facilitate understanding. As such, then, everything that goes into the production of the account that helps to understand past philosophy is part of the history of philosophy, and it would be very difficult to try to exclude the preparation of editions, translations and biographies from that process. This does not mean, however, as already noted, that the task of the historian of philosophy becomes less philosophical. That task is to provide an account of past philosophical ideas, and that account, in order to qualify as part of the history of philosophy, must be philosophical. I shall return to this point in Chapter Five, when we turn to the various approaches that may be used in doing history of philosophy.

There are other genres of the history of philosophy that are more widely accepted and vary according to the degree of generality and comprehensiveness at which they aim. First and most general of all are what might be called *general histories*. These trace the historical development of philosophical issues and ideas through various authors, schools, and times. Their aim is to provide an understanding of philosophical changes within a larger historical context. In this genre are included general histories of philosophy as well as more specific histories of a period or a country. Because of the extent of the materials covered, this genre cannot provide the kind of details and analyses that other, more restricted types of studies can provide.

A second genre might be called *comprehensive studies*. These studies also cover periods and extend to large spans of time, but they concentrate on a particular problem or issue. So they might trace the development of the problem of universals, say, from Boethius to Thomas Aquinas or they might compare the views on that issue in the twelfth century, sometimes concentrating on a particular school of thought and other times on a century or a region. In all cases, however, the aim is to provide a comprehensive account.

A third genre is also common. It concerns itself with the exposition of an author's overall philosophy. These studies, too, may make reference to the views of contemporaries of the author in question or even of predecessors and successors. The difference between these and "comprehensive" studies is that their main purpose is the exposition and understanding of the views of one author, even if in order to do that they have to refer to the ideas of other authors and to the point of view accepted during an age or in a particular society or place. The center of attention of these studies is the philosophy of one individual. Comprehensive studies, on the other hand, aim to provide an understanding of the philosophy of a period, an age, a school, and so on, rather than of the views of one individual.

The fourth genre is still more restricted than the previous one. It seeks to examine in detail an author's position only with regard to one issue or idea. Its emphasis, then, tends to be more analytical and detailed. That does not mean, again, that reference is not made to other authors or doctrines, but the focus of attention is always the problem or idea at hand and the author under consideration.

I shall return briefly to these genres in Chapter Five and show which methodological approaches best fit them. Now it is time to turn our attention to the relation between philosophy and its history, which will be explored in the next chapter.

NOTES

1. This sort of position is defended by Renford Bambrough in "Universals and Family Resemblances," *Proceedings of the Aristotelian Society* 61 (1960–1961), 207–222; reprinted in Michael J. Loux, ed., *Universals and Particulars: Readings in Ontology*, rev. ed. (Notre Dame, Ind., and London: University of Notre Dame Press, 1970), pp. 106–124.

2. Jorge J. E. Gracia, Prolegomena, *Individuality: An Essay on the Foundations of Metaphysics* (Albany: SUNY Press, 1988), pp. 10–12.

3. Richard Rorty, Introduction, in Rorty, Schneewind, and Skinner, eds., *Philosophy in History*, p. 8.

4. Naturally, reference to events and happenings will also entail references to the persons, things, and circumstances involved in those events and happenings.

5. Strictly speaking, I would have to say "an account of *a series of* past events" and not just "an account of past events," because historical accounts are accounts of history in the first sense, that is, of a series of past events. Yet, although history in the first sense refers to series of events, in the second sense it is also taken to refer to accounts of single past events. In order to preserve this possibility in my description, I refer to history in the second sense simply as an account of past events. It should also be clear that accounts of past events are themselves part of history in the first sense, since they are themselves historical events. I shall return to this point later.

6. Cf. Karl Popper, *The Poverty of Historicism* (London: Routledge & Kegan Paul, 1957), pp. 143–144. This understanding of history is by no means universally accepted. Christian Wolff, for example, excludes explanation from historical accounts and considers it part of philosophy rather than history: "Philosophical knowledge differs from historical knowledge. The latter consists in the bare knowledge of the fact. The former progresses further and exhibits the reason of the fact.... He who knows the reason of a fact which is alleged by another man has historical knowledge of the philosophical knowledge of another." *Preliminary Discourse on Philosophy in General*, trans. Richard J. Blackwell (Indianapolis and New York: Bobbs-Merrill, 1963), p. 5. The distinction between knowledge of a fact and of a reasoned fact comes from Aristotle, *Posterior Analytics* I, ch. 13, 78a23. For a discussion of the issues involved in the distinction between chronicle and history, see Arthur C. Danto's *Analytical Philosophy of History* (Cambridge: Cambridge University Press, 1965) ch. 7. The question of the nature of narrative has been widely discussed in contemporary philosophy. For a summary of the controversy, see Hayden White, "The Question of Narrative in Contemporary Historical Theory," *History and Theory* 23, no. 1 (1984): 1–33.

7. The issue of what constitutes historical explanation has preoccupied many philosophers in the recent past. I do not discuss that issue in this book, but those interested in it may consult Ernest Nagel's *The Structure of Science: Problems in the Logic of Scientific Explanation* (New York: Harcourt, Brace and World, 1961), particularly ch. 15; John Herman Randall's *Nature and Historical Experience* (New York: Columbia University Press, 1958); M. G. White's *Foundations of Historical Knowledge* (New York: Harper & Row, 1965); and the papers by Berlin, Passmore, Hempel, Hart, and others in William H. Dray, ed., *Philosophical Analysis and History* (New York and London: Harper and Row, 1966), among others. Among Continental philosophers the work of Foucault, Habermas, Gadamer, and Ricoeur is particularly relevant.

8. Cf. the already cited work by Meiland, *Scepticism and Historical Knowledge.*

9. One way might be to think of a universe in which all minds were

connected in some way, like TV sets are, so that whenever one mind thought of something the same thought would occur in all other minds. Actually, when Christian writers speak about the beatific vision they sound as if what they are talking about is this sort of thing.

10. Let me make clear that I am using the term 'proposition' here generically to refer to statements and sentences as well as to the meaning of those statements and sentences. For present purposes the distinctions among mental, nonmental, and natural and artificial languages, as well as between propositions, statements, and sentences, will be ignored. None of the points that are made in the course of the discussion is contingent on such distinctions.

11. These and the other examples that are provided throughout this chapter should not be taken to be paradigmatically exhaustive. They are meant to be precisely what I have called them: "examples" of the sorts of propositions that one finds in histories, philosophy, and histories of philosophy.

12. For an extended discussion of the selective character of historical accounts, see William Dray, "The Historian's Problem of Selection," in Ernest Nagel, Patrick Suppes, and Alfred Tarski, eds., *Logic, Methodology and Philosophy of Science, Proceedings of the 1960 International Congress* (Stanford, Calif.: Stanford University Press, 1962), pp. 595–603.

13. Contrary to this point of view, Hayden White has argued that history properly is not fundamentally different from philosophies of history. See *Metahistory: The Historical Imagination in Nineteenth-Century Europe* (Baltimore: Johns Hopkins University Press, 1973), p. xi and elsewhere. For a rebuttal of this point of view, see Maurice Mandelbaum, "The Presuppositions of Hayden White's *Metahistory*," in *Philosophy, History and the Sciences: Selected Critical Essays* (Baltimore: Johns Hopkins University Press, 1984), pp. 97–111. Although I disagree with Hayden White's point of view, I recognize that to do history of philosophy properly one must develop some ideas concerning the philosophy of history, as I do in Chapter 6 of this book.

14. Note that I have also kept separate historiography and the philosophy of history, although in the literature they are not always distinguished (see Dray's article "Philosophy of History" in Paul Edwards, ed., *Encyclopedia of Philosophy* [New York and London: Macmillan, 1967], vol. 6, p. 247). What I call *historiography*, also referred to as *critical*, *analytical* or *formal philosophy of history* in the literature, deals with the nature and methodology of historical explanation, with the justification of historical knowledge, and with the logic of historical discourse. In short, historiography, as already noted, is a branch of epistemology that deals with a particular type of knowledge. On the other hand, what I call *philosophy of history*, also referred to as *speculative, synoptic*, or *material philosophy of history* in the literature, tries to discover the way in which events unfold and are related, detecting patterns of significance in historical development as well as purpose and meaning in it. The philosophy of history is not concerned with the conditions of historical knowledge, but with the description and understanding of the forces that shape history, that is,

with the laws that govern historical development. As such, the philosophy of history is not a branch of epistemology but of metaphysics or philosophy of nature, depending on the terminology one prefers, since it is metaphysics that is supposed to tell us how the world is. The philosophy of history, understood as I do here, goes back to the ancients although it is practiced to this day. Perhaps the best known example of this type of inquiry is Augustine's *The City of God,* trans. J. H. S. Burleigh (London: The Westminster Press, 1953). In this century, both Spengler's *Decline of the West,* special ed. (New York: Alfred A. Knopf, 1939) and Toynbee's *A Study of History* (London: Oxford University Press, 1935–1961) fall into this category. Historiography, however, is rather recent as a discipline. Although it goes back to Vico's *New Science,* trans. from the 3d ed. (1744) by Thomas Goddard Bergin and Max Harold Fisch (Garden City, N.Y.: Anchor Books, 1961), it is only in the nineteenth century that it flourishes in the work of Dilthey, Rickert, and others. In this century, some of the most influential works in this area have been Croce's *The Theory and History of Historiography,* trans. Douglas Ainslie (London: G. G. Harap and Co., 1921); Collingwood's *The Idea of History* (Oxford: Clarendon Press, 1946); and Mandelbaum's *The Problem of Historical Knowledge* (New York, Evanston, and London: Harper & Row, 1967, originally published in 1938). There are at least three reasons why historiography and the philosophy of history are not always distinguished in the literature: (1) They are usually put together in order to contrast them with history proper; (2) both of them deal with the universal, whereas history deals with the individual; and (3) their relation to history is similar. Let me explain (3) further. Historiography is related to history (understood as an account of past events) in the same way in which science is related to scientific data. And it turns out that the philosophy of history is related to history (understood in this case as a series of past events) also as a science is related to scientific data. In both cases history, although understood differently, functions as the data on which historiography and the philosophy of history base their speculation. It is important, however, to understand the differences between these two disciplines in order to prevent methodological confusions. Points (2) and (3) became clear in my mind as a result of a conversation with Ky Herreid.

15. This is also Ernest Nagel's conclusion in *The Structure of Science,* p. 549.

16. Some ideas seem to me to be clearly philosophical. For example, the Aristotelian notion that physical objects are composed of matter and form seems to me to be a philosophical idea. And some ideas do not seem to be philosophical at all, such as the notion that water boils at 100°C. But concerning many other ideas the case is not so clear. Maurice Mandelbaum has posed this problem as the problem of what counts as a philosopher rather than as a philosophical idea. This way of posing the problem has both advantages and disadvantages. The main disadvantage is the difficulty it creates with authors such as Montaigne, who are not strictly speaking philosophers but many of whose ideas are not only philosophical but influenced well-known philosophers. See Mandelbaum's "The History of Philosophy: Some Methodological Issues," in *Philosophy, History and the Sciences,* pp. 120–130.

17. See, for example, Augustine's *On the Teacher.*

18. Plato and Augustine concluded that, since knowledge of ideas does occur, we must have direct access to them. And Averroes, aware that various human beings may understand the same idea, even though there is no way this idea can be passed from one to the other through physical means, concluded that all human beings must have one and the same intellect.

19. Michael Ayers, "Analytical Philosophy and the History of Philosophy," in Rée, et al., *Philosophy and Its Past,* pp. 54 and 58 ff.

20. Paul Shorey, *What Plato Said* (Chicago: University of Chicago Press, 1933). Compare that with G. M. A. Grube's *Plato's Thought* (Boston: Beacon Press, 1958). Michael Ayers seems to support this brand of antiquarianism when he criticizes H. H. Price for wanting to get at what an author "really meant" even if it "is perhaps not quite what he said." "Analytical Philosophy and the History of Philosophy," p. 50. The controversy between those who favor a strict adherence to what a philosopher said and those who favor a more interpretative approach becomes explicit in G. H. R. Parkinson, *Logic and Reality in Leibniz's Metaphysics* (Oxford: Clarendon Press, 1965), see p. 117 particularly; and R. Robinson, *Plato's Earlier Dialectic,* 2d ed. (Oxford: Oxford University Press, 1962), particularly p. 5. See J. J. Mulhern's discussion of the issue in "Treatises, Dialogues, and Interpretation," *The Monist* 53, no. 4 (1969): 631–41.

21. Daniel W. Graham, "Anachronism in the History of Philosophy," in Peter H. Hare, ed., *Doing Philosophy Historically* (Buffalo, N.Y.: Prometheus Books, 1988), pp. 137–148, and Hayden White in *Metahistory.* Among earlier authors who have argued this way are Charles Beard and W. H. Walsh. For Beard, see "Written History as an Act of Faith," and "That Noble Dream," *American Historical Review* 39, no. 2 (1934): 219–229 and 41, no. 1(1935): 74–87, respectively. The first was reprinted in Hans Meyerhoff, ed., *The Philosophy of History in Our Time* (Garden City, N.Y.: Doubleday Books, 1959), pp. 14–51; and the second in Fritz Stern, ed., *The Varieties of History* (Cleveland and New York: Meridian Books, 1956), pp. 315–328. For Walsh, see *An Introduction to Philosophy of History* (London: Hutchinson's University Library, 1951).

22. This argument is sometimes cast in a linguistic context. It is argued that language is a historical and cultural product and, therefore, cannot be used to bridge the gaps between the present and the past. For a recent discussion of various attempts to argue that philosophical language can transcend history, see Mark Jordan, "History in the Language of Metaphysics," *Review of Metaphysics* 36, no. 4 (1983): 849–866.

23. For a different strategy in dealing with anachronists, see Danto, *Analytical Philosophy of History,* chs. 3 and 6.

24. Ian Hacking makes this point in the parable, "The Green Family," in "Five Parables," in Rorty et al., eds., *Philosophy in History,* pp. 104–107.

25. Cf. Peter Winch, "Understanding a Primitive Society," *American Philosophical Quarterly* 1 (1964): 307–324. Most transcultural studies, including the enterprise known as comparative philosophy, assume a core of similarity among human beings. See, for example, John S. Major's "Myth, Cosmology, and the Origins of Chinese Science," *Journal of Chinese Philosophy* 5, no. 1 (1978): 1–20.

26. Giovanni Battista Vico, *The New Science*, paras. 332–333.

27. In fact, there are many views concerning what historians of philosophy are allowed in their historical task. One extreme believes that their task is purely descriptive, excluding not only truth value evaluations but evaluations of every kind as well as interpretations. At the other extreme are those who, convinced that the objective recovery of the past is impossible, advocate complete license when it comes to the interpretation and evaluation of the past. In between these extremes are all sorts of different positions.

28. Martial Guéroult, "The History of Philosophy as a Philosophical Problem," *The Monist* 52, no. 4 (1969): 566.

29. Daniel Garber, "Does History Have a Future? Some Reflections on Bennett and Doing Philosophy Historically," in Hare, ed., *Doing Philosophy Historically*, pp. 27–43. See also Franklin L. Baumer, "Intellectual History and Its Problems," *Journal of Modern History* 21, no. 3 (1949): 191 ff.; and Edward H. Madden, "Myers and James: A Philosophical Dialogue," in Hare, ed., ibid., p. 299.

30. Yvon Lafrance, *Méthode et exégèse en histoire de la philosophie* (Montreal: Les Éditions Bellarmin, 1983), p. 27. Lafrance's "positivism" should not be confused with the positivism propounded by nineteenth century authors like Henry Thomas Buckle. The positivism of Buckle involved an attemt to understand historical development in terms of purely physical laws. See Chapters 1 and 2 of the Introduction to his *History of Civilization in England* 3d ed. (London: Longmans, Green & Co., 1866). Lafrance's point of view goes back to the emphasis on scientific history characteristic of historians like Leopold von Ranke and John Bagnell Bury. For Ranke, see "Vorrede zur ersten Ausgabe," in *Geschichten der romanischen und germanischen Völker von 1494 bis 1514* 3d ed. (Leipzig: Duncker & Humblot, 1885), pp. v–viii. For Bury, see "The Science of History," in H. Temperley, ed., *Selected Essays of J. B. Bury* (Cambridge: Cambridge University Press, 1930), pp. 3–22.

31. Garber, "Does History Have a Future?" p. 37.

32. Ibid., p. 30.

33. Michael Frede, "The History of Philosophy as a Discipline," *Journal of Philosophy* 85, no. 11 (1988): 669.

34. Yvon Lafrance had put forth a similar argument in *Méthode et exégèse en histoire de la philosophie*, pp. 15–27. His argument is that philosophy functions in some sense under the illusion that there is one absolute and uni-

versal truth (p. 21) and as such is charged with personal bias. History, on the other hand, is concerned only with the examination of linguistic facts (historical works) and so historians must abandon every personal theory when approaching their subject matter. Therefore, Lafrance advocates a "nonphilosophical history of philosophy" (p. 26).

35. Apart from those I include here, other grounds also are frequently used by historiographers to argue that value judgments play an indispensible role in historical accounts: (1) the selection of events to be accounted for is made in terms of values, (2) the choice of relevant conditions to account for those events is made in terms of values, and (3) the characterization of those events is value laden both because it is presupposed by an individual who has a particular value perspective and because the events themselves are purposeful. Such arguments have been proposed, among others, by Max Weber, S. F. Nadel, Edwin A. Burtt, Leo Strauss, and Karl Mannheim. Ernest Nagel presents a thorough discussion of them in *The Structure of Science*, ch. 13, pp. 485–502. See also Dray, "Philosophy of History," p. 250 and *Philosophy of History*, ch. 3 (Englewood Cliffs, N.J.: Prentice-Hall, 1964), pp. 21 ff.

36. This applies also *mutatis mutandis* to works that we call "great," for to say that a work of philosophy is great does mean that it reveals to us something that we did not know before. Of course, some may want to argue that 'great' in a historical context means simply that the work had considerable influence. That, indeed, may be the case in some circumstances, but certainly not in others. There are works that have had enormous influence, such as Hitler's *Mein Kampf*, that are anything but great, and there are works that have had little historical influence and yet may be great.

37. This is one of Michael Ayers's concerns. See his "Analytical Philosophy and the History of Philosophy," pp. 55–56.

38. Robin George Collingwood, *The Idea of History* (Oxford: Clarendon Press, 1946), pp. 282–283.

39. Richard Rorty, "The Historiography of Philosophy: Four Genres," in Rorty et al., eds., *Philosophy in History*, p. 55.

40. J. B. Schneewind, "The Divine Corporation and the History of Ethics," in ibid., p. 175.

41. Indeed, this is the basis of some of Lafrance's arguments against an interested or philosophical history of philosophy, for he holds that there are no general standards according to which all philosophical systems can be judged. Each system must be judged only by the internal criteria used to put it together. *Méthode et exégèse*, pp. 16 and 19. The problem with this position is that, if the only legitimate criteria at the disposal of historians were internal, there would be no way of comparing different systems of philosophy unless they adopt the same criteria. Historians, then, become trapped within systems and have no way of comparing the relative strengths of historical developments.

42. A variant of this case occurs when an author holds two incompatible positions at two different times, say P at t^1 and ~P at t^2. In such cases the historian should be able to say not only that the author held P at t^1 and ~P at t^2, but also why he did so and whether the author improved his overall position by changing from P to ~P. For it is altogether possible that the author made a mistake in changing his views, or he might have forgotten that he had held P by the time he held that ~P, or he may have changed his mind based on incorrect information, and so on. The historian must pass judgment on all these things and to do that requires also judgments about the truth value of P and ~P.

43. Jonathan Rée has argued that one of the reasons why the history of philosophy is different from other histories is that it is done by philosophers, whereas the history of music, say, is not done by musicians. See his "Philosophy and the History of Philosophy," in Rée et al., *Philosophy and Its Past*, pp. 1–2. I fail to see a drastic difference between them in that respect, however. If to be a philosopher means to write nonhistorical philosophical materials, then many historians of philosophy are not philosophers, just as many historians of music are not musicians. But if to be a philosopher means to understand, analyze, and judge philosophical views, then it would seem a requirement of historians of philosophy that they be philosophers. But so it would seem that historians of music must be musicians insofar as they need to be able to understand, analyze and judge musical compositions. Either way, the case of the historian of philosophy is not different from that of the historian of music.

44. Jonathan Bennett, "Response to Garber and Rée," in Hare, *Doing Philosophy Historically*, p. 62. See also Voltaire, "De l'utilité de l'histoire," in *Dictionnaire philosophique*, in Adrien Jean Quentin Beuchot, ed., *Ouvres de Voltaire*, vol. 30 (Paris: Lefèvre, 1829–1840), pp. 207–209.

45. For a discussion of this distinction, see Nagel, *The Structure of Science*, pp. 492 ff.

46. It should also be distinguished from the view advocated by Martial Guéroult, according to which we must treat the history of philosophy as containing truth but must refrain, *qua* historians, from making truth value judgments about it. I cannot subscribe to Guéroult's position because I cannot understand how we can treat something as true without at the same time making a judgment concerning its truth value. For Guéroult's position, see "The History of Philosophy as a Philosophical Problem," pp. 563–587, particularly pp. 584–585.

47. Another way of putting this is to say, as Danto has done, that there is a distinction between "objective" and "biased." See *Analytical Philosophy of History*, p. 96.

48. This is, indeed, what leads Lafrance to his positivism. In particular, he is concerned with the distortions resulting from Thomistic and Marxist readings of history. See his *Méthode et exégèse*, p. 17.

49. S. F. Nadel recognizes this need in social anthropology in *The Foundations of Social Anthropology* (London: Cohen & West Ltd., 1951), p. 54.

50. Richard Rorty, "The Historiography of Philosophy: Four Genres," in Rorty et al., eds., *Philosophy in History*, p. 49.

51. Thomas Aquinas, *Expositio super librum Boethii de Trinitate*, q. 4, a. 2, *responsio*, ed. B. Decker (Leiden: Brill, 1959), p. 143.

52. Thomas Aquinas, *De ente et essentia*, ch. 2, ed. M. D. Roland-Gosselin (Paris: J. Vrin, 1948), p. 11.7, and *Summa theologiae* I, 29, *ad* 3 and 30, 4, ed. De Rubeis et al. (Turin: Marietti, 1932), vol. 1, pp. 206a and 215b.

53. See the various articles on interpretations of the Thomistic principle of individuation by Owens, Wippel, and others, in Jorge J. E. Gracia, ed., *Individuation in Scholasticism: The Later Middle Ages and the Counter-Reformation*, Analytica Series (München and Wien: Philosophia Verlag, forthcoming 1992).

54. Maurice H. Mandelbaum, "The History of Ideas, Intellectual History, and the History of Philosophy," *History and Theory*, Beiheft 5 (1965): 44–45.

55. Phlogiston was a mysterious substance used by modern physicists and philosophers to explain the presence of heat.

56. That, of course, does not ensure that the historian is in fact reconstructing the text that the author intended to write, but only the one that the author actually wrote. I shall return to the relation of the text to the author and the status of the so-called intended text in Chapter Four.

Chapter Two

Philosophy and Its History

Having discussed the natures of history, philosophy, and the history of philosophy in the last chapter, I now take up the much disputed relationship between philosophy and its history. Any serious attempt to understand what the history of philosophy can contribute to philosophy must begin with an understanding of this relationship, as the growing literature on the subject clearly indicates. I divide the discussion into three parts. The first examines the current perception of the issue at stake; the second presents a proposal for the understanding of the relation of philosophy to its history; and the third illustrates the consequences of not understanding properly that relationship. I defend three main theses concerning the relationship between philosophy and its history: (1) that philosophy and the study of its history are not incompatible, (2) that the study of the history of philosophy is not necessary for philosophy, and (3) that philosophy is necessary for the study of the history of philosophy.

Prima facie some might be tempted to think that the theses I defend are rather obvious, or trivial, or both. After all, does not the very notion of "history of philosophy" involve the notion of "philosophy"? Is it not evident that the notion of "philosophy" makes no reference to the history of philosophy? And, finally, is it not the case that both philosophers and historians of philosophy have found no difficulty, let alone incompatibility, in mixing both disciplines in practice?[1] However, as will become clear in the course of the discussion, the theses I present are by no means obvious or trivial and have serious and numerous opponents both at present and in the past. Moreover, the issues involved in them extend to important questions of methodology that should not be overlooked in a discussion of the historiography of philosophy. Let me begin, then, with a discussion of the current state of the issue.

I. STATUS QUAESTIONIS

Two extreme and conflicting positions have been adopted by philosophers with respect to the relationship between philosophy and its history. The first denies that there is or that there should be any relation between them. The second holds that the relation between philosophy and its history is one of necessity: there cannot be philosophy apart from its history nor history of philosophy apart from philosophy. I call the first view the *incompatibilist position* and the second the *historicist position*. There are ample representatives of both views not only in the history of philosophy, but also in current philosophical circles.

A. The Incompatibilist Position

Those who favor this perspective sometimes begin by pointing out that whatever philosophers do or accomplish is irrelevant to what historians of philosophy do or accomplish, and vice versa.[2] For example, they ask, What does Thales's thought about the basic stuff of the world have to do with current questions of philosophy? Indeed, arguing from analogy, they note that no serious astronomer today pays any attention to what Ptolemy thought about the heavens, so why should a contemporary philosopher pay attention to Thales or Aristotle? According to this point of view, there is nothing relevant that the history of philosophy can contribute to philosophy. (I shall return to these kinds of arguments in Chapter Three.) And something similar could be said concerning the contribution of philosophy to its history. For, so the argument goes, how could contemporarily developed concepts and ideas help in the proper understanding of concepts and ideas developed in a different age and context? Historians of philosophy, then, have no need for philosophy as such, just as philosophers have no need for the history of philosophy.

Still, some consider this conclusion insufficient and go beyond the charge of irrelevance to argue that what philosophers do or accomplish is not just irrelevant but actually pernicious to and downright incompatible with what historians of philosophy do or accomplish, and vice versa. Philosophy, like astronomy and the other sciences, is concerned with the investigation of the ultimate nature of the universe and its components, and therefore deals with the truth value of claims about such an ultimate nature. But the history of philosophy is concerned rather with what past philosophers have thought about the ultimate nature of the universe and its components *apart from* whether what they thought is true or false. The propositions about whose truth value historians of philosophy are concerned are propositions that describe what past philosophers believed. Thus, whereas philosophers are concerned about the truth value of propositions of the type 'X is Y,' historians of philosophy are concerned about the truth value of propositions of the type 'X stated that P.' These two types of propositions illustrate well that the aims of philosophers and historians of philosophy are different, at odds, and cannot be reconciled. The use of history in philosophy leads to confusion, resulting from the simultaneous pursuit of two distinct and conflicting aims that require different and interfering procedures.[3] Likewise, the application of philosophical concepts to the history of philosophy tampers with historical accuracy, distorting history by presenting it in a light foreign to it and thus leading to anachronisms.

This position, in the extreme form in which I have described it, is not as popular these days as it once was. Generally, those who support it break down into two camps. The first argues for the incompatibility of philosophy and the history of philosophy from a philosophical point of view. The arguments given by these authors are based on views concerning philosophy and the history of philosophy that make them conflict. Philosophy is interpreted as a scientific discipline, universal in intent and scope, insulated from the spatio-temporal and cultural circumstances in which it takes place. Its aim, as already noted, is to discover universally applicable truth. Consequently, the philosopher, like the scientist, must concentrate on the present. The history of philosophy, on the other hand, is concerned with the past and its individual idiosyncracies. Thus, the history of philosophy, with its theories, views, and distortions, is often portrayed as an obstacle to clarity and understanding. Past perspectives and views interfere with a fresh look at the facts and the discovery of truth. Philosophy must start from scratch, with a clean slate, unencumbered by past mistakes, errors, and unsupported presuppositions.

This kind of position has always been popular among those whom I have called *positivists* in the Introduction; that is, philosophers who want to make of philosophy a science modeled after what today we call the natural sciences. In our own century the logical positivists are prime examples of this position.[4] Not that they always avoid the discussion of past views. Indeed, the study of the philosophical past is sometimes and even frequently useful, they believe, because it illustrates so well the mistakes the philosopher can make.[5] But that is the only use the history of philosophy can have, for philosophizing does not begin or proceed with the positive help of the history of philosophy. This attitude is not restricted to our century or to positivists, however; its influence extends even to some authors whom I have classified as forming part of the pre-Kantian philosophical mainstream. A case in point is Descartes, who does not by any means hold that the history of philosophy is incompatible with philosophy, but nonetheless seems to regard it in most cases as a waste of time and sometimes as an obstacle to philosophical progress.

> [An author's] plan of collecting into a single book all that is useful in every other book would be a very good one if it were practicable; but I think that it is not. *It is often difficult to judge accurately what others have written, and to draw the good out of them without taking the bad too.* Moreover, the particular truths which are scattered in books are so detached and so independent of each other, that I think one would need more talent and energy to assemble them into a well-proportioned and ordered collection...than to make up such a collection out of one's own discoveries. I do not mean that one should neglect other people's discoveries when one encounters useful ones; but I do not think one should spend the greater part of one's time in collecting them. *If a man were capable of finding the foundation of the sciences, he would be wrong to waste his life in finding scraps of knowledge hidden in the corners of libraries; and if he was* [sic] *no good for anything else but that, he would not be capable of choosing and ordering what he found.*[6]

Obviously Descartes does not think much of the study of the philosophical past as a means of helping the philosophical present. History is a mixed bag of good and bad. Those who cannot discriminate between the good and the bad in it should not be exposed to it, and those who can do not need it. So, let the dead bury the dead, we might say, and turn to the present, for that is the business of philosophy according to Descartes: to look within, starting without any of the presuppositions that its past has imposed on it.

The second group of authors who support the incompatibilist position argue from the side of history rather than philosophy: They likewise reject the simultaneous and joint pursuit of philosophy and its history. Interestingly, their arguments are based on conceptions of philosophy and its history similar to those adopted by the philosophers, but their concerns are with the pernicious effect of philosophy on the history of philosophy rather than vice versa.[7] They argue, for example, that the aims of both disciplines are incompatible and that mixing them destroys history. The aim of history is fundamentally to present an accurate description of what happened in the past, whereas the aim of philosophy is to discover truths about the universe. Their view of philosophy is primarily interpretative and evaluative:

to discover and understand truth; that is, to formulate and judge the truth of claims about the world. Their view of history is descriptive: the disinterested account of the past.

In conclusion, those who maintain the incompatibility of philosophy and the history of philosophy, whether they are philosophers or historians, generally base their views on the notion, contrary to what I have argued in Chapter One, that history is an essentially disinterested pursuit whereas philosophy is not. For them, no history, including the history of philosophy, can go beyond the nonevaluative and noninterpretative description of the past. On the other hand, it is of the essence of philosophy to interpret and evaluate. For this reason the simultaneous and joint pursuit of both disciplines is impossible.

B. The Historicist Position[8]

Just as there are those who reject any relation between philosophy and its history, there are also those who find that such a relation is indispensible for the effective pursuit of one or the other.[9] They point out that the study of philosophy is in fact and must always be centered in its past, since from the moment that a view is formulated or defended its formulation or defense already is a part of history. There is not and cannot be any real cleavage between philosophy and its history; their presumed separation is an artificial one created by those who wish to divide the recent history of philosophy from its more distant past. All philosophy, from the moment it makes its appearance, is history of philosophy.

Although versions of this argument are occasionally presented in discussions of the issue that concerns us here, the argument is seldom given much weight by those who wish to prove that philosophers cannot do philosophy independently of its history. For the argument does not justify the study of the entire history of philosophy or even most of it. Indeed, what the argument would show, if it were sound, is that doing philosophy cannot be considered incompatible with the history of philosophy, but it certainly would not prove that to do philosophy one must necessarily study anything but the most recent history of philosophy. However, most historicists want to support the view that it is not just the recent history of philosophy that is necessary, but all history, including and perhaps particularly the distant history of philosophy. That is the reason why they have drummed up other arguments in favor of their position.

The most effective defense of the historicist position is inspired by Hegel, but has been restated in various ways by his followers. A most recent formulation goes something like this: Philosophy consists in the rearticulation of a view about ourselves and the world. But such rearticulation presupposes two things: first, an understanding of past articulations and, second, a liberation from them. Since these two conditions cannot be met without the study of the history of philosophy, the very activity of philosophizing intrinsically depends on the study of the past. Charles Taylor has eloquently presented this point of view in a recent article, where he summarizes the argument at stake in the following words:

> Freeing oneself from the model [within which one operates] cannot be done just by showing an alternative. What we need to do is get over the presumption of the unique conceivability of the embedded picture. But to do this, we have to take a new stance towards our practices. Instead of living in them and taking their implicit construal of things as the way things are, we have to understand how they have come to be, how they come to embed a certain view of things.... But that means a genetic account; and one which retrieves the formulations through which the embedding in practice took place. Freeing ourselves from the presumption of uniqueness requires uncovering the origins. That is why philosophy is inescapably historical.[10]

Philosophy cannot escape its history because in order to redesign the way it looks at the world it must first distance itself from previous designs, and that distancing requires their understanding. This view, then, does not argue for a purely scholarly or historical approach to philosophy. It understands that the aim of philosophy is to move forward and come up with something new, but that very process, it argues, entails the understanding and therefore the study of the past.[11]

Underlying this position is the conviction that neither philosophy nor its history is to be done disinterestedly. Philosophy, of course, is interested in truth and therefore in evaluation, but so is the history of philosophy. It would not do to say that the history of philosophy is only a propaedeutic, if necessary, step in the philosophical enterprise; for to say that would entail that philosophy and the history of philosophy are not identical, as Taylor and Hegel wish to say, but only that the history of philosophy is a part of philosophy. To support the claim of identity requires much more than that and for this Taylor's argument, even if it were to be considered sound, is insufficient. To establish identity he would have to demonstrate that philosophy involves no activity and reaches no conclusions beyond the activity and conclusions of the historian of philosophy.

Of course, there are those who wish to argue that philosophy and its history are identical precisely in the just stated way. For them, philosophy is trapped in its history, and the liberation of which Taylor speaks, and which is implicit even in Hegel's view that the Absolute becomes conscious of itself, is not possible. The way they support their position is by arguing that our concepts and ideas and the very language in which we express them are historically bound by their genesis and development, and, therefore, we cannot possibly go beyond them. No liberation is possible, since the concepts used to produce such liberation would themselves be the result of the historical process. One cannot step out of history just as one cannot step out of language, as Wittgensteinians would say. The supposed liberation brings forth nothing new.

This is not Taylor's argument, however. As already stated, his argument does not show that philosophy and the history of philosophy are one and the same. If sound, the argument would show only that philosophy is necessarily dependent on its history and, thus, that the study of the history of philosophy is necessary for philosophy.

From this brief and obviously oversimplified presentation of the issue involved in the relation between philosophy and its history I hope that three points have become clear. The first is that there seem to be two rather incompatible and extreme positions with respect to this relation. One rejects any relation and the other makes the relation necessary. So that there is no middle ground where the two may meet and compromise.

The second point is that the issue can be presented from two different perspectives. On the one hand, it can be presented as the problem of whether and to what extent the history of philosophy can contribute to or become integrated with philosophy. On the other hand, it can be presented as the problem of whether and to what extent philosophy can contribute to or become integrated with its history. The first perspective in fact is the one reflected in the title of the recent conference to which I referred in the Preface: Doing Philosophy Historically. The issue posed from this perspective is of concern primarily to philosophers, because it is the nature of philosophy that is at stake. But the same issue can also be presented from a different perspective, although it is often confused with the first and frequently discussed in the same context. What is at stake in it is the extent to which, altering the title of the conference, the history of philosophy can be done philosophically. Posed in this way, the issue concerns primarily the historian of philosophy, for it is the nature of that history that is in question.

Third and last, it should also be clear that the solution to this question depends very much on what one understands by history and philosophy. As Chapter One already has provided a preliminary understanding of the terms of the relation under dispute, we can turn directly to the proposal I wish to make concerning the understanding of the relation between philosophy and its history.

II. PHILOSOPHY AND ITS HISTORY

The issue involves the relation of philosophy and its history and the questions just asked had to do with whether philosophy and its history are incompatible or are necessarily related to each other. Let me begin by addressing the issue of incompatibility first.

A. Incompatibility

From what has been said concerning philosophy and the history of philosophy in Chapter One, it follows, first, that there is no incompatibility between philosophy and its history. If the propositions of philosophy and those of its history are as different as we have said they are, then it should not be possible to find that they contradict each other and therefore that they are incompatible. A brief perusal and integration into a single set of the nonevaluative propositions of philosophy and the history of philosophy given earlier as examples will illustrate the point:

1^{hp}. X stated that P (where, for example, P = God is omnipotent, omniscient, and benevolent).

1^{p}. P (where, for example, P = God is omnipotent, omniscient, and benevolent).

2^{hp}. X stated that Q (where, for example, Q = God is not the cause of evil).

2^{p}. Q (where, for example, Q = God is not the cause of evil).

3^{hp}. X's stating that P is the reason that X gave for holding that Q.

a^{hp}. X held that Q.

3^{p}. P, therefore Q.

b^{hp}. X held that Q because X held that P.

c^{hp}. X held that P because Y held that P.

4^{hp}. M, a contemporary of X, stated that X did not hold that P.

d^{hp}. X's holding that P led to the abandonment of ~Q by subsequent philosophers.

e^{hp}. What X meant by C was D.

5^{hp}. N, another of X's contemporaries, stated that he disagreed with M concerning M's view that X did not hold that P.

6^{hp}. R, a later historian of philosophy, stated that M was right in holding that X did not hold that P.

7^{hp}. S, another later historian of philosophy, stated that he disagreed with R's view concerning M.

An analysis of these propositions shows that there are no contradictions in the set. Indeed, if we take the propositions that are given as examples of propositions contained in the history of philosophy, it is clear that even those propositions that have the same subject (1^{hp}, 2^{hp}, a^{hp}, b^{hp}, c^{hp}) do not contradict each other. Of course, it is altogether possible to have a set of propositions of this sort in which contradictions occur. For example, if we added to the set another history of philosophy proposition, say 8^{hp} (X did not state that P), that proposition would contradict 1^{hp}. Likewise, it is easy to think of examples (P and ~P) in which philosophical propositions contradict each other, even though the propositions present in the preceding set (1^{p}, 2^{p}, and 3^{p}) do not. What is not possible is to have a contradiction between propositions belonging to the history of philosophy and propositions belonging to philosophy, for reasons to which I shall turn shortly.

Something similar applies to evaluative propositions. Putting together the examples we gave earlier of evaluative propositions for both philosophy and the history of philosophy we get the following set:

A^{hp}. X's view, that P, is true.

A^{p}. P is true (where, for example, P = God is omnipotent, omniscient, and benevolent).

B^{hp}. X's argument A is valid.

B^{p}. Argument 3^{p} is invalid.

C^{hp}. X's argument A' is unsound.

C^{p}. P lacks proof.

D^{hp}. X was perspicacious when he asked question Q.

D^{p}. Doctrine 1^{p} is incoherent.

E^{hp}. X was right in formulating problem N in the way he did.

F^{hp}. X was unclear on issue I.

G^{hp}. X is an excellent philosopher.

H^{hp}. X contradicted himself.

I^{hp}. X's view, that P, was useful in the development of Y's view, that Q.

J^{hp}. M, a contemporary of X, was wrong in thinking that X's view, that P, was false.

K^{hp}. R, a later historian, who thought that M was right, was wrong.

L^{hp}. X's view about S shows that Western thought had undergone substantial progress.

M^{hp}. Y's view indicates a step backward in the development of philosophy.

N^{hp}. R was right in thinking that X held that P.

In this set, as in the previous one, we find that there are no contradictions, even in cases where the propositions have the same subject (e.g., B^{hp} and C^{hp}), although it would be easy to add examples of propositions, for example O^{hp} (X's argument is invalid) that would contradict some of the propositions belonging to the set (O^{hp} contradicts B^{hp}). However, contradiction is possible only in cases in which the propositions belong to the same discipline, whether the history of philosophy or philosophy. Contradictions do not occur accross disciplines. The reason that there can be no contradiction between philosophical propositions and those found in the history of philosophy has to do precisely with the character of those propositions. In the first place, there is a whole category of historical propositions, the descriptive, that has no counterpart in philosophy. Thus it is not possible to find propositions in philosophy that would contradict the propositions in history that I call descriptive. For a contradiction to take place the contradictory propositions must be about the same thing, and descriptive and nondescriptive propositions (e.g., 1^{hp} and C^{p}) cannot be about the same thing.

In second place, all propositions in the history of philosophy either contain an explicit or implicit reference to time, provenance, and individuals or at least are found in a context where such references are present. For, indeed, their function, as we saw in Chapter One, is to provide an account of past ideas. Historians of philosophy, like philosophers, will interpret and make value judgments while engaged in that task, and, in so doing, will discuss purely philosophical issues, but their judgments, unlike those of philosophers, will always concern the past. If the past ceases to be their concern, then they cannot be called historians to that extent and in that respect. A proposition that does not, directly or indirectly, make reference to the past and is not found in a context where the past is the primary concern, cannot therefore be considered historical. But, as the examples of philosophical propositions given above indicate, philosophical propositions have no reference to the past. Hence, again, we see that propositions that belong to the history of philosophy and philosophical propositions cannot be about the same thing and thus have the kind of meaning that would make contradiction possible.

For these reasons, then, there cannot be any incompatibility between philosophy and its history. That there can be no incompatibility between them, however, does not answer the question of the necessity of their relation, so we must turn to that next.

B. Necessity

We saw earlier in this chapter that those who argued for a necessary relation between philosophy and its history adopt a historicist attitude. Their view is that philosophy and its history are not different in any significant way and to engage in one is the same as engaging in the other. But, if what was said in Chapter One is correct, then this position is mistaken. In order to grasp its error more clearly we must look at the issue in terms of the end pursued, for the end of philosophy is clearly different from that of its history.

Formulated from a philosophical perspective, the pertinent question that needs to be asked is whether the history of philosophy is necessary for philosophy. And the answer is readily available. First, if, on the one hand, the function of philosophical propositions, in accordance with what was said earlier, is to present interpretations of the world in terms of human experience, to describe the logical relations used to present such interpretations, and to evaluate such ideas and their relations and, on the other hand, the aim of the history of philosophy is to present an accurate account of past ideas, where reference to a past time, provenance, and individuals are of the essence, it is obvious that philosophy is not necessarily dependent on its history. For the philosopher *qua* philosopher does not need to refer to the history of philosophy, its actors, authors, or their ideas to present interpretations of the world, to describe the logical relations among propositions that present such interpretations, or to evaluate ideas and their relations.

Nor will it do to argue against this (1) that all philosophy is historical from the moment that it is formulated, or (2) that philosophy, owing to its dialectical nature, must refer back to its history; or even (3) that the concepts and ideas philosophers use to philosophize have a historical origin and therefore imply a dependence of philosophy on its history. In spite of the spatio-temporal and dialectical character of philosophy and of the historical origin of the concepts and ideas it uses, the philosophical enterprise as such is not concerned with giving an account of the past and does not need to rely on it to go about its business. So, even if philosophy as a human enterprise is itself a historical phenomenon, which moreover refers to the past and uses concepts and language that have historical origins, none of that makes of philosophy history or renders it necessarily dependent on its history. This should become quite clear when one compares philosophical and historical propositions, and a quick look at the paradigmatic examples provided in Chapter One will underscore the point.

Those who want to make of philosophy a historical enterprise, moreover, often confuse the historicity of the practice of philosophy with the historicity of its content, the dialectical dimension of philosophy with its history, and the historical concepts philosophy must necessarily use as points of departure with the history of philosophy. The practice of philosophy, like any other human enterprise, is historical but that does not mean that the content produced as a result of that enterprise involves history. Likewise, the dialectical dimension of philosophy involves the give and take present in dialogue, but the partners of that dialogue need not have arisen from the past. Finally, the use of concepts that historically predate the practice of philosophy at a particular time and place does not entail that those concepts constitute a history of philosophy. In order to philosophize, human beings must use the concepts present in their culture, thus the practice of philosophy always entails prior concepts. But those concepts need not be philosophical in any significant sense; they can be ordinary, religious, and so on; and therefore should not be thought to constitute philosophical thought.

Finally, someone might wish to argue (4) against the view that holds philosophy is in no need of its history that at least one branch of philosophy does; namely, the philosophy of history. Indeed, this objection appears sensible at first glance, for it seems obvious that the philosophy of history needs history as its subject matter. But on reflection its force is not so evident. One may try to answer the objection in several ways. One may retort, first, that even though the philosophy of history is a branch of philosophy, philosophy is not the philosophy of history, so the conditions that apply to one do not necessarily apply to the other. Second, one may respond that what the philosophy of history presupposes is not the history of philosophy, but rather history, and that does not affect the thesis defended in this chapter. That thesis is that philosophy does not require the history of philosophy, not that it does not require history. For the objection to be good, then, it would have to be recast as arguing that the philosophy of the history of philosophy presupposes the history of philosophy. But even in these terms one might still have two ways out. First, again one could argue that the conditions that apply to philosophy and those that apply to the philosophy of the history of philosophy are not the same. Second, it is possible, at least logically, to speculate about the history of philosophy even when in fact there is no such history or the history is fictitious: One could construct a history of philosophy out of thin air and use that construction to philosophize. In that sense one would not be able to argue that the philosophy of the history of philosophy requires an actual history of philosophy, but only an imagined one.

These answers to objection 4 have various degrees of force. None of them, however, addresses the central confusion that gives rise to the objection. The confusion concerns two different types of necessity, which I call *objective* and *methodological*, respectively. Objective necessity is the type of necessity that characterizes the relation between an inquiry, study, or discipline of learning on the one hand, and the object of that study, inquiry, or discipline on the other. In this sense there is no question that the history of philosophy is not only necessary for the philosophy of the history of philosophy, but for philosophy in general. Indeed, if the history of philosophy is part of the world and the business of philosophy is to provide an interpretation of the world, then the history of philosophy is part of the object that philosophy studies. But, of course, this is not the sense of necessity against which I have been arguing here. That sense of necessity is methodological necessity. Methodological necessity is the type of necessity that characterizes the relation between two studies, inquiries, or disciplines of learning. It is methodological because what is involved here is the interdependence of method. Thus, for example, physics is methodologically dependent on mathematics and medicine on chemistry. But, as I have tried to show, philosophy has no relation of dependence on the history of philosophy in this sense.

Now, the objection we have been discussing is based on the confusion between objective and methodological necessities, arguing that the history of philosophy is necessary for philosophy because it is an object of philosophical study. But that, of course, does not invalidate the thesis I am defending here, namely, that the history of philosophy is not methodologically necessary for philosophy.

That the history of philosophy is not necessary for philosophy does not mean, second, that the history of philosophy is irrelevant to philosophy. Indeed, the history of philosophy should be of great use to the philosopher, for among other things it furnishes diverse formulations of positions and arguments that facilitate the philosopher's task, and in many instances it may supply the solution or the seeds of the solution the philosopher is looking for, or it may show that certain views are oversimplistic, or that certain arguments are unsound. The history of philosophy, then, although nonessential to philosophy, is a source of what might be called basic data for which the philosopher can find good use. It is where the philosopher does field work, as it were. This can be easily seen if we look back at the integrated sets of propositions in philosophy and the history of philosophy given earlier, for the intimate relationship among them is evident. This does not mean that the history of philosophy is philosophy, or that it becomes philosophy when it is used by philosophers. The history of philosophy remains history, but precisely as such it can be of use to the philosopher. I shall return to the issue of the usefulness of the history of philosophy for philosophy in Chapter Three, where I examine in more detail various theories concerning the justification for the study of the history of philosophy.

With respect to history, on the other hand, the situation is somewhat different. For, although the propositions contained in the history of philosophy are different from philosophical propositions in that some of them are purely descriptive and all of them either have reference to time and provenance as well as to individuals or are found in contexts where such reference is present, they also contain philosophical concepts and the understanding of those concepts necessarily falls within the province of philosophy considered as a discipline. Indeed, as we saw in Chapter One, the history of philosophy involves not only description but also interpretation and evaluation, and none of them can be carried out without the help of philosophy. The history of philosophy, then, entails philosophy; otherwise, it reduces to the repetition of terms and phrases without an understanding of what those terms and phrases mean. Consequently, although the history of philosophy may be useful only to philosophy, philosophy is essential to its history; for the propositions that compose the history of philosophy entail in turn certain philosophical propositions that are implicit in them.

Take, for example, the proposition 'X held that God is omnipotent, omniscient, and benevolent.' Someone, I imagine, could report that so and so stated that proposition without himself or herself understanding the notions of omnipotence, omniscience, and benevolence. But this would be equivalent to reporting a proposition in a foreign language and, therefore, could not be called understanding or history. To understand the proposition we must also understand that to be omnipotent is to be such and such and likewise with the other notions used in the proposition. The account of past ideas requires understanding, interpreting and evaluating, tasks that can be accomplished only through the exercise of philosophy itself. The history of philosophy entails an understanding of what is being said and, therefore, a conceptual framework and analyses of the terms it uses. Here is where philosophy becomes indispensible for it. The history of philosophy of necessity is philosophical, unless, of course, it is either bad history of philosophy or no history of philosophy at all.

The fact that the history of philosophy needs philosophy in the ways I specified should not, however, cloud the distinction between philosophy and its history. That distinction has to do with the different aims of the disciplines and the necessary reference to time, provenance, and individuals that characterizes the history of philosophy. Historicists are right in saying that thoughts and statements from the moment they occur are historical. Indeed, since thoughts and statements always occur at a certain time and in a certain place, they are by force bound to historical coordinates. Accordingly, these very words that I am putting down on paper at this moment and the thoughts that accompany them in my mind are historical. But this does not mean that the intensions of the signs and the content of the thoughts are historical. That is, when I think, for example, that 2 + 2 = 4, there is nothing historical about what I think even though my thought is historical in the sense that it has occurred at a certain time in a certain place and is part of the past from that moment on. On the other hand, when I think about what I had for dinner *last night*—a delicious homemade pizza made by Clarisa—and how much I liked it *at the time*, both my thought and the content of my thought are historical. Perhaps we might distinguish these two types of historicities by calling them *extensional* and *intensional*, respectively. Extensional historicity is the type of historicity that applies to events and entities in the world, and intensional historicity is the type of historicity that applies to the content of our thoughts and the meaning of statements about the world.

Historicists frequently confuse these two types of historicities and argue that all philosophy is history of philosophy because all our thoughts are historical. But the historicity that characterizes our thoughts is only extensional. And, although we do have many thoughts that are also intensionally historical, there are many that are not. Indeed, the sorts of thoughts whereby we establish relations among ideas discussed in Chapter One are examples of nonintensionally historical thoughts. Thus, if this distinction is understood, then the distinction between philosophy and its history can be preserved. The history of philosophy consists of an account of ideas that is intensionally historical, whereas philosophy consists of an account of ideas that is historical only extensionally. This is what is meant by saying that the history of philosophy is concerned with the past, whereas philosophy is not.

Note that, according to the view I have presented here, in order for an account to be classified as historical there is no particular temporal distance required between the production of the account and the events or ideas of which it proposes to provide an account. An account of what I just thought, for example, is as historical as a present account of what Plato thought. The differences between the two accounts do not lie in their historicity, but rather in their distance from the event they describe. As such, they pose the same problems of reconstruction—description, interpretation, and evaluation. Nor does it matter much whether those engaged in providing historical accounts are or are not the actors of the events being accounted for. In this sense, autobiography is as historical as biography, and the later Wittgenstein's views about what the early Wittgenstein thought are also historical provided those thoughts are concerned with constructing an account of what the early Wittgenstein thought. If they are not, that is, if there is no concern with accounting for the past, then they are not historical in the intensional sense identified earlier.

That the reconstruction of the very recent past poses problems similar to those involved in the reconstruction of the distant past can be demonstrated by an experiment I carried out in a graduate seminar at Buffalo in the spring of 1989 and can be repeated easily in any classroom. It consisted of carrying on a class discussion during which students were asked to take notes. After half an hour, we stopped the discussion and went around the table asking each student to read his or her notes and to reconstruct the discussion. The result was quite revealing. Although these were graduate students familiar with the materials we were discussing, it became apparent that their notes differed in substantial respects. Indeed, we quickly found ourselves arguing about whose account was right and whose account was wrong. Moreover, we realized that even when we put together all the notes there were obvious gaps in the record and, more serious, there were disagreements as to the interpretation of key aspects of the discussion that had taken place. Interestingly enough, often the disagreements were settled not on the basis of the written record, but on the basis of *what made sense,* which supports my thesis that evaluation is an essential part of the task of the historian of philosophy.

In conclusion, philosophy and the history of philosophy are different enterprises, but this does not entail that philosophy is not necessary for its history. Indeed, in my view it is. Unfortunately, not many contemporary philosophers and historians of philosophy are aware of the need to understand the relation between philosophy and its history as I have outlined it here, and, as a result, they misunderstand not only their respective tasks but even the character of the work they have produced. These problems are not restricted to rather obscure and little known figures in the field, but are displayed in the work of well-known and respected philosophers and historians. A case in point that I had the opportunity to examine recently is Henry Veatch's *Aristotle;* therefore, I shall turn to that work to illustrate how Veatch's misunderstanding of the nature of the book on Aristotle he has produced and of his task in producing such a book affect the way he goes about defending the main thesis he proposes in the work.

III. AN ILLUSTRATION: VEATCH'S *ARISTOTLE*

My argument in the remaining part of this chapter will be, first, that Veatch thinks that in his book on Aristotle he is primarily doing philosophy or at least something much more philosophical than just history of philosophy, and that he thinks this because his uses of the history of philosophy are philosophical. Second, I shall argue that in fact Veatch is not primarily doing philosophy but rather history of philosophy, even though he uses philosophy in his understanding of that history. Third, I shall point out two misconceptions concerning the history of philosophy that are at the root of Veatch's view concerning the nature of his book and that Veatch shares with many contemporary philosophers: (1) the view that history should be entirely descriptive, and (2) the notion that the history of philosophy has little value for philosophy. And fourth, I shall indicate how all of this affects at least one of the claims he makes concerning Aristotle's philosophy.

How can it be shown that Veatch thinks that he is not primarily engaged in a historical study? Simply by what he says. The very subtitle of his book, *A Contemporary Appreciation*, suggests that he has something more than history in mind. This is supported by explicit statements found throughout the book. He tells us, for example, that "philosopher-historians and historians of ideas continue to write learned books about [Aristotle, but]...rather than approach Aristotle in this way, why may we not treat him as if he were a contemporary philosopher?"[12] A bit later he writes that his "brief account of Aristotle's life and influence...is not an account whose purpose is simply to fix Aristotle's place in history; instead it is intended to remind us of just who and what this man is who we claim should once again become a dominant force on the contemporary philosophical scene."[13] And later still, "to preserve Aristotle as a historical figure is really to embalm him as a philosopher."[14]

Thus, it would seem that Veatch regards his aim as not historical or at least not as just historical, but rather either as something different or at least as something more than that; that is, I take him to mean that his aim is "philosophical." At the basis of Veatch's belief is his desire to establish the truth of certain views that he claims Aristotle defended, a task he seems to think is not in the province of the historian.

Now, some historians of philosophy will probably agree with Veatch in that his book contains claims about Aristotle's ideas that they would regard as going beyond what Aristotle said. The primary thesis itself of the book seems to reflect such an interpretative approach, for it claims that "Aristotle is, *par excellence,* the philosopher of common sense"[15] and for most historians of Aristotelian thought, this thesis goes well beyond what Aristotle explicitly held. The reasons are several. In the first place, Aristotle uses no terminology that would express the notion of common sense to which Veatch refers. Indeed, as Veatch himself recognizes, the term 'common sense' is used to translate a Greek term that refers to something that has nothing to do with what Veatch means by common sense. Nor does Aristotle adhere explicitly to the principle that Veatch identifies as fundamental to a common sense philosophy, the maxim that "what to all men everywhere in their sane moments is known to be the truth is, indeed, really the truth."[16] Moreover, if Veatch were right concerning the role of common sense in philosophy, then the function of philosophy would be restricted to the empirical task of finding out what all men everywhere in their saner moments know or think they know to be the truth, but in fact Aristotle engages in no such empirical enterprise.[17]

Moreover, the argument of the historians would continue, the concepts and views that Aristotle proposes in his philosophy are as far from an ordinary commonsensical view of the world as any philosopher can get. It is true that Veatch tries very hard to show that Aristotle's doctrines are commonsensical. But, although he succeeds in many cases, it is just not possible to view all, or even most, of Aristotle's philosophical views as commonsensical. How can one argue the commonsensical character, for example, of Aristotle's doctrine of the ultimate end of human beings as "the whole uninterrupted activity of theoretical knowledge and pure contemplation"? [18] And what of notions such as matter, form, or the unmoved mover? If these are commonsensical notions, then so are Bergmann's "bare particular" and Scotus's *haecceitas.*

Finally, some historians, and even Veatch himself, might point out that *Aristotle* contains judgments about the value of philosophical doctrines. Indeed, the overall conclusion of the book is that Aristotle's philosophy is "perhaps not merely a live option, but even the only option open to a man of healthy common sense with respect to the realities of things generally and of our human situation particularly."[19] In introducing such value judgments, so the argument would go, Veatch has gone beyond history and engaged in philosophizing.

To this I would like to respond that, as we saw earlier, the history of philosophy is not restricted to description, but also contains interpretations and evaluations. The presence of interpretations and evaluations in a history of philosophy, therefore, does not render the history less historical. For the interpretations involved are supposed to go beyond what authors have said in order to reconstruct hidden assumptions and views that underlie and explain explicit statements. Thus, Veatch's use of the notion of common sense, even though not explicit in Aristotle, does not render his account unhistorical. It could turn out, of course, that Veatch is wrong about Aristotle and common sense, but that does not alter the historical character of his enterprise.

Likewise, evaluations involve propositions in which claims concerning the value of the views of historical figures are expressed. Consequently, Veatch's judgments with respect to the value of Aristotle's philosophy can hardly disqualify his account from being primarily historical. Indeed, much of what Veatch is doing is entirely in keeping with what the history of philosophy has done in its best moments and, therefore, should be.

All of this, however, only points out that the considerations that led Veatch to interpret his book on Aristotle as not primarily historical in character are not sound, but this is not enough to establish that the book is not a primarily philosophical book. The proof of that, however, is easily available in that the book concerns Aristotle's ideas, even though those ideas are also thought to be true ones. The thrust of Veatch's account is always concerned with the description, interpretation, and evaluation *of Aristotle's views,* even though the evaluations involve positive recommendations as to what we should think ourselves. Nor could one argue, I believe, that this is a work of philosophy in which the history of philosophy is used to illustrate the positions discussed. For the book is simply not organized in that way. Indeed, what the book does is to present Aristotle's views in a favorable light and to recommend that we adopt them, but that procedure is still overwhelmingly historical in character, contrary to what Veatch seems to think. Even a superficial perusal of the text will confirm the overriding concern on Veatch's part with the time and provenance of his claims. For, indeed, it is Aristotle's views that are discussed, evaluated and commended.

But we may ask, if what I have said concerning Veatch's book is correct, namely, that what Veatch has carried out in his book on Aristotle is primarily a historical task, why the disclaimers to the contrary? Why should Veatch try so hard to present his account of Aristotle's views as something more than or different from simply history of philosophy?

I believe the reasons are two. The first originates in the widespread, but mistaken belief that history is entirely descriptive and should contain neither interpretations nor value judgments. The second has to do with a rather poor view of the history of philosophy, in which the discipline is seen as something largely irrelevant and useless, a discipline of interest only to antiquarians. Indeed, the picture of the historian that is indirectly revealed by the first paragraph of Veatch's book confirms my point.

> Poor Aristotle! Having for so many centuries been a dominant force, in Western philosophy and in Western culture generally, he now reminds one rather of an enormous dinosaur. He is not exactly extinct, but he seems hardly to be alive philosophically any more. In consequence, like nearly all dinosaurs, as well as like countless dead philosophers, Aristotle would seem to be reduced to little more than a great, hulking museum piece in the history of Western culture. Classical scholars still translate him and edit his texts; and of course philosopher-historians and historians of ideas continue to write learned books about him; yes, even philosophers themselves—at least during their childhood in the profession—usually find themselves taken around by one of their elders on a tour of the museums of Western philosophy, where they are almost certain to find old Aristotle prominently displayed in a enormous glass case.[20]

The history of philosophy is not reducible to mere description, and it has a vital and important function assisting philosophy in its quest. Veatch's desire to interpret and evaluate Aristotle's philosophy, then, and his wish to make Aristotle's thought come alive for us today need not entail an interpretation of the history of philosophy as philosophy or as something more than what it is, namely, history. We can still have our history of philosophy and also our interpretations and evaluations of the ideas contained in it together with a philosophical understanding of them, as Veatch himself has demonstrated so well in his book.

Now we come to the last point I want to make in this chapter; namely, that Veatch's understanding of both the history of philosophy and the nature of his *Aristotle* tend to weaken in some ways the arguments of his book and undermine the main thesis he defends in it.

From the analysis given in Chapter One, it should be clear that the history of philosophy contains descriptive, interpretative, and evaluative propositions and that it also requires an understanding of philosophy. A good historical account of past philosophy requires descriptions that are accurate and historically documented, interpretations that are consistent, lucid, and that enlighten us about the reasons for and the character of certain philosophical ideas, and, finally, sound evaluations of those ideas, their historical impact, and their philosophical worth.

Descriptive accounts that are accurate and historically documented require in turn a careful presentation of historical data backed up with explicit evidence. In the case of philosophy, it is necessary to present or refer to not only the primary texts that make explicit the ideas being described by the historian, but also the evidence gathered from the opinions of contemporaries as well as historical authorities who have had something to say about those ideas or their authors.

The development of interpretations that are consistent, lucid, and enlightening requires explanations of how hitherto hidden concepts and ideas explain the nature of the philosophical framework of which an account is being given, as well as the reasons why that particular framework was adopted and defended. If interpretations lack this dimension their use is limited.

Moreover, sound evaluations require clear statements of the criteria used to measure the value of philosophical ideas and an explanation of how those ideas fit the adopted criteria. Otherwise we are unable to judge if such evaluations are appropriate.

Finally, the philosophical nature of the history of philosophy requires the explicit presentation and analysis of the basic concepts used in the description, interpretation, and evaluation sought. Indeed, for a historical account to be at all sound it must be presented in the context of a conceptual framework whose tenets and ideas are explicitly discussed. The existence of the framework makes possible the production of an intelligible account and its explicit presentation functions as a controlling device of the objectivity, fairness, and honesty of the account. This will become more clear in Chapter Five when we examine various approaches to the history of philosophy.

Does Veatch's *Aristotle* adhere to the principles outlined? Does it fulfill the requirements of a sound historical account of Aristotle's philosophy? Most parts of Veatch's account without a doubt are prime examples of what sound history of philosophy should be. But, and this is my main objection, Veatch's account, although generally successful, fails when it comes to the main thesis that he defends. And I suspect the reason is that, as I claimed earlier, Veatch does not quite understand that his task is historical and, therefore, neglects those aspects of a historical account that are necessary for it to be successful. His view that his book is not historical, or at least not primarily historical, leads him to think that he does not need to back up the main thesis he proposes in it with the kind of textual evidence that should accompany sound history, for example. Moreover, most likely for the same reasons, he leaves unstated the criteria of evaluation according to which he measures the value of some of Aristotle's ideas. Finally, and most important, he does not present explicitly the conceptual framework that he uses to interpret Aristotle's philosophy as commonsensical.

A quick look at Veatch's thesis will illustrate these points. The thesis, as mentioned earlier, is that "Aristotle is, *par excellence*, the philosopher of common sense." Clearly, this is a historical thesis that aims to characterize Aristotle's philosophy; it is interpretative insofar as Aristotle did not describe himself or his philosophy as commonsensical, and it involves an evaluative element because Veatch also claims that Aristotle's philosophy "is not merely a live option, but even the only option open to a man of healthy common sense."

Now, the problem that arises with this thesis is that Veatch's substantiation of it does not fulfill all the requirements of a sound historical account. In the first place, he does not give any textual evidence, either primary or secondary, to support the thesis. Yes, he does show quite successfully that many of Aristotle's basic concepts correspond to concepts present in our ordinary view of the world. Thus, for example, the Aristotelian notion of substance corresponds roughly to the ordinary notion of thing. And so likewise with others. But this is not enough to support the view that Aristotle's philosophy can be best described as a philosophy of common sense. We need the texts from Aristotle that support that view, as well as evidence drawn from existing authoritative interpretations of Aristotle's aims and philosophy.

Second, Veatch does not discuss anywhere in the book the criteria by which he is led to conclude that Aristotle's philosophy is the only option available to the man of healthy common sense. He does try and very often succeeds in showing that Aristotle's ideas make sense, but that is not enough to substantiate his much stronger claim at least on two counts: That a view makes sense does not necessarily mean that it is commonsensical, and certainly it does not entail that it is the only view open to individuals with a healthy common sense.

Finally, and this is perhaps the most important weakness that I see in Veatch's substantiation of his thesis, Veatch does not present an explanation of the basic concept of common sense that he uses to interpret Aristotle's thought. Nowhere does he explain in detail what common sense is and nowhere does he specify for us how to distinguish common sense from personal, social, and cultural viewpoints. How can we judge that Aristotle's philosophy is a philosophy of common sense if we do not know what Veatch means by common sense? Indeed, this is the crux of the matter, because the notion of common sense is one that has been widely discussed in the history of philosophy, and no agreement has been reached about it. To use this controversial notion, without giving us a clear understanding of it, to characterize and make intelligible for us Aristotle's philosophy does not make sense. Indeed, I would go so far as saying that it does not seem to be commonsensical at all!

For all we know after reading Veatch's book, although it may be true that Aristotelian philosophy is a philosophy of common sense *par excellence* and that it is the only one open to a man of healthy common sense, as Veatch claims, we still have no definite proof that it is so. And this, if I am correct, can be traced to a methodology arising from Veatch's disparaging opinion of the history of philosophy and his view that his *Aristotle* is not a historical work.

Having reached the conclusion that philosophy is necessary for the history of philosophy whereas the history of philosophy is not necessary for philosophy, and having illustrated the problems that can arise when one fails to understand that relationship properly, we might go back to the question as to the reasons why philosophers should pay any attention to the history of philosophy. That question concerns nothing other than the justification and value of the study of the history of philosophy. I undertake the discussion of this issue in the next chapter of this book, to which I turn presently.

NOTES

1. Indeed, as one of my critics has stated: "the upshot of Professor Gracia's intricate instructions on this score [i.e., doing philosophy historically]—arrived at after no little backing and filling—would seem to amount to little more than the truism that to do philosophy historically, of course one cannot very well avoid doing something in the *history* of philosophy; and equally and at the same time, insofar as it is something in the history of *philosophy* that one is doing, one cannot very well avoid doing some philosophy as well." Henry B. Veatch, "Response to Commentators," in Hare, ed., *Doing Philosophy Historically*, p. 127.

2. Wittgenstein states in the *Notebooks 1914–16*, trans. by G. E. M. Anscombe, ed. G. H. von Wright and G. E. M. Anscombe (Oxford: Basil Blackwell, 1961), p. 82e: "What has history to do with me? Mine is the first and the only world! I want to report how *I* found the world. What others in the world have told me about the world is a very small and incidental part of my experience of the world. I have to judge the world, to measure things."

3. Cf. Paul G. Kuntz, "The Dialectic of Historicism and Anti-Historicism," *The Monist* 53, no. 4 (1969): 658.

4. This view is frequently attributed to analysts in general, not just to logical positivists. See Peter H. Hare, Introduction to *Doing Philosophy Historically*.

5. This point is echoed outside the ranks of logical positivists as well. Cf. Jonathan Bennett, "Response to Garber and Rée," p. 62.

6. René Descartes, Letter from 1638, in *Descartes: Philosophical Letters*, ed. and trans. Anthony Kenny (Oxford: Clarendon Press, 1970), pp. 59–60. My emphasis.

7. See the works by Garber and Lafrance to which reference has been made in Chapter One.

8. Historicism is a complicated phenomenon that often presents confusing and conflicting claims. The position I describe here should not be identified with any view of any author in particular, although as presented has much in common with many authors whose views are routinely described as historicist. For a discussion of the origins of historicism, see Georg G. Iggers, *The German Conception of History: The National Tradition of Historical Thought from Herder to the Present*, rev. ed. (Middletown, Conn.: Wesleyan University Press, 1983), particularly the Introduction. For the impact of historicism on contemporary philosophical thought, see Robert D'Amico, *Historicism and Knowledge* (New York and London: Routledge, 1989).

9. See, for example, Jonathan Rée, "Philosophy and the History of Philosophy," p. 30, and Michael Ayers, "Analytical Philosophy and the History of Philosophy," pp. 48–49 and 63.

10. Charles Taylor, "Philosophy and Its History," in Rorty et al., eds., *Philosophy in History*, p. 21.

11. For other recent statements and defenses of this view, see Louis Dupré, "Is the History of Philosophy Philosophy?" *Review of Metaphysics* 42, no. 3 (1989): 463–82; and Lesley Cohen, "Doing Philosophy Is Doing Its History," *Synthese* 67 (1986): 51–55. Cohen's point is that "philosophy is essentially historical because it cannot forget (or should not be allowed to forget) the actual historical (that is, temporal) *development* of the questions that concern us," as "not to know the history of philosophy is not to understand *why* the questions we are endeavoring to answer are worth answering—or asking" (p. 53). From a somewhat different angle, Étienne Gilson argues that the history of philosophy is a necessary introduction to philosophy, without which no valuable contribution to the field has been made. See "Introduction to *A History of Philosophy*," in Armand A. Maurer, *Medieval Philosophy* (New York: Random House, 1962), pp. vii and viii.

12. Henry B. Veatch, *Aristotle: A Contemporary Appreciation* (Bloomington and London: Indiana University Press, 1974), p. 3. Similar statements occur in "Introduction: On Trying to Be an Aristotelian or a Thomist in Today's World," in *Swimming against the Current in Contemporary Philosophy: Occasional Essays and Papers* (Washington, D.C.: Catholic University of America Press, 1990), p. 3.

13. Ibid., p. 5.

14. Ibid., p. 9.

15. Ibid., p. 12.

16. Ibid.

17. Of course, other views of the function of common sense do not necessarily preclude reaching conclusions that are not part of what "all men everywhere in their saner moments know or think they know to be the truth." For example, G. E. Moore, as Jonathan Bennett pointed out to me, had an important role for common sense in philosophy and yet he reached all sorts of conclusions that were not part of what could be regarded as commonsensical truths. Indeed, as long as those conclusions did not contradict common sense, he felt they were not in conflict with the commonsensical view of the world, even if they themselves were not commonsensical. However, Veatch seems to hold a much stronger view of the function of common sense than Moore. As I see it, one needs to distinguish three positions with respect to the use of common sense in philosophy. One holds that all philosophy should begin with the examination of the commonsensical view of the world. In this sense, common sense is the origin of philosophy, for all philosophy begins with the examination of our ordinary beliefs about the world. Another view holds that common sense is a strong criterion of philosophical truth in such a way that all philosophical propositions must be found in the ordinary commonsensical view of the world. Consequently, if a philosophical proposi-

tion is not found among the propositions that compose such a view, or if it contradicts a proposition that is part of such a view, the proposition is to be regarded as either nonsensical or false. Finally, there is a view that holds that common sense is a weak criterion of philosophical truth in such a way that: (1) if a philosophical proposition is part of the commonsensical view of the world it is true, (2) if a philosophical proposition contradicts the commonsensical view of the world it is false, and (3) if a philosophical proposition is not part of the commonsensical view of the world, but does not contradict common sense, it may be true. I believe Aristotle held the first view, Moore held the third, and Veatch holds the second.

18. Veatch, *Aristotle*, p. 124.

19. Ibid., p. 199

20. Ibid., p. 3.

Chapter Three

Doing Philosophy Historically: The Justification and Value of the History of Philosophy

The general attitude of nonphilosophers toward philosophy is quite different from the attitude they generally have toward science, art, and literature in that they expect philosophy to justify itself. Most persons do not find the need to justify the pursuit of science, for example. Indeed, its practical applications are so evident in society that it appears to be almost self-evident that science is not only a good thing but something that should be actively pursued. How, for example, could I be comfortably writing these words in the middle of a Buffalo winter without the help of science and its offspring technology, which provide me with light, heat, and a word processor? True, once in a while one finds criticisms that *prima facie* seem to be directed at science. But on closer examination they usually turn out to be directed not against the pursuit of science itself, but rather against what are perceived to be abuses of it or against the unwelcomed results of those abuses. The pursuit of science as such is seldom questioned, let alone criticized. Something similar is true of art and literature as well, for we receive an immediate enjoyment and gratification out of them that renders questions concerning their value superfluous. There seems to be no pressing need to ask Michelangelo or Tolstoy for a justification of their work—a look at Michelangelo's *David* or a reading of Tolstoy's *War and Peace* convince even the most skeptical observer of the value of the enterprises that produced those works.

The perception that there is no need for a justification of science is quite obvious in the academy, where many students and administrators seem to take for granted that the budget for faculty lines and equipment in science departments should be constantly increased. And, although neither literature nor art enjoy the privileged budgetary conditions of science, even the most technically oriented schools and their administrators pay lip service to the benefits of exposing students to them and thus to the need to support them. Students too have no trouble seeing the practical value of science and the aesthetic value of art and literature. They see in technological knowledge the key to their financial future and they regard art and literature as means that will make their lives more pleasant and interesting.

Unfortunately, many administrators and students have difficulty understanding the role of philosophy in the curriculum. Some administrators occasionally underline the value of the discipline, speaking about "integration," "values," and "a coherent world-view," but such platitudes seldom translate into budgetary realities. If they maintain philosophy at all it is usually because other schools do and they do not wish to appear any less progressive. A look at the number of faculty lines assigned to philosophy in most public universities and a comparison to the lines assigned to science and, say, modern language departments, clearly illustrate the administrative priorities in academia in the United States today.

As far as students are concerned the situation is even worse. Not having been exposed to the discipline in high school and having a generally technical and business orientation, they seldom take philosophy courses, and those who do, find them so difficult and so far removed from their ordinary experience that they rarely try again. All this results in limited demand for philosophy courses and continually shrinking budgets for departments where the discipline is taught. The question that everyone presses on philosophers, then, is, Why philosophy?

As if this were not bad enough, the situation of the history of philosophy is much worse, for it occupies within philosophy a position similar to that of philosophy within the spectrum of the sciences and humanities. Most practicing philosophers take for granted the value of and need for philosophy and only a few of them raise questions concerning its justification. Indeed, when these questions are raised they are the result of nonphilosophical pressures rather than of the inner needs of philosophers themselves. But when it comes to the history of philosophy the matter is quite different. After all, if the business of philosophy is to advance the discipline, whatever that may entail, why do we have to study past views and ideas which in most cases are outmoded or blatantly false? Shouldn't we concentrate on what is happening and relevant now rather than the past? Haven't we superseded old questions and controversies? Certainly present-day astronomers do not go back to Galileo when they pursue their discipline, and it is doubtful whether any physicists in the forefront of the discipline today spend much time poring over Aristotle's *Physics*. Nor do astronomers concern themselves with medieval astrological theories—they leave that task for popular heads of state or their wives—and few if any have ever read the classic works of Kepler and Copernicus. Only historians of science take seriously the history of science.

This same unhistorical approach is characteristic of practitioners of contemporary art and literature. True, in some cases artists and writers find sources of inspiration in works of the past: Picasso redid *Las Meninas* and Bernstein gave a new rendition of *Romeo and Juliet*, for example. But what artists and writers do with the past cannot be compared to the job of the historian of philosophy. Artists go to the past primarily for inspiration. The historical work is used most frequently as a point of departure for a new and original composition in which the contemporary author gives free reign to artistic expression. This contrasts quite clearly with the careful attention to philosophical sources given by the historian of philosophy, whose major aim is to provide an accurate account of past ideas. Indeed, the work of the historian of philosophy is similar to that of the historian of art and literature, not to the work of the artist or literary writer. And in neither case does there seem to be a compelling reason, from the side of the nonhistorical disciplines, to delve into their history. So we may ask, Does the history of philosophy have something to offer to philosophy that the history of physics, art, and literature do not offer to physics, art and literature? In short, is there a justification for the study of the history of philosophy by philosophers?

Note that the justification for which this question asks is not just the purely historical one in which the study of the history of philosophy would be seen as satisfying the general human curiosity to know about the past. It is true that the history of philosophy, just like any other history, can be justified in those terms. But that does not help us here. For what we wish to know is whether the history of philosophy can be justified as an appropriate pursuit for philosophers and others whose interests are more than antiquarian. In the previous chapter we saw how philosophy and its history are not incompatible and we also determined that philosophy is necessary for the history of philosophy. Our present question has to do with the use that the history of philosophy can have for philosophy when, as we know from our earlier discussion, the history of philosophy is not necessary for philosophy.

I. THE NEGATIVE VIEW

One answer to this question is negative. The history of philosophy does not offer anything more to philosophy than what the history of physics offers to physics and the history of art and literature offers to those disciplines. Indeed, that is the primary reason, so the argument goes, why it should not be pursued at the same time that philosophy is being pursued.

The reasons given for this negative conclusion are usually one or more of the following: (1) The study of the history of philosophy stultifies creativity; (2) it prevents discoveries; (3) it is irrelevant to present concerns; and (4) it wastes precious time.[1] These reasons cannot be summarily dismissed, for there are many examples of philosophers who have indeed fallen into one or more of these traps. The lack of philosophical creativity, for example, is a commonplace among those who work in the history of philosophy. As we shall see in Chapter Five, the excessively scholarly approach of some historians of philosophy leads them to function primarily as paraphrasers and commentators of other philosophers' work, and renders them unable to interpret and translate the past into conceptual categories that may be intelligible and useful to the present. This dependence on the past can lead to extremes, where historians feel they can express themselves only with the words and terms of the authors they study. Sometimes this is done for rhetorical effect, but often it becomes a crutch without which the historian is mute. Most of those who exemplify this problem behave as they do because of their inordinate respect for the authority of their source. They forget that in philosophy the argument from authority is the weakest one can give.

Furthermore, if connections with the past become too strong, not only is creativity stifled but discovery is prevented. Those who live in the past and think in terms of its categories see the world always from the same perspective. They recognize only what is familiar, missing anything new. They are like carts traveling in deep ruts from which they cannot escape. There are countless examples of this phenomenon in the history of philosophy and it is particularly evident among those historians who have a definite commitment to a particular philosopher from the past. The problem, however, is not their commitment, but their inability to think in terms of new patterns and structures. Thus, for example, many neoscholastics are frequently unable to accommodate and sometimes even to understand contemporary philosophical notions. Their attempts to do so boil down to attempts to translate contemporary concepts and ideas into already familiar scholastic language. In doing so they often miss precisely the important and new elements of the views they examine. Not that it is not possible to translate the present into the past. If, as I have claimed, it is possible to translate the past into the present, there is no logical impossibility of doing the reverse. Such translation is not impossible;

the difficulty is that an excessive emphasis on translation and finding correlations between the present and the past distorts the present, preventing the appreciation of its unique contribution to the history of philosophy. Many historians of philosophy, then, enclosed as they are in the past, cannot break away from it both to chart new courses in philosophy and to appreciate and understand those that others have already charted.

Third, it also is true that a good proportion of past philosophical history is irrelevant to current concerns. Philosophers who dwell only on the past tend often to be concerned with issues and problems that have nothing or little to say to the present. For example, what purpose can it serve for us today to dwell on the rather abstruse doctrine of the multiplicity of human intellects, so hotly debated first by Islamic authors and later by scholastic philosopher-theologians during the Middle Ages? This whole controversy seems to be predicated on the excessive respect and concern for certain obscure Aristotelian texts from *De anima* on the composition of the human mind and on various philosophical and theological assumptions that do not govern philosophical thinking any longer. Something similar could be said about the medieval doctrine of illumination, so intensely debated at the time but that now strikes us as an oddity in the history of human thought. And the same could be said about Descartes's innate ideas or Kant's categories, for that matter. If one's concern is with these and other abstruse and largely irrelevant issues, so the argument goes, one is prevented from confronting the pressing philosophical problems of the day. Not that every philosophical issue discussed in the past is abstruse or irrelevant. Indeed many are still relevant today. The point is that those philosophers who spend their energies and time in the past alone miss the very many issues that are alive today and were never part of the past. Some of these, for example, have surfaced owing to scientific and technological developments of which the past was not aware. The moral issues involved in genetic engineering, for instance, or matters related to artificial intelligence are entirely new and never occurred to philosophers until relatively recently. In short, the concern with the history of philosophy leads to the kind of antiquarianism that freezes in the past those who suffer from it, preventing them from dealing with the problems of the present and future and rendering their thought irrelevant to contemporary concerns.

Finally, the time at our disposal is very limited and the history of philosophy is vast and complicated. The serious undertaking of the study of even a small portion of the history of philosophy, indeed of the thought of a single philosopher, can easily consume the energies of an entire life and leave no time to investigate philosophical issues.

Universities are filled with individuals whose areas of expertise sometimes extend to no more than one author and even to a single period of his or her life. How close to the development of a comprehensive and consistent account of the world are these individuals? If the job of the philosopher is precisely to develop a comprehensive and consistent account of the world, the study of the history of philosophy seems to be a waste of time. There may be truth in the history of philosophy that could help us in fulfilling the philosophical goal, but the problem is that we do not know where to find that truth, how to separate it from what is false or useless, and the effort and energy required to do so far outweighs the potential rewards. Those individuals, then, whose interests are philosophical, who are concerned with the development of a comprehensive and consistent account of the world, have no choice but to devote themselves to the systematic investigation of the discipline rather than the investigation of its history.

But, of course, none of these problems is necessarily connected with the use of the history of philosophy by philosophy, and those philosophers who turn to them in order to reject the value of the history of philosophy for philosophy miss the advantages that such history does have for it. Take the first one: that the study of the history of philosophy stultifies creativity. This would seem to be true in many cases as already noted, but experience teaches us that there are many other cases in which it is not true. For example, if there ever were an age concerned with and bound by the past it was the Middle Ages. The notion of authority, understood as sanctioned past views and the texts that expressed them, dominated the period. Indeed, the weight of the past was so overwhelming at the time that it was generally accepted as a rule of procedure that one should not contradict it. Thus we seldom, if ever, find anyone explicitly disputing the views of Augustine or any of the other Church Fathers. The most that we find are "interpretations," some of which in fact are not faithful to the letter or the spirit of the text or author in question, but nonetheless try to maintain the appearance of agreement with it. The general attitude of medieval authors toward the past was that it was immensely valuable and often incontestable. They saw their function as one of facilitating the harmonization of authoritative views from that past and their preservation. The notions of "discovery" and "originality" that so frequently dominate the concerns of contemporary philosophers were foreign to them. Yet, it is incontestable that medieval authors, in spite of their concern with the past, broke new ground in many areas of philosophy and displayed the kind of originality that could be the envy of many of our contemporaries. The conclusion, then, that the study of the past necessarily or even mostly stultifies creativity is contradicted by experience.

Indeed, just as in the arts the study of past achievements actually can help rather than hinder artists in their creation of new works, so there is no reason why the history of philosophy should be an insurmountable stumbling block and not a helpful aid in the pursuit of creativity. The study of the history of philosophy, as we shall see in a moment, in fact may help in that process of creation.

Something similar could be said concerning the second charge: that the study of the history of philosophy prevents discoveries. It is true, again, that in many cases the excessive concern with the past has a nefarious influence on discovery. But, as the example of the Middle Ages illustrates, it certainly is not a necessary result of such a study. For example, Aquinas's enormous respect for Aristotle, to whom he referred as "the Philosopher," did not prevent him from introducing new and revolutionary notions in his philosophical thought that can be regarded not just as un-Aristotelian but may even be interpreted as anti-Aristotelian. The view that existence is an act really distinct from essence and that the principle of individuation is matter considered under determinate dimensions are two such notions, for example. Similarly, Heidegger's explorations of medieval and ancient philosophy have resulted in strikingly unusual views that cannot be considered in any sense as repetitions of the views of ancient and scholastic authors.

As far as the third charge is concerned, that the past is irrelevant to the present and takes us back to a frame of mind foreign to the concerns of the present, the answer is that this is simply not true. Of course, many concerns of the past are philosophically irrelevant for us today, and also many current concerns did not preoccupy the past. Both of these points are clear from the examples mentioned earlier. But it is also quite true that much of what the past discussed is also of concern to us today and many of the views arrived at by past philosophers are defensible even today. Who is to say, for example, that Plato's momentous question in the *Republic*, "What is justice?" is irrelevant for us? And who is to say that Thrasymachus's cynical answer, "Justice is the interest of the stronger," is not a contending position today? The fact is that the core of philosophy is composed of certain types of questions and issues that seem to remain largely unaltered throughout history, and this is the reason why the statements and views of philosophers who lived hundreds and thousands of years ago are still pertinent to our discussions. This, indeed, is the main reason why they are still read today. But more on this later. For the moment it is sufficient to point out that the study of the history of philosophy does not seem irrelevant to present concerns, nor does it, as concluded earlier, necessarily stand in the way of discovery and creativity. I shall deal with the fourth charge later; now I turn to ways in which the history of philosophy may be defended.

II. THE AFFIRMATIVE VIEW

The most widespread view concerning the usefulness of the history of philosophy for philosophy is that, indeed, the history of philosophy can and does contribute substantially and beneficially to philosophy. The attempts to substantiate this position fall roughly into three categories. One of these gives practical reasons to argue in favor of the study of the history of philosophy and thus I call it the *pragmatic justification*. Another tries to find the theoretical bases for the use of the history of philosophy in philosophy and so I refer to it as the *theoretical justification*. In addition, there is a third group of arguments, of which I give only two, that do not easily fall into any single category but which I gather under the heading of *rhetorical justification* for reasons that will become clear as we discuss them. I begin with this third category, move to the pragmatic justification next, and end with the theoretical justification.

A. The Rhetorical Justification

The rhetorical justification for the study of the history of philosophy takes various forms of which I refer only to two: the first views such a study as inspirational and the second finds in it support and respectability for contemporary views.

1. History of Philosophy as a Source of Inspiration. According to this justification, the primary function of the history of philosophy is as a source of inspiration for subsequent philosophers. This inspiration is not to be understood primarily in terms of content as a source of information and truth—that is a different view, which I discuss later. The source of inspiration involved here is more of a "romantic" sort. Past philosophers are seen as role models, whose lives, works, and struggles serve as examples of what other philosophers should be and do. To perceive them as individuals of flesh and blood, working toward a lofty goal of knowledge and truth inspires us to pursue the same goals as philosophers: They become our heroes. As Rée has put it: "[Their] doctrines are presumed true, even if their meaning is a mystery; and anyway, the focus of attention is not the doctrines, but the hero's style of life and death. Devotees are tormented by a fear—indeed, a certainty—that they are unworthy of their master."[2]

Although I have not seen this justification of the history of philosophy explicitly articulated in the fashion in which I have described, it is easy to imagine that those like Rée, who favor the romantic approach to the history of philosophy to be discussed in Chapter Five, will tend to adopt this sort of apology for the study of the philosophical past. And, indeed, there is considerable value in this argument. For, although not all philosophers have led lives that could serve as sources of inspiration to other philosophers, many have. Socrates, of course, is the prime example of someone who not only led an unimpeachable life but who was willing to die for his principles. And there are many other examples of similar devotion to philosophy and principled behavior among the ranks of philosophers of the past. Philosophers of any age can certainly find the strength and courage to defy opposition and bigotry by examining examples of such strength and courage in individuals who preceded them. We must remember that philosophers are not disembodied minds and that they are subjected to the same emotional influences as other human beings. As Augustine would have pointed out, the pursuit of truth and goodness requires not only the motion of the intellect but also the concurrence of the will, and the will needs an object of desire in order to move. It is this object of desire that the history of philosophy makes clear to us through the concrete examples of many worthy philosophical lives.

On the other hand, if what the history of philosophy provides for us is only a source of inspiration, we may ask, Does it merit the kind of detailed study and analysis of views and arguments that is the norm in historical studies? Why bother, after all, with all those doctrinal details, if what is important is only the history of the philosophical struggle and the character of individuals? Why not turn the history of philosophy into a kind of secular hagiography? The very etymology of the word suggests that to be "inspired" means to get into the spirit of someone or of something, and such an effect is not easily accomplished except through the observation of the way other human beings have faced the challenges presented to them. It is not their thought, then, that functions as a source of inspiration, but their behavior in various circumstances and the way they arranged to meet their goals. It would not seem necessary to know anything about Bertrand Russell's views, for example, to be able to admire his courage in the face of opposition and his willingness to fight for unpopular causes of whose value he was convinced. If this is so, most of what goes under the name *history of philosophy* is useless; we need to concentrate only on those aspects of that history that have romantic and inspirational potential.

This conclusion, however, seems preposterous for three reasons:

First, because biographies are only a small portion of the history of philosophy. Second, because if the aim of the historian were to write inspirational books about past lives, we would need very little research on anything but biographical data, having to concentrate only on those philosophers who led inspirational lives and on the details of their lives that could serve as inspiration to the past. It would be doubtful that if this were the case, anyone would pay attention to Kant, for example. For what inspiration could we derive from the rather quiet and inactive life he led? He almost never set foot outside his native city, he did not get involved in political or other sorts of controversies, and he does not seem to have been tortured by psychological or religious concerns. Outside of the content of his philosophical thought, punctuality seems to have been his only quality worthy of admiration and that can hardly be the subject of inspiration. Third, since what is inspirational to one age may not be so to another, it would be difficult to know exactly what is ultimately valuable in a philosopher's life. For example, it would be difficult for many contemporary philosophers to be inspired by Augustine's piety or Seneca's docile acquiescense in carrying out Nero's order to commit suicide. The most we could expect would be an ever changing number of biographical accounts, and that certainly does not seem to be what the history of philosophy is about.

2. History of Philosophy as a Source of Support and Respectability. As with the inspirational justification, I do not know of any philosopher who has explicitly and unambiguously claimed that the only or even primary justification for the study of the history of philosophy is the search for support and respectability. Probably the reason for this absence is that such a justification strikes one as either cynical, weak, or both. Yet, the use of the history of philosophy as support is *de facto* frequent in philosophy. Even those philosophers who pride themselves in their unhistorical approach occasionally make references to historical figures. And no wonder, since corroboration by the past lends present views an aura of continuity, validity, and common sense that helps to establish them. To find past figures who lived under different conditions and worked within vastly different conceptual frameworks agreeing with one's views is reassuring. Moreover, if the figures in question were towering intellects, generally respected for both their genuine search for truth and extraordinary philosophical acumen, there is even more reason to enlist them in our support. By standing on the shoulders of giants we can appear to be very tall, indeed.

Although the search for validation and support from the past is present in every age, there can be little doubt that it is in the Middle Ages that we find the most extreme case of it. This period of Western intellectual history, as already stated, was dominated by the notion of authority: the view that certain positions are to be regarded either as true or as so close to the truth that they cannot be contradicted and should be respected. Ultimately, an authority was a text that had been backed by the character of the author and sanctioned, either explicitly or implicitly, by the Church. At the top of the hierarchy of authorities were the Christian Scriptures, considered as divinely revealed by God. Next came the early commentaries on the Scriptures and elaborations of Christian doctrine, that is, the work of the Fathers of the Church. Below the Fathers was the work of Masters, who taught at the medieval universities, and, finally, the writings of pagan philosophers, individuals like Aristotle, Averroes, and Avicenna. Within this authoritative framework, the job of the Christian philosopher-theologian was taken to be one of building on what already had been accomplished, harmonizing whatever views appeared to be discordant and presenting an overall compendium of Christian thinking. This goal gave rise to the *summae* of the period, where much space is taken by quoting texts from the Scriptures, the Fathers, and other authoritative sources. Indeed, it is almost impossible to find the presentation of any important point of view in the Middle Ages unaccompanied by references to the past. It should be noted, however, that the interest of these authors was not historical; they used past authors and texts as props that supported their own views and lent respectability to their theories.

Obviously, in an age where one of the criteria of intellectual acceptability was the sanction of authority, this kind of procedure worked well. But if the assumption concerning the value of authority is discarded, this procedure collapses. Since in philosophy the argument from authority is the weakest argument possible, the usefulness of the study of the history of philosophy, if based only on the presumed authority of the past, disappears. Indeed, even some medieval authors realized that the use of texts as props is valuable only in disciplines like theology that are essentially authoritative—in philosophy textual props have little value.[3]

In short, the justification of the study of the history of philosophy based on the support and respectability that it may bring to current views is no justification at all. In many ways it subverts the true aim of philosophy—the search for truth—presenting the discipline as a kind of rhetorical procedure aimed at the defense of predetermined views, and it is the rhetorical aspect of this justification as well as of the inspirational one that invalidates it. If we cannot find that the study of the history of philosophy contributes significantly to the practice and progress of philosophy, then there is no reason to go back to it. The fact that the history of philosophy may function as a source of inspiration, support, and respectability does not contribute in any significant way to the development of philosophy. If the history of philosophy is to have any value for philosophy, such value must be found elsewhere.

B. The Pragmatic Justification

The pragmatic justification for the study of the history of philosophy takes at least three different forms. One visualizes the study of the history of philosophy as a practicum in the art of reasoning, another sees it as a source of information and truth, and a third regards it as good conceptual therapy either to restore philosophy's health or to keep it from lapsing into some kind of malaise. In all three cases the justification is based on practical considerations related to the usefulness that the study of the history of philosophy can have for philosophy. It is for this reason that I refer to it as the *pragmatic justification.*

1. History of Philosophy and the Art of Reasoning. The argument here is well known. The history of philosophy provides the philosopher with innumerable case studies of good and bad reasoning from the study of which the philosopher can profit. There is, after all, only one way of getting an argument right, and, although there are many ways of getting it wrong, their number is also limited. Moreover, some mistakes and fallacies tend to repeat themselves, and the subtlety of others is such that they are difficult to spot. The history of philosophy is a veritable vast gold mine in which the philosopher can see some of the most ingenious forms of argumentation presented by the best minds of every age. Going over these arguments, understanding them and their strengths and weaknesses, helps philosophers learn and practice the ways of argumentation. This learning and practice is transformed into actual skills, which lead to the formulation of a methodology whereby philosophical problems are to be settled. Just as the art of teaching has to be learned not just by a theoretical awareness of how to teach but also by practicing the learned theory, so the philosopher can learn a great deal from the practical experience that comes from the study of the history of philosophy.[4]

This is a standard argument based on long-established procedure and experience, particularly in the classroom. Philosophers learn to philosophize, to identify arguments, to judge their validity, and so forth, by examining philosophical texts, and those texts are for the most part historical texts far removed from the time in which students of philosophy find themselves. True, many textbooks of logic, for example, make up arguments for students to use. Nor is there any logical necessity that the arguments on which students of logic and philosophy practice should be taken from the history of philosophy. But it is also true that the best logic textbooks are those that use examples of reasoning already in existence and not examples designed *ad hoc*. The reason is simple: *Ad hoc* examples are contrived and often lack the genuine character and freshness that characterize what philosophers have said in good faith while engaged in philosophizing. Moreover, the vast reservoir of historical arguments presents students with a variety that is certainly diminished if they were to be restricted to contemporary texts. There are famous—often notorious—pieces of reasoning found in the history of philosophy that have challenged philosophers throughout the ages and that certainly present unique opportunities for students of the discipline to practice their skills. Who has not been puzzled, for example, by Anselm's argument for the existence of God or Descartes's *cogito?*

This justification of the study of the history of philosophy is particularly powerful because it concerns the knowledge of the formal structure of arguments and the logical skills that any philosopher ought to have. For these formal structures and skills are not subject to the passage of time or affected by the assumptions and views that permeate the circumstances surrounding the philosopher. As such, they cannot be regarded as "outdated," as may happen with the actual doctrines and views held by philosophers in a particular historical period. Thus, although the content of the arguments given by, say, Aristotle in support of the unmoved mover might be based on dated physical theory and therefore unacceptable to us at present, the form of those arguments is not tainted by such content. Hence we can learn from that form even when ignoring the content in which it is cast.

There is a strong pedagogical argument, then, from the point of view of logic in favor of the study of the history of philosophy. The weakness of the justification rests, first of all, on the lack of any essential connection between the study of logical form and the history of philosophy. Indeed, it is often logicians themselves who most frequently ignore altogether the history of philosophy. For, even if it were convenient to use examples from the history of philosophy in their procedures, such use is not necessary and in some instances is even regarded as counterproductive. The rationale for this conclusion is that form is frequently closely tied to content, and so the content of historical arguments about which we are not completely clear could muddle our understanding of the form in which they appear. It is much better after all, so the argument goes, to use contrived arguments, particularly if they are expressed in unambiguous symbols, than to try to unravel muddled pieces of reasoning from the past.

A second problem has to do with the narrow interest that this pedagogical skill-related justification has in the history of philosophy. For, according to it, only those aspects of that history that can serve for practicing logical skills can be of use. Why do we need, then, all the details about doctrinal content that seem to be so important to historians of philosophy? In fact, is there any reason why we should worry about historical accuracy at all? If the object of the study of the history of philosophy is only to practice one's skills at reasoning, the accuracy of the historical account would seem superfluous. Indeed, the very notion of providing an account appears irrelevant. If that is so, this kind of justification is useless for what has traditionally been known as the history of philosophy.

In short, the justification of the study of the history of philosophy based exclusively on its pedagogical usefulness with respect to logical form and argumentation fails miserably. From the logician's point of view it fails because it is not clear how the history of philosophy can help in the development of logical skills; and from the historian's point of view it fails because it is not clear that a history of philosophy that is useful pedagogically to learn reasoning skills would be anything like what we generally take to be the history of philosophy.

2. History of Philosophy as a Source of Information and Truth. The study of the history of philosophy by philosophers also frequently is justified by pointing out that it provides philosophers with information concerning views, problems, solutions to problems, and actual arguments with which they may not otherwise be acquainted. The value of the history of philosophy, then, does not rest on the opportunity it provides to practice philosophical method, to exercise one's mental muscles as it were, but on the fact that it presents philosophers with information about issues, alternative positions, and ways to defend them related to their concerns, which might have escaped their attention. As Corcoran puts it, "Attempts to understand ancient theories seem to force us to reconsider fundamental and enduring questions."[5] It is a matter of experience that acquaintance with other contemporary philosophers' reactions, views, and concerns expands, deepens, and sharpens a philosopher's philosophical horizon, awareness of problems and alternatives, and overall philosophical position. But if this is so obvious in the case of contemporary ideas and works, there is no reason why the same could not be said about the past.

To this must be added that knowledge of the history of philosophy prevents the present from repeating the past and wasting valuable time and effort on what has already been discovered. To paraphrase a well-known saying: Those who do not know the philosophical past are condemned to repeat it. Philosophers who do not wish to travel the same roads traveled by others before them would do well to study the history of philosophy. The history of philosophy is a rich reservoir of truth that can easily teach us lessons that otherwise would take a great deal of effort to learn.[6]

The difference between the present and the past in this context is the extraordinary wealth of the past if compared with the present. There are 2,500 years of philosophy in which contemporary students of philosophy may immerse themselves, while what is considered the present may in fact consist only of the philosophical production of a very few years.

Besides, the past offers a variety of perspectives that are substantially different from the present, thus forcing a reexamination of present views, underscoring their character and raising questions concerning their viability. Even Descartes, who as we saw earlier had little use for the history of philosophy, acknowledged the value of studying the past in this respect:

> to hold converse with those of other ages and to travel, are almost the same thing. It is useful to know something of the manners of different nations, that we may be enabled to form a more correct judgment regarding our own, and be prevented from thinking that everything contrary to our customs is ridiculous and irrational,—a conclusion usually come to by those whose experience has been limited to their own country.[7]

Philosophers who have been exposed only to the views of their contemporaries are like those individuals who have never traveled outside their own countries and have no knowledge of other languages, literatures, and cultures. They develop a kind of philosophical provincialism that prevents them from seeing their own mistakes and the unexamined assumptions on which many of their views rest. The study of the history of philosophy, then, functions as a liberating art that opens up new possibilities and poses new challenges. As Garber has put it:

> Many of the philosophical beliefs we now take for granted are not shared by figures in the past. By studying the past, taking the past seriously, we are led to reflect on our beliefs, in just the

> same way as we are led by travel to reflect upon our customs. Such reflection need not lead to a change in our beliefs. The fact that some past geographers thought the earth flat, or past physicists thought that there is such a thing as elemental fire that by its nature rises, these historical observations should not move us to give up our present conceptions of geography or combustion. But reflection on some of the things people have believed should at least cause us to ask ourselves *why* we believe the things we do, and *whether* our grounds are sufficient to support the explicit or implicit beliefs we have and assumptions we make...the history of philosophy can be important not because it leads to philosophical *truths,* but because it leads to philosophical *questions.*[8]

All of this makes considerable sense; nonetheless, the case made by this justification is not airtight. After all, it can always be pointed out that, just as there may be some pragmatic reasons to look back into the history of philosophy, there are other, also pragmatic, reasons why one should not do so. For example, there is the problem of time limitations raised earlier: In what period or area should students concentrate? Which philosophers, positions, and problems should be given attention, and which should be ignored? The history of philosophy is too vast and one can easily get lost in it, losing sight of the aim originally intended. Indeed, this seems to have been the fate of many philosophers, who as a result became historians and never succeeded in moving out of the purely historical study of the philosophical past. There is, therefore, a real danger of being swallowed by the history of philosophy. The contemporary philosophical panorama amply illustrates the fact that most philosophers confine themselves to the study of very narrow areas within the history of philosophy, writing erudite articles on what Descartes thought about this or what Plato thought about that, often consigning themselves to what some philosophers consider to be minutiae. The study of the history of philosophy, according to many, is a two-edged sword that at worst should be avoided and at best should be handled carefully; and the justification of philosophy based on its consideration as a source of information does not make a convincing case against this sort of objection.

3. History of Philosophy and Therapy. Finally, there are those who hold that the most important practical justification for the study of the history of philosophy is the therapeutic effects of such a study, either as a healing process or as a preventive measure against possible deterioration. On the one hand, those who see it as primarily a healing procedure generally assume that philosophy has undergone a process of deterioration, so that at present it is either sick, confused about its nature and role, or both. Under these conditions, there is a need for therapy in order to restore philosophy's former vigor and health. The way to do this, as Heidegger has attempted, is to go back to its origins; for in the history of philosophy we can find first of all how philosophy began, its original aims, and what early philosophers thought about it. The study of these origins may reveal the original intuitions concerning the discipline that led its founders to pursue it, as well as the needs that prompted its foundation. The understanding of those original intuitions and needs, unmixed by subsequent speculation and artifice, in turn could hold the key to the proper understanding of philosophy. Besides, from the study of the history of philosophy we can also learn the steps by which philosophy has arrived at its present state of decay. The study of the history of philosophy can provide us with a picture of what philosophy at its best is supposed to be and, therefore, with the goals it should pursue as well as the methods it should employ to pursue them. And by uncovering the causes that have separated philosophy from its intended path, leading it astray, we can devise strategies to render those causes ineffective.

On the other hand, those who see the study of the history of philosophy as furnishing a preventative against future deterioration do not necessarily assume that the present state of philosophy is unwholesome; their concern is only with future decay. They agree with the former group, however, in finding in the study of origins and subsequent historical developments the key to maintaining the health of the discipline, because through the understanding of those origins and developments we in turn may reach a proper understanding of the nature of philosophy as well as of the procedure it should employ.

Both of these views make sense if one shares their assumptions. For the understanding of a procedure generally helps either in restoring it to the state for which it was designed or prevents its deterioration. There can be no doubt that such an understanding can function under certain circumstances as a necessary condition of efficient practice. And here the analogy of health that runs through this justification is particularly helpful. Take, for example, any bodily organ. It is accepted wisdom that to prevent its deterioration we must understand precisely the nature of the organ and its function. And the same goes for restoring it to good health when for some reason it has undergone deterioration. Likewise, for philosophy, we must begin by understanding it and to do that we must pay attention to the way it functions; and this can be achieved only, according to this point of view, through the examination of its history.

But again, one may want to ask, Even granting that philosophy is sick or that it can get sick, is the remedy to be found necessarily in its history? The case for history as cure is far from clear. Moreover, in which part of the history of philosophy should philosophers concentrate? The pre-Socratics? Plato and Aristotle? The Middle Ages? The Enlightenment? The medicine seems too unclear and too vast to do any good; before we finish administering it, the patient could very well be dead.

Particularly troubling are two problems. First, the notion that philosophy is at present in a state of ill health, for this is certainly a judgment with which many philosophers would disagree. Many of them would appear to support the opposite view, namely, that philosophy is thriving and has achieved a degree of sophistication, precision, and development unmatched in any previous historical period of development of the discipline. There is plenty of evidence to back up this judgment. For, although we may disagree as to the ultimate value of the philosophical ideas in circulation today, it is unquestionable that there are more practicing philosophers and more philosophical publications today than at any other time in the history of the discipline.

Likewise, second, there is considerable disagreement with respect to the way the history of philosophy can restore the former health of philosophy or prevent its present health from deteriorating based on the study of the origins of the discipline and its subsequent historical developments. Some would argue that it is not clear how the study of its origins and its subsequent development can help us to uncover either what philosophy is or its proper methodology. The study of such origins and developments would give us only descriptive knowledge about those origins and developments, but not necessarily or even primarily the kind of prescriptive knowledge we require if we are to know the nature of the discipline and its proper methodology.

There is no question that the three pragmatic justifications we have discussed have considerable merit, and even the most recalcitrant opponents of the study of the history of philosophy would probably agree with some of the observations they make. The first two justifications have a particularly strong appeal. It takes very little experience in doing philosophy to learn that acquaintance with the history of philosophy helps to develop argumentation skills and deepens one's breadth and depth of understanding of philosophical issues and positions. The third justification, on the other hand, is considerably more controversial both because of the assumption of those who use it concerning the poor state of philosophy in the present and also because of its views about the way in which the history of philosophy can bring philosophy back to health.

Be that as it may, however, even if we were to accept the conclusions of all three pragmatic justifications, such acceptance would not seem to be enough to justify the study of the history of philosophy. A more theoretical justification is needed, that is, the justification should rest on something more than expediency; it should be tied to the very nature of philosophy and its history. Not that we would find that philosophy requires the study of the history of philosophy. We have already seen that it does not. Rather, what we would like to find are reasons, based on the nature of philosophy and its history, that make the study of the history of philosophy naturally useful for philosophy. To those sorts of considerations I turn next.

C. The Theoretical Justification

The *theoretical justification* of the study of the history of philosophy finds its ammunition in the nature of philosophy itself and in the nature of philosophical practice. I consider here four forms that this sort of justification may take: The first two to which I refer are based primarily on the nature of philosophical practice, and the last two are based on certain conceptions of the nature of philosophy.

1. Ontogeny Recapitulates Phylogeny. Ontogeny is the process whereby an individual entity develops from its origin, through various stages, into the complete individual entity it is. Phylogeny is the process whereby a type of entity develops from its origin, through various stages, into the complete type of entity it is. Thus to say that ontogeny recapitulates philogeny is to claim that the process whereby an individual entity develops into a complete individual repeats in some sense the process whereby a type of entity develops into the complete type of entity it is.[9] For example, it has been argued that because, biologically speaking, the human species is the product of a process consisting of various stages of development, the production of an individual human being mirrors in some way that process of development. Indeed, so the argument goes, if we observe the stages of development through which a human embryo passes, we can pair them off with stages in the development of the human race.

This sort of argument can be applied as well to knowledge and, in particular, to the case at hand: One could argue that the acquisition of philosophical knowledge by an individual goes through stages that mirror the stages through which the human race as a whole has gone in its understanding of philosophy.[10] If this is so, then it makes a great deal of sense to study the history of philosophy, for in doing so we would be saving ourselves considerable effort.

This argument is appealing in many ways, and if we could be sure of the truth of its fundamental premise, namely that ontogeny recapitulates phylogeny, it would quite easily constitute the best or at least one of the best theoretical justifications for the study of the history of philosophy. The problem, of course, is that the status of that premise is unclear, and it is unclear primarily because the very notion of "recapitulation" on which the premise hinges is itself unclear. First of all, the notion of recapitulation seems to be based on some similarities between the phylogenic and ontogenic processes, but it is not obvious what those similarities are. Second, even if there were similarities between the processes, there also are important differences between them. The differences stem in part from the fact that in the case of phylogeny we are dealing with a group, whereas in the case of ontogeny we are dealing with an individual. Moreover, the process of phylogeny takes place over a long period of time whereas the process of ontogeny takes a shorter span of time. These differences suggest that at best phylogeny and ontogeny are analogous in some fundamental ways—at worst, of course, the processes are fundamentally different and have only surface analogies that do not reflect the basic nature of the processes themselves. In either case, we are dealing with analogies whose natures need to be determined, and, under those conditions, it seems inappropriate to argue that going through one procedure necessarily would help the other. If that is the case, we would have no firm basis for arguing that studying the history of philosophy would actually help us in our philosophical development.

In short, the claim on which this justification of the study of the history of philosophy rests is too unclear and controversial to serve as basis of a justification for the study of the history of philosophy at present. Until the principle on which the justification is based is established on firmer ground, we must turn to other alternatives to justify the study of the history of philosophy.

2. Dialectical Nature of Philosophy. Another attempt at a theoretical justification for the study of the history of philosophy is based on the view that philosophy is a dialectical discipline. That philosophy is dialectical may be interpreted, however, in various ways, of which two are particularly pertinent here. According to one, philosophy is a discipline in which dialogue is of the essence: To do philosophy is to engage in dialogue and thus exchange ideas. Philosophy cannot proceed by itself; it needs the give and take so evident in the

Platonic writings. According to the other, the dialectical nature of philosophy means that philosophy moves according to certain laws of thought, certain patterns that lead toward a goal. Both of these interpretations of the dialectical nature of philosophy can be used to justify the study of philosophy's history.

a. Philosophy and Dialogue. The argument here is that, since dialogue is essential to philosophy and in a dialogue the better the partner the better the result, the study of the history of philosophy is enormously beneficial to philosophy, for the history of philosophy provides the best possible partner in dialogue for contemporary philosophers.[11] The advantages of using this partner are extraordinary if compared to those of using our contemporaries. In the first place, the history of philosophy presents us with a wealth of arguments and positions that cannot be equalled by even the cummulative effect of the thought of all contemporary philosophers. Of course, some arguments and positions of contemporary philosophy are original and therefore not found before the present time. But their number pales when compared with the number of arguments and positions that the past has to offer us.

Second, there is also a matter of quality. In the history of philosophy we know we are dealing with the best minds of the different periods we study, whereas we are not yet sure who the best minds of our times are; we are too close to them to be able to judge them accurately. This consideration brings me to the third point that needs to be made in connection with this justification; namely, that we are too close to our contemporaries and their views to enter with them into the kind of dispassionate objective and rational dialogue that one would expect of philosophers. But, of course, to do so with the past is much easier, so the argument goes, for we are not emotionally related to its figures as we are to our contemporaries.

I do not wish to dispute the claim that philosophy is essentially dialectical in the stated sense, although I think it is far from certain that it is so. But even leaving that claim unquestioned, two weaknesses of this position seriously undermine it. The first is involved in the application of the notion of "dialogue" to describe the relation of the philosophical present with the philosophical past.

The primary and most clear case of dialogue occurs when two speakers engage in conversation. Thus we speak of dialogue as a primarily verbal phenomenon, although we also call "dialogues" the written reports of what is supposed to be a verbal affair. Obviously, there is no serious reason why a dialogue could not take place through writing or other appropriate means. Certainly we can establish and maintain a dialogue by correspondence. Nor is it necessary, as the example of correspondence illustrates, that there be a determinate time element involved. One can carry on a dialogue through years and the exchanges do not have to be separated by specifically short time spans, although it is true that if the times between exchanges grow too long we speak of "interrupting" a dialogue and "resuming" it again. Actually what seem most important, indeed essential, to a dialogue are two things: (1) that the parties engaged in it respond to each other, and (2) that there be the real possibility that the respective positions of the parties engaged in the dialogue be modified and changed. This is what distinguishes a true dialogue from two monologues respectively recited by speakers to each other. Where two persons are so set in their beliefs that there is no real possibility of any change in position by *both* parties, we usually do not think of the exchange as a dialogue. To have a dialogue both parties must be open to change. This is frequently lacking in the recent and acrimonious exchanges between the pro-choice and anti-abortionist parties, for example. In this case many anti-abortionists hold on to their position on the basis of religious beliefs that are not negotiable. And many supporters of choice ground their commintment on emotional and personal needs. Under these conditions dialogue between those two parties is impossible, for neither is willing to introduce modifications in position; indeed, they cannot even contemplate the possibility of a change of opinion. The exchanges between these groups under these circumstances are not dialogues, but rather statements of their respective views; and the arguments that are given in support of them have as an end merely persuasion or intimidation, not communication.

If in order to have a dialogue we must have responses and the possibility of changes of position, it becomes clear that it is impossible to have a dialogue with figures in the history of philosophy: They cannot react to what we say and they cannot possibly change their views as a result of our arguments. Therefore there is not and there cannot be genuine dialogue between the present and the past. True, historians of philosophy sometimes speak of "establishing a dialogue" with the past, but in those instances the word 'dialogue' is being used, or should have been used, metaphorically.[12] I do not mean to say that philosophers, when they study the history of philosophy, do not seriously aim to understand past philosophers. Many of them do. Nor do I reject the procedure of developing questions that one may then try to answer on the basis of what one knows of a past philosopher's position. That is, indeed, a very useful philosophical and historiographical procedure. But neither of these procedures involves a dialogue with the past, for the past cannot change. And even if we were to make the past answer us through the process indicated, we could never be sure, unless the question we asked of the past and its answer were actually recorded somewhere, that the answer we surmise is the answer that past philosophers would have given to our question. That indicates clearly that the past does not really respond to us and that neither of the two conditions required for a dialogue to take place is fulfilled in the study of the history of philosophy.

The other objection against this justification for the study of the history of philosophy is no less significant. It objects that even if philosophy is to be considered fundamentally dialectical in nature, that does not mean that it is with the past that it needs to establish a dialogue. Philosophy could be essentially dialectical and yet satisfy that nature by involving a contemporary dialogue. Of course, there may be advantages in dealing with the past, but it is not necessary that we do so.

In conclusion, the justification for the study of the history of philosophy based on its dialectical nature fails to point out how philosophy can profit from the study of its past. To say that philosophy is fundamentally dialectical in nature is not sufficient to indicate that it is helped by its history. In the end it boils down, in many ways, to the sort of pragmatic justification that we examined earlier, lacking the theoretical dimension that those justifications also failed to have.

b. Philosophy and the Dialectic. The second dialectical justification for the study of the history of philosophy takes a different road. It argues that the study of the history of philosophy is useful to philosophy because it provides the philosopher with knowledge of how philosophy works. That is, the philosopher can see in the history of philosophy how philosophy moves along certain preestablished patterns. These patterns are what supporters of this position call "the dialectic" and consist in a logic of development and progress. How this logic of development and progress is analyzed varies from author to author but the best-known example is the one proposed by Hegel. According to him, philosophy, just like everything else in history, moves in a threefold pattern beginning with a stage called *thesis*, followed by a stage that negates it, called *antithesis*, and finally reaching a final stage, called *synthesis*. The synthesis is both the end of a dialectical process and the beginning of another in which the synthesis of the old functions as a thesis of the new.

The value of the history of philosophy, according to this view, is that it reveals to us the dialectical pattern of development and progress of philosophy and brings us to a higher state of consciousness concerning what has been achieved already in the past and the inexorable process that philosophy must follow in its development. This higher consciousness helps us, of course, in our task as philosophers, preventing us from repeating the past, saving time for us, and helping us see how we need to proceed.[13]

Two problems with this justification undermine it seriously, however. The first is rather obvious: This justification relies on the view that philosophy always develops according to a preestablished dialectical pattern, and that is far from clear. Indeed, the claim that philosophy, like everything else in the universe, follows a dialectical pattern is highly speculative and relies on a complex metaphysics. To use such a speculative claim to support some other claim is methodologically unsound, for one would have to buy an entire metaphysical interpretation of the world in order to buy the justification for the study of the history of philosophy. In other words, this justification for the study of the history of philosophy is parochial to a certain philosophy and loses its attractiveness and effectiveness if used outside the parameters within which that philosophy functions. Thus, for our general purpose it is useless.

The second problem is less obvious but certainly more serious than the first. Let me formulate it in terms of a question: If both philosophy and its history move necessarily according to a preestablished dialectical pattern, then what use is the knowledge of the history of philosophy, or of the pattern that it follows, to philosophers? In other words, if philosophers proceed inexorably according to the dialectic, then knowledge of the past and that dialectic can contribute nothing to the process in which they are engaged. The determinate nature of the process precludes the possibility that philosophers may improve performance or save time. Indeed, in this context to say that the study of the history of philosophy is useful or necessary is either meaningless or incoherent. For, if philosophers engage in it, they do it because they are determined to do it; and if they do not, again they are determined not to do it. Under these conditions it makes no sense to try to answer the question of why they should study the history of philosophy. For that question presupposes that they can choose to study or not study it, whereas this position regards such a study as a predetermined fact, outside the province of our will. From the point of view of those who accept the dialectical position, it would seem impossible to provide a justification for the study of the history of philosophy. The only thing possible is to provide a description of the role that the history of philosophy plays in the development of philosophy; and providing this description, like anything else in the historical process, also is determined.

3. Philosophy as the Consciousness of Science. A third theoretical justification for the study of the history of philosophy is based on a rather unusual view concerning the relation of philosophy to science and technology. The argument points out that the understanding and management of science and technology is possible only on the basis of historical experience and that historical experience is supplied by the history of philosophy. What is rather original in this point of view is that the need for the study of the history of philosophy is not based on the historical nature of philosophy itself, as has been repeatedly argued by historicists. Nor is it supported on the basis of the cultural nature of philosophy as culturalists argue. Rather, the need for and value of the history of philosophy is supported on the basis of its relation to science and technology and their eminently historical character. It is because science and technology are historical phenomena that the history of philosophy has value, for it is the only study capable of integrating and producing an understanding of the significance of scientific and technological developments. Scientific knowledge, therefore, is not seen as absolute and universal, but as a social product bound to the cultural circumstances in which it arises. Likewise, with technology, only in the historical context where it appears and develops, and only through the consciousness of the ideas that brought it about can its significance be understood. Furthermore, only the history of philosophy can carry out that task.

There is no question that this point of view is not only original but also has some merit. It is true that science and technology do not come out of an ideological and cultural vacuum.[14] And it is also quite clear that only the philosopher and in particular the historian of philosophy can try to understand the large cultural and historical matrix within which science and technology arise. Some might want to argue, however, that this task belongs to the historian of science rather than the historian of philosophy. But proponents of this position answer that this is not so, because the history of science is too insular. Although the history of science aims to provide an account of the development of science, its restricted subject matter prevents it from providing the kind of broad cultural understanding that philosophy can supply. The significance of science and technology can be judged only by a discipline broad enough to deal with the overall ideas developed in a culture, and this is a function that only philosophy can carry out.

I am not entirely satisfied by this kind of reply, but that is the least of my worries concerning this justification. I am willing to accept, for the sake of argument, that supporters of this position can explain how the history of science cannot do for science what the history of philosophy can do for it. What bothers me is that, as the most recent defender of this position acknowledges, this view relies on the assumption that "the natural sciences and the technology based on the natural sciences, possess an irreducible historical dimension... [that is,] they cannot adequately be understood, without being viewed as unique historical events."[15] Here is where the greatest weakness of this position rests, for it is not at all clear that scientific knowledge is so irreducibly historical that its significance cannot be understood except in the context provided by the history of philosophy. Indeed, it seems to me that, although some dimensions of the significance of particular scientific and technological developments cannot be appreciated except through the context provided by philosophy and its history, there are many aspects of scientific knowledge and technology whose significance can be understood apart from the philosophico-historical context in which they arose. Note that I am not claiming that all scientific knowledge is like that; not even that most of it is like that. I am claiming only that *some* of it is like that or at least could be like that. The jury may still be out on this matter, but the mere possibility of it coming to a decision contrary to this position undermines its very strong claim. Since the philosophical community regards this issue as very controversial, it seems inappropriate to use it as the basis of support for a claim such as the one under discussion.

On the other hand, it does seem quite sensible to argue that the significance of much science and technology is completely missed if not placed in the context that the history of philosophy provides for it, thus the study of the history of philosophy has value in this respect. Moreover, since part of the philosophical task is to understand the significance of science and technology, it is clear that the study of the history of philosophy is useful not just for understanding scientific and technological developments but also philosophy. Still, this justification is more pragmatic than theoretical and, thus, leaves the study of the history of philosophy in the realm of expedience. For a more effective justification we have to turn to a position based on a cultural analysis of philosophy.

4. The Cultural Dimension of Philosophy. The fourth and what appears to me to be the most theoretically effective justification for the study of the history of philosophy argues that philosophy is closely allied to the culture in which it is produced, and, therefore, the study of the history of philosophy helps us free ourselves from conceptual provincialism, facilitating the understanding of our own ideas and their limitations. The study of the history of philosophy has a liberating effect on philosophy, helping it to pursue a more objective and balanced course.

There are two versions of this justification, which depend on the degree to which philosophy is held to be tied to the cultural conditions and circumstances within which it arises. The first, held by most philosophers who favor this approach, conceives philosophy as inextricably culturally bound. The second, which is the position I favor, is that, although closely related to culture, philosophy has some degree of independence. I call the view held by the first group the *culturalist position*. I call my own view the *modified culturalist position*.

a. The Culturalist Position. The backbone of the culturalist position is the belief that philosophy, just like everything else based on human experience, is bound by particular spatio-temporal coordinates. Being so bound implies that its truth claims about the world also are bound to particular spatio-temporal circumstances, with the result that there are no universal and absolute philosophical truths. Truth is always concrete and the product of a viewpoint, an individual perspective arising from particular circumstances and inextricably tied to them. This is so even in the case of mathematical truths, as Ortega suggested.[16]

Naturally, since philosophy is culturally bound, the study of philosophy is closely tied to the study of culture and, just as history is of the essence for the study of culture, so it is for the study of philosophy. The study of the history of philosophy, then, is essential to philosophy, according to culturalists.

An interesting result of the success of this view has been the rise of the notion of "national" philosophies, philosophies that express the national spirit and culture. Thus we find the concern in the last hundred years for "German philosophy," "French philosophy," "Italian philosophy," and so on. A particularly persistent case of this phenomenon is found in Latin America, where the search for a specifically "Latin American philosophy" has been a major preoccupation since the 1940s.[17]

Ortega's view that all truth is culturally bound and depends on a particular perspective, introduced in Latin America by many of Ortega's Spanish disciples and particularly by José Gaos, is to a great extent responsible for the popularity of the culturalist position in that part of the world. A philosophy that emphasizes the value of the particular and idiosyncratic lends itself quite easily to support the aspirations of cultures with weak philosophical traditions. Consequently, many Latin Americans adopted this view unhesitatingly, adapting it to their conceptual needs. This is how the idea of a Latin American philosophy as a philosophy peculiar to the Latin American continent came about, a philosophy different from that of other cultures, and particularly opposed to Anglo-American philosophy. This philosophy is supposedly the product of Latin American culture, which is in turn the product of the cultural perspective from which Latin Americans think. Ortega's perspectivism, then, was a strong instrument in the search for an autochthonous philosophy that can reflect unambiguously the idiosyncratic characteristics of Latin American culture.

There is much that is commendable in the culturalist position. It is obvious that philosophy always functions in the context of a given culture, receiving from it impulse and direction. Philosophy does not spring up by itself; it is the product of human reflection, which in turn always is particular, belonging to one person or another in specific situations and cultural circumstances. It is Plato and Aquinas who philosophize, and it is the circumstances in which they found themselves that prompted them to do so: for Plato, Socrates' teaching and death, among others; for Aquinas, his belief in the Christian faith and the influx of secular knowledge in the thirteenth century that threatened that faith. But the particular origin of philosophy does not entail that the content and intent of philosophical reflection are necessarily relative to this or that person, or to the conditions where that philosophical reflection is produced. This is an important point that requires more detailed discussion for two reasons: First, the culturalist justification for the study of the history of philosophy is not only one of the most popular among historiographers who defend the value of that study, but also has substantial merit; second, my own view has similarities with this position, so I must make clear exactly how my view differs from it.

Let me begin by distinguishing four basic types of propositions that will illustrate both the nature of the culturalist claim and its weakness: absolute, relative, universal, and particular.

A proposition is absolute when its truth value does not depend on factors other than those described in the proposition. Note that I am not saying that the truth of the proposition in question must be independent of all circumstances, for there are many synthetic propositions whose truth depends on particular facts even though they are absolute. An obvious case is the proposition 'Ky is sitting.' The truth of this proposition does not depend on the meaning of its terms (that is, it is not analytic), but on Ky's state. But the proposition is not relative, since its truth value does not depend on factors other than those described by the proposition. Other examples of absolute propositions are the following:

a^1. *La Traviata* is an opera in four acts.

a^{2}. Operas are divided into acts.

a^{3}. Mary married John at twenty-two.

a^{4}. Women marry at twenty-two years of age.

a^{5}. Mary is pregnant.

a^{6}. Pregnancy occurs when an egg is fertilized by a sperm.

a^{7}. The intensity of the fluorescent light over my desk is X.

a^{8}. Fluorescent lights have an intensity of X.

a^{9}. The universe is infinite.

a^{10}. No universe can be infinite.

Regardless of the actual truth value of these propositions, their truth value is independent of any perspective or point of view associated with the proponent of the proposition. Whether or not this or any other universe is infinite, or whether or not Mary is pregnant, for example, does not depend on anything other than the universe, Mary, and the circumstances in which they find themselves; and not on the circumstances or the perspective of observers external to the situation.

In the case of relative propositions, on the contrary, truth value depends on circumstances related to an observer, that is, the truth of those propositions depends not only on factors described by the propositions but also factors external to them. The proposition 'Ky is sitting to the left of Tim' is a relative proposition, because its truth depends on the relative position of the observer who proposes the proposition with respect to Ky and Tim. The observer may be in such a position that Ky may appear to be behind, in front of, or to the right of Tim rather than to his left. Other examples of relative propositions are the following:

r^{1}. The acts in *La Traviata* are too long.

r^{2}. The acts in operas are too long.

r^{3}. Mary's decision to marry John at twenty-two was a mistake.

r^{4}. Marriage at twenty-two for women is a mistake.

r^{5}. Mary's decision to have an abortion was a mistake.

r^{6}. Abortion is a crime.

r^{7}. The fluorescent light over my desk is too bright.

r^8. Fluorescent lights are too bright.

r^9. This universe is large.

r^{10}. No universe is small.

In all these cases, the truth value of the propositions depends in part on something other than what the propositions describe. What this something other is varies from case to case. It can be a scale of some sort that determines whether universes are large or small. Or it can be a principle that stipulates something about the natures of crime and abortion. In the earlier case of the proposition that described Ky's position with respect to Tim, it had to do with the location of the observer who proposed the proposition. In all cases, it is clear that a perspective or principle is at work that operates from outside what the propositions describe but plays a role in determining their truth value.

Absolute and relative propositions in turn may be universal or particular. A universal proposition is one whose subject refers indistinctly to all the members of a class. A particular proposition is one whose subject refers distinctly to one or more individuals. All the even numbered propositions in the preceding lists are universal; the odd numbered propositions are particular. Thus, for example, a^4 ('Women marry at twenty-two years of age') is universal, but a^3 ('Mary married John at twenty-two') is particular. And this goes also for a^1, where 'La Traviata' refers to an individual opera, and a^9, where 'The universe' refers to one individual universe and not to all universes.

The combinations of these four different classes of propositions yield four different types of propositions: absolute-particular, absolute-universal, relative-particular, and relative-universal. The examples that were given earlier, then, can be broken down into the following categories:

Absolute-particular

a^1. *La Traviata* is an opera in four acts.

a^3. Mary married John at twenty-two.

a^5. Mary is pregnant.

a^7. The intensity of the fluorescent light over my desk is X.

a^9. The universe is infinite.

Absolute-universal

a^2. Operas are divided into acts.

a^4. Women marry at twenty-two years of age.

a^6. Pregnancy occurs when an egg is fertilized by a sperm.

a^8. Fluorescent lights have an intensity of X.

a^{10}. No universe can be infinite.

Relative-particular

r^1. The acts in *La Traviata* are too long.

r^3. Mary's decision to marry John at twenty-two was a mistake.

r^5. Mary's decision to have an abortion was a mistake.

r^7. The fluorescent light over my desk is too bright.

r^9. This universe is too large.

Relative-universal

r^2. The acts in operas are too long.

r^4. Marriage at twenty-two for women is a mistake.

r^6. Abortion is a crime.

r^8. Fluorescent lights are too bright.

r^{10}. No universe is small.

Now let us turn to philosophical propositions and see if they fit the categories of propositions that we have examined. There seems to be no difficulty in finding examples of philosophical propositions that are both absolute and universal. Take for example, the following two:

Every cause has an effect.
$\sim(P \cdot \sim P)$

In either of these two cases it is obvious that the subjects of the propositions, whatever they may be, do not refer distinctly to one or more individuals, but rather indistinctly to any member of a class. Moreover, the truth value of the propositions does not depend on anything external to the propositions. Both of these propositions could be interpreted as analytic, and indeed analytic propositions make good examples of absolute-universal propositions. But it is not necessary that all absolute-universal propositions be analytic. For example, the proposition "All physical entities are composed of matter and form" is not analytic, since the truth of the proposition does not depend exclusively on the meaning of its terms, but it is both absolute and universal according to the criteria we have established.

There is no real difficulty either in finding examples of propositions that are relative and universal. Take, for example, the following two:

> Killing is wrong.
> Abortion is wrong.

In each of these cases the universal character of the propositions is clear; neither one of them refers to a particular act to the exclusion of other acts. Moreover, they are both relative because in either case the judgments that they contain are based on circumstances external to the propositions and that have to do with the persons who propose them. For example, if the first proposition is considered from a perspective where the preservation of life is taken to be more valuable than anything else, then killing will be interpreted as wrong. But if the situation is considered from a perspective that adopts a principle according to which happiness for the greatest number is identified as the highest good, then killing will not necessarily be interpreted as wrong, since in certain circumstances the termination of life can produce more happiness for the greatest number than its prolongation. This is so, for example, in the case of a terminally ill, very old patient who is suffering great pain and whose treatments are producing financial chaos for his family. A similar argument could show that the second proposition given as an example, 'Abortion is wrong,' falls easily into the relative-universal category.

I should add at this point that the classification of propositions such as 'Killing is wrong' as relative does not necessarily entail ethical relativism. In the first place, the point I am making is not about ethics, but about logic. Second, I have not claimed that *all* ethical propositions are relative. And, third, even if all ethical propositions were relative, that would not entail that all perspectives on which they depend are equally justifiable.

Examples of the category I have named absolute-particular are more difficult to come by, but nonetheless can be found. Consider the following two:

> God is omnipotent.
> The universe is finite.

Both of these propositions easily meet the absolute and particular criteria. I am not concerned with whether they are meaningful or not, of course. My only concern is with finding propositions that philosophers generally deal with that illustrate the categories I have proposed, and it seems to me that these propositions do so. Both have individuals as subjects and their truth value is independent of anything but what the propositions purport to describe. The first is true if, indeed, God is omnipotent and the second is true if the universe is finite.

Finally, we reach the last and probably more controversial category: relative-particular. I propose the following two examples:

> Socrates's sentence to death was unjust.
> Picasso's *Guernica* is not a great work of art.

I imagine that there are very few philosophers alive today who would disagree with the first proposition and who would not disagree with the second.[18] Posterity has ruled on the side of Socrates and the great artistic value of Picasso's *Guernica* is generally acknowledged. But that is really neither here nor there. The important point for us is that both of these propositions are particular and relative. They are particular because they are concerned with Socrates's sentence to death and Picasso's *Guernica;* they are relative because they both make value judgments that depend on criteria external to the propositions.

From all this we may conclude that philosophy includes all four types of propositions, and this means that those who adopt the culturalist position are mistaken. They are mistaken in that, in their zeal to understand philosophy as relative to culture and dependent for its truth value on particular circumstances, they end up maintaining the extreme position that *all* philosophy, that is, every philosophical proposition, is relative and particular. But, as we have seen, the truth value of some philosophical propositions does not depend on particular circumstances; that is, not all philosophical propositions are particular. A great number, perhaps the majority, of philosophical propositions are universal; most philosophical conclusions are universal or aim to be so and, therefore, transcend particular circumstances.

At this point it is pertinent to refer back to a distinction introduced in Chapter Two, between intensional and extensional historicity. For culturalists, like historicists, seem to confuse them. Extensional historicity is the type of historicity that applies to events and entities in the world, including the statements we make and the thoughts we think. Intensional historicity, by contrast, is the type of historicity that applies to the content of our thought and the meaning of the statements we make. Now, I claimed in Chapter Two that historicists confuse these two types of historicities, arguing that all philosophy is history of philosophy because all our thoughts are historical, but they are wrong, because the historicity that applies to our thoughts is only extensional. And, although all our thoughts are extensionally historical, since they occur at a particular time and in a particular context, the content of many of those thoughts need not be historical even though many of them may be so. Thus, for example, although the thought I have when I write "2 + 2 = 4" is historical, the content of that thought, namely that 2 + 2 = 4, is not historical. On the other hand, both the thought I have and the content of the thought are historical when I think that I was in Paris two weeks ago.

The distinction between intensional and extensional historicity can be used to understand the mistake of the culturalist position. For culturalists confuse the extensional characteristics of our thought, which are always historical and therefore particular and relative, with the intensional characteristics of our thought, which need not always be historical and therefore particular and relative.

Culturalists could still claim, however, that all that has been said here is irrelevant to their position, for it is all based on an analysis of the surface grammar of propositions whereas the culturalist position is based on a deeper understanding of language. Thus, even though on the surface certain propositions appear to be universal or absolute, in reality they all contain a cultural bias, because they are composed of linguistic terms whose meaning is culturally determined. Even terms like 'pregnant' and 'fluorescent light' are products of a culture and, therefore, depend on a cultural perspective for their meaning.

In response to this retort I would like to bring up the following points. The first is that what I have tried to do in the discussion concerning various types of propositions is to point out that there are certain irreducible intentional ways of talking about the world and that among those there are some that are not perspectival. When we say that Mary is pregnant or that fluorescent light is characterized by such and such intensity, we do not mean to say something the truth of which is to be judged only according to a certain point of view. We mean to state something that is the case *regardless* of anyone's point of view. Indeed, either Mary is pregnant or not, and we need only wait a few months to see whether our claim about her pregnancy is true or false; her pregnancy is not a matter of perspective.

The problem with the culturalist position in its extreme and pure form is that it distorts the intentionality of our claims, making them all perspectival regardless of their intent. In many ways the perspectival program is very much like the ideal language program of the logical positivists. They both want to translate ordinary language into a language of their own creation, which has metaphysical and logical properties and implications different from those of ordinary language. The difference between the two is not in their programs, but in the type of language they identify as ideal. For the logical positivists it is the language of symbols purged from traditional metaphysical connotations; for culturalists it is a language in which all propositions turn out to be relative and particular. The one thing that can be said in favor of the logical positivists is that they tried to put their program into effect, a reason why the shortcomings of their position became obvious even to them. Culturalists, on the other hand, usually content themselves with making theoretical claims and have never systematically tried to develop the language that their view would seem to imply they should develop. Perhaps because of this, their claims are still taken seriously in some quarters, for they have remained sufficiently abstract to mask their implications and deficiencies.

But this is not all that I want to say against the culturalist claim. I would like to add also that experience militates against it, for if the culturalist position were true, translations from one language into another and transcultural communication would be impossible. And yet, they are not. It is true that both procedures involve enormous difficulties, but it is also true that they are carried out effectively. Such successes, even if partial, point to the fact that, although the signs we use to communicate have a cultural origin and many of the concepts they are meant to communicate do so as well, some concepts transcend cultural parameters. We may find cultures in which Mary's pregnancy is referred to as a swelling, for example. But we can be sure that the swelling in question is distinguishable from the swelling of a finger and carries with it the expectation of the birth of a child at some later time.

I touched on the basis for transcultural communication in Chapter One and thus it is not necessary to repeat what was already stated there. What is important for us is to make clear that the culturalist claim as stated is unacceptable.

The failure of culturalism does not mean, however, that the extreme opposite to *culturalism,* which I call *universalism,* is free from severe shortcomings. In fact, by taking the completely opposite approach to culturalism and holding that *all* philosophical propositions are absolute and universal, universalism also falls into an intolerable extreme. Its main mistake consists precisely in refusing to accept that philosophy originates from particular conditions and that, therefore, every philosophical generalization is based on one or several particular situations.[19] The description of the situations on the basis of which a generalization emerges is as legitimately a part of philosophy as the general conclusions harbored by the discipline. This is why we find in philosophy not only universal and absolute propositions, but also particular and relative ones, which in many cases provide the foundation for universal or absolute propositions. It is in the nature of scientific pursuits, whether philosophical or not, to proceed in this fashion, for science and philosophy are human endeavors, and we humans are historical individuals bound by historical circumstances. Of course, this does not mean that we cannot transcend historical circumstances. Indeed, we do it the moment we formulate universal principles and laws. But it must be remembered that philosophy also includes the sort of relative and particular propositions we have examined earlier.[20]

In rejecting the culturalist position we do not have to reject all that culturalists hold and adopt the universalism just described. We can recognize that there are aspects of culturalism that are correct, for the view that philosophy is closely allied to culture is a useful one as long as it is not taken to mean that philosophy is so culturally dependent that every conclusion it reaches is culturally bound, thus lacking universal value. The culturalist position's view that all philosophical propositions are culturally bound, revealing the cultural perspective in which they arise, is an extreme point of view that is difficult to justify and easily assailed. Fortunately, we do not have to adhere to an extreme version of the culturalist position to justify the study of the history of philosophy, for that defense requires only that we hold the much weaker claim that philosophy is closely related to culture. The view of which that claim is the backbone I call the *modified culturalist position.*

b. The Modified Culturalist Position. The claim that philosophy is closely related to culture can be easily defended, independently of the stronger claim that philosophy is necessarily culturally bound, in two ways. First, the types of propositions that compose philosophy clearly tie the discipline to a spatio-temporal and cultural location. The strong relative and particular components of philosophy cannot be ignored. Philosophy begins with the particular and the relative. Nor is its ultimate aim solely, even if it is its primary aim, the universal and the absolute, as universalists claim. Philosophers also seek to apply the universal and absolute principles they discover or formulate to the particular reality in which they live. Philosophical reflection often is prompted by particular problems arising out of the situation philosophers experience, it moves from them to the formulation of universal and absolute principles and truths distant in many ways from that situation, but frequently it returns to the original concerns that gave rise to it in the first place. For example, the sudden death of a dear person may prompt reflections about death in general that are later applied to the particular case. The types of proposition that we find in philosophy, then, show clearly the close relations of the discipline to culture.

Second, we may illustrate the close relation of philosophy to culture by referring to the dependence of philosophy on language. Without language, without linguistic signs of one sort or another, the task of philosophizing would seem impossible. Perhaps it could be argued that thought is possible without language and, if that is the case, then philosophical inquiry may still be possible, for philosophy would not be dependent on language for its existence. I am not sure that this claim is supportable but, even if we were to hold that, indeed, philosophy can be carried out mentally without language, the absence of a language would prevent any kind of communication among philosophers, at least in a world of the sort in which we live. Philosophy without language would become a solitary task available only to the single person. We may conclude, then, that philosophy *does* depend on language, at least to the extent that philosophers communicate their ideas to others *through* language. Now, if the means of philosophical communication is language and language, as I believe everyone would accept, is a cultural expression, it cannot but be concluded that philosophy must be closely related to culture. Through language ideas are communicated and preserved once a means for codifying that language in writing has been devised, so that the bases of culture and civilization, that is, the conceptual schemes through which society interprets, evaluates, and manages its surroundings, are preserved.

Linguistic signs, put down and codified, have meaning and significance only insofar as there is a community of individuals that understands the concepts for which the signs stand, and insofar as that community takes what principles and rules the signs reveal into consideration in its behavior. But communities change, their members are in a constant state of evolution, whereas their codified signs remain and are passed down to future generations that have to appropriate them by understanding their meaning and applying them to their own circumstances. Language is a historical phenomenon, for the linguistic signs we use today have a history and so do the concepts for which they stand.

The overall view of the world developed by each culture, and by each generation within a given culture, is colored by the language it learns to use and by the heavy cultural baggage that language carries. The human mind may be a *tabula rasa* at birth, but immediately after birth it begins to acquire a series of principles, concepts, ideas, and directives with the help of language.

Having illustrated the close relation of philosophy to culture, it should be easy to see why the study of the history of philosophy is so useful to philosophy. In the first place, the study of the history of philosophy brings us face to face with the origin of the basic terms and concepts that compose our intellectual framework. Moreover, the history of philosophy uncovers how they have evolved and changed over the years, reaching their present state. In short, the study of the history of philosophy is an invaluable tool in the understanding of our ideas.

But that, as already mentioned, is not the only function the study of the history of philosophy has. Perhaps as important as it, this study liberates us from the shackles of cultural provincialism. By revealing to us the way philosophers thought in the past and how they came to do so, it makes us aware of the limitations of our intellectual cultural heritage. The study of the history of philosophy uncovers for us hidden assumptions and presuppositions at work within our culture, which could not become evident except through the comparison of our ideas with the thought of different periods and cultures. It forces us to rethink our ideas, deepening our understanding of them and bringing to the fore their shortcomings. As Skinner has pointed out, "the indispensible value of studying the history of ideas" is that it makes us realize "what is necessary and what is the product merely of our own contingent arrangements."[21]

The justification and value of the study of the history of philosophy, then, rests primarily on the cultural dimensions of the philosophical enterprise, which are revealed in the relative and particular character of some philosophical propositions and in the cultural nature of language. Of course, the pragmatic justifications given earlier also underline the value of the study of the history of philosophy. There is no question that the study of the history of philosophy can serve as a practicum for the art of reasoning, as a source of philosophical information and truth, and may help us see areas where we may have gone wrong. And we must accept too that the history of philosophy can serve as inspiration to philosophers as well as add persuasive support to philosophical arguments and views. Although philosophy consists in the search for truth rather than in edification or persuasion, edification and persuasion are not necessarily in conflict with philosophy and, as pointed out earlier, at times may serve the discipline. But it is ultimately in the need to transcend cultural provincialism and to understand the terms that we use in discourse that we find the indisputable grounds of the importance of the history of philosophy for philosophy.

But we may ask, does not the modified culturalist justification for the study of the history of philosophy in fact boil down to a pragmatic justification? For to say that the study of the history of philosophy helps philosophy in its task by helping to liberate it from cultural provincialism seems to be the same sort of justification used, for example, by those who argue that in the history of philosophy one finds a large repository and variety of arguments that help philosophers practice their skills? On the surface the answer to this question would seem to be affirmative. Indeed, as long as we argue that the history of philosophy is *of use,* it would seem that we are dealing with a pragmatic justification of its study. However, there are important differences between the pragmatic and theoretical justifications, which separate as well the modified culturalist justification from the pragmatic ones. Of these differences the fundamental one is that pragmatic justifications are based on a matter of convenience. The history of philosophy is a rich and therefore useful and convenient source of arguments, information, and truth for philosophers. But that is as far as the pragmatic justification goes. There is no particular reason, apart from the richness of the source and its convenient availability, why philosophers should turn to the history of philosophy. On the other hand, the theoretical justification goes beyond these pragmatic considerations and argues that the very nature of philosophy and its practice justify the special use that the study of the history of philosophy has for philosophy. In particular, the modified culturalist justification argues that the close association between philosophy and culture, exemplified among other things by philosophy's use of language, make the study of the history of philosophy particularly valuable for philosophers. Not, of course, that that study is necessary for philosophy. That issue was settled already in the previous chapter in two ways: first, by showing that there is no relation of methodological necessity between philosophy and the history of philosophy; and, second, by distinguishing between the extensional historicity and intensional nonhistoricity of philosophy. Still, the history of philosophy is especially useful for philosophers because of the very character of the discipline.

But even if one accepts the distinction between pragmatic justifications and the modified culturalist justification, questions remain. These are related to some of the arguments used to undermine the power of the pragmatic justifications given earlier. For it seems that some of those arguments also can apply to the modified culturalist justification.

Two arguments in particular seem pertinent. The first indicates that the careful attention that historians pay to the views and arguments of historical figures hardly seems warranted by the needs of the philosopher who turns to history only for pragmatic reasons.

Could not something similar apply as well to the modified culturalist justification? That is, could one not argue that there is no apparent reason why the modified culturalist should turn to the study of the history of philosophy with the zeal that historians so often exemplify?

The answer to this objection is that, although for pragmatists historical details may constitute obstacles to their task, modified culturalists would argue that the study of historical details is essential to theirs. Indeed, if they study the history of philosophy in order to transcend their own cultural provincialism, that study must be as detailed, objective, and complete as possible. It would involve the faithful reconstruction of the past in order to compare it with the present, and the establishment of the historical links between that past and the present. Modified culturalists, therefore, on the basis of the reasons that they give for the study of the history of philosophy, need to adopt and apply the most stringent historiographical procedures, for the usefulness that the history of philosophy has for them lies precisely in their ability to get that history right.

But, then, one might want to retort—and this is the second argument used to undermine the pragmatic justification for the study of the history of philosophy—that the temporal constraints to which philosophers are subjected would prevent them from carrying out the task that would be required for the modified culturalist justification to work. In the first place, those constraints would affect the choice of materials: Which periods, authors, and materials should the philosopher study? Second, the work of historians is so demanding and covers so much material that the philosopher runs the risk of being swallowed by historical work, thus abandoning philosophy.

But again, the answer to this objection is not difficult. For I do not claim that the philosopher should become a historian of philosophy. That is the point of view of some historicists and was rejected in Chapter Two. My point is rather that the study of the history of philosophy is especially useful for philosophers. That means that it is not necessary for philosophers to become engulfed in the history of philosophy. They profit from its study, and that study must be as objective, rigorous, and complete as possible in order to provide the kind of materials that would help philosophers in their philosophical task. But the study of the history of philosophy is not the aim of philosophers. Their primary interests are in philosophy, not its history, and they turn to that history only to the degree that it is useful to their task as philosophers. This means, of course, that they must choose what to study and those choices must be made on the basis of philosophical needs. The history of philosophy is vast, but philosophers are justified in turning only to certain parts of it, since their aim is not the complete reconstruction of the philosophical past, but the advancement of philosophy.

But how should philosophers do history of philosophy, then? And how should historians do history of philosophy? I argued in Chapter One that the history of philosophy must be done philosophically, so that even historians cannot but do the history of philosophy philosophically. And I have argued in this chapter that the study of the history of philosophy is especially useful to philosophy. What I need to clarify still is whether there are methodological differences between the history of philosophy done with a historical aim and the history of philosophy done for philosophical reasons. Moreover, I must show how a philosophical history of philosophy incorporates evaluation and interpretation without endangering the objectivity required of history. I intend to make these matters clear by discussing the methodology of the history of philosophy. But before I turn to that issue in Chapter Five, I believe we must discuss a fundamental task of the historian of philosophy: the interpretation of philosophical texts. This is the subject of the next chapter.

NOTES

1. For texts that illustrate these reasons, see the references to Descartes, Kant, and the logical positivists given in the previous two chapters and the Introduction. A more recent instance is found in Michael Scriven's belief that the history requirements in the philosophy curriculum are a barrier to philosophical development. See "Increasing Philosophy Enrollments and Appointments through Better Philosophy Teaching," *Proceedings and Addresses of the American Philosophical Association* 50, no. 3 (1977), 233. Allan Wood, in "Russell's Philosophy," in Bertrand Russell, *My Philosophical Development* (New York: Simon and Schuster, 1959), p. 274, says: "[Russell's] lack of systematic philosophical education was an advantage, and nothing can do more to stultify original thinking than a thorough knowledge of past philosophers acquired too early in life."

2. Jonathan Rée, "History, Philosophy, and Interpretation: Some Reactions to Jonathan Bennett's *Study of Spinoza's 'Ethics'*," in Hare, *Doing Philosophy Historically*, p. 44.

3. For example, Thomas Aquinas, *Summa theologiae* I, 1, 8.

4. A variation on this justification is John Yolton's point that the study of the history of philosophy produces the skill of understanding others through the practice it encourages on how to read texts. See "Is There a History of Philosophy? Some Difficulties and Suggestions," *Synthese* 67 (1986), 20.

5. John Corcoran, "Future Research on Ancient Theories of Communication and Reasoning," in John Corcoran, ed., *Ancient Logic and Its Modern Interpretations* (Dordrecht and Boston: D. Reidel, 1974), p. 187. Edwin Curley defends this point of view by indicating that the history of philosophy sharpens our perceptions of issues, the range of possible positions, and the advantages and disadvantages of each position, in "Dialogues with the Dead," *Synthese* 67 (1986): 33–49, particularly 38.

6. The didactic justification for the study of history is one of the most frequently found in the literature. See, for example, Voltaire's "Conseils à un journaliste," in M. Beuchot, ed., *Ouvres de Voltaire*, vol. 37, pp. 362–367.

7. Descartes, *A Discourse on Method*, p. 6. (This text is followed by a statement which reemphasizes Descartes's general antihistorical attitude, however.) John Stuart Mill makes a similar point, noting that a "necessary part of the philosophical character is a thoughtful regard for previous thinkers, and for the collective mind of the human race." Indeed, the philosopher needs to strengthen "the weak rule of his own intellect" by paying attention to "modes of thought most opposite to his own. It is there that he will find the experiences denied to himself; the remainder of the truth of which he sees but half." *Dissertations and Discussions* (New York: Henry Holt, 1882), pp. 376, 377 and 379. See also Paul G. Kuntz, "The Dialectic of Historicism and Anti-Historicism," where he discusses the import of Mill's texts, on pp. 663–665.

8. Daniel Garber, "Does History Have a Future?" p. 36. The same point was expressed earlier by C. S. Lewis, "On the Reading of Old Books," in *First and Second Things: Essays on Theology and Ethics*, ed. Walter Hooper (Glasgow: Collins, 1985), pp. 27–28.

9. This idea was popularized by the biologist Ernst Haeckel in his controversial work, *The Riddle of the Universe*, trans. Joseph MacCabe (New York: Harper & Brothers, 1900). Haeckel's exact formulation (p. 81) is as follows: "*Ontogenesis is a brief and rapid recapitulation of phylogenesis*, determined by the physiological functions of heredity (generation) and adaptation (maintenance)."

10. There are many different understandings of the idea that ontogeny recapitulates phylogeny, particularly when applied to knowledge. For example, in a recent discussion of mathematical instruction, Edwin E. Moise interprets this principle as "the notion that things have to be taught in the order in which they were discovered." See the panel discussion on "New Directions in College Mathematics," in Robert W. Ritchie, ed., *New Directions in Mathematics* (Englewood Cliffs, N.J.: Prentice-Hall, 1964), p. 51. Imre Lakatos points out that both H. Poincaré and G. Pólya applied Haeckel's "fundamental biogenetic law" to mental development and particularly mathematical mental development. See Lakatos's *Proofs and Refutations: The Logic of Mathematical Discovery*, ed. J. Warrall and E. Zahar (Cambridge: University Press, 1976), p. 4, n. 2. For Poincaré, see *Science et Méthode* (Paris: Flammarion, 1908). For Pólya, see "The Teaching of Mathematics and the Biogenetic Law," in I. J. Good, ed., *The Scientist Speculates* (London: Heinemann, 1962), pp. 352–356.

11. An interesting variant of this position has been recently defended by Henry Veatch in *Swimming against the Current*, pp. 1–12. His view is that what he calls "the Aristotelian dialectic" is preliminary to philosophical investigation (p. 4). Its function is to clear away the aporias that are the point of departure of philosophy, making room for the disclosure of truth (p. 11). Naturally, clearing up those aporias requires understanding the opinions from which they result and thus in turn requires a study of the history of philosophy (p. 7).

12. For recent examples of this way of speaking, see Dominick LaCapra, "Rethinking Intellectual History and Reading Texts," in Dominick LaCapra and Steven Kaplan, eds., *Modern European Intellectual History: Reappraisals and New Perspectives* (Ithaca, N.Y., and London: Cornell University Press, 1982), pp. 49 ff.; Edwin Curley's "Dialogues with the Dead" cited earlier; and A. Peperzak, "On the Unity of Systematic Philosophy and History of Philosophy," in T. Z. Lavine and V. Tejera, eds., *History and Anti-History in Philosophy* (Dordrecht: Kluwer Academic Publications, 1989), p. 27. This point also applies to the word 'conversation.' Some philosophers speak of having a "conversation" with the past, with past philosophers, or even with a text. See, for example, Michael L. Morgan, "The Goals and Methods of the History of Philosophy," *Review of Metaphysics* 40 (1987), 721; W. H. Williams, "Comment on John Yolton's 'Is There a History of Philosophy? Some Difficulties and Suggestions,'" *Synthese* 67 (1986): 26; and V. Tejera, "Introduction: On the Nature of Philosophic Historiography," in the volume edited by him and Lavine.

13. Lawrence H. Powers has added an original and intriguing wrinkle to this view in his recent "On Philosophy and Its History," *Philosophical Studies* 50 (1986): 1–38, particularly 1–13. According to him, philosophy needs the history of philosophy because "philosophical positions need to be adequate accounts of the history of arguments" that support or undermine those positions. Thus the philosopher, *qua* philosopher, needs to turn to the past.

14. Cf. Thomas S. Kuhn, *The Structure of Scientific Revolutions*, 2d enlarged edition (Chicago: University of Chicago Press, 1970).

15. Lorenz Krüger, "Why Do We Study the History of Philosophy?" in Rorty et al., eds., *Philosophy in History*, p. 78. Among other defenders of this position is Friedrich Engels, *Dialectics of Nature* (New York: International Publishers, 1940), Introduction.

16. José Ortega y Gasset, *El hombre y la gente*, ch. 3, in *Obras completas*, vol. 7 (Madrid: Revista de Occidente, 1964), p. 115.

17. Iván Jaksić and I gathered the most influential texts in the historical development of this position in *Filosofía e identidad cultural en América Latina* (Caracas: Monte Avila, 1987).

18 I. F. Stone has recently tried to build a case for the prosecution in *The Trial of Socrates* (Boston: Little, Brown & Co., 1988).

19. That sciences include both universal and singular propositions was made clear by Nagel in *The Structure of Science*, pp. 547–551.

20. I perhaps should make clear in passing that the inclusion of particular propositions in philosophy does not militate against the point made in Chapter One to the effect that philosophical propositions cannot contradict propositions that are part of the history of philosophy, because the first are not concerned with time, provenance and individuals, whereas the second are. The reason is that, even though philosophy includes particular propositions of the sort mentioned and thus is concerned with individuals in some respects, it is not concerned with time or provenance. It should be remembered that the aim of philosophy is the formulation of universal propositions rather than particular ones, whereas the aim of history is just the reverse.

21. Quentin Skinner, "Meaning and Understanding in the History of Ideas," *History and Theory* 8, no. 1 (1969): 3–53.

Chapter Four

Texts and Their Interpretation

If, as I argued in Chapter One, the history of philosophy studies ideas from the past, then historians of philosophy face a serious problem concerning their object of study for two reasons. In the first place, because we can never have direct empirical access to the past unless that past is close to us and we have taken part in it. In order to know the past in which we have not participated we must rely on the testimony of those who had direct access to it and who have left records of what they witnessed. In the second place, the problem arises because ideas are not things, events, or facts for which we can have direct empirical evidence, even if we are contemporaneous with them. The most we can have is a kind of indirect empirical evidence. We do not perceive ideas, what we perceive are certain phenomena that suggest to us certain ideas. If I ask you, for example, "Do you approve of what the president did?" and you frown in return, I conclude that you do not. But it is altogether possible that you in fact do approve of the president's action, although you wish me to think that you do not and thus mislead me by making the frown. My conclusion, that you do not, then, can be taken only as an interpretation of what you are thinking based on certain empirical evidence that is related only indirectly to what you think. Therefore the study of the history of philosophy is very difficult, more difficult than the study of the type of history that relies on events for which there can be direct empirical evidence at the time when they happened; for not only cannot historians of philosophy from the present have direct access to the past, but even if they had it they would not have direct access to the ideas that are supposed to be the object of their study.

The study of the philosophical past, then, like the reconstruction of what I think on the basis of what I say, involves an interpretation and the bases of that interpretation are texts. But at least two other factors also play important roles in the interpretation of texts, namely, their authors and audiences. Hence, in order to provide an understanding of the nature of texts and their interpretation, we need to discuss the author, the audience, and their relations to texts and their interpretation. Accordingly, this chapter is divided into four parts, dealing respectively with the text, the author, the audience, and the interpretation of texts. Its overall purpose is to provide an understanding of what an interpretation is, its object and aims, as well as of the complex set of difficulties that historians of philosophy encounter when they try to produce interpretations of texts and thus do history of philosophy.

I. THE TEXT

A text is a group of signs selected, arranged, and intended by an author in a certain context to convey some specific meaning to an audience. The specific meaning of the text depends on three factors: (1) the particular meaning and function of the signs of which the text is composed, (2) the arrangement of those signs, and (3) the context of the text.[1] I say *meaning and function* of the particular signs because there are signs that do not have independent meaning but rather acquire meaning only in conjunction with other signs that they modify. In such cases their function as modifiers consists of altering the meaning of other signs. Take, for example, syncategorematic signs like the indefinite and definite articles. Neither 'a' nor 'the' has independent meaning, but they do change the meaning of the term 'man' when used in conjunction with that term. 'Man,' 'a man,' and 'the man' mean quite different things.[2]

A more subtle, although still rather obvious, point that I wish to stress is that the meaning of a text does not depend only on the independent meaning and function of the signs of which it is composed, whether they have independent meaning or not, but depends also on the particular arrangement of those signs. For example, if I say "Only men are allowed in this club," it is clear that what is meant is that all those allowed in this club must be men and, thus, women are excluded. But if I change the place of 'only' in the proposition and say "Men are allowed only in this club," what is meant is that men are allowed in no place other than in this club, leaving open the possibility that women also may be allowed in it.

An equally important point is that the meaning of texts depends as well on their context. For example, when a mother says to her dear child "If you touch that, I will kill you," it is clear that she is using a metaphor to mean that some minor punishment will be given to the child if he disobeys her. But when a bank guard says to a thief he caught *in flagranti* and who is reaching for a gun "If you touch that, I will kill you," he means exactly what he says. The context, then, is extremely important in the determination of the meaning of texts.

These examples serve to illustrate that the meaning of a text depends on the independent meaning and function of the signs of which it is composed, on the particular way in which those signs are arranged, and on its context. They also underline the fact that a text should not be confused with its meaning. The meaning of a text is what we are supposed to understand when we understand the text. We do speak of "understanding a text," but what we mean by that is that we have understood what the text means, what it expresses. The status and nature of what we understand when we understand a text is a matter of seemingly endless controversy among philosophers and one that I can hardly be expected to settle in passing, so I shall stay away from it here. However, whatever the ultimate status and nature of that may be, for historians of philosophy what we understand when we understand a text must be conceived as philosophical ideas, as pointed out in Chapter One, for it is philosophical ideas that they seek to understand and for which they wish to provide an account.

Now let me go back to the signs that compose a text and say that they may be classified in various ways. They may be written, spoken, or mental; conventional or natural; linguistic or nonlinguistic; and universal or individual, giving rise to correspondingly different types of texts. I discuss each of these characterizations next.

A. Written, Spoken, and Mental Texts

Texts may be physical, that is written or spoken, or mental. Consider the following examples:

1. 2 + 2 = 4
2. 2 + 2 = 4
3. Two and two make four.
4. Two plus two add up to four.
5. Dos y dos son cuatro.

In 1–5 we have five token texts, four type texts, and one single meaning. By *token* and *type* I mean the standard understanding of these terms. Terms and expressions function as tokens, for example, if they cannot be placed both before and after the copula in an identity sentence such as 'A is A.' And terms and expressions function as types in turn when they do not meet that condition and thus can be placed both before and after the copula in an identity sentence. Accordingly, texts 1–5 are not the same token text. Indeed, every time I write a text, even if it is like other texts, I have a different token text. Tokens occur only once. On the other hand, 1 and 2 are token texts of the same type text, that is, they are similar, which makes for four type texts in the group, since none of the others belongs to the same type: there are differences in the English texts 3 and 4, and text 5 is in Spanish. As far as the meaning of these texts is concerned, however, all texts from 1–5 are identical.

Just as there can be token and type written texts like the ones we have seen, so can there be token and type spoken texts. In this case, instead of the written marks on a piece of paper or other writing material there would be certain sounds uttered by a speaker. So, for example, when I say text 1 aloud, I have uttered a token spoken text, and the same happens when I say aloud text 2, or for that matter any text from 1–5. But the sounds I make when I say texts 1 and 2 or when I repeat texts 1 or 2, are similar instances of a type of sound, which in fact is the sound counterpart of the type written text of which 1 and 2 are tokens.

The case of the mental text is more difficult to grasp, but should not be significantly different from the cases of written and spoken texts. The mental text is not composed of written marks on some writing surface or sounds uttered through the vocal organs of a person, but of certain thoughts or images present in a mind. The token mental text is a mental phenomenon, an image or thought that someone, say, a psychologist interested in the nature of mental phenomena, investigates or thinks about while carrying on certain investigations. Moreover, when mental phenomena that are the counterparts of token written or spoken texts are similar, they are instances of a type of mental phenomenon of which token mental texts are also instances, namely, the type mental text.

The question that arises at this point is whether there can be a distinction between token and type mental texts on the one hand and the ideas subjects think when they understand the texts. It arises because it seems difficult to distinguish between a mental text and the ideas that it conveys if those ideas are also mental. The question is important because if there is no difference between mental texts and ideas, then a text can be only written or spoken. I believe, however, that the distinction to which I referred earlier between a text and its meaning can help us understand also the distinction between mental texts and ideas.

A text, whether written, spoken, or mental, is a group of signs used to convey a certain meaning. The meaning of the text is what the text tells us, what it makes us, or is supposed to make us, think about. The text is a group of marks on a page, or a group of sounds uttered, or a group of mental constructs that function as signs that express its meaning. As such the text and its meaning are not the same, even when the text too is a mental and not a physical phenomenon. What the philosophical text means are certain ideas that are distinct from the text. Now, that there is a mental text distinct from its meaning, that is, the ideas that it is supposed to convey, should be clear from the fact that we can think of the mental text as a separate entity from the ideas it conveys. This was illustrated earlier when I introduced the distinction between mental and physical texts, but perhaps another example will clarify this matter further.

Take token written text 1. That token written text consists of the marks that actually are made on the paper; it is the actual picture that is given there, composed of ink marks drawn and arranged in a certain way. But the meaning of that text is something that is neither material nor composed of marks made by ink on that particular page. Indeed, the meaning of token texts 1–5 is one and the same. Moreover, the type text is a type text not because it has the same meaning as texts 1–5, otherwise there would be only one type text for all those token texts, something that we saw is not the case. A text is a type text because it is the sort of composition of which token texts are instances. In 1–5 there are only four type texts, as already noted.

Now the same can be said about token mental texts and their meaning. For example, let us suppose that a token mental text is an image of token written text 1. We can think of that token mental text without thinking about what it means. For when we think about it, we could be thinking about certain marks or signs, and not about what the text expresses. I am not arguing that all token mental texts or type mental texts are images of written token and type texts. They certainly could be images of sound type and token texts, for example. Indeed, they may not even be images at all. But this is a question that does not directly concern us here and, therefore, will not be addressed. The pertinent point I wish to make is that, first, there is a mental text that is different from the physical text (whether written or spoken) and, second, the mental text is distinct from the meaning of the mental text, just as the written and spoken texts are different from the meaning of those texts. The meaning of a philosophical text, as stated, consists of the ideas that the text helps us understand, so that it may turn out that the meaning of mental, spoken, or written texts, whether token or type, is the same, even if the texts are not of the same type.

B. Conventional and Natural Texts

Having established that texts can be written, spoken, or mental, we need to determine whether they are conventional or natural. In order to do this we must establish, first, whether the signs of which texts are composed are natural or conventional and, second, whether the arrangement of those signs into a text is itself natural or conventional. Whether the signs of which texts are composed are classified as conventional or natural depends very much on what one means by *conventional* and *natural*. If by *natural* one means something that occurs in nature without human input and design as it were, and by *conventional* one means something that has been specifically made by human beings, that is a result of human art, then it is clear that a text could be composed of either conventional or natural objects. For, although many signs may be entirely due to human fabrication, it is perfectly possible to use natural objects as signs. For example, a text could be composed of a pile of rocks used to mark a turn on a road travelers must make. In this case the text is composed of natural objects. Likewise, a certain natural arrangement of pebbles found on the beach could be used as a text. In this case each pebble would be assigned a certain meaning that, when combined with the meanings of the other pebbles that are part of the arrangement in a certain context, would yield an overall meaning resulting both from the meaning of the individual pebbles and from their arrangement in that context.[3] It is not necessary for a text to be composed of signs or pictures entirely created or designed and arranged by human beings.

On the other hand, if 'natural' and 'conventional' refer to the particular connection between the thing to be used as a sign and the meaning for which it is supposed to stand, then it is clear that all texts are composed of conventional signs. For no thing, whether made by humans or not, is in fact necessarily connected to a particular meaning. The connection to meaning is a result of human design, intention, or activity and can be subject to change according to that design, intention, or activity.

There are philosophers who have held a different point of view, however, maintaining that there are indeed natural signs in the sense that they have a necessary connection to a particular meaning. Perhaps the best known supporter and one of the earliest defenders of this view is Augustine, who saw the whole natural world as a sign of supernatural reality. According to this position, which was widely accepted in the Middle Ages, everything is both what it is itself and also a sign of something else, a higher and deeper truth.[4]

This position is neither contradictory nor incoherent, but it relies on certain views that cannot be supported on the basis of reason unaided by faith, and, thus, it is perfectly possible to hold the contrary view. But if that is so, then the view is weakened, since there can be no necessary connection, as the position claims there is, between signs and their meaning.

Supporters of this point of view might want to reply to this objection, however, that the supernatural or religious dimension of their position is not necessary and thus the view does not need to rely on faith; a purely natural interpretation of it can be given.[5] Take, for example, the case of a leaf falling off a maple tree. Is that not a natural sign of the coming of autumn. And is not thunder a natural sign of an impending storm?

Although the expression 'natural sign' frequently is used in ordinary discourse to refer to cases such as these, even in such cases I would like to argue we have a conventional connection between the sign and its meaning. The falling of a maple leaf is a sign of autumn and thunder is a sign of an impending storm because we have established a connection between them on the basis of certain observations and, therefore, use the phenomena in question to indicate something of interest to us. A different culture, for example, might see the falling of a maple leaf or thunder as signs of other events or even as indications of the divine will to punish and reward them. That there is a causal or any other kind of natural connection between natural phenomena does not entail that the phenomena in question are necessarily related as sign and meaning. That connection is made only by convention based on human agency.

The same reasoning that we have applied to the signs that compose texts with respect to their conventional or natural character also may be applied to the arrangement of those signs and, therefore, need not be repeated. Let it suffice to point out that the arrangement, even in cases where it naturally occurs, is connected to a meaning only as a result of human ingenuity and design. In short, even when texts are composed of natural objects and found in a natural arrangement, the connection of a text to a certain meaning is the result of human activity, making texts conventional in that sense.

Finally, the importance of the context in determining the meaning of texts further emphasizes their conventional nature. For, indeed, it is the context, determined by human attention, that can make texts of natural objects.

C. Linguistic and Nonlinguistic Texts

This brings me to another point, already brought up indirectly in what has been said, namely, that texts are not necessarily composed of signs belonging to natural languages. A text could very well be composed of pictures that depict natural objects, as indeed some early texts were. Moreover, the meaning of the signs of which a text is composed could be established by stipulation even if the signs are taken from a natural language, as when I say that from now on I shall use the term 'cow' to refer to sheep even though all English speakers use it to refer to cows. What is inevitable, however, is the linguistic character of texts, for signs are linguistic phenomena insofar as they have meaning and serve to communicate. Texts should not be confused with language, however; there are significant distinctions between the two that may be made evident through the following considerations.

Texts are composed of linguistic elements, but languages are not composed of texts. A language consists of (1) a set of terms with specific meanings and functions and (2) a set of rules governing the mutual relations among those terms as well as the arrangements into which those terms may be placed. Texts also are composed of terms, which I have called *signs*, but unlike languages texts do not contain rules, although knowledge of the rules according to which they have been put together may be necessary in order to understand them. A language, therefore, is much more than the texts that have been written, spoken, or thought in that language. A text is a product that humans put together, whereas language is an instrument that humans use to produce texts. As a result, a text has a unique and rigid structure that is given and cannot be altered without altering the text. Language, on the other hand, is flexible and is meant to be used in different arrangements. Although there are general rules to which language has to adhere and that govern the arrangements of the terms of which it is composed, language is a flexible instrument that can be changed according to the purposes of the moment. Consequently, even though languages have relatively limited numbers of terms and rules, they can be combined in a virtually infinite number of ways to create texts. Texts, by contrast, have a kind of resistance to alteration that is not characteristic of language and which, I believe, is the result in part of their peculiar ontological status. Let me say a couple of things about the ontological status of texts before we proceed.

D. Universal and Individual Texts

What I mean by the *ontological status* of texts is whether they are individual or universal. As noted elsewhere, I regard something as individual if and only if it is a noninstantiable instance of an instantiable, whereas I regard universals as capable of instantiation, that is, as instantiables.[6] "Peter," for example, is individual because he is a noninstantiable instance, whereas "human being" is a universal because it can be instantiated, indeed it is instantiated in Peter. The same could be said about "this white color" (a noninstantiable instance) and "the color white" (an instantiable). The question that we have to address concerning the ontological status of texts is whether they are noninstantiable instances or are capable of instantiation. If the first, then they are to be regarded as individual; if the second, then they are universal.

The issue of the ontological status of texts is raised because on the surface it is not clear whether texts are individual or universal. Unlike the examples of universal and individual given earlier, texts share some of the characteristics associated with individuals and some of the characteristics associated with universals. On the one hand, texts are historical entities, just like Peter or this white color, and thus would appear to be individual. And yet, on the other hand, they seem to be capable of multiple instantiation; indeed, there appear to be all sorts of instances of the same texts as the existence of multiple copies of a book indicates. In the sense that they appear on the surface to be both individual and universal, texts are very much like works of art. For works of art seem to be individual and at the same time subject not just to instantiation but even to multiple instantiation.[7] The original of Picasso's *Guernica*, for example, is in El Prado, but there are reproductions of it in various places, including one in my office where I keep a postcard that I tacked onto the bulletin board. Insofar as some of these reproductions are completely indistinguishable from the original, could we not say that they are instances of that original and, therefore, that Picasso's *Guernica* is instantiable and consequently universal? And yet the original of *Guernica* is a historical artifact that exists only in one place at a time and has other marks normally associated with individuals.

The case with texts is even more puzzling, because the original printing of a text and subsequent printings of it for all intents and purposes are indistinguishable.[8] And not only that, but the whole notion of the value of the original that so concerns the art world is totally immaterial in the case of a text, whose value is in what it says rather than in the material composition through which it accomplishes that task or the historical originality of the material composition. Of course, collectors value old editions, but such value involves other factors in addition to the nature of the text, such as the rarity of the copy in question. Under these circumstances we may go back to the original question and ask, again, Is the text universal or individual?

The answer to this question becomes clear if we keep in mind the distinctions, first, between the text and its meaning to which I have already referred and, second, between written, spoken, and mental texts. Let me begin by repeating what was noted earlier; namely, that there is no reason why different signs cannot have the same meaning or why the same sign cannot have different meanings. Indeed, synonyms clearly indicate that different signs can have the same meaning and equivocation shows that the same sign can have different meanings. This is not only possible but commonplace. Therefore, we could in principle accept that, although we may have written, spoken, and mental texts, their meanings need not be different; nor do we have to conclude that they need to be the same for that matter. But even if they have the same meaning, that should not entail that the meaning of those texts is the universal of which the texts are instances. The situation in fact is quite different.

First of all, we have a distintion between three different *types* of texts: the written, spoken, and mental. But within those types we have many, indeed a potentially infinite, number of individual texts, as many as the market would bear to have printed in the case of written texts, as many readings of the texts as audiences may demand in the case of spoken texts, and as many mental texts as persons who actually think about them. Those written, spoken, and mental texts are all individual insofar as they are not instantiable themselves. In the case of the written texts, for example, they could be burned or mangled or whatever. In the case of the spoken texts, they could be left unfinished or spoken in a peculiar way, for example. And in the case of mental texts, they could be in different minds and subject to different temporal coordinates. As individual instances, moreover, they presuppose corresponding universals, but the universal is not the same for the three types of texts. For the written text it would be a written type of universal even though the universal would not be something written anywhere. For the spoken texts there would be a spoken type of universal, which similarly would not be spoken anywhere. And the same could be said about the mental universal corresponding to the mental instances of it. In no case, however, is the meaning of the texts their universal, since the meaning of all the texts can be one and the same and the texts belong to three different natural kinds—the auditory, the visual, and the mental—and therefore constitute three different types.

Texts can be both universal and individual, then, depending on the text involved. The universal text is that of which the physical (written or spoken) or mental texts are noninstantiable instances. The universal, however, is not the meaning or ideas that the various individual texts are supposed to convey, but rather an actual type of the physical or mental individuals in question. This can be easily illustrated with texts 1–5 to which I referred before. The universal of those texts is not the meaning of the texts or the ideas that they are supposed to convey, namely, that two and two make four, for then there would be only one type for all the texts. But, as we saw earlier, in texts 1–5 we have four different types of texts, two consisting of mathematical symbols, two in English, and one in Spanish. And the same could be said for the corresponding spoken or mental texts. There is, therefore, no single universal of the written, spoken, or mental texts considered as such, even though they may have the same meaning.

In short, if we are referring to token texts such as texts 1–5 discussed earlier and their spoken and mental counterparts, texts are individual. But if we are referring to type texts or their spoken and mental counterparts, then they are universal.

E. The Historian's Text

Having proposed a characterization of texts, we may now ask which text is the immediate object of study of historians of philosophy. The answer is that historians of philosophy are not interested in token texts, whether written, spoken, or mental, and therefore in individual texts, although it is individual texts to which they have access and on which they work directly. The individual text is of concern to archeologists, paleographers, and others interested in the cultural and historical significance of individual artifacts. The concern of historians is with the type text, namely, the universal text, although their interest in it is not in the text as a type of written, spoken, or mental material, but as a set of signs that conveys a certain meaning that originated in a certain author at a certain particular time. It is in the meaning that historians of philosophy are interested. And that goes as well for the individual text that the author produced. Insofar as it is individual, historians of philosophy have little concern with it; they are concerned only with a universal and only as a vehicle of ideas, although the historical origin of those ideas is of the essence to their task, otherwise they would not be acting as historians of philosophy, but only as philosophers.

But this answer is not completely satisfactory, even if on the surface it might look adequate. The reason is that it assumes, among other things, that there is one and only one universal text and that the text reveals the mind of the author. If these assumptions were correct, the task of historians would boil down to the study of the ideas of an author, his work as it were, by examining the instances of the universal text he or she produced. The individual text, as representative of its type, therefore, should be the center of the historians' investigations and reveal to them the mind of the author.

The reality of the situation, however, is that there is no such thing as "the text." There may be at least four different texts that, because of their number and their varying degrees of accessibility, complicate the task of historians enormously, for each of them in principle could not only be an instance of a different universal text, but also yield a different set of ideas. The texts I have in mind are the following: the text historians have, the text the author wrote, the text the author intended to write, and the text the author should have written. I call them respectively, the contemporary text, the historical text, the intended text, and the ideal text.

1. The Contemporary Text. By the *contemporary text,* I mean the text available to historians when they set out to study the history of philosophy, although I do not mean by it any translation of it; I mean the text as historians have it in the original language. One of the interesting things about the contemporary text is that in many cases historians usually do not have one but several texts. This is particularly so when they are dealing with texts that originate from periods of history that preceded the invention of the printing press, although it is even the case in some texts produced subsequent to that event.

The reason that historians may have several texts usually is that there may be several textual traditions of the same work, going back to some original source, perhaps the autograph, that may have been lost, and various editions based on those different traditions produced at different times. For example, there are today several editions of Thomas Aquinas's *Summa theologiae,* such as the Piana (1570), the Leonine (1888–1903), and the Ottawa (1941). The differences among these and other available editions of the same work result from the fact that there is no autograph of the work and there are more than 200 extant manuscripts of the complete text (except for the Supplement, of which there are only 42) and another 235 fragments of various parts of it.[9] The task of the editor with a text of this sort, found in this state, is to produce a stemma or family tree of manuscripts and reconstruct the best possible text on that basis.

The notion of "the best possible text," however, raises some serious questions that need to be answered. For the best possible text is not necessarily the one written by the author nor the one that had the greatest historical impact. A critical edition that reconstructs the best possible text might be a patchwork that never existed and has no historical relevance. Thus the historical value of many nineteenth century critical editions of medieval and classical texts that were put together with the methodological goal of producing the best text possible is quite limited. Many subsequent editors, in order to avoid this kind of problem, have produced editions that center on a good and historically important text, a so-called copy text, making on it as few corrections as possible and adding variants with other manuscripts for the benefit of historians and interpreters.[10] Nonetheless, the idea that the best possible text is a composite of all the texts and textual traditions available is alive and well.

From the historiographical point of view what is important to note is that even the contemporary text is not a single text. What historians have, rather, is a family of texts that are related in various ways and may be more or less historically accurate and more or less historically relevant, although their degree of accuracy is not necessarily and directly proportional to their historical relevance.[11]

2. The Historical Text. The *historical text* is the text that the historical author actually wrote or dictated.[12] I do not mean by this the actual marks the author may have made on a particular piece of paper or parchment or the actual sounds that he or she emitted in dictating the work to a scribe who was putting it down. What I mean is the type of mark that the author or the scribe wrote down or the type of sound that was emitted and changed into marks by a scribe. If we were to understand the historical text as the individual marks and sounds that make up the autograph or the first copy of the text produced, then there would be only one such text in existence; indeed, no reproduction of it, carried out by a xerox machine for example, could be called the historical text. What I have in mind, then, is what I earlier called the *type* or *universal text* rather than the token or individual text, the type of the token text produced by the author or a secretary. There are cases in which we do have autographs from authors; but I would call the autograph as well as any accurate transcription of it instances of the historical text.

Note also that I have referred only to written or spoken texts. The reason is that, although mental texts are as historical as written or spoken ones, the historian has no access to them except through written or spoken texts (the single exception to this occurs when the historian is also the author—in which case the source is memory). So, for all intents and purposes, the historical text is the written or spoken type text.

Obviously, from what has been said concerning the contemporary text, it is clear that, particularly when historians are dealing with texts written before the invention of the printing press, the historical text seldom is the same as the contemporary text. There are exceptions, of course. If there is an autograph or an accurate copy of it, it would appear that historians do have the historical text. Moreover, if historians know that they have a text that was corrected by the author shortly after it was composed, even if not originally written by the author, they also can say that they have the historical text. The procedure whereby an author revised notes originally taken by a student was common in the Middle Ages, for example. The revised notes were called *ordinatio* and the unrevised notes were called *reportatio*. In some cases works became known by those names perhaps in order to stress the degree of their historical fidelity. This happened to Duns Scotus's *Opus oxoniense*, which came to be known as the *Ordinatio* and to another version of his *Commentary to Peter Lombard's "Sentences"*, which came to be called *Reportata parisiensia*.

In many cases, however, the situation is not so simple, indicating that there may be no single historical text but actually several. A case in point occurs with some of Thomas Aquinas's works. In some instances he wrote an autograph of the work, but then had the text copied by a secretary and made changes on the copy rather than on the autograph. Indeed, there is evidence that points to subsequent changes made at various times during his life. In such a situation there is no single historical text of a particular work. What we have are several texts corresponding to the various times at which the author made alterations.

3. The Intended Text. The *intended text* is a still different text from the contemporary text and from the historical text. As its name suggests, it is supposed to be the text the author intended to write but did not write. The notion of an intended text distinct from a historical text arises when one begins to consider the unintended mistakes authors make while producing a text: authors may say or write something they may not intend, they may use words that are not exactly the ones they want because they cannot think of better ones at the time, they may omit words or phrases by mistake, they may get confused with the punctuation, and so on. There are many mechanical ways in which authors can get sidetracked and produce texts that are different from what they intend to produce. More important still, there are always matters that have to do with the difference between what authors want to say or write and the means they have at their disposal to say or write it. Once they have used a certain expression, the expression becomes part of the text, but authors sometimes would have preferred saying what they said differently, although at the time of composing the text the expression they were looking for did not occur to them. This is particularly evident when they use ambiguous expressions, for then if one asks them later, "Did you mean P or Q, when you said R?" the author sometimes will answer P, sometimes Q, and only occasionally R. Only when the author answers R may we surmise that the ambiguity is intended, although even then we never can be absolutely sure that the author was aware of it at the time of the text's composition.

As further substantiation for the notion of an intended text and its distinction from the historical text, historiographers point to the fact that authors frequently correct the text after it has been composed. As in the case of Thomas used earlier, they go back and change things around, sometimes altering the meaning significantly. This is taken to signify that texts do not accurately reflect what authors intended at the time of composing them, although again one never can be sure whether authors intended something different from what they wrote or said in the first place, or simply changed their minds about it later on.

All this sounds quite reasonable, but one can also argue that there is no such thing as the intended text, for the simple reason that authors never have clear and complete texts in their minds prior to the moment in which they actually produce them. At most they may have more or less vague ideas of what they want to do, perhaps a mental outline of how the text should be structured, but the actual text is produced only at the moment of writing, speaking, or thinking it.

The process whereby an author composes a text could be conceived as that of the artist who wishes to produce a sculpture. He has a general idea of what he wants to do; say, to produce a composition commemorating a certain victory in battle. He also has an idea of the number of persons he wants in the sculpture, whether he wants them clothed or nude, and a general sense of the pose they should adopt. Moreover, he has decided he will use marble as his material and that the figures should be life-size. But this is all quite vague. If we were to ask him to describe to us the sculpture, he would give us only generalities. On the basis of those generalities we could, perhaps years later, pick out among many sculptures some among which could be the one he finally made, but we could never be sure which was the one he made if we were presented with somewhat similar sculptures. The reason is that the sculptor's description is too general and does not identify those features of the sculpture that set it apart from others. Now, the reason that his description is too general is that he does not have a complete and detailed idea of what the sculpture will look like when he finishes it, even if he has tentative sketches of what he wishes to produce. And he does not and cannot because the particular sculpture that the sculptor produces is not the result of his idea alone, but also involves the materials with which he works as well as the creative process itself that produces it. Let me explain.

Once the sculptor has an idea about what he wants to do, he proceeds to see what piece of marble he can get. He has a budget, so his choices are not unlimited. Moreover, when he gets to the quarry to look for an appropriate piece of marble he finds that only five or six pieces are available, all in slightly different colors, shapes, and sizes. He wanted white marble, but most marble has veins of one sort or another, and now he has to decide whether to choose the one with gray, green, or pink veins. If he chooses the grey or the green he is restricted by the size and shape of those pieces, whereas if he chooses the pink he will have more freedom in the composition because of the size of the block. But he decides to go with the gray anyway—he cannot see how a serious and sobering subject like war, even in victory, can be rendered in anything but grays and whites. Once the artist has the marble, he needs the models, so he goes out to a modeling agency and asks to look at the pictures of the models they have that he could use. He does not really know with exactitude what he is looking for except that he needs six men. When he sees a face or a body, he sometimes discards the photograph immediately, sometimes he looks at it for a while and discards it all the same, but at other times he saves it. After a while he has accummulated a group of twenty-odd possible models that he thinks he could use based on the pictures he has seen. Then he proceeds to interview the models in person and, after examining them, he settles for the six he thinks he needs. Eventually he gathers all six in his studio and makes them stand in the pose he envisioned, but he finds that the arrangement does not work. In the first place there seem to be too many figures, and in the second place some of them are wrong for the composition. Their bodies looked appropriate when considered separately but together they do not go well. One is too tall and another too short, for example; then there are the faces. In particular he needs one face to express a certain emotion and none of the faces of the models selected expresses it well. Discouraged, the artist dismisses two of the models and asks the others to come back at some later date. He is tormented and worried about the face he needs, in particular because he cannot picture it in detail. But he gets lucky. His daughter brings home a new boyfriend that night, and he realizes that the boyfriend has the face he needs. Because the young man is eager to ingratiate himself with the family, he consents to pose for the sculptor and our artist has his group. But he again has doubts about the pose, and so on. Indeed, the process of rethinking and rearranging does not end until the work is finished. Each decision closes certain alternatives, but also opens areas where further decisions are required.

I could go on describing the creative process but I do not believe it is necessary. The point I wished to illustrate is that a work of art is the result of much more than an idea: It is the effect of many factors. There in fact is no intended work as such, only a more or less vague idea that slowly takes shape and is modified and transformed into an actual work of art through a complex process. For the artist of our example there were compromises concerning color and size; there were choices about composition, models, and poses; and all these were determined in part by circumstances beyond the control of the artist. He did choose, but his choice was restricted and molded by the actual circumstances within which he had to make the choice.

This conclusion applies also to a text. There is no text before the author sets out to produce and actually produces one. The author at first has a vague idea of what he wants to do, but only when he sets out to produce the text, whether in his mind, on a piece of paper, or on a tape recorder, does the text begin to take shape. For then he is forced to make compromises similar to those the artist has to make. True, the materials with which the author and the artist work are different. Artists work with such things as marble, paint, models, and they try to convey a certain plastic form whereas authors work with pencils, papers, computers, and language, and they try to convey a certain meaning. All the same, the materials the author uses, including language, are not significantly different from the materials at the disposal of artists. For even language is composed of elements that are very much like the marble, its color, and the faces, the bodies, and the expressions of the models used by the sculptor. It is composed of elements some of which have meaning, as a face contorted in a certain way may suggest sadness. Other elements have meaning only in the context in which they are found, just as the marble acquires significance only when it is shaped in a particular form.

Many factors, then, influence authors while they compose texts, playing a causal role in various aspects of the composition. The text, just as a work of art, is not caused by the author alone. The author is only one of the causes that produces it. As Aristotle would say, the author is merely the efficient cause of the text and in addition to the efficient cause other causes also play key roles in bringing about the effect.

It makes very little sense to talk, then, about the texts that authors "intend" to produce rather than the ones they actually produce. There really are no such intended texts that predate the production of historical texts. There are cases, of course, in which one might want to argue that there were plans for a work to be completed that was left incomplete because of the death of the author or some such eventuality. But this does not go against the conclusion reached for two reasons. The first is that when there are outlines, notes, and plans, the production of the text has already begun. Indeed, one may want to argue, although I am not prepared to do that here without further reflection, that notes, plans, and outlines are early versions of a text. The second is that, until the work is actually produced, extant outlines and notes as to how the work is to be completed are mere guidelines that the author feels free to modify or even discard as the work progresses. Thus even when a work has been interrupted for some reason, it would be difficult to argue convincingly that there is an actually particular work intended. The work of art, just like the text, is what gets produced, the rest is only more or less vague speculation.[13]

Many examples of both texts and works of art could be cited to illustrate this point. A very dramatic instance is the plans that Gaudi left for Barcelona's Sagrada Familia, a church that has been under construction for about a century. Gaudi left many sketches and prescriptions concerning the way the building was to take shape, and he even completed some parts of it before his death. But the architects that have been struggling with the building since Gaudi's death have found that they must make endless numbers of decisions about what to do as the process of construction goes on, many of which had not and perhaps could not have been anticipated by Gaudi.

The distinction between the intended text and the historical text arises, like much of what has to do with hermeneutics, from various assumptions. The first has to do with scriptural exegesis, which is guided by the principle that there is a divine being who reveals his perfect views through an imperfect medium. Thus, although the text that the divinity intends to reveal is inerrant and perfect in every way, the actually revealed text may be mistaken because of human instrumental agency. This idea is applied to nondivinely revealed texts with the consequence that it is assumed that an author, just like God, had an intended text in mind before the text was produced.

The second assumption behind the view of the intended text is that the ideas authors intend to communicate are texts, even though they may not be linguistic. Thus a set of ideas that an author may have in mind to express are considered to be the intended text that gets translated into a linguistic text either in his mind or outside of it. The nonlinguistic set of ideas is what the author intends to translate into a linguistic text, although the ideas might get mangled in the process of translation.

Third, it is also believed that the cause must explicitly and actually precontain everything that is present in the effect. Thus, the author, in order to act as a cause of a text, must have a completely actual text he intends to produce before he sets out to produce the historical text.

The third assumption becomes particularly strong when it is coupled with the fourth, which I already have disputed, that the author is the sole cause of a text. If there is only one cause, and the cause must precontain actually everything present in the effect, it is obvious that the author, who is the sole cause of the text, must have an actual text he intends to produce before he produces the historical one.

But these four assumptions are quite misguided. Let me take them one by one. Concerning the first, let us assume that God did reveal the Scriptures and had a text in mind that the scriptural writers took down as well as they could, although they made occasional mistakes. Even if that were the case, it would tell us nothing about how a human author proceeds and certainly does not entail that authors have an intended text in mind of the sort we have discussed before they actually produce a historical text. It is true that some authors (e.g., Russell), like some artists (e.g., Mozart), seem to have a completed text in their minds before they put it down in writing, for example. But this is a misleading counterexample. For in such cases what they have in their minds is a mental text that has already been produced and consigned to memory. They do not have to go through the process of correction, and so on, that other authors go through with their written or oral drafts because they wait until the mental text is completed before setting it into writing. In cases like that of Russell, this is often the result of habits acquired through exposure to an educational system where one is not supposed to write or say anything that is not in good form. But none of this supports the claim that authors have an intended text before they actually produce one either mentally, orally, or through writing.

The second assumption rests on one or two confusions. The first is the confusion between an author's intentions and a text. That an author has the intention to convey certain ideas when he sets down to construct a text seems indisputable.[14] But this does not entail that the author has a text in mind that he intends to convey, for the intentions of the author need not be texts. Indeed, the mental phenomena that correspond to an author's intentions do not have the characteristics associated with a text. For example, the intention to pursue a course of action is not the mental image of the text 'to pursue a course of action.' The second confusion blurs the distinction between an author's ideas and a text. That authors have some ideas they intend to convey when they set out to produce a text is not very controversial. But this does not mean that those ideas constitute a text. For example, the idea of "two" is not a mental image of the Arabic number '2' or of any other of the signs used to convey it. As pointed out earlier, a text should not be confused with its meaning, that is, with the ideas it proposes. And it is those ideas that are intended and that the historical text may or may not effectively convey, even though the author certainly intended the text to convey them.

The status of the third assumption is again controversial and we cannot be expected to settle its validity here. What we can do, however, is to point out that, since the author is not the single cause of the text, as the fourth assumption claims, even if we were to accept that a cause must actually precontain whatever is in the effect, it does not follow that the author has to precontain it. Whatever is in the completed historical text must be actually precontained in the total set of causes of the effect and not in the author alone. Therefore, the conclusion that the author must have a complete and actual text that he intends to produce before he produces the historical text is gratuitous.

Let me finish, then, by repeating that the distinction between the intended text and the historical text is unwarranted. The most that could be accepted is, first, a distinction between the historical text and a certain vague and fragmentary set of ideas that the author has prior to the production of the historical text, and, second, a distinction between a historical text as produced and the historical text purged of any mechanical or clerical mistakes that may have crept into it during the process of production. The distinction between the latter two is in fact the distinction between a text that has been carefully composed or corrected and one that has not, and should not serve as basis for arguing in favor of the puzzling notion of an intended text.

4. The Ideal Text. The *ideal text* is the text the author should have written, not the text the historian has, the text the author actually wrote, or the presumed text the author intended to write. It may be considered ideal for two reasons: First, because it has never actually existed. It is a mere construction, speculatively posited by someone other than the author. Second, because it is supposed to be a perfect model of the more or less bad copy that the historical author produced. The second meaning of *ideal*, then, is Platonic.

The ideal text is posited by a philosopher or someone interested in a text who looks at it as an imperfect textual formulation of a certain view or argument. The notion of an ideal text in this sense is based on the position that an author's textual formulations of his or her views always are more or less imperfect copies of some perfect textual formulation of those views. Thus when we adopt a philosophical position about justice, say, we express it textually in a way that is necessarily imperfect and inadequate, although there is a perfect and adequate way of expressing it. Note, moreover, that there is an important difference here with orthodox Platonism. For orthodox Platonism there are ideas only of what is absolutely perfect and true whereas the notion of an ideal text implies that there can be perfect textual formulations of even false and, therefore, imperfect views. Thus, although utilitarianism is false and therefore imperfect in some sense for that reason, there is an ideal and perfect textual formulation of the position of which Mill's formulation fell short.

The ideal text, considering both that it has never existed and those who posit it accept it as such, functions in fact as a kind of regulative notion used to understand, interpret, and evaluate a historical text. It serves to underline where authors may have gone wrong and where they might have not, by comparing what they did with what they should have done. It also serves to construe what authors may have wanted to say but failed to say adequately. The notion of an ideal text relies on the assumption that authors are trying to reach perfect formulations of the views they were trying to describe in their texts.[15] The ideal text as such is a useful hermeneutical and historiographical tool, although its use can lead to abuses.

The main challenge to those who try to reconstruct an ideal text as understood here is to raise the question as to what extent they can legitimately depart from the historical text in their speculative fancy. For, if the modifications introduced in the historical text are too drastic, there is the danger that the ideal text may no longer be the perfect textual formulation of an imperfect view of which the historical text is an imperfect copy, but simply the perfect textual formulation of a perfect view of which the historical text should be the copy. This brings me to an important question concerning the criteria to be used for the selection of the components of the ideal text and for the modification of the historical text in accordance with it: Should the criteria include personal, cultural, or just philosophical principles? The ideal text would look very different indeed, depending on the type of criteria used, and it is by no means obvious at the outset that one set of criteria should be used rather than another.

There is some point in arguing that the ideal text should be determined by taking into consideration personal and cultural elements, for example. After all, a text is always produced by a certain individual person in a certain cultural milieu and itself is a cultural product. So it would seem appropriate that cultural considerations enter into its determination. An ideal text from such and such a time and such and such a place should reflect that time and place. On the other hand, some will argue no doubt that personal and cultural considerations have nothing to do with the production of an ideal text. Because the aim of philosophers is philosophical, the criteria to be used to construct the ideal text, and modify the historical text accordingly, should be strictly philosophical.

But what does 'philosophical' mean in this context? Does it mean "logical"? If that is the case, then the job involved in the production of an ideal text consists in going through the historical text, straightening out any logical mistakes that might have crept into the ideas it is supposed to convey. It would also involve discarding all the *non sequiturs* and putting in all the conclusions that were carelessly left out, but are logical conclusions and implications of the premises and asumptions of the views described in the text.

But 'philosophical' may mean more than "logical." It may mean not only cleaning up the logic and making explicit enthymematic premises and conclusions, but also clarifying the formulations that are found in the text but remain obscure. This procedure might involve substituting or expanding certain definitions in order to clarify various notions and views and so on. Or 'philosophical' may be interpreted also as involving the addition of arguments that are more cogent than the ones provided in the text and even the correction of certain views expressed by the text on the basis of our own experience and knowledge.

When we go beyond logic and include in the task of constructing the ideal text such procedures as clarification, supplementation, substitution, and correction, I believe we are well beyond the task of constructing the perfect textual formulation of the more or less perfect views that the historical text tried to express. We are in fact trying to construct the ideal text of which *all* texts, dealing with the specific subject matter with which a particular historical text deals, are copies. In this sense we are not looking for the best textual formulations of imperfect views, but rather for the text that best expresses truth. In short, we have reverted to orthodox Platonism.

From all this it should be clear that, as in the other cases of texts discussed, the ideal text turns out to be more than one. It can be the personally and culturally accurate text, it can be the logically correct text, it can be the clear and complete text, and finally, it can be the text that expresses the truth. There are at least four different ideal texts, then, depending on the criteria applied, although in each case one and only one text is best supposed to fulfill the criteria in question.

Note also that the ideal text should not be confused with the meaning of the historical or any of the other texts we have discussed.

Texts and meanings, as pointed out earlier, are not the same. The meaning of the historical text is a set of ideas, and the meaning of the ideal text is also a set of ideas. Now, the assumption behind the notion of an ideal text is that the ideas meant by the historical text are just more or less imperfect copies of the ideas meant by the ideal text. But even as imperfect copies, if one were to accept this assumption, they cannot be considered to be the same as the ideas meant by the ideal text. The meanings of the historical text and the ideal text *are not,* therefore, the same, even if that of the first *should be* the same as that of the second.

II. THE AUTHOR

If there is a text there is an author, for the author is the creator of the text. But because there is more than one text, then there cannot be just one author.[16] Indeed, if we look closely at the various texts just discussed, we can see the correlative problem of identifying and characterizing the various authors that give rise to those texts.[17] I would like to distinguish four different authors: the historical author, the pseudo-historical author, the composite author, and the interpretative author. These four authors, as we shall see, do not correspond exactly to the four texts discussed earlier.

A. The Historical Author

The *historical author* is the person who produced the historical text. This person in fact may turn out to be several persons, since it is not unusual to have several individuals cooperate in the composition of a text. This procedure is quite frequent in science, but it is also followed in some literary works. The case of the voluntary cooperation of several persons in the production of a text should be kept separate from cases where a text is subjected to modifications by persons other than the original author without the knowledge and consent of that author. In these cases those who modify the original text are also "historical authors," but they are not the authors of the original historical text, only of modified original historical texts. For the consideration of such cases, then, it is useful to introduce a distinction between "the original historical text" and "derivative historical texts." The author of the former in turn could be called *the historical author* and the authors of the latter *subsequent historical authors.*

Although the historical author may turn out to be a group of persons rather than a single person, he (I shall refer to him in the masculine singular to avoid confusion) is not to be confused with the composite author that will be discussed shortly—he is only one of the authors or group of authors that make up the composite author. The historical author is not only the author of the historical text, but also of the presumed text that he intended to produce but never did. Note that this author existed—he was an actual person who lived at a certain time in history. However, although he actually lived, we do not know him exactly as he was for various reasons.

First of all, there is much of him that we do not know, a fact that gives rise to historical controversy. Take Aristotle, for example: Do we know how he felt about Alexander? Do we know whether he preferred to eat lamb or fish? What clothes did he wear on the day he fled Athens to prevent the city from sinning against philosophy twice? And so on. Moreover, what we know about him has been filtered through much speculation and lore. It is also colored by the ideas we have about his thought. He may appear to us more commonsensical and approachable than Plato, but was he really that way? Isn't our perception of him and his character shaped in a way by an interpretational tradition that began even during his lifetime? I do not mean to suggest that we do not know anything about Aristotle or that all we know about him is a matter of conjecture. Least of all am I suggesting that such conclusions apply to all authors. What I am suggesting is that the author of the "historical text" is a real historical figure, but that our knowledge of that historical figure is at best an approximation to what the author in fact was. The composite figure that we know or think we know is what I call the *pseudo-historical author*. The historical author is presented to us only in the persona of the pseudo-historical author.

B. The Pseudo-Historical Author

The *pseudo-historical author*, unlike the historical author, never existed. As I just stated, he is a composite of what we know or think we know about a historical author. Many historiographers would rather refer to the pseudo-historical author as the historical author, for they want to restrict the meaning of history to an account of events and eliminate the notion of history as the events of which an account may be given. But that, as indicated elsewhere in this book, seems to be a contradictory position that only confuses the issue. If we maintain the distinction between history as a series of events and history as the account the historian provides of those events, then we can speak of the historical author as the figure who is part of history in the first sense and of the pseudo-historical author as the figure who is part of history in the second sense. The pseudo-historical author, then, is the author we think wrote the historical text. We know him from the descriptions that his contemporaries and other historians have left us as well as from the clues we find about him in the text he is supposed to have composed. It is altogether possible that the historical author fits all or most of the descriptions that make up the pseudo-historical author, although something always would be left out—say, the exact color of his liver at the moment he wrote the word *saraballae* in his treatise *De Magistro*. But it is also possible that the historical author does not fit most or even any of the descriptions we have of him except for the attribution to him of the authorship of the text in question. Indeed, even that may be questionable.

A good example of the sort of case that raises the issues to which I have been referring is that of the notorious Pseudo-Dionysius. *Pseudo-Dionysius* is the name historians have given to the author of a group of four important treatises written in the early part of the Middle Ages: *On the Divine Names, On Mystical Theology, On the Celestial Hierarchy,* and *On the Earthly Hierarchy*. Throughout the Middle Ages he was identified with Dionysius, whom St. Paul is supposed to have converted to Christianity in Athens according to *Acts* 13:34. Indeed, it was not until the Renaissance that the identity of Dionysius was questioned by Lorenzo Valla. Today we know that he could not have been the man converted by St. Paul, since his works depend on Proclus, dating him to at least 400 years after his conversion was supposed to have taken place in Athens. Who is the author of these texts, then? For over a thousand years it was Dionysius, but today we believe it was probably an ecclesiastic from Syria who lived around the fifth century A.D. The medieval persona is clearly a pseudo-historical author, but even the picture we have of him today must be considered little like the actual historical figure who wrote the mentioned texts and called himself Dionysius in order to give his works the weight of authority necessary to ensure their survival and influence. Indeed, the historical author of the treatises must have had a keen sense of the importance of the pseudo-historical persona.

The discussion of the various descriptions that make up the pseudo-historical author brings me to three points. The first is that I take the descriptions that make up the pseudo-historical author generally to be intended by the historians who propose them in good faith to communicate information concerning the historical author; it is only through occassional bad faith or because of unintended mistakes made by historians that they do not describe accurately the historical author. It is the historical Voltaire that historians wish to describe when they describe the author of *Candide,* even though they might make mistakes in those descriptions owing to incomplete or faulty information or to faulty historical methodology. Of course, not infrequently historians willfully distort the historical record to present a figure in a good or bad light for nonhistorical reasons. For example, the picture painted of Stalin by many North American historians is hardly flattering, whereas Russian historians until recently tended to whitewash many of Stalin's actions and look at them as minor *pecadillos.* Such willful distortions produce as effective pseudo-historical authors as the descriptions presented by historians who act in good faith do. Indeed, sometimes they are more effective, because the historians who produce them take advantage of certain desires and aspirations in the audience for which they produce the historical account. But that should not obscure the fact that in most cases historians act in good faith.

The second point that I wish to bring up is that, strictly speaking, there are as many pseudo-historical authors as there are versions of the historical author. Each historian, indeed each person, who has an idea of who Stalin or Voltaire was, has constructed a pseudo-historical author that may or may not be the same as the picture constructed by someone else. Indeed, the same person may hold different views about the same historical figure at different times. The number of pseudo-historical authors, then, is potentially infinite, although in fact it reduces to a fairly small set, reflecting current knowledge and interest.

The third point is that, since the pseudo-historical author never existed, he could not have written any of the texts attributed to him. He could not have written, of course, either the contemporary or the historical texts. Nor could he be considered the author of the intended text, for that text is little more than a phantom posited by those historians who find certain mistakes or infelicities in the text with which they are dealing. Of course, sometimes on the basis of the idea of the historical author they have, namely on the basis of the pseudo-historical author, historians will argue for a particular reading of a text rather than another, trying to discover the intention of the author from an analysis of their idea of that author (the pseudo-historical author). But that is all a construction based on conjecture in which historians may be mistaken. So it cannot really be argued convincingly that the pseudo-historical author is the author of the intended text.

Nor can it be argued convincingly that the pseudo-historical author is the author of the ideal text, for the ideal text is supposed to be the text that the historical author should have written and the pseudo-historical author is the historians' own conception of what the historical author actually was. The ideal text cannot be the product of an author that is supposed to be historical and is actually taken to have produced the historical text.

C. The Composite Author

The *composite author* is the author of the contemporary text. As we saw earlier, the contemporary text is the version or versions of the historical text that we have, resulting from the vicissitudes to which the historical text has been subjected. The players in the composition of the contemporary text are three: the historical author who produced the historical text, the various scribes or typesetters involved in the transmission of the historical text from the moment of its production to the present, and the editors who have tried to put together a definitive or at least historically accurate version of the text. Each of these players or groups of players has an important role in the construction of the contemporary text and, therefore, must be considered partial authors of that text. The contemporary text is the result not of the activity of one person, but rather of the cummulative efforts of all the individuals mentioned.

The role of the historical author is to produce the historical text, whether original or derivative, but that is just the beginning of the process that gives us the contemporary text. The different scribes or typesetters that copied the historical text from which other scribes and typesetters made other copies, and so on, are also responsible for part of the shape the contemporary text has. In the process of copying they make mistakes, they miss words, they missread expressions, they add or eliminate punctuation, and in some cases even add clarifications and glosses. This sort of thing was more frequent before the printing press was invented (in fact it was standard procedure then), when texts were copied by hand and each process of copying involved the potential of substantial changes. But even after the printing press came into being, typesetters continue to make frequent mistakes, and some authors do not have the opportunity, patience, inclination, or even expertise to correct them.[18] So, even concerning recent texts, the distinction between the historical text and the contemporary text is significant and, thus, also the distinction between the historical author and the author of the contemporary text. Because of the mistakes and changes among various versions of the text, the need arises for the work of an editor, who plays the role of third author-component of the composite author. The role of the editor is to choose among various readings of a text, collating the various versions and deciding what he considers the best measured by criteria established by himself or by the editorial tradition within which he works.

The editorial labor involved in the modern production of ancient and medieval texts is extraordinarily important because only seldom does the autograph version of a text survives. In most cases what we have are many manuscripts that contain widely differing readings of a particular passage. In those circumstances, the editor constructs the family tree (stemma) of manuscripts, determining which branch is the best with the ultimate goal in mind of reconstructing the best possible version of the text. This involves not only enormous knowledge of the language, thought, and style of the author in question, but also knowledge of the subject matter discussed by the author. The editor is called on to choose among various readings of a text, to correct mistakes, to straighten out unintelligible or corrupt passages, and in general to give us a sensible and credible version of a text. In order to do this the editor has to act in many instances as the author of the text, thinking through what he takes to be the proper reading and phrasing. The editorial role is particularly important in cases where there is only one extant manuscript, for then the editor becomes the sole arbiter of how the text is to be read. All this indicates that, of the three authors that make up the composite author, the editor is second in importance only to the historical author.

Before we leave the composite author I would like to state something that seems rather obvious but should not go unsaid, namely, that it is highly unlikely that the composite author ever exist as a single person. Nevertheless, we are justified in talking about this author because in the contemporary text we have a text that is not the result of the efforts of any one individual. Of course, it is logically possible for the composite author to turn out to be one person, namely, the historical author (if the historical author is also one person). A historical author himself could have made copies of the autograph and later on tried to collate them with a view to producing an accurate version of the original text he composed but has since lost. But this situation, although logically possible, is not likely to occur. Moreover, even if it occurred, it could still be argued that when the historical author turns out to be the same person who also copies and edits the text, he plays different roles when copying and editing than when composing. So, although in this case there is only one person, the author of the contemporary text is still a composite of three different roles.

D. The Interpretative Author

The *interpretative author* is the author of the ideal text. I call this author *interpretative* because the ideal text exists only in the mind of the interpreter; that is, the philosopher or historian who, on the basis of the criteria discussed earlier, reconstructs how the text should have read. The ideal text, then, is a construct in someone's mind, and that mind is its author, because that mind produces it while it scans the contemporary text it examines.

It should be noted, however, that the interpretative author does not always have in mind the reconstruction of the ideal text. Most often his aim is to reconstruct the historical text. In such cases he functions merely as an editor, although often, owing to the criteria he employs, he ends up reconstructing an ideal text rather than the historical one. In order to keep the roles of editor and author of the ideal text separate I reserve the term 'interpretative author' for the second.

Platonists will want to argue, no doubt, that it is not interpreters of the text that create the ideal text. Interpreters merely avail themselves of the ideal; they do not create it, but simply discover it through a kind of mental dialectic.

I have no *prima facie* objection to understanding the ideal text in this way and holding that the interpreter is not the author of the ideal text but only a kind of conveyor of it. Indeed, the status of the ideal text and the relationship between the text and the interpreter pose a host of interesting philosophical questions that are in need of discussion, but are related only marginally to the issues that concern us here. For our present purposes I shall ignore them and leave open the possibility that the interpreter is not really an author but merely a conveyor of the ideal text. Of course, if that is the case, then the question arises as to the identity of the author of the ideal text and whether in fact such a text requires an author. Plato would have the text without an author, Augustine would have God as the author of the text, and others would follow other paths. But all that is immaterial to us at present.

Having discussed the text and the author, let me turn to the audience. Here again we are going to find a multiplicity of both persons and types.

III. THE AUDIENCE

The audience is the real or imaginary group of persons who in fact do read or are meant to read a text. Etymologically, the term 'audience' refers to a group of listeners. This meaning of the term goes back to a time when the primary form of acquaintance with the work of an author was through the spoken word. From the time in which the printing press was invented, however, until the time when the use of the radio became widespread, written texts became the primary way of learning about an author's work. And, although contemporary media have changed that to a certain extent, in science and philosophy it is still true to say that the audience for an author's work consists largely of readers. At any rate, for present purposes, the distinction between readers and listeners is immaterial and, thus, I shall refer to an audience as a group of readers, although what I say about it will apply *mutatis mutandis* to listeners as well.

It should be mentioned at this point that there are authors who claim that their business is not with an audience at all. Practitioners of the *nouveau roman,* such as Alain Robbe-Grillet, believe that for a writer the aim is to write and whether an author is read or not is actually unimportant. (Robbe-Grillet's third novel, *Jealousy,* sold only 300 copies in the first year even though he was already famous.) Thus, from this point of view it would seem that an audience is neither necessary nor important for the author, and if that is so, then its consideration could neither be necessary nor important for the understanding of a text and its interpretation.

These observations, however, are based on a conception of audience that excludes the author as part of the audience of a text. But, as we shall see shortly, the author, even when a practitioner of the *nouveau roman,* functions as audience at least in part. Hence, there is always an audience for a text, even when the author has no conventional audience in mind at the time of composition.[19]

What characterizes an audience is that it is meant to understand the text. The author, on the other hand, when acting as author, is related to a text as its creator and therefore has as aim to compose and mold it in some way. This does not mean that the audience must be considered passive, as some historiographers used to think. On the contrary, the audience approaches the text actively, but its relation to the text and the aim it has *qua* audience are different from those that characterize an author. The active character of an audience is involved at two levels: First, the interpretation of the signs of which the text is composed, for this involves an activity of connecting a sign to its meaning. Second, the audience must fill the *lacunae* that characterize all texts. Texts are rhetorical; they are like maps, on which only prominent landmarks are recorded and that, if taken by themselves, provide at best a general outline of the conceptual terrain they chart and are at worst unintelligible. It is the task of the audience to fill in the *lacunae* in the text, supplying the details that have been left out and without which the full meaning of the text would remain undisclosed.

In sum, then, the audience is not passive, but this does not mean that its activity must be equated to that of authors, as some philosophers seem to think.[20] The pendulum of contemporary philosophical opinion seems to have swung too far in favor of an active role for the audience. An audience is active in the understanding and interpretation of a text, but does not create it. The text is already an accomplished reality, even if incomplete and subject to diverse interpretations, before the audience encounters it; and the audience's role is not to change it but to grasp its meaning and significance. As such, the distinction between the audience and the author cannot be obliterated. In spite of this, however, the author can and does play the role of audience, as we shall see immediately.

The audience of a text may be divided into at least five different categories. To facilitate their discussion I have named them as follows: author as audience, intended audience, contemporaneous audience, intermediary audience, and contemporary audience.

A. The Author as Audience

From the moment an *author* has put something down in writing, has said something, or even has thought about the parts of the text he is composing that are already established, even if only provisionally, and goes back to it, he becomes an audience for the text. If the text is written, it acquires a status that is more independent of the author than if it is spoken or thought. But even a spoken text or a thought text could be examined by an author as an audience examines it. When spoken, it could have been recorded on a tape or on the author's memory, and when thought, it may be recorded in the author's memory. In all these cases, the author who approaches the text may function as audience insofar as he goes to it with the aim of understanding it. Indeed, the whole process of composing a text involves the author in a continuous switching back and forth between the roles of author and audience, whether as writer and reader, speaker and listener, or thinker and rememberer. In order to see the effect of what he says and how he says it, he needs to look at it as observer rather than composer. In many ways, the effectiveness of authors depends to a great extent on their dexterity at this switching of roles and understanding the needs of the audience. Good writers, for example, say only what needs to be said in order to convey a certain meaning; they use what the audience already knows in order to determine what to write; they are economical and effective. Bad writers, on the other hand, repeat what the audience already knows and fail to say what is necessary for the audience to understand. The ability of the author, then, to become audience and see his work as an audience would, is very important. There is nothing paradoxical or odd in considering the author as audience, although he is not the audience precisely insofar as he plays the role of author, but only insofar as an acquaintance and identification with the needs of the audience will help him in his role of author properly speaking.

Even in cases where the author does not compose a text with an audience in mind as is the case of the practitioners of the *nouveau roman,* the process of composition, revision, and correction force on him the role of audience. The difference is that in such cases the author does not seek to impersonate someone other than himself whom he, consciously or unconsciously, identifies as the audience of the work. Yet, the critical stance that leads him to make changes indicates that he has separated himself from the work and adopted the role of audience.

Not only in the process of composition, however, can an author function as audience. After a work has been completed, an author often goes back to it, interpreting and judging it, thus assuming the role of an audience in still another sense. The classic case in contemporary philosophy is Wittgenstein, who was concerned in his later career with attacking some of the theses he had defended in his earlier work.[21] A more common example is that of the author who, after writing a book, spends some of his time clarifying or defending what he said in it.

B. The Intended Audience

The *intended audience* is the person or group of persons for whom the author composes the work. The author may sometimes ostensibly dedicate the work to someone. In that case he probably intends for that person to read it, if we are dealing with a written work, and either profit by it or do something for the author. Many famous books of philosophy, and not a few infamous ones, were dedicated to powerful figures from whom the authors intended to seek fortune, protection, and other favors.

Apart from persons to whom a work may be explicitly dedicated, authors often have in mind specific groups of people as audience. Philosophers usually write for other philosophers, scientists for scientists, and so on. Only literary authors generally aim to a wider audience, but even then there are audience restrictions that have to do with education, culture, and language, among others.

What distinguishes the intended audience from the other three that still remain to be discussed is that the intended audience need not become acquainted with the text in question. The intended audience may never come into contact with the work and in fact may be no more than a figment of the author's imagination. There may not be any persons of the sort intended as audience by the author, and, if there are, there is no assurance they will come in contact with the text.

All the same, in some situations an understanding of the intended audience helps historians in the interpretation of a text, for it presents them with the group of persons that the author thinks would be most affected by his work. In that sense the intended audience reveals some of the author's ideas as to the intention of the text and how it should be approached. If, for example, historians know that a text is intended for professional philosophers who work within a certain philosophical tradition and share certain assumptions about method, they will be in a better position to interpret and evaluate it. They will try to supply those methodological assumptions that the author took for granted the audience would supply.

It should be noted, moreover, that the audience intended by an author need not be contemporary with the author. Authors may intend their texts to be read at future times, as is the case when something is written and placed in a sealed vault with the intention that it should be read only at some future date. Thus the category of intended audience should not be considered to exclude the categories that follow; it may overlap them.

C. The Contemporaneous Audience

The *contemporaneous audience* is composed of all those persons who are contemporaneous with the historical author and have or could have become acquainted with the text. They share with the author much that other, later audiences do not share with him. Living during the same time period, even if in a different country and culture, would seem to entail some basic and common elements, although this may not always be the case. The illiterate Tibetan, for example, will have very little in common with the Nobel laureate in literature even if they are contemporaries, and it is probably true that, conceptually, a contemporary Aristotelian will have more in common with Aristotle than with an illiterate Tibetan.

By the contemporaneuos audience, however, I do not mean to refer to persons who are culturally and educationally far removed from the historical author. I mean members of his and similar social groups who have the basic educational and cultural tools to be capable of understanding the text in question. Under these conditions, this audience is better prepared to understand the text than subsequent audiences.

D. The Intermediary Audience

The *intermediary audience* consists of the group of persons who have or could have become acquainted with the text, but who are neither contemporaneous with the author nor contemporaries of the historian. They are, thus, separated from the author not only by individual idiosyncracies but also by time. Living at a different time and under different conditions, the context within which they reach the text is different from that of the historical author's contemporaneous audience, and it is also different from the context in which the historian's contemporaries would read it. How different the context is will vary not only with the temporal separation between the intermediary audience and the moment in which the historical text was produced, but also with the degree to which the ideological assumptions and climate of the age have changed. Temporal distance is not directly proportional to conceptual distance. Some temporally very distant ages may be closer together conceptually than other ages that are temporally closer.

E. The Contemporary Audience

The *contemporary audience* is composed of the group of persons who have or could have become acquainted with the work and are contemporaries of the historian, but who are neither the author nor his contemporaries. In some cases it will consist simply in the generation of persons that comes after the contemporaneous generation. If that is the case, then there will be no intermediary audience between the contemporaneous and the contemporary ones. But in all cases except for that one, there will be at least one generation of persons acquainted with the text between the contemporaneous audience and the contemporary audience, allowing for an intermediary audience in between.[22]

The difficulty for the contemporary audience is not only one of temporal or ideological distance between the text and itself, but also the fact that it has at its disposal interpretations of the text provided by both the contemporaneous and the intermediary audiences, and sometimes even by the author himself. Furthermore, the number of interpretations increases as time passes. These interpretations can be both helpful and unhelpful to the contemporary audience in its understanding of the text. They can help insofar as they establish bridges between the contemporary audience and the historical text, as I already noted in Chapter One, but they can also be obstacles insofar as they may be mistaken and may lead the contemporary audience into directions that would take it farther rather than nearer the meaning of the historical text.[23]

IV. THE INTERPRETATION OF TEXTS

Having discussed texts, their authors, and audiences, I can turn to their interpretation, which is the primary object of concern in this chapter. The questions that give rise to more disagreements among historiographers concerning interpretations have to do with their nature and object, with the factors involved in them and the role they play, and with their aim. Let me begin, then, with their nature.

The term 'interpretation' is the English translation of the Latin *interpretatio,* from *interpres,* which in turn and etymologically meant "to spread abroad." Accordingly, *interpres* came to mean an agent between two parties, a broker or negotiator and by extension an explainer, expounder, and translator. The Latin term *interpretatio* developed at least three different meanings. Sometimes it meant "meaning," so that to give an interpretation was equivalent to give the meaning of whatever was being interpreted. *Interpretatio* was also taken to mean "translation"; the translation of a text or a word into a different language was also called an interpretation. Finally, the term was also used to mean "explanation," and by this an interpretation was meant to bring out what was hidden and unclear, to make plain what was irregular. All these meanings point to the fact that in an interpretation there must be three elements: whatever is being interpreted, something other than what is being interpreted that is added to it, and an interpreter or broker that mediates between the two. Since our concern here is with the interpretation of texts, I shall identify the object of interpretation with a text.

In an interpretation of a text, then, we have a text, something in addition to the text, and an interpreter.[24] The text is ontologically part of the interpretation, just as the *definiendum* is part of the definition, for in order to add to a text, the text must be presupposed. Now, what is added to the text, just as the text itself, can be something mental, written, or spoken. For our purposes, whether it is the first, second, or third of these is not very important. What is important is that it is something other and something more than the text under interpretation.

The text itself, whether written somewhere, spoken at some time, or mentally present in some mind, is not an interpretation. The interpretation comes in when the interpreter begins to analyze the text and its elements into terms or concepts that are not explicit in the text. For example, to reproduce Boethius' statement, "*Atque ideo sunt numero plures, quoniam accidentibus plures fiunt*," is not an interpretation.[25] To translate it into, "Wherefore, it is because they are plural by their accidents that they are plural in number" is a kind of interpretation, since it changes the original into a different set of linguistic terms whose denotations and connotations may not be the same as those of the original Latin sentence, but that are meant to be equivalent in meaning, considered as a whole, to the original text. And if we go further and say, for example, that what Boethius has in mind in that text is to say that the principle of individuation is a bundle of accidents, we are without a doubt providing an interpretation of Boethius's text, for the text contains no such formulation of Boethius's doctrine.

Interpretations of texts, then, involve texts, something added to them, and an interpreter. However, as we saw earlier, the historian can deal with at least four different texts, assuming, contrary to what was said earlier, that each category contains only one: the contemporary, the historical, the intended, and the ideal. So we must ask which of these texts should be the object of the historian of philosophy's interpretation.

The answer to this question is that the text to whose interpretation the efforts of historians should be directed is the historical text. However, since historians may not necessarily have that text, but only a contemporary text, their interpretation must be based on the contemporary text, although keeping in mind that the overall aim is to provide interpretations of the historical text. There is nothing unusual about this. Historians often have bad editions of a text that depart in substantial ways from the historical text, but which they must use as long as the historical text is not available. Indeed, in many cases there is no hope of ever recovering the historical text, as is the case with the works of most pre-Socratic philosophers, and we must make do with what we have. Moreover, in cases where there are several historical texts that reflect the evolution of an author's thought through a period of time, historians must take them all into consideration, keeping in mind the evolutionary process that they reflect.

The function of the intended and the ideal texts in the process of interpretation, on the other hand, should be primarily regulative and instrumental. The aim of historians is not the reconstruction of an ideal text regardless of its perfection, for that would be outside the historical task. Historians are concerned with the past as it existed, not with the past as it should have existed. Nor should historians aim to reconstruct the text that the author presumably intended to produce but never did, for as we saw that text never existed, not even in the mind of the author. The concern of historians is with the text that was actually produced, the historical text. However, insofar as the historical text is not always available, historians can profit from considering what they can surmise about both the intended and the ideal texts. These texts are reconstructions of what historians believe the historical author was trying to do or should have been trying to do. As such they allow historians to correct what appear to be mistakes and supply missing elements that help in the understanding of the text. But historians must keep in mind that the historical task involves the development of an interpretation of the historical text and resist the temptation to see that task as the reconstruction of the intended or ideal texts. To fall into the latter trap leads surely to the distortion of history. But that need not happen if the interpreter keeps in mind the merely regulative and instrumental function of the intended and ideal texts.

In the interpretative task historians are also aided, and sometimes hampered no doubt, by their knowledge of the author and the audience. As far as the various authors we discussed are concerned, the only two that provide them with useful information are, first, the two members of the composite author about whom historians may have some information, namely, the editor and the scribe, and, second, the pseudo-historical author. They have no complete and direct picture of the historical author and, as mentioned earlier, the interpretative author is the historian.

Knowledge of the audience should be particularly helpful because of the elliptical character of texts. With rare exceptions, texts are meant to be read or heard by an audience, and they thus presuppose a certain context that allows for shortcuts and *lacunae* intended to be filled by the assumptions and views of the audience. Knowledge of the intended audience is especially useful because it reveals some of the assumptions made by the historical author in the composition of the text. Knowledge of the contemporaneous audience is also helpful because it reveals, in an indirect fashion, something about the historical author and puts in perspective whatever contemporaneous interpretations of the text were produced. This last point also applies to the knowledge of the intermediary audience. Finally, no less important than the others is the knowledge of the contemporary audience, particularly the self-knowledge of historians, for such information helps to make explicit the assumptions and prejudices of historians and prevents them from distorting their view of the past. As we shall see in the next chapter, it is essential that the methodology used by historians of philosophy make provisions to ensure as much as possible the neutralization of these biases and assumptions.

So far I have discussed the text, the author, and the audience, and I have indicated how these relate and must be used by the interpreter, that is, by the historian of philosophy. Now I must say something about what the interpretation adds over and above the text.

What an interpretation adds to a text in fact is another text. The added text can be mental, spoken, or written, but it is neither the contemporary nor the historical texts. It is a new text added by the interpreter to make sense (meaning), translate, or explain the contemporary (or historical, depending on what is available) text. Nor should this text be confused with the intended text or the ideal text. Indeed, even if the interpretation were presented as a reconstruction of the ideal text or the intended text, it would not be either one of them. It could not be the ideal text because the ideal text is supposed to take the place of the historical or contemporary texts in places where such texts are corrupt or make no good philosophical sense; it is not supposed to clarify or explain them, as an interpretation ought to do. Nor could it be the intended text, for, like the ideal text, the intended text is supposed to take the place of the historical text and therefore is not meant to clarify it. The actual function of the intended and ideal texts is purely regulative, as stated earlier. Those texts help the historian to come up with an interpretation in cases where there are doubts concerning the meaning of the text and the evidence available is inconclusive, but they are not what is added to the text in an interpretation of it.

An interpretation of a text, then, boils down to the text with its commentary. If the historical text is not available, the interpreter tries to reconstruct it and explain it on the basis of the available texts. If it is available, then the interpreter simply tries to explain it. But we may ask, Don't the additions to a text present in an interpretation change the original text and therefore destroy the possibility of understanding its original meaning and consequently of recovering history as it was? Can the historian really add anything to a text and still understand the historical text as it should be understood? Can we go beyond the original text and add anything to it without actually changing it? Indeed, some might argue that the only course we have of understanding a text without distorting it is that of reproducing the text, becoming Pierre Menards and nothing more, for any addition would transform the text, thereby eliminating the possibility of understanding it in its historical dimension.[26]

This brings me to what I call the *interpreter's dilemma:* Either the interpreter simply reproduces the text (in his mind, for example), adding nothing whatever to it, or he glosses it. If he adds nothing to it, as the antiquarians would wish, he can't really say he understands it in its purely historical dimension, since he is not the author of the text or even a member of the contemporaneous audience of the text that, because they were acquainted with the meaning of the signs used in the text, knew its meaning. But if he adds to it, as the anachronists favor, he clearly distorts the text and again loses access to its historical meaning. Can the interpreter escape this dilemma and avoid both antiquarianism and anachronism? I believe he can because the dilemma, like most dilemmas, is based on a misunderstanding of the situation.

In order to explain how the interpreter's dilemma can be escaped, let me begin by pointing out that the aim of an interpreter is to re-create, first, the mental acts of the author of the text, not as creator of the text, but as audience. The reason that the interpreter does not want to re-create the author as creator is that the creator *qua* creator was involved in many different mental acts that were only propaedeutic to the production of the text he finally produced. And those acts, since they involved the rejection of some options about how to construct the text, for example, are largely irrelevant and indeed could be distracting to the development of an understanding of the historical text.

The interpreter could also have in mind the re-creation, second, of the acts of understanding through which the audience for which the work was intended went through or was expected to go through. Remember that the author usually has in mind an audience, and the interpreter needs to become that audience, composed of the author and his contemporaries, in order to understand a text in its historicality.

In trying to re-create the acts of the author as audience and of the contemporaneous audience for himself and his own contemporary audience (because the aim of a historian is not only to understand the historical text himself but also to make it available to the historian's contemporaries), the historian needs to create a causal complex that will produce in the audience of his interpretation acts of understanding similar to those acts that the historical author and the contemporaneous audience underwent when they came into contact with the text. But in order to do this it is necessary to add to the original text elements that will make it possible to re-create those or similar acts. For the distance in time and culture, and so on, that separates the contemporary audience from the historical text would ensure that, if that audience had access to the text as it was historically, the audience would develop acts of understanding that surely would be different from those that the author and his contemporaneous audience developed. This is similar to what would happen if the historical author and his contemporaneous audience had access to a text contemporary to the historian, for in that case they would understand it differently than the historian and his contemporary audience would do unless a gloss of it were provided. The function of the additions that the interpreter supplies, then, is to ensure that the same or similar acts of understanding expected of those who were contemporaneous with the historical text would be reproduced in the contemporary audience. The view that I have stated can be summarized in what I call the *principle of proportional understanding*. According to this principle:

> An interpretation of a text (composed of a historical text and the interpretative additions of an interpreter) should be to the contemporary audience with respect to the production of their contemporary acts of understanding as the historical text is to the historical audience (composed of the author as audience and the contemporaneous audience) with respect to the acts of understanding of the historical audience.

Perhaps this principle will be more easily understood if we break it down as follows:

$$\frac{\text{historical text}}{\text{author + contemporaneous audience}} = \text{acts of understanding of author + contemporaneous audience}$$

$$\frac{\text{interpretation (i.e., historical text + interpretative additions)}}{\text{contemporary audience}} = \text{acts of understanding of contemporary audience}$$

What the principle of proportional understanding establishes is that, in order for an interpretation of a historical text to be accurate, the ratio of the interpretation to the contemporary audience (that is, the acts of understanding it produces in such an audience) must be similar to the ratio between the historical text and the author and contemporaneous audience (that is, the acts of understanding it produces in the author and that audience).

The aim of the interpreter, then, is to create a text that produces in its audience (the contemporary audience) acts of understanding similar to those produced by the historical text in the author when he functions as audience and in the contemporaneous audience of the historical text. The interpreter creates the textual object that produces the kind of thoughts and judgments in the contemporary audience that the author and his audience had and made.

Now we can see more clearly why interpretation is an integral part of the historical task of understanding texts, for its aim is to bridge the conceptual and cultural gaps that separate the historical text from a later time at which it is being read, heard or even remembered. It also explains why interpretations need not be anachronistic simply by virtue of the fact that they add to the original text, since the function of their additions is precisely to produce acts of understanding in the contemporary audience similar to those the historical text produced or should have produced in the contemporaneous audience.

It must be clear also, however, that the task of the historian of philosophy goes beyond that of textual interpreter. The task of the historian is not only to produce a textual interpretation, but over and above that a historical account of past philosophical ideas, as was stated in Chapter One, and this involves much more than a textual interpretation. In order to make what I mean clear I would like to introduce a distinction between "textual" and "historical" interpretations. A textual interpretation is precisely the sort of interpretation that I have been talking about: It is an interpretation of a text that makes the text accessible to a contemporary audience by adding to it whatever is neccessary in order to get results in contemporary minds that are similar to the mental phenomena present in the author and the contemporaneous audience when they thought about the text.

A historical interpretation, on the other hand, is much more than a textual interpretation, for it seeks to reconstruct the intricate weave of thoughts and ideas and relations not recorded in the text that makes the history of philosophy more than just a series of atomically discrete texts. The ultimate aim of historians of philosophy is to produce an account of past ideas and that account includes not only textual interpretations, but also the reconstruction of the larger context in which the text was produced, the ideas that the author did not put down in writing or uttered in speech, the relations among various texts from the same author and other authors, the causal connections among ideas and texts, and so on. Historians seek more than the reproduction of the acts of understanding of the author and the contemporaneous audience of a text; they want to produce also other acts of understanding that neither the author nor the contemporaneous audience had or could have had precisely because of their historical (temporal, cultural and spatial) limitations and that are possible for the historian and his contemporary audience to have owing to their different historical location and perspective.

In short, textual interpretation is only the beginning and only one element of historical interpretation. The task of historians of philosophy is much larger than to offer interpretations of texts, but if they are going to get anywhere with their task they must begin with those interpretations.

Let us suppose, then, that we adopt the principle of proportional understanding and that we accept the distinction between textual and historical interpretations, we may still ask, Is there one or many textual interpretations?

The answer to this question as formulated will depend on how many commentaries on a text have been done and would have to be determined on the basis of empirical evidence. If we asked, for example, whether there is one or many interpretations of Aristotle's *Metaphysics,* it is obvious from even a cursory review of the literature that there are many. But neither this type of answer nor the question that it answers is very interesting to the historiographer. What the historiographer would like to know rather is whether there is and can be only one *definitive* interpretation of a text or whether there is room for more than one. Of course, if 'text' is taken to refer generically to all the texts that we have discussed, clearly there can be as many interpretations as there are texts. And the same applies to the contemporary text, which turned out to be multiple rather than single. For the question to have any philosophical and historiographical interest it must refer either to a single historical text or to one of its contemporary versions. Understood in this sense the issue that the question raises is at the heart of the historiographical inquiry and relates in many ways to similar issues that can be raised concerning science and philosophy. In science the question involves whether what the physical scientist, for example, produces or seeks to produce are more or less approximations to *the one definitive* interpretation of nature, or whether what physical scientists produce are various versions of *equally correct* interpretations of nature. With philosophy a similar question could be posed. Is there one correct philosophy or are there many?

One way of approaching this question is by looking at the success of various interpretations. But that, of course, cannot give us an affirmative answer because so far there is no interpretation in science, philosophy, or the history of philosophy that is unquestionable. Nor do the extraordinary difficulties involved in providing a textual interpretation, to which I pointed out earlier, support optimistic predictions concerning future interpretations in the history of philosophy. Indeed, much of the philosophical effort since Kant has been spent in showing in one way or another that we have no way of arriving at a final and definitive interpretation in science, philosophy, or the history of philosophy.

But there is another way of looking at this question. If what I have argued concerning the nature and function of interpretations is correct, then it is not possible to think that there can be one definitive interpretation of a text as long as there are cultural and conceptual differences between the contemporaneous audience of the historical text and the audience contemporary with the historian. For each new audience will require a new interpretation that will bridge the gaps between it and the contemporaneous audience of the historical text. The only way in which there could be one definitive interpretation of a text would be if its audience always had the same cultural and conceptual character, but that, although not logically impossible, is not in the cards. Of course, there is no reason why there cannot be a definitive interpretation of a text for a particular time and place, that is, an interpretation that best helps to bridge the gaps between the text and the audience of that time and place. And there is no reason either why there cannot be interpretations that are more enduring than others. Indeed, some interpretations may be such that they can bridge the gap between the historical text and several subsequent audiences rather than just one. Moreover, the notion of a possible single definitive interpretation is methodologically significant, for this notion both propels ongoing efforts of interpretation, preventing complacency, and furthers the critical spirit that should animate any interpretative search. Care should be taken, however, that the adherence to this notion be nondogmatic and nonideological. Its function, as that of the ideal text, is regulative rather than substantive. If kept at that level, its effects can be very useful, otherwise they can be nefarious.

Let me finish by going back to the beginning of the chapter. There I pointed out that historians of philosophy faced a serious problem in the historical task, namely, that they did not and could not have direct empirical access to the object they are supposed to study. In the subsequent discussion I have tried to show how the solution to that problem is to be found in the development of textual interpretations whose purpose is to bridge the gap between the understanding of texts in different historical periods. I also indicated the factors involved in the development of those interpretations and the nature of the texts on which they are supposed to be based. Moreover, since interpretations involve choices and those choices can be made only on the basis of evaluations, it becomes clear that historical accounts involve both interpretative and evaluative judgments of the sort we discussed in Chapter One. Thus we see here further confirmation of the overall thesis I set out to support in this study, namely, that the task of the historian of philosophy is philosophical, involving evaluative judgments. Still to be determined, however, is how a philosophical history of philosophy can be carried out without endangering its objectivity and accuracy. The answer to that question is contained in the next chapter, where I deal with the issue of philosophical methodology.

NOTES

1. Two qualifications are in order at this point. First, it may be possible to argue that there are texts composed of only one sign, such as 'P,' which stands for the order to print in my word processing program. In that case the meaning of the text would not depend on any kind of arrangement or organization. However, the view that texts may be composed of only one sign is disputable. Paul Ricoeur is against it in "On Interpretation," in Baynes, et al., eds., *After Philosophy*, p. 359. Second, I am using a rather ordinary way of talking about meaning here because of its convenience. I do not believe that I need to develop a theory of meaning in order to carry out my purpose in this chapter, and so I dispense with it.

2. There are contexts, however, where 'man,' 'a man,' and 'the man' may have the same meaning. For example, in the propositions 'Man is a rational animal' and 'A man is a rational animal,' both 'man' and 'a man' mean the same thing. In cases such as these, the context is the determining factor.

3. In the case of the pile of rocks, presumably the arrangement was the result of human activity. In this situation, the objects are clearly natural, but the arrangement is a matter of human design.

4. For Augustine, see *On the Teacher;* and for a later statement of the Augustinian view, see Bonaventure, *Retracing the Arts to Theology,* in Sister Emma Thérèse Healy, *St. Bonaventure's "De reductione artium ad theologiam," A Commentary with an Introduction and Translation* (St. Bonaventure, N.Y.: Saint Bonaventure College, 1939).

5. Peirce seems to have held such a view. Cf. D. Greenlee's *Peirce's Concept of Sign* (The Hague and Paris: Mouton, 1973).

6. Gracia, *Individuality,* pp. 43 ff.

7. Ibid., pp. 102–103. See also Nicholas Wolterstorff, "Toward an Ontology of Art Works," *Nous* 9, no. 2 (1975): 115–142; Joseph Margolis, "The Ontological Peculiarity of Works of Art," *Journal of Aesthetics and Art Criticism* 36, no. 1 (1977): 45–50; and Edmund Husserl, "Formale und transzendentale Logik: Versuch einer Kritik der logischen Vernunft," *Jahrbuch* 10 (1929): 1–298, see 17 ff. in particular. English trans. Dorion Cairns, *Formal and Transcendental Logic* (The Hague: Nijhoff, 1969). Wolterstorff's view is that works of art are universal; Margolis's view is that they are tokens of a type that exists embodied in physical objects; for Husserl, works of art are "ideal individuals," to be contrasted with "ideal universals" of which the triangle as such and color as such are examples. As I have pointed out in the place noted, the ontological status of a work of art depends very much on what one understands by 'work of art.' As we shall see, something very similar applies to texts.

8. I am assuming that differences in script (uncial vs. Gothic, for example) do not alter the text. To show how this is so is beyond the boundaries of this paper.

9. James A. Weisheipl, *Friar Thomas D'Aquino: His Life, Thought and Work* (Garden City, N.Y.: Doubleday and Co., 1974), p. 362.

10. For the notion of "copy text" and its implications, see Thomas Tanselle, "Greg's Theory of the Copy-Text and the Editing of American Literature," *Studies in Bibliography* 28 (1975): 167–229.

11. In addition, there are the mental memories of the individuals who may have heard or read various versions of the text. These are all cases of mental texts that may vary according to diverse factors.

12. As I point out later, the historical author may actually be more than one person, but I leave the discussion of this matter for the section on The Historical Author.

13. This is the reason why the meaning of the text cannot be reduced to the author's intentions, as P. J. Juhl correctly argues in "The Appeal to the Text: What Are We Appealing to?" *Journal of Aesthetics and Art Criticism* 36, no. 3 (1978): 277–287. The classic defense of the identity of the meaning of a text with its author's intention is found in Eric Donald Hirsch's *Validity in Interpretation* (New Haven, Conn.: Yale University Press, 1967). At the other extreme of this dispute is Monroe Beardsley, who holds that the text by itself determines its meaning and that the author's intention is irrelevant for determining such meaning. See his *Possibility of Criticism* (Detroit: Wayne State University Press, 1970).

14. See Monroe C. Beardsley, *Aesthetics: Problems in the Philosophy of Criticism*, rev. ed. (New York: Macmillan, 1980), pp. 17–28.

15. I am referring here to what Richard A. Watson calls "formal structures." See his "Method in the History of Philosophy," pp. 9–10.

16. For recent discussions of authorship, see Michael L. Morgan, "Authorship and the History of Philosophy," *The Review of Metaphysics* 42, no. 2 (1988): 327–355; and Alexander Nehamas, "Writer, Text, Work, Author," in Anthony J. Cascardi, ed., *Literature and the Question of Philosophy* (Baltimore and London: Johns Hopkins University Press, 1987), pp. 267–291.

17. In what follows I largely ignore the complex relation between author and text. For a seminal essay on this issue, see Michel Foucault, "What Is an Author?" in Donald F. Bouchard, ed., *Language, Countermemory, Practice* (Ithaca, N.Y.: Cornell University Press, 1977), pp. 113–138.

18. Peter Hare brought to my attention one of the best examples of this attitude and the unfortunate consequences that follow from it: Alfred North Whitehead and the poor state in which he left *Process and Reality*. See the Editors' Preface to the Corrected Edition of the book, by D. R. Griffin and D. W. Sherburne (New York: Free Press, 1979), pp. v–x.

19. There is one exception to this rule. It happens when an author composes a text in a kind of stream of consciousness mode, where he never goes back to what he has produced or considers it in any way.

20. Echoes of this view are found in most postmodernists and deconstructionists. For an extensive defense of the contrary view, see Louise M. Rosenblatt, *The Reader, the Text, the Poem: The Transactional Theory of the Literary Work,* ch. 4 (Carbondale and Edwardsville: Southern Illinois University Press, 1978), pp. 48–70.

21. Kenneth Barber brought to my attention a more recent one. Edwin B. Allaire talks about the author of a paper he wrote years before and about the paper as if he were not the author of it. See "Berkeley's Idealism Revisited," in Colin M. Turbayne, ed., *Berkeley: Critical and Interpretative Essays* (Minneapolis: University of Minnesota Press, 1982), p. 197.

22. Of course, the matter is not so simple, for the contemporaneous audience may be composed of individuals of different ages, some of whom one could argue could become also part of the intermediary audience or contemporary audience. This possibility underscores once more the artificial character of historical categories. All the same, I believe it does not seriously undermine the points I have made here.

23. Bennett, "Response to Garber and Rée," p. 66.

24. For a survey of contemporary theories of interpretation, see Svante Nordin, *Interpretation and Method: Studies in the Explication of Literature* (Lund: Lund Universitet, 1978). Some key names in the literature on this topic are Monroe C. Beardsley, Joseph Margolis, Charles Stevenson, and Morris D. Weitz. See the bibliography at the end of this book for the pertinent works.

25. Boethius, *De Trinitate* I, in *The Theological Tractates,* trans. H. F. Stewart and E. K. Rand (Cambridge, Mass.: Harvard University Press, 1968), p. 6.

26. Pierre Menard is a character in Jorge Luis Borges' story "Pierre Menard, Author of the *Quixote,*" in *Labyrinths* (Norfolk, Conn.: New Directions, 1962), who tries to rewrite Cervantes's novel. The story suggests that even the recomposition of a text by anyone but the historical author goes beyond the historical text and constitutes an interpretation even if it does not differ from it in any way.

Chapter Five

A Philosophical History of Philosophy: Uses and Abuses of the History of Philosophy

The approaches used by historians of philosophy vary widely, and historiographers have not failed to notice the differences among them. In fact, various attempts have been made, some of them quite recent, at classifying and examining the main approaches used by historians. However, most of those attempts have been inadequate. Their problems range from the omission of some obvious approaches to the lack of clarity in their description. In this chapter I wish to remedy this situation to some extent by proposing a new, more complete taxonomy of these approaches and a preliminary examination of their strengths and weaknesses. No doubt those familiar with the pertinent literature will note similarities between the categories I use in the classification and those used in other classifications, but I hope they will also notice the new elements I propose here for the first time. In cases where the categories I propose resemble already proposed categories or where I in fact have used ideas originating in other authors, I identify the pertinent sources.

The task of providing both a taxonomy and an evaluation of the various methods used in the study of the history of philosophy might seem to some to be of little theoretical value and perhaps even irrelevant to the philosophical issues raised by the study of the history of philosophy. In fact, the question of method is not only bound inextricably to the philosophical issues raised in philosophical historiography, but also particularly important in this book, for we cannot rest with a mere general justification of its overall thesis, that the history of philosophy must be done philosophically. To back up this thesis properly, we must also present a specific blueprint of how it is to be done.

I would like to begin by pointing out that I have been able to identify at least thirteen different approaches used by historians of philosophy in the practice of the discipline. Although these approaches are easily distinguishable logically, in practice they are seldom found in isolation. Historians of philosophy frequently mix two or three approaches, and sometimes even more, although in most cases one can easily notice the predominance of one approach over the others. Only rarely, however, are historians themselves aware of the methodological assumptions and procedures under which they work. Most often their concerns are directed toward their historical work and not toward the metahistorical issue of the proper methodology of history.

The thirteen approaches in question fall into two major categories. Three deal with the history of philosophy from a nonphilosophical standpoint, and the rest maintain a primarily philosophical perspective. All aim to provide an account of ideas, but the first three approaches provide an essentially nonphilosophical account. They do this by supplying explanations of the occurrence of ideas in terms that are of no interest to the philosopher *qua* philosopher; the accounts are based on considerations that are not intrinsic to the nature of the philosophical ideas themselves. By contrast, the other ten approaches account for the same ideas in terms of the very nature and character of philosophical ideas themselves, of their relations, and of the way in which philosophers deal with those ideas.

I proceed by presenting, first, those approaches to the history of philosophy that are nonphilosophical. Their discussion is relatively brief since, considering the primarily philosophical character and intent of this book, an extended discussion of them would be out of place. The discussion of the nonphilosophical approaches is followed by a more detailed discussion of the remaining ten approaches. I regard all the approaches, whether philosophical or not, as inadequate when taken separately, but their discussion will help us formulate, in the section of the chapter that follows their discussion, the requirements that a correct approach should have. Finally, I present and illustrate what I consider the most fruitful approach to the study of the history of philosophy.

Before I enter into the discussion of the various ways of doing history of philosophy, however, I would like to make clear that the various approaches discussed here are not intended to be either exhaustive or exclusive. They are certainly not exhaustive, for, I am sure, there are many more approaches than I have listed. Nor are they exclusive, for as already noted often one will find several of them in the work of a single historian. It is precisely because of their lack of exclusivity in particular that one seldom, if ever, finds a pure example of any of them. The characterizations I provide are intended, therefore, more as abstractions, benign caricatures if you will, that, as such and precisely because of their exaggeration, make us notice factors that otherwise would have escaped us.

I. NONPHILOSOPHICAL APPROACHES

I call the three *nonphilosophical approaches* to the history of philosophy I wish to discuss cultural, psychological, and ideological. Their common feature is that they provide nonphilosophical accounts of philosophical ideas from the past. I should add that I confine the discussion to the three mentioned, but many other approaches of a similar nature are either actually employed or at least possible in principle. An example of an approach actually employed that I do not discuss is the sociological. Such an approach involves accounting for past ideas in terms of social phenomena. Thus Voltaire's skepticism might be explained in terms of his French origin and Hume's empiricism might be traced to sociological phenomena prevalent in British society at the time he lived. Alternatively, one could also try to explain their ideas in terms of their genetic and biological makeup, although little has been done in this area so far, probably because of our still rudimentary knowledge of biology and genetics. But I can see a future in which there will be attempts to explain the differences among the ideas held by different philosophers in terms of their biological makeup and genetic heritage. After all, it is widely accepted that special talents, such as musical or mathematical ability, have to do with biology. So there is no reason why we should not see at some point studies purporting to explain philosophical talent in biological and genetic terms. Indeed, some might go so far as to attempt to show how X holds that P because of some describable biological configuration or phenomenon, such as a certain neural structure or a particular genetic makeup.[1]

Still, all this, at least in the area of biology and genetics is not yet possible and, therefore, there is no need to consider this approach at this time. With sociology, by contrast, the situation is different, but again there is no need to discuss a sociological approach here both because it is not widespread and also because the more popular cultural and psychological approaches we discuss illustrate well, although indirectly, the sort of procedure that a sociological approach would involve.

Finally, let me add that both the cultural and psychological approaches are useful to the historian of philosophy insofar as they help to determine what past philosophers thought. My criticism of them, as will become clear, is not that they are not useful, but that they do not provide a philosophical account of past philosophical ideas.

A. The Culturalist

The cultural approach to the history of philosophy is dominated by one concern: the understanding of past philosophical views as expressions of the complex cultural matrix from which those views arose. The emphasis of this approach is not on the understanding of philosophical ideas as uniquely distinct, *qua* philosophical ideas, which address or seek to address specific philosophical questions and problems posed by individual persons. On the contrary, this approach views philosophical ideas as parts and products of a culture, as representative phenomena of an age and period. The by-product of this primary goal is that historians who adopt this approach concentrate on description and to a certain extent on interpretation, but are generally opposed to evaluation. The culturalist wants to understand past philosophies as part of a general account of cultural development, but has no interest in the value of those philosophies. The concern with tying philosophical ideas to other aspects of culture, such as art, literature, science, and religion, leads also to the treatment of those ideas in general terms.

The culturalist, moreover, is interested in the whole picture and for that reason often neglects the details. This leads in turn to neglect of arguments and more idiosyncratic views. Culturalist accounts have little use for detailed or even cursory examination of past arguments and the ideas of individual philosophers. They are interested mostly in general conclusions that they can relate to other cultural phenomena; their perspective is fundamentally interdisciplinary.

Finally, the explanations that culturalists give of how and why this or that idea arose and so on have to do with cultural forces external to philosophy and what philosophers consider to be their task *qua* philosophers. For example, if they were to try to explain why medieval authors held that the human soul is immortal, they would point to the medievals' religious beliefs rather than to the philosophical reasons they gave for holding such a position. Indeed, those reasons would be considered useless unless they could be used to shed some light on the "spirit" or "mind of the times." Philosophy and philosophical ideas are seen as symptoms of something much more important for the historian to grasp. Bréhier put his finger on the fundamental trait of the culturalist while describing Comte's approach:

> Comte understands by philosophy not so much the technical systems of the specialists in philosophy, but a mental state diffused throughout society that will manifest itself in judicial institutions, literary works, or works of art just as well as, if not better than, in the philosophers' systems. A philosophical system could, it is true, show this state of mind with particular clarity, because it puts together traits scattered elsewhere and presents them in full light; but it will never be studied except as a symbol and a sympton.[2]

This emphasis on what the French have come to call *faits de mentalité,* became essential to the historical method favored by the *Annales* historiographical school. According to the members of this school, the object of all history is to reveal the collective mind or spirit of the times. As such, "the mentality of an individual, although he may be a great man, is what he has in common with other men of his time."[3] The importance of studying great writers and philosophers, then, is that they reveal to us the general conscience of the cultural and social group of which they are part.[4] Lucien Febvre, one of the founders of the *Annales* school, offers a biting criticism of the method employed by some historians of philosophy who forget the cultural context of ideas:

> Of all the workers who retain, whether or not it is qualified by some epithet, the generic term of historians, there is none of them who does not justify it in our eyes in some respect—except, often enough, those who, setting themselves the task of rethinking for their own use systems sometimes many centuries old, without the least care to take note of the relations of these systems to the other manifestations of the epoch which gave them birth, thus find themselves, quite precisely, doing exactly the opposite of what a historian's method demands; and who, seeing these productions of concepts that are born of disembodied intellects and then live their own lives outside of space and time, forge alien chains whose links are at once unreal and sealed.[5]

And he praises Étienne Gilson's *La philosophie du moyen âge* precisely for putting ideas in what he regards as the proper context:

> It is not a question of underestimating the role of ideas in history. Still less is it a question of subordinating that role to the action of interested parties. It is a question of showing that a gothic cathedral, the markets of Ypres, victims of the great barbarism, and one of these great cathedrals of ideas such as Éti-

> enne Gilson describes for us in his book—these are daughters of a single era, sisters who grew up in the same family.[6]

The task of historians of philosophy, then, is not to judge ideas nor to see them as idiosyncratic occurrences produced by individuals. Rather, their task is to bring out the connections between those ideas and the cultural mentality of which they are representations. And the reason, as Ortega and his followers are fond of pointing out, is that ideas are not caused by abstract notions, for ideas are not disembodied abstractions, but acts that human beings perform in determined circumstances with a view to definite ends.[7] Thus a history of philosophy that speaks of ideas only abstractly, as entities separate from the circumstances that originated them is neither history nor philosophy. The task of the history of philosophy, then, is precisely to make explicit the relations among ideas, considered as concrete human responses and reactions, to the circumstances that prompt them, revealing thus the conceptual foundations of the culture in which they arise.

This is all very interesting and useful, and in many cases the conclusions and explanations provided by culturalists are not only absolutely correct but also enlightening. Indeed, it is quite clear that the main reason why medieval authors believed that the human soul is immortal was precisely that they were Christians and lived in a society where Christian values and ideas ruled. But that, to the philosopher, is only of limited interest: For that reason it has little philosophical value and therefore little interest. It would no doubt illustrate how nonphilosophical factors play a role in philosophy, but it would tell us nothing about the philosophical reasons that medievals gave for believing in the immortality of the soul. From the philosophical standpoint what is important is not that the medievals believed in the immortality of the soul because they were Christians, but rather the philosophical reasons they gave to support the view that the human soul is immortal as well as the value of those reasons. The type of causal explanation favored by culturalists, then, sets them apart from those who wish to take a philosophical approach to the history of philosophy.

But that is not all for, as argued elsewhere in this book, historians cannot hope to understand past philosophers unless they assume the role of philosophers themselves, understanding what philosophers are after and the considerations that carry weight in their discourse. Indeed, as Passmore has pointed out, cultural historians tend to fall into gross mistakes when describing the philosophical past precisely because they do not understand the practice of philosophy.[8] Therefore, in rejecting a philosophical understanding of the philosophical past, culturalists misunderstand it.

B. The Psychologist

The development of psychology as a separate social science and the initial controversies surrounding psychoanalysis in the latter part of the nineteenth century and the beginning of the twentieth have stirred a general interest in psychology that has extended to other fields. The history of philosophy has not escaped this impact, with the result that some historians of philosophy spend considerable time and effort trying to show how psychological factors affect ideas in various ways. I call this sort of approach to the history of philosophy "psychological," and its practitioners "psychologists."

There is much of interest in the results achieved by the application of this procedure. After all, most of us have some curiosity to know something about the inner workings of the minds of those whose ideas we admire. In particular in philosophy it would seem *prima facie* quite appropriate to investigate such phenomena, considering that the notions of "philosopher" and "sage" have traditionally been intertwined. We like to know, therefore, not only about Socrates' ideas, but also about how he came to hold those ideas and how he put them into practice. Furthermore, to establish the psychological reasons why Socrates held the ideas he did, for example, might make clear to us why someone else, of a different frame of mind, might not do so, and so on. All of this is, indeed, important for the accurate reconstruction of the historical record. The question that comes up, however, is whether such considerations have any philosophical value and contribute, therefore, to a philosophical understanding of the history of philosophy.

My answer to that question is that I do not see clearly how such psychological considerations and causal explanations can contribute to a truly philosophical history of philosophy. If we accept the principle that the task of the history of philosophy is to produce an account of past philosophical ideas and that, as argued in Chapter One, such an account must be philosophical and thus include not only description but also philosophical interpretation and evaluation, then it seems quite clear that psychological factors to a large extent are irrelevant to such an account. Such factors no doubt would help us in reconstructing the causal framework that gave rise to the philosophical ideas of an author, but they would provide only a psychological understanding of their appearance, leaving unexplained the philosophical reasons why the authors in question may have held the ideas they did. Such an account, then, would be useful for the special historian who is interested in psychological history or for the general historian who wishes to have a complete account of past events. But the historian of philosophy is not generally interested, *qua* historian of *philosophy*, in factors other than philosophical ones; he or she is expected to provide philosophical interpretations and evaluations and not just descriptions of the past.

Not that all nonphilosophical factors are irrelevant. Since historians of philosophy are concerned with the relations among the ideas of different authors and diverse periods of time, considerations such as spatio-temporal location and so on are important for them. For example, in order to establish the relations between Kant and Hume it is important to know when they lived, the languages they knew, the direct or indirect contact that Kant may have had with Hume's writings, the books that Kant read that may have made reference to Hume, and so on. None of these factors is strictly speaking philosophical, but it is clear that they have an important bearing on any reconstruction of the relation of Kant's ideas to those of Hume and therefore must be dealt with by the historian of philosophy.

The case of psychological phenomena is different, however. The historical phenomena that we have just mentioned are important because they make clear the locational circumstances within which ideas took place, and they serve to establish, among other things, contact among philosophers. They do not, however, explain the philosophical reasons why a philosopher held a particular view. For this reason they cannot become rivals of the philosophical reading of the history of philosophy. The psychological approach, on the other hand, does exactly the opposite, presenting as reasons that a philosopher held such and such a view some psychological factor or factors other than whatever philosophical reasons the philosopher gave for holding it. In this sense, there is a radical difference of perspective between the psychological historian and the philosophical historian: The psychologist will identify as a reason for a past philosopher holding a certain view that he or she was, say, paranoid, whereas the philosopher will say that he or she derived that view from certain assumptions about the nature of reality, for example.

Perhaps a concrete illustration will make the point clear. A few years ago, W. W. Bartley wrote a book about Wittgenstein that caused quite a stir. The stir came about because Bartley claimed in the book that Wittgenstein was not only psychologically homosexual but actually engaged in homosexual activity and with rather rough types. Considering Wittgenstein's stature, his reputation for a kind of pure moralism and delicate cultural sensibilities and tastes, and the devoted following that he had had, the reaction against the book was immediate and vicious. The protests were almost exclusively concerned with the defense of Wittgenstein's character, and charges were made against Bartley for historical inaccuracy and shoddy scholarship. Interestingly enough, what was mostly lost in the controversy was the implication of Bartley's procedure; namely, that somehow an understanding of the details of Wittgenstein's life, including his homosexuality, helps us grasp better some of his philosophical ideas.[9] From the historiographical point of view, of course, it is this claim that is interesting, but in the heat of the controversy it was largely ignored by almost everyone.[10] For our purposes, the importance of this example is that it illustrates the fundamental assumption of a psychological approach; namely, that knowledge about the psychology of philosophers will provide an understanding of their philosophy.

Now, if we take understanding to involve a causal explanation, this sort of claim would boil down to the view that Wittgenstein's homosexuality was the cause of some of his philosophical ideas. And, indeed, this is precisely what A. W. Levi argues concerning Wittgenstein's ethics. His view is that Wittgenstein's homosexuality and the guilt he felt because of it are responsible for his view of ethics as excluding anything that may have to do with facts; for this conception of ethics allowed him to escape the condemnation of rational discourse.[11]

But can we say that we have a better understanding of the philosophical reasons that support Wittgenstein's view of ethics, or that he thought supported it, from knowing that he was homosexual and that he may have been psychologically predisposed or determined to hold those views? If Levi is right, something not above dispute, surely we are enlightened in a psychological way by this analysis, but even in that case we can draw no philosophical lesson from it. Thus this kind of psychological analysis has little value for the historian of philosophy whose aim is to produce a philosophical history in which *philosophical* understanding, interpretation, and evaluation are of the essence.

In short, even if we could find a causal relation between some psychological phenomena and some philosophical ideas, something that is not easy to establish, such relation would still be largely irrelevant for the history of philosophy. For the history of philosophy requires a historico-philosophical account of ideas, not a historico-psychological one. The difference between these two accounts can be brought out by the fact that, as established in Chapter One, the history of philosophy includes value judgments about ideas, but psychohistory does not. The psychohistorian is interested only in describing which psychological fact produced which philosophical idea and not in the philosophical value of those ideas. There is a deep chasm therefore, between a psychological approach to the history of past philosophical ideas and the history of philosophy.

C. The Ideologue

The primary characteristic of the ideological approach to the history of philosophy is that it involves a commitment to something other than the understanding of the history of philosophy. The history of philosophy is studied because that is thought to be the way to achieve some other goal to which the ideologue is ultimately pledged. In some cases the goal is selfless and worthy of admiration, but in others it is selfish and cynically egotistical. Most often it is a mixture of the two, resulting from a lack of clear awareness in those who adopt this approach of where they stand and what their aims are. Ideologues, unlike philosophers and historians, are not looking for truth or discovery; they already have reached the conclusions they desire. They make use of the history of philosophy only for rhetorical reasons, that is, to convince an audience of what they have already accepted. As a result, there is in this approach a strong emphasis on defense, and we find a frequent recourse to formulas that, after a while, become meaningless clichés. We also find in it an excessive sensitivity to criticism as well as a marked belligerence against any remark that can be construed even remotely as critical.

A very interesting case of the ideological phenomenon took place among Latin American intellectuals in the nineteenth century.[12] Latin America at the time, as is still the case today, was plagued by political instability, social inequality, and economic woes. Preoccupied with the solution to these problems, Latin American intellectuals imported from Europe a set of ideas that they called *positivism*. These ideas were supposed to point the way toward a successful solution to Latin America's political, social, and economic problems. Positivism was a hodgepodge concocted from the thought of such diverse authors as Comte, Spencer, Haeckel, Mill, and others. Its main emphases were two: (1) an emphasis on "positive" science, meaning empirical science, as opposed to philosophy and metaphysics, in the area of knowledge; and (2) an emphasis on order in the political sphere so as to promote overall progress. Positivist ideas swept Latin America and they were studied, spread, and defended not only by intellectuals but by governments as well. The Brazilian flag to this day carries the motto "Order and Progress," a remnant of positivist influence. In Mexico, positivism became the "official philosophy" of the government of the dictator Porfirio Díaz. Some of those who joined the new ideology and studied the ideas of Comte, Spencer, and other authors favored by positivists did so because they were convinced the positivist program was the only way to end political instability and economic backwardness in Latin America. This was obviously a commendable motive. Others, however, had personal gain in mind, the perpetuation of the *status quo* that allowed them to occupy and preserve a privileged position in society. Theirs, of course, was not a selfless motive. Regardless of the motive, however, the object of commitment of Latin American positivists was external to the ideas they adopted to bring about that object. The ideas they adopted, studied, defended, and discussed were mere means to something else, in this case the development of Latin American society.[13] The interest of Latin American positivists in the history of thought that preceded them was ideological.

The nonphilosophical aim of the ideological approach allows for the use of nonphilosophical means to spread philosophical ideas. Proselytizing and even force are not out of the question. Moreover, there is also the possibility of a cynical purpose in ideology and that there be no real and true belief in the ideas adopted and studied. For the ideologue what is important is the object of commitment, which is neither philosophy nor history.

The reasons for the development of an ideological approach are quite understandable. We all can easily understand the temptation to use and endorse ideas to bring about benefits to ourselves. And most of us no doubt can favor the use of ideas to bring about needed changes in society. But the benefits of this approach seem unrelated to the history of philosophy; they have to do with social and practical gain, not with the deeper understanding of past ideas themselves. Indeed, it is difficult to see how ideas can be truly understood when the overall aim of the one who studies them is something other than their understanding. There are no clear advantages, then, to the ideological approach as far as the history of philosophy is concerned, and the disadvantages of it seem all too clear.

Perhaps the most serious of the disadvantages associated with ideology, and certainly the most often cited, is the loss of objectivity implied by this approach. The emphasis on useful results, whether meant for the social group or the individual, detracts from the objective understanding of ideas in themselves, leading to interpretations and evaluations marred by mercenary considerations derived from the value they have for something else. The perspective from which they are examined, then, precludes the objectivity required to understand and describe them. This attitude in many ways is a step backward to the time preceding the discovery of science by the pre-Socratics, for it is characterized by a nonliberal understanding of knowledge and the history of thought where knowledge and history have value only insofar as they can be used for some practical purpose. This devaluation of objectivity may not just result in an unintended distortion of the past, but sometimes leads to intended revisions of it in order to bring it in line with the views required to achieve desired ends. It should be clear, however, that the ideological approach does not imply revisionism. Ideologues do not necessarily need to revise history in order to carry out their program. They can use what they know about the past exactly as they know it, or, alternatively, they can use their knowledge selectively. In either case, one can hardly argue that such use implies the revision of the historical record; it implies a nonhistorical aim but not a revisionary one.

Another disadvantage of the ideological approach is the impossibility of conducting a true dialogue with those who adopt it. The overall practical aim to which ideologues are committed stands in the way of communication. True dialogue involves an exchange of ideas with a view toward mutual and deeper understanding. There is in dialogue the implication of the possibility of change in perspective as already noted in Chapter Three. But ideologues make no room for such possibility. Their interests are in indoctrination with a view to the achievement of practical results. If they engage in dialogue at all, they do so only as a means of achieving their predetermined goal and only insofar as it does not interfere with that goal. There is no give and take for them; ideologues are takers, they take whatever they can get at whatever cost.

It is precisely this closed attitude and the kind of duplicity with which some ideologues participate in dialogue that has earned them a bad name and the disdain of serious historians of philosophy. For the conscious and willing use of the history of philosophy for aims extraneous to that history is repugnant to the historical spirit. It reveals a cynical and sophistical attitude toward historical knowledge or a naive, quasi-religious commitment to a cause, which are insurmountable obstacles to doing history of philosophy. As noted in Chapter One, the history of philosophy involves description in addition to interpretation and evaluation, but idealogues are concerned only with the last two. Moreover, the interpretative and evaluative judgments they reach are based on nonphilosophical considerations, thus rendering the historical accounts they produce nonphilosophical.

II. PHILOSOPHICAL APPROACHES

The main characteristic of the *philosophical approaches* to the history of philosophy is that, in contrast to nonphilosophical approaches, they try to provide philosophical accounts of past philosophical ideas.

There are ten philosophical approaches to the history of philosophy that I would like to examine in particular. I have given the following names to their practitioners in order to facilitate the discussion: Golden Age nostalgic, romantic, scholar, doxographer, apologist, literary critic, dilettante, idealist, problematicist, and eschatologist. These names are meant to suggest the fundamental thrust of the procedure used in each case, but care must be taken to avoid some of their inappropriate connotations.

These ten different approaches can be gathered into two general groups, depending on their aim and the character of the methodology they use to achieve it. One group, composed of the Golden Age nostalgic, the romantic, the scholar, and the doxographer, I call *historical*. The other group, composed of the apologist, the literary critic, the dilettante, the idealist, the problematicist, and the eschatologist, I call *polemicist*. Let me begin with the historical group.

A. Historical Approaches

The aim of those who adopt a historical approach is fundamentally historical, as the name indicates, although that should be understood in a philosophical context. All approaches within the group of philosophical approaches aim to provide a philosophical account of the history of philosophy where the identification of and concern with philosophical reasons and ideas is regarded as essential. This distinguishes these approaches from the nonphilosophical approaches considered earlier. But in the historical group that aim is secondary and pursued only insofar as it serves an overriding historical aim. There is a fundamental emphasis on historical accuracy, faithfulness to sources, and the construction of an accurate account of the philosophical past. Philosophical enlightenment is only secondary and, when present, is considered to be precisely a consequence of the correct understanding of the past. The stress is on description rather than interpretation and evaluation, although, as we shall see, some of these approaches fail precisely because their excessive reverence and enthusiasm for the past prevents them from approaching and describing it with any degree of objectivity. Indeed, some of those who favor the romantic approach go so far as to reject the possibility of any objectivity and description, thus subverting the very aim they originally sought to achieve. Of the four approaches mentioned that fall into this group, those used by the Golden Age nostalgic and the romantic display and even encourage an emotional involvement with the past. The other two tend to favor a detached and nonemotional attitude toward it.

1. The Golden Age Nostalgic. The *approach of the Golden Age nostalgic* has some characteristics in common with the ideological approach, but their differences are many and more substantial than their similarities. The most prominent feature of the ideological approach that distinguishes it from that of the Golden Age nostalgic is its nonhistorical character. Its main concern in studying the history of philosophy is not to establish, understand, and evaluate that history, but rather to defend and promote certain views to achieve some ends that are nonhistorical. Its attitude toward the history of philosophy implies a kind of contempt for it, since practitioners of this approach feel free to use history for reasons foreign to it. But this is not true in the approach of the Golden Age nostalgic. Indeed, those who favor the latter approach look upon some historically distant past as the time when philosophy reached its zenith. Convinced of the value of past achievements, they seek to recover the past in its "ancient glory."

Still, this very attitude of excessive reverence for the past, which may reach extraordinary extremes and becomes at times almost religious, leads them to see the period of the history of philosophy they admire only in positive terms, thus distorting the reality they seek to understand and preserve. Anything different from it is interpreted either as propaedeutic to it, if it precedes it, or as a deterioration of it, if it follows it, a fact that establishes similarities between this approach and the eschatological approach to be discussed later. The exaggerated positive emphasis that characterizes this approach precludes the analysis, understanding, and criticism of the shortcomings of the period regarded as the Golden Age. Consequently, the objectivity so necessary for the study of the history of philosophy is lost. This loss is not the result of a consciously malicious decision where objectivity is purposefully rejected, rather it is an unintended corollary that follows indirectly, but nonetheless effectively, from the excessive enthusiasm of the nostalgic for the Golden Age. In the Golden Age approach objectivity is implicitly subverted.

Those who adopt this approach look at the past with awe, but we may ask, Why do they do it? The obvious answer is that they are impressed with it, finding in it what they do not see among their contemporaries. Usually, this attitude is not confined to philosophy, and in philosophy it does not refer to the thought of a single individual. The attitude is generally adopted toward a whole era in all or most of its cultural expressions: art, architecture, literature, political theory, and so on. It has often been the case that this approach characterizes a whole historical period that looks on a previous historical epoch as a Golden Age. The most obvious case in point is the Renaissance, where ancient culture was glorified and imitated to the last detail.

In the Renaissance one can see quite clearly both the advantages and disadvantages of this approach. Among the advantages perhaps the most important is the possibility of understanding and seeing aspects of the past that have escaped others. The devotion and reverence characteristic of the nostalgic approach, the open sympathy that it entails, lead to an appreciation of the inner springs that compose the intellectual machine of a past age, making plain ideas and reasons that otherwise would escape the uninvolved observer. The imitation of the ancients that so often accompanies this approach uncovers not only their ideas, but the obstacles they encountered and the techniques they devised to overcome them. Finally, this attitude leads to new discoveries of various sorts, such as previously unknown relations, hidden dependencies, and subtle achievements that only the devout admirer could expect to detect.

All this is finely exemplified by Renaissance humanists, with their admiration for Classical thought and their devotion to its study. Indeed, thanks to the humanists many ancient texts were recovered and their ideas taken seriously again.[14] It was as a result of the humanists' extraordinary sensitivity to the nature of ancient thought and writing that proper authorship was assigned to texts previously assigned to the wrong authors and forgeries were uncovered. The fates of the *Donatio Constantini* and the *Liber de causis* were sealed forever during the Renaissance, to name just two of the most notorious texts affected by the approach practiced by humanists.

But just as the nostalgic approach has advantages, so does it have serious disadvantages. In the first place, it tends to stifle creativity and progress and, in the second place, as already noted, it tends to distort the value of anything not belonging to the period regarded as the Golden Age. Both points can be easily illustrated by reference to the Renaissance. Take the second one, for example. It is well known that in their devotion to antiquity Renaissance humanists came to regard the period between antiquity and their own age disparagingly as barbaric, uncivilized, uncouth, and lacking any philosophical and artistic value whatsoever. They expressed their attitude clearly by calling the period the *Middle Ages*, the ages in between the two glorious ages of the Renaissance and Classical antiquity. But now, after the Renaissance prejudice against the medieval period has eroded and new textual discoveries have been made by non-Renaissance scholars, we know the richness, variety, originality, and high philosophical, let alone artistic, sophistication that characterized the culture of those ages "in the middle." Indeed, from the philosophical standpoint, the general consensus today is that the Middle Ages was much more original, complex, and interesting than the Renaissance ever was. The thought of the humanists appears to us today as unoriginal, contrived, and somewhat superficial if compared with that of thirteenth and fourteenth century scholastics, for example. Ironically, some historians of philosophy today regard the Renaissance as a transitional period between the Middle Ages and Modern philosophy, in a way somewhat similar to the way in which Renaissance humanists considered the Middle Ages.

But let us not forget the first disadvantage noted, namely, the lack of originality that tends to characterize the work of those individuals and ages dominated by the nostalgic approach. Such lack of originality does not always and necessarily characterize all the products of periods where the dominant approach is nostalgic, however. In the case of art, for example, the Renaissance, in spite of its admiration for and imitation of ancient works, was able to achieve new heights of artistic expression unmatched in any previous historical period. Yet, in many instances excessive admiration leads to slavish imitation and the sacrifice of creativity. This result is quite evident in most Renaissance philosophy, where the attempt to recreate the literary style and ideas of the ancients frequently stifled originality.

2. The Romantic. The romantic approach has much in common with the approach of the Golden Age nostalgic. Like the nostalgic, the romantic looks at the past with emotional involvement, an object of love and commitment. On the other hand, the romantic tends to focus on individual authors, who are treated as heros, whereas the nostalgic usually centers attention on a past period of history that he or she regards as a Golden Age. The romantic is concerned with the individual and his or her life more than his or her ideas, as we saw in the text of Jonathan Rée cited in Chapter One.[15]

The romantic looks at the interpretation of the past as a kind of performance where sympathy, creativity, and literary form are more important than objectivity, fidelity, and content. The reading of a text becomes something personal where, just as happens with the reading of novels, poetry, and other works of literature, one looks for experiences and emotion rather than cut-and-dried logical understanding. This procedure makes sense according to those who follow it, because pure objectivity can never be achieved. Nor is it possible to be absolutely faithful to a source. The key to the reading of the history of philosophy is rather inventiveness and creativity:

> No thoughts, least of all philosophical ones, can be definitely represented, since no system of representation is definitive; or conversely...all thinkers, especially philosophical ones, can be

> aware that their thoughts might best be represented in ways that they cannot even imagine. This is why anachronistic interpretations, whether in art or in theory, can reveal aspects of a work that historically authentic interpretations may conceal.[16]

This does not imply that no fidelity is possible, but it does mean that historians of philosophy can and should let sympathy guide their interpretations and feel free to open themselves to creativity.

Again Rée provides us with a good example of the way the romantic approach works when applied to a historical work of philosophy such as Spinoza's *Ethics:*

> The romantics...see the world of the *Ethics* as controlled by an author who is not...a level-headed, civilized, and clubbable member of a democratic intellectual community, ready to have his claims tested like anyone else. Their Spinoza is a complacent mystic, a self-absorbed saint whom we thank for understanding our difficulties and never blame for having caused them in the first place. The romantics will not expect their interpretation of the *Ethics* to appeal to someone who has no sympathy with such a figure, and who believes that philosophical thoughts ought always to be represented in a language uncluttered by such complexities as metaphor, narrative, or irony. They may even claim that good philosophy always calls upon forms of representation which involve fictions, and that it can succeed only for readers who are willing to control their disbelief. And they may concede that the necessary fictions (Spinoza's concept of intuitive knowledge, for example) can be incoherent; but they will insist that there are important truths which can be apprehended only by proceeding *as if* they were true.[17]

Undoubtedly, the romantic approach brings something different to the history of philosophy, namely, an emotional empathy with past philosophers that no other approach seems to provide to such a degree. The historical task requires sympathy in order to get at the depths of a philosophic thought. One must internalize that thought and in a sense appropriate it in order to discover all its hidden connections and springs. Moreover, romantics understand that creativity has a role to play in the history of philosophy. Historians must also be creative, for the study of history involves moving into a substantially different world, where the modes of thinking and concepts to which historians are accustomed may not operate. Discovery involves inventiveness, the ability to see new possibilities, to move out of set patterns of thought and try new ones. Because the line between objectivity and fidelity on the one hand and subjectivity and creativity on the other is by no means clear, there is no question that the romantic approach emphasizes important elements in the historical task. The problem is that it does not balance them with other emphases that are essential to that task, and thus goes too far.

Indeed, the extreme romantic will say that the descriptive task of the history of philosophy is impossible and evaluation cannot be separated from interpretation. But, under these conditions we are left hanging in the air, without an anchor to secure our speculative creativity about the past. Can it be possible for us, then, to separate actual history from fictional history? Are we not condemned by the romantic to treat all romantic histories as equally valid, since they express the particular visions of individual romantics and one romantic is as good as any other? Or are there criteria that can help us distinguish between true romantic histories and false romantic histories or between accurate romantic histories and inaccurate romantic histories? And since romanticism is a personal matter, on what grounds can one argue that one history is romantic and another not, or that one is more romantic than another? According to what some romantics tell us, the epitome of nonromantic history is Bennett's view of Spinoza's thought as a hypothetico-deductive system. But, for all we know, Bennett wrote the book with tears in his eyes, so impressed was he by the greatness of the system and Spinoza's acumen! Would that make his book an instance of romantic history?

The exclusion of works such as Bennett's on Spinoza from romantic histories according to those who favor them indicates another important shortcoming of the romantic approach: The sympathy and emotional stir favored by romantics seems to be misplaced. Does it make sense to appreciate a dog because it resembles a cat? Similarly it seems to make no sense for the historian of philosophy *qua* historian of philosophy to sympathize and appreciate philosophers for anything other than their philosophy. What importance does it really have for historians of philosophy that a particular philosopher was tall or short, handsome or ugly, good or bad, crooked or honest? Just as what is important in physicists for other physicists are their views about nature, so in philosophers what is important for other philosophers and for historians of philosophy as well is their philosophy. Their character, looks, or anything else are mere curiosa that need not be considered essential components of a historical account of their philosophical ideas.

The emphasis of the romantics on the lives and character of philosophers indicates that their interest in the past is really not philosophical. The romantic historian is very much a person in love, but love is neither a necessary nor a sufficient condition for the philosopher or the historian of philosophy to carry out their tasks; indeed, it could function as an unwelcomed distraction and obstacle on the way to truth. The historian of philosophy needs a cool head and a sharp intellect, not the passion of love.

In short, romantic history seems to be either bad history or just history with a sentimental bent. The good aspects of this approach are already present in other approaches to the history of philosophy and the bad ones are so serious that there is little to recommend this approach taken by itself.

3. The Scholar. The *approach of the scholar* is strongly historical, more so than any of the other historical approaches to the history of philosophy. Its aim is to uncover and understand the history of philosophy, to provide, in Rorty's words, "a historical reconstruction" of the past, in which history is the key notion.[18] Thus, the scholarly approach does not bring into history the undesirable elements characteristic of the ideological approach. Its primary advantage over the approach of the nostalgic is that it does not share with it the excessive reverence and devotion characteristic of those who study "the Golden Age." This frees those who adopt the scholarly approach from the constraints of predetermined value judgments and allows them to appreciate more objectively the connections among historical ideas. The devotion and allegiance of scholars is not to a particular thinker or age but to history, to the past as a whole. What they want to do is to understand the past as it was, without mixing it with anachronistic impurities brought into it, such as value judgments, prejudices, preconceived notions, and any other elements that would cloud the objectivity needed by the students of history, preventing them from observing, understanding, and presenting the past as it was, on its own terms. This distinguishes them from the romantic, whose sympathy is for an individual. The sympathy of the scholar is not for historical figures, but for the historical procedure itself. The task that historians who adopt the scholarly approach see for themselves is one of description, completely objective description, purged from any element of interpretation and particularly of evaluation. Indeed, as a recent defender of this position has noted,

> the question of the ultimate truth or falsity of the doctrines is simply not at issue; the only thing that is important is whether or not our account has made the beliefs intelligible. Sometimes this will call for a judgment that *on his own terms,* some premise

> or inference a philosopher uses may not be available to him, properly speaking. [But] if we are interested in historical reconstruction...the falsity of a premise then universally accepted is not a relevant part of the story.[19]

The task of the historian of philosophy is to describe what the past thought as determined by what it said and by what is revealed in the documents and events of the period. Anything beyond this is not history of philosophy but literature, philosophy, or something else. Creativity, an essential element in literature, art, and philosophy favored also by romantics, is not to play a role in historical work except with regard to devising new methods and technologies to uncover the past. Note, then, that unlike the Golden Age nostalgic, the respect and devotion of the scholar is not for the particular *thought* and *ideas* of an age or a period; nor is it, in contrast with the romantic, for a historical figure. As far as historians who adopt the scholarly perspective are concerned, the value of the ideas they study is irrelevant to their task. Their respect and devotion goes rather to the *record* and its accurate establishment. The texts that reveal that record become the center of attention and the only basis for knowing and studying the past. Any departure from the text, any interpretation not explicitly backed up by it, any judgment not found in it, must be expunged from the historical account. For this reason those who favor this approach have been accused of antiquarianism—a narrow and exclusive interest in the past, as we saw in Chapter One. And their critics point out that this attitude restricts substantially the range of operation of the historian, confining it usually to the production of critical editions, translations, and biographies and the resolution of textual problems and issues of authorship.

Many arguments are offered in support of the scholarly approach. Some are dialectical insofar as they try to establish the correctness of this approach by attacking other approaches that conflict with it. But other arguments reason directly for this position. One such argument offered recently points out, as noted in Chapter One, that the importance of the history of philosophy is not that it may lead to philosophical truths, but that it may lead to philosophical questions of which we may not have been aware. Now, in order to get at those questions, so the argument goes, we must adopt a "disinterested" approach, that is, one in which evaluation is eliminated altogether and even interpretation is reduced to description. For this is the only possible way in which we can understand historical figures on their own terms and thus penetrate the questions and issues with which they were concerned.[20] When historical studies are tainted by "interest," we tend to see selectively and therefore distort the understanding of the past. The only way to profit from the study of the past is to understand it as it was. That study, by confronting us with questions that are foreign to us, provides us with an invaluable perspective on the issues and problems of our own time.

This attitude leads to the creation of a historiographical method in which the work of the historian boils down to three tasks: conceptual translation, rearrangement of texts, and tracking down influences. Indeed, much of the history of philosophy produced so far falls precisely in one or more of these categories. By conceptual translation I understand not just the actual word-by-word rendition of a text into a different language from the one in which it was written, but also close paraphrases of the original text into a new language or into a modern version of an older language. The task of the historian in this case is simply, as it were, to modernize the language of the text in order to make it understandable to those not conversant with the language or vocabulary and usage present in the text. The paraphrase is necessary to make this modernization possible, since many words do not have one-to-one counterparts in modern vocabulary and also to facilitate transitions often absent in old and cryptically written works. A vast number of historical works in philosophy fall into this category. One has only to look at original sources to find that what many historians have done in their studies of them is to paraphrase closely the source and nothing else.

Obviously the conceptual translation of texts, as we have understood it, is a valuable task and one that should not be discouraged. Not everyone can understand historical texts, since not everyone possesses the necessary tools to do so and the acquisition of such tools requires considerable time and effort. Historians who engage in the conceptual translation of works render a valuable service to the philosophical community by making available materials that otherwise would not be accessible. Moreover, it should also be clear that to do this kind of work requires not only sophistication in philology but also in philosophy, for translation requires knowledge and understanding of concepts and not merely of word usage. The question as to how far the translator should go, however, is a matter of dispute among historiographers of philosophy. Those historiographers who adopt the scholarly perspective tend to favor a conservative approach to translation, where the emphasis is on trying to capture the conceptual framework of the past rather than appropriate it and render it into contemporary terminology. They see conceptual translation as providing at most a close paraphrase in which the main concepts of the original, and even the language, are preserved as far as possible.

By the *rearrangement* of texts I mean an approach a bit more free than the close paraphrase that I have called *conceptual translation*. In this case historians do not restrict themselves to rendering the text intelligible to the modern reader; they also seek to present interpretations of the text and to answer philosophical questions not explicitly raised by the author but that are nonetheless of interest to modern philosophers. The way this is done is by looking for other texts that answer those questions or interpret the passages whose understanding is sought. This method has been the traditional favorite of theologians. Since they deal with sacred scriptures, considered to be divinely revealed, they do not feel that they can "put words into the text." Under those conditions the only alternative is to interpret the text through other passages found in the same work or in other works of the same author. This exegetical method allows historians also to answer questions not explicitly posed by the historical author but that have become the subject of debate. Thus, one may want to know what Plato thought was the principle of individuation, even though he does not seem to have raised the issue of individuation explicitly. It may be the case, of course, that he says nothing that may reveal his view on this matter. Indeed, he may not have had a view on the matter and may not have been aware of the issue at all. But it is also possible that he did say something in passing that reveals he was aware of the issue and held a view about it. This kind of situation poses no problem for those who adopt this approach since, whatever the outcome of the investigation, the procedure always involves references to the text. Historians who follow this method take certain liberties and incur certain dangers, for there is always the possibility of quoting out of context, but the danger is counterbalanced by a strong respect for the text and its context.[21]

Finally, the scholarly approach also permits tracking down influences in the history of philosophy. Questions concerning who got what from where are a primary concern of historians who adopt the scholarly approach. However, those who adhere strictly to it will accept only hard data as evidence for their conclusions. They do not consider similarities of doctrine and style to be evidence of influence. They are willing to consider only explicit references, internal or external, that point to a direct connection between authors.

The scholarly approach favors total immersion. Historians who proceed in this way seek to immerse themselves in their texts to such an extent that they impersonate their authors and speak only their words. This is the quintessential scholarly attitude and one that has been ridiculed by Jorge Luis Borges in a notorious short story to which I already referred, where Pierre Menard, an expert on Cervantes's period, aims to rewrite *Don Quixote*.[22] The perfect historian, according to this point of view, is one who can reproduce every text the author in question ever wrote, manipulating them at will, as their author would have done were he alive. The historian becomes in a sense like a computer that contains the complete works of an author and can reproduce any text or part of it.

Clearly there are many advantages to the scholarly approach. Above all of them are its reliability, its accuracy, and its historical objectivity. The scholar goes by what authors said, not by what they may have thought and we think they may have meant. And those sayings are so internalized that they become the historian's own conceptual framework. Supposedly, then, we have a perfect understanding of the past, if by understanding of the past one means thinking exactly as the past thought. But, we may ask, is that what the history of philosophy is about? Should historians of philosophy be restricted to rearranging texts and rethinking thoughts and nothing else? Can such a procedure result in true understanding? Philosophical understanding involves the elements of interpretation and evaluation discussed in Chapters One and Four, and the pure scholar must reject both. Textual immersion, even at its best, then, fails if taken by itself insofar as it does not provide us with a complete account of the philosophical past.

These are serious charges against the scholarly approach, but there is at least another one that is even more serious: Even the more strictly scholarly approach involves elements that are incompatible with the explicit agenda of this approach. I discussed this difficulty in Chapter One, but in the present context the bases for this accusation can be easily illustrated by referring to the three tasks of the scholar mentioned earlier: translation, rearrangement of texts, and tracking down influences. At first impression these activities seem harmless and perfectly concordant with the scholarly aim of pure description unmixed with any interpretation or evaluation. But on closer examination it becomes clear that all three of these tasks involve at least an element of interpretation. This is quite obvious in tracking down influences and rearranging texts. For to rearrange something involves following an order different from the one it has, and this is no less true of the texts of an author than of anything else. A purely descriptive task could not but reproduce the original arrangement; anything else involves interpretation. Indeed, it is at least arguable that it also involves an evaluative element, since it clearly favors one arrangement over another and a new one over the one the texts originally had. The elements of interpretation and evaluation are even more evident in tracking down influences. For to say that a particular author borrowed an idea from some other author involves the comparison of texts and ideas and their interpretation so that their similarities and disimilarities can be established. There is also an element of evaluation when historians judge, as those engaged in this task inevitably do, that the author misinterpreted or was faithful to the source, for these judgments involve values of precision, accuracy, and so on.

It is not, however, only the rearrangement of texts and the tracking down of influences that fail to meet the purely descriptive aim of the scholar. Even translation, and particularly "conceptual" translation, requires interpretation, as we saw in Chapter One. The use of any linguistic sign other than the original involves a potential shift in meaning that may change the import of the text. If we want to be absolutely faithful to a source we need to reproduce it as it is, without alterations of any kind. As Graham has pointed out:

> An extremist who would not admit modern concepts into his explanations will end up, for instance, having to explicate Aristotle in Aristotelian terms.... Even this is not enough; for the English terms will be but imperfect renderings of the Greek. Thus to be faithful to the program one must explicate Aristotle in Greek. But not just any Greek will do; it will have to be fourth century Attic Greek—written by a native speaker of an Ionic dialect, and so on.[23]

Even more, the historian will have to refrain from "explicating" at all, since any elaboration would certainly involve the use of terms not found in the original or, if all the terms used are found in the original, at least a rearrangement of those terms.

The approach of the scholar, then, is not only inappropriate for the historian of philosophy, but in fact is inconsistent with the scholar's own explicit agenda. It is for this reason that approaches of a different character have been devised and favored by many historians of philosophy.

4. The Doxographer. The main characteristic shared by all doxographical approaches is their emphasis on uncritical description. In contrast with the more probing and critical character of the polemical approaches that will be discussed later, doxography aims to present views and ideas in a descriptive fashion without aiming to evaluate them critically. Indeed, in keeping with its historical emphasis, doxography often discourages interpretation. Unlike scholars, they do not aim to provide accounts at all, but are content to describe philosophies from the past.

There are two quite different understandings of the doxographical approach in the historiographical literature. One is a traditional understanding of doxography, presented clearly by Passmore in a relatively recent article.[24] I call this *life and thought doxography.* The second is a new interpretation of doxography put forth by Rorty.[25] I call it *univocal question doxography.* To these I add a third type of doxography, which I call *history of ideas doxography.* Let me begin with the traditional interpretation of doxography.

a. Life and Thought Doxographer. The fundamental characteristic of *life and thought doxography* is its concentration on the lives and what are regarded as fundamental ideas of various authors that are discussed *seriatim.*[26] No attempt is made to discuss the arguments on the basis of which the philosophers reached their conclusions, nor is there much in the way of subtle interpretation or evaluation of their positions. Moreover, although the aim of life and thought doxographers is historical, insofar as their concern is to provide accurate information about the past, they treat philosophers and ideas to a large extent as atomic events not connected with each other. They generally ignore the historical circumstances that may have had a bearing on philosophers' thinking, and their ideas are treated as single occurrances to be listed as part of a kind of creed to which the particular philosophers are supposed to have adhered. It is true that, as Passmore has pointed out, practitioners of this approach do gather philosophers into "schools" or groups, but this is done rather mechanically and serves more to separate them than to reveal the historical connections among various individual philosophers. Thus, for example, Locke, Berkeley, and Hume are put and treated together in the group of "British empiricists" because they all adhered to a particular view concerning human understanding, and Descartes, Malebranche, and Leibniz are put and treated in a separate group of "Continental rationalists" because they all held a common view of human knowledge that differed from that of the empiricists, while ignoring the individual connections between members of the two groups. A very important factor in life and thought doxographies is temporal succession. Authors are ordered according to a chronology rather than in an order that expresses the historical interrelations among them.

One of the earliest and best examples of this kind of doxography is Diogenes Laertius's *Lives and Opinions of Eminent Philosophers.* This book consists of a chronologically arranged series of short descriptions of the main facts and views of ancient Greek philosophers. The book begins with a short preface in which Diogenes defends the Greek origin of philosophy. Indeed, he goes so far as to claim that the human race itself began with the Greeks. But in it he also provides a very summary and sketchy classification of the branches of philosophy (physics, ethics, and logic), of philosophers (dogmatists and skeptics), and of the philosophical schools of the times (Megarians, Epicureans, and so on). After the preface, he proceeds to discuss philosophers *seriatim*. These discussions are primarily informative and dominated by biographical data. For example, almost half of the chapter devoted to Aristotle is concerned with the facts of his life, including a reproduction and discussion of his will, and the other half provides a list of Aristotle's works and sayings attributed to him. The discussion of the philosophy of Aristotle, properly speaking, occupies less than one-sixth of the chapter, which makes it grossly inadequate. Consider that the only comments that Diogenes makes concerning the *Prior* and *Posterior Analytics* are as follows: "As an aid to judgment he left the *Prior* and *Posterior Analytics*. By the Prior Analytics the premisses are judged, by the Posterior the process of inference is tested."[27] These statements are not only inadequate but also misleading, for what Aristotle does in the *Prior Analytics* is not to judge premises, but rather to provide us with a classification and evaluation of argumentative structures.

All this sounds pretty bad, and it is to a certain extent. There is no question that this kind of history of philosophy does not reveal the actual historical connections among past philosophers and their ideas. Indeed, this approach distorts our view of the way in which philosophical ideas arise and develop because it does not present them as solutions to the problems that philosophers intend to solve with them. An accurate historical account of philosophical ideas must present ideas in their proper context as solutions to problems if that was in fact how they were meant. As such, the life and thought approach may be considered not only unhistorical but also historically distorting. Moreover, this approach is also philosophically superficial, since it does not dwell at depth on ideas and arguments and avoids both the sort of interpretation and evaluation that I claimed in Chapters One and Four are essential requirements for the history of philosophy.

On the other hand, we should not be too harsh on this approach. In the first place, it should be understood that some of those who have adopted it have had a very limited aim in mind. They have not been trying to reconstruct the history of philosophy or to present an account of it in the sense we have established here. Their aim has been rather to provide some basic information about past philosophers and their ideas. They were writing informational sources, the sort of thing that is still found today in encyclopedias and similar works of reference. And certainly that information is useful and the task of assembling it is not only perfectly legitimate but also historically relevant. We need to have works of reference where we can go to look up dates, titles of books, summaries of someone's ideas, and biographical information. And this is indeed what we find in some of the classical doxographical works, such as the mentioned one by Diogenes Laertius and Walter Burleigh's *De vita et moribus philosophorum*. These works served as models for similar works in later centuries that functioned basically as biographical encyclopedias of philosophy.

The problem with life and thought doxography is not what it accomplishes, but the fact that it may be taken for more than it is and historians will consider themselves satisfied with it. For the history of philosophy entails much more than what the doxographer of this sort provides: It requires philosophical analyses of ideas and their reasons, as well as historically accurate accounts of the relations among authors and their views. As Passmore has correctly pointed out, "doxographical information constitutes, as it were, the margins of our knowledge, and no quantity of it will give us any sort of understanding"[28] but, I would add, it does nonetheless have a place in the historical corpus.

b. Univocal Question Doxographer. The second doxographical approach is what I call *univocal question doxography*. Those who adopt it have some things in common with the eschatologists, who will be discussed later. Both groups approach the history of philosophy with a certain point of view in mind, and neither believes in completely disinterested history. But there is a fundamental distinction between these two approaches. Eschatologists generally consider their own point of view as the end product of a continuous process of philosophical development, and they have a self-justificatory aim in mind. In contrast, univocal question doxographers have no self-justificatory aim, nor do they see their thought as the culmination of a historical process of development. Their approach, then, is not as philosophically interesting as that of the eschatologists. Partly because of this, however, they have a greater sense of historical objectivity than eschatologists, since they have no particular ax to grind, as it were.

The single most important characteristic of univocal question doxography is its insistence in making the past answer questions and address issues that became evident only in subsequent historical periods. Typically, as Rorty has pointed out, they formulate a question, such as "What did X think the good was?" and then proceed to substitute X by the various philosophers of the period they are studying.[29] Their historical account consists of the answers that they squeeze out from all the philosophers they examine. The resulting lists (X believed the good was *M*, Y believed the good was *N*, Z believed the good was *O*, etc.) are generally uninteresting and contribute little to an understanding of the dynamics through which philosophers reach their positions, the arguments they use in their support, or even the character of the answers themselves.

The main assumption of this procedure, of course, is that all philosophers at all times are concerned with the same issues and that those issues are not affected by the historical circumstances surrounding them. Philosophical questions for the doxographer of this type are to be considered *sub specie aeternitatis*. This is why I have used the expression *univocal question* to describe this approach, for according to this perspective, all philosophers are taken to be concerned with the univocally same philosophical questions.

Note, moreover, the important differences between the life and thought approach and the univocal question approach. In the first the overriding emphasis was on data, biographical and philosophical, arranged in chronological order and by school. In the univocal question approach, systematic concerns become more important, and the beginnings of an interest in problems, oversimplified as questions, begins to show.

Univocal question doxography has been harshly criticized by some historiographers, but it should be noted that not all of it is bad. Indeed, in many ways it is a more objectively historical approach than that used by many other historians. Its lack of interest in defending a particular point of view and the absence of a "progressive" perspective mean practitioners of this approach can examine the past dispassionately, allowing for a more accurate picture of it. Through this approach it might be easier to arrive at the past as it was itself, rather than what we would like it to have been. The dangers of univocal question doxography lie rather in its insistence on getting answers from the past to questions and issues that may have been foreign to it, thus distorting the conceptual framework within which past figures were working. Note that there may be nothing wrong in asking questions of the past based on subsequent concerns. What is wrong is to insist that the past must answer them and answer them within contemporarily established parameters. Thus, there is nothing wrong in asking whether Plato had a principle of individuation, for example. What is wrong is to squeeze out of Plato's texts such a principle and then regard the answer as Plato's answer, even if Plato may have never thought about individuation and may have never proposed a principle of it.

The univocal question doxographer's insistence on putting questions to the past and bringing some order and intelligibility to vast expanses of the past by means of those questions is commendable. The objectionable aspects of the procedure are that it is overdone and the integrity of the past is not respected, partly because of oversimplification and partly due to neglect of the idiosyncratic circumstances within which philosophical issues surface and are addressed. It is fine to consider whether one can put a wood cube through a circular hole whose radius is equal to half the side of the cube, but it is stupid to insist on trying to get the cube through the hole.

One should be careful, therefore, not to overreact to univocal question doxography by rejecting, as Collingwood did, the possibility that several philosophers from different times may be addressing the same or at least a similar question.[30] This would push one into the kind of historicism that would render the history of philosophy impossible, and against which I argued in Chapter Two.[31] But in order to reject univocal question doxography one need not go to such extremes. It is enough to indicate the need to take into account the local historical context in the history of philosophy and to recognize that philosophical problems are enormously complex and often defy simplification.

c. History of Ideas Doxographer. Still a third doxographical approach is that of the so-called *historian of ideas*. The characterization of this approach perhaps is best presented in the words of Philip P. Wiener, one of the foremost practitioners of and proselytizers for this approach. In the Preface to the monumental *Dictionary of the History of Ideas*, which he edited, he makes clear the special contribution of the historian of ideas: "the historian of ideas makes his particular contribution to knowledge by tracing the cultural roots and historical ramifications of the major and minor specialized concerns of the mind."[32] The purpose of this type of study, moreover, "is to help establish some sense of the unity of human thought and its cultural manifestations in a world of ever-increasing specialization and alienation."[33]

This purpose is carried out concretely, as in the *Dictionary of the History of Ideas*, by trying "to exhibit the intriguing variety of ways in which ideas in one domain tend to migrate into other domains. The diffusion of these ideas may be traced in three directions: horizontally across disciplines in a given cultural period, vertically or chronologically through the ages, and 'in depth' by analysis of the internal structure of pervasive and pivotal ideas."[34]

From this description of the procedure that the historian of ideas follows, it should be clear that the procedure differs in important ways from the procedures followed by the other two doxographical approaches discussed earlier. The practitioner of history of ideas doxography goes well beyond the mere recording of the ideas of particular authors, trying especially to see the continuity of these ideas in history as well as investigating their origins and development. Likewise, this approach can be distinguished from univocal question doxography in two respects: First, historians of ideas do not necessarily have in mind a particular question that they ask of every author they study. Their concern is less with questions than with concepts, even though their interest in concepts will lead them no doubt to investigate and discuss the questions that may have given rise to particular ideas. Second, as Wiener points out, at least one mode of history of ideas research seeks to examine these ideas in depth by analyzing them in detail in order to understand their internal structure and, we could perhaps add, their appeal. In that regard historians of ideas go well beyond the rather mechanical procedure followed by univocal question doxographers. Finally, it is important to note that the interest in cross-disciplinary connections ideally safeguards this approach from the kind of cultural insularity of the other two doxographical approaches, where questions of culture and historical circumstances tend to be ignored.

These positive characteristics popularized this approach earlier in this century. Indeed, at the hands of a master like Arthur Lovejoy, whose *The Great Chain of Being: A Study of the History of an Idea* (1933) is regarded as a model of the implementation of the method, this approach reached a level of sophistication that helped spread it among intellectual historians. Moreover, its emphasis on continuity and the understanding of influences helped bring the kind of order and sense to intellectual history for which many historians had long craved.

On the other hand, as with other doxographical approaches, there are problems with this one. Most of the problems stem from the treatment of ideas as somehow atomic units that are assumed to be passed, either whole or in part, from author to author, without undergoing substantial changes in themselves. For, although some ideas seem to be that way, others are not. When confronted with history of ideas doxography and how it tends to treat ideas, one cannot help but be reminded of Plato's view of ideas as absolute, immutable, and timeless, and of his confinement of relativity, change, and time to a different and lesser realm than that occupied by ideas. Indeed, although the historian of ideas certainly is concerned with their historical development, in the background there is always the sense that these historical developments are mere accidental happenings that do not affect ideas in themselves. Ideas affect those who hold them, but seem to be immune from influence themselves, having a life of their own.[35] This kind of "anthropomorphism," to use a term of Huizinga, is quite widespread among history of ideas doxographers.[36]

There is also the temptation in this approach, stemming from its emphasis on continuity, to disregard the differences that mark the thought of most authors and particularly of those who use the same linguistic formulas to express themselves. This problem may be aggravated by the relatively little interest of those who practice this method in the philosophical analysis of ideas. True, as Wiener points out, "in-depth" analysis of the internal structure of ideas is one way in which the history of ideas may be practiced. Significantly, however, he lists this as the third of three different ways of practicing the discipline and never makes such analysis a requirement of the other two. In fact, it is characteristic of many practitioners of the history of ideas to omit this sort of in-depth analysis, a reason why they often miss the true import of those ideas.[37] Part of this problem results from ignoring, as already mentioned, the questions and problems that gave rise to ideas in the first place and from treating ideas as self-contained phenomena. For these reasons I have classified the method used by historians of ideas as a kind of doxography, whose primary emphasis is on uncritical description rather than analysis. Yet, the importance and value of this procedure should not be underestimated. All that is good in it, and there is much of that as we have already seen, should find its way into any procedure that claims to be better.

Let me turn now to a different set of approaches, where the historical dimension of historical accounts is emphasized less than the philosophical one. I am referring to the polemical approaches.

B. Polemical Approaches

In contrast with the aim of the historical group, the aim of the *polemical*[38] group is not primarily historical; the philosophical concerns in it override the historical ones. As a consequence, the methods this group employs in dealing with historical figures and ideas tend to emphasize the sense and value of those ideas rather than their historicity. Their approach tends to be primarily interpretative and evaluative, whereas the historical approaches tend to be purely descriptive or at least aim to be so. The polemical group is composed of the apologist, the literary critic, the dilettante, the idealist, the problematicist, and the eschatologist.

1. The Apologist. The primary focus of the approach used by the *apologist* is defense: the defense of certain ideas or thinkers. The emphasis on defense is so strong that frequently the defense of those ideas and thinkers overrides the main historical task of understanding the past. The ideas and the views of the thinkers in question often are presented in standard formulas that are repeated as if they were articles of faith. Indeed, the analysis of what the formulas mean is neglected because the aim toward which all effort is directed is the effective defense of those ideas and authors against what are regarded as hostile attacks. Those who use this approach in the study of the history of philosophy become extremely sensitive to criticism, so that even questions about clarification are generally regarded as hostile challenges and treated as objections to be answered rather than as requests for elaboration and analysis. They seem to be concerned only with finding in the history of philosophy the ammunition they need to defend the idea or author they support against those who challenge them.

Very often the apologetic attitude characteristic of this approach is associated with a particular philosopher whose thought is regarded as so fine and true that it is beyond improvement. This attitude goes well beyond what has been called the *principle of charity*. This principle stipulates that one should always give the best interpretation possible of an author or a text. It rests in turn on two other principles. The first is the assumption that past philosophers were as acute and as philosophically perceptive as present philosophers and, therefore, that they most likely would be aware of any of the problems and difficulties of which present philosophers are aware. Thus, if a present philosopher finds difficulties with certain issues, it is assumed that the historical author was also aware of those difficulties. That being the case, of course, his or her view should be read in the best possible light so that the difficulties in question can be resolved or avoided.

The second principle is the methodological rule that it is always best to give the strongest possible interpretation of an argument or a view, particularly if the argument or view undermines a position that we currently hold. If our aim is to see our position fully tested, the best way to do that is to meet it head on and answer the strongest objections that could be brought against it. This is more than to follow the dictum, Know thine enemies; it is to hold that one should give battle to the strongest forces that can be mustered against oneself, so that the victory will be decisive and not Pyrrhic. Besides, there is always the possibility that we might be wrong and thus that the development of the strongest possible case for a position contrary to ours might make us see where we are mistaken.

Apologists, however, go well beyond the principle of charity. They adhere rather to what I call the *principle of infallibility*. According to this principle, historical authors are regarded as infallible. Indeed, the possibility that they could be wrong in any way, that they could have given an argument in which the conclusion does not follow, or that their views could be false or incoherent is ruled out at the outset. Any suspicion of a mistake is interpreted as a fault on the part of the historian, rather than on the part of the authors, and must be resolved by changing the historian's methodology and approach.[39] In short, this attitude is very much like that of the religious devotee toward sacred scriptures, the reason why Peter Hare likes to call historians who adopt this attitude *cultist*. Of course, this is an extreme position and one that not all apologists adopt, but there are, indeed, many cases of historians of philosophy who implicitly adopt the principle of infallibility.

One of the best known philosophers who has had the fortune (or misfortune, depending on the point of view) of being the object of the apologetic attitude is Thomas Aquinas.[40] During his lifetime Thomas had a considerable following that increased steadily, in spite of minor setbacks, during the 400 years following his death and again after the middle of the nineteenth century. Two factors contributed enormously to the development and increase of the apologetic spirit among his followers. The first was that he was a member of the Dominican Order. After his death, the Dominicans adopted him as their official doctrinal spokesman, their doctor and teacher, and used him in their struggles with other religious orders, such as the Franciscans. Thomas's thought became identified with the very perspective proposed by Dominicans, and, therefore, an attack on his ideas was taken as an attack on the Dominican Order itself.

The second factor that contributed to the development of the apologetic attitude among Thomas's followers is that in 1879 Pope Leo XIII declared his philosophy to be of lasting value and thus eminently compatible with Catholic teaching. He called Thomism a *philosophia perennis*. The immediate consequence of the Pope's pronouncement was that a good portion of the vast intellectual resources of the Catholic Church were directed to the study and support of Thomas's views, giving his thought a unique place among that of other doctors of the Church. Consequently, to this day, and in spite of some recent setbacks, there seem to be more publications about Thomas and his thought than about any other single figure, with the possible exception of Marx, in the history of philosophy.

Even before Leo XIII officially pronounced that Thomas's philosophy had perennial value, however, the attitude of many Thomists toward Thomas was clearly apologetic. Perhaps the best example, although not one that ended in complete sterility, is that of John of St. Thomas (1589–1644). In his *Cursus theologicus, Tractatus de approbatione et auctoritate doctrinae d. Thomae*,[41] he explicitly outlined the five marks of a true disciple of Thomas Aquinas and identified as his main purpose to explain and develop the teaching of the master whose name he had adopted. The true disciple of Thomas, according to John, must (1) look back to the continuous line of succession of previous disciples who adhered strongly to Thomas's doctrines; (2) be energetically intent on defending and developing Thomas's views rather than disagreeing cautiously with them or explaining them in a lukewarm manner; (3) stress the glory and brilliance of Thomas's doctrines rather than his own opinions and novelty of interpretation; (4) follow Thomas, arrive at the same conclusions, explain Thomas's reasons, and resolve any apparent inconsistencies in his views; and (5) seek a greater agreement and unity among Thomas's disciples.

Clearly, John of St. Thomas was intent on defending Thomas's views and ruled out the possibility of disagreement with those views. If one looks at John's philosophy, one finds that he tried very hard to adhere to these principles because his admiration for Thomas's views had no limit. Unfortunately, the results of that attitude were not always as orthodox as he would have liked or as successful philosophically as a nonapologetic approach toward Thomas's views might have made them, as we shall see shortly.[42] But these failures have not deterred many modern Thomists from not only following in Thomas's footsteps, but also from adopting the apologetic attitude outlined by John of St. Thomas.

The case of Thomas is quite extreme, but many other past philosophers have suffered a similar fate, although to a lesser degree: Plato, Aristotle, Hegel, and, more recently, Wittgenstein, for example. The list could be very long, indeed.

The reasons why the apologetic attitude develops are quite understandable. After all, the figures who enjoy such faithful following are usually philosophers of the first rank who without a doubt have uncovered important truths and presented us with conceptual syntheses that have universal appeal and value for all times. To a great extent the power of their thought and ideas engenders the loyalty that turns their supporters into apologists. Moreover, some advantages follow from adopting the apologetic attitude in the study of historical figures. In the first place, loyalty and commitment make possible understanding that otherwise might be missed. One should not underestimate the close relations between the will and the intellect. To know and to will are two different things, and not always is the will to know a requirement of knowing. But in some cases the will to know is a requirement of knowing, and in other cases it is at least helpful. Thus, the desire to understand an author because of a preestablished sympathy for or commitment to his or her views should be helpful in the achievement of that understanding. In this sense, the apologetic attitude enjoys advantages similar to those of the Golden Age nostalgic and the romantic approaches.

In addition, and this is perhaps the most important and beneficial aspect of this approach, apologetic partisans treat their heros as contemporary philosophers and their ideas as living conceptual alternatives. They engage them in the contemporary problems that concern their own times, extending the thought of past thinkers into fields and areas into which they did not venture. This is an important advantage, for, if the history of philosophy includes interpretative and evaluative philosophical statements as I claimed it does in Chapter One, then it is essential to it that we treat its figures as living philosophers and its ideas as viable intellectual alternatives.

On the other hand, the disadvantages of this approach outbalance its advantages and have contributed to the creation of a bad reputation for those historians and philosophers who openly display it. These shortcomings stem from excessive concern with evaluation and interpretation to the detriment of the descriptive dimension of the historical task. The most obvious disadvantage of this approach is that its unwavering commitment to certain ideas blunts any balanced critical appraisal, indeed it prevents it, vitiating the perspective of the historian from the start and precluding the objectivity required in any historical pursuit. Moreover, its faithful adherence to well-established formulas coupled with its emphasis on defense rather than critical analysis and understanding, often lead to a lack of a true understanding of the import of the very formulas defended.

Another unwanted consequence of the apologists's unwavering commitment is the lack of serious consideration, let alone appreciation, of views other than those proposed by authors they favor. This attitude becomes aggravated in particular when those ideas seem to contradict the views of the favored author.

Finally, a predominantly apologetic attitude precludes the possibility of real and serious dialogue with other philosophers. There can be no dialogue between two parties one of which knows it has the truth and whose only aim is to defend it or proselytize those who disagree with it. Dialogue, as pointed out in Chapter Three, depends on the possibility that those who engage in it may increase their understanding, correct their mistakes, or change their position. Otherwise, there is only an apparent exchange of views without an effective attempt at communication, that is, at understanding each other's positions and advancing the truth. It is the prevention of dialogue that has traditionally worked most effectively against those who adopt an apologetic approach, isolating them from other historians and philosophers who come to the conclusion, after attempting to communicate with them, that any real exchange of views with them is impossible.

Most of these problems of the apologetic approach are well exemplified in John of St. Thomas's treatment of Thomas Aquinas's principle of individuation, but here I shall restrict the discussion to the fact that it distorts Thomas's view. That should serve as sufficient illustration of the point I am making.

John of St. Thomas's discussion of Thomas's explicitly stated principle of individuation, namely matter designated by quantity, reflects his desire to find an interpretation of Thomas's view that is immune to the kinds of objections arising from the violation of two important principles. The first is that in a substance-accident metaphysics the principle of individuation must be substantial. The second is that the principle of individuation could not be anything formal because what is formal is not individual. Thomas's view seems to violate both of these principles since quantity is both formal and accidental, so in order to render Thomas's view unassailable, John changes Thomas's formula to the following: "matter radically designated by quantity."[43] The addition of *radically* to the formula is meant to counter these objections by making matter's designation closer to substance and less formal (the word *radicaliter* in Latin as well as its English counterpart come from the term for "root"). However, a careful study of Thomas, as some scholars have indicated, shows that Thomas's view was not only phrased differently, but that the formula provided by John could actually have been unacceptable to Thomas.[44] For, during his career, Thomas seems to have moved away from an understanding of designated matter as undetermined dimensions and toward determined dimensions, that is, away from a substantial view of the designation of matter and toward an accidental one.

In spite of the shortcomings of the apologetic approach it should be considered fully philosophical and, therefore, different from the nonphilosophical approaches discussed earlier. Although this approach emphasizes defense, such a defense and the account that the apologetic approach gives of the past are philosophical insofar as the reasons discussed for the views of past philosophers are philosophical reasons and not psychological, cultural, and so on. The apologist is after defense, but defense understood in philosophical terms.

It is true that the apologist shares with the ideologue, for example, the strong emphasis on defense, but apologists are not as strongly oriented toward proselytizing as ideologues. Morever, apologists engage in partisan defense because they are committed to a certain idea or system of thought proposed by an author rather than to factors alien to those ideas, as is the case with the ideologue. Finally, the apologists's commitment to ideas primarily, and only secondarily to the author who discovered or proposed those ideas, generally separates them from romantics.

2. The Literary Critic. Historians of philosophy that approach the history of philosophy as *literary critics* share an interest in looking at historical texts as literary productions in which literary form is fundamental and content is purely a function of form.[45] The rationale behind this position is that writers of philosophical texts, consciously or unconsciously, use literary form and style to convey the overall message they want to communicate, for form and content can never be entirely separate; all content has to be transmitted through language and language always presents a certain articulation. Thus, it is through the form, as a literary text, that one should approach philosophical writing. Those historians who do not use this approach, so claim literary critics, miss the structural import of philosophical works, entirely bypassing their true significance.

This approach has become quite popular in some contemporary philosophical circles, particularly among philosophers who belong to what I called in the Introduction the "poetic tradition" in philosophy. As poets, they see a philosophical work as primarily rhetorical and, therefore, consider the job of the historian of philosophy to be that of the literary critic who uncovers the stylistic and literary structure of the work in order to reveal its complete import.

Obviously, there is considerable merit in this position. Philosophical texts are literary productions of one sort or another, and authors convey their ideas through the literary form. Undoubtedly, the content of texts is tied closely and perhaps inextricably to their form, and it is part of the task of the historian of philosophy to study that form in order to understand better both what the authors had in mind and what they created apart from what they thought. Indeed, part of the argument of those who favor this approach is precisely that texts, once written, are independent entities which may have a meaning and significance that go well beyond what their writers intended or were aware of when they were writing them.[46]

All this, of course, makes sense, as we saw in Chapter Four. The emphasis on the connection between form and content in particular, as well as the independence of the text once completed, seem valid points. There are many philosophers whose work cannot be properly understood without paying careful attention to the form they used to convey their views. The most obvious case in point is Plato, whose dialogues are full of literary devices that, if misunderstood or ignored, can mislead the historian. Taking an irony as nonironic may be sufficient to undermine the whole interpretation of a Platonic dialogue.[47] And the characters of the dialogues often are quite well developed and have significance for the understanding of the text. Indeed, the study of Plato without regard to the literary form that he used certainly will lead to interpretative disaster. Moreover, the same can be said about many other philosophers, such as Nietzsche, who expressed themselves in complex literary genres.

Likewise, with regard to the independence of a work once completed, one should not fall into the so-called *intentional fallacy*, confusing the meaning and significance of texts with what their authors intended. For authors may have intended to say or write something that they did not say or write. But even more than that, authors may have used language that in fact does not convey accurately a certain idea for which they were groping. It makes sense, then, to look at texts and their structure independently of what their authors may have said elsewhere about what they had in mind, for these reasons as well as those discussed earlier in this book. Indeed, since we can have access to the intentions of authors only through texts, texts should be at the center of the historian of philosophy's attention.

The consideration of the literary form of a text, then, seems to have a great bearing on the historian of philosophy. Indeed, even in cases where literary form seems to have played no intended important role, the nature of the text at hand and its structure need to be taken into account in any serious historical account of an author's ideas. For, doesn't knowing the structure of Aristotle's *Metaphysics* help us in understanding what he was trying to do in its various books as well as the impact those books had in the subsequent development of philosophy? And doesn't the understanding of the medieval *quaestio* help us identify better the positions being defended by thirteenth century scholastics?

There is considerable merit in the literary critic's approach, but if used in isolation, strictly as described, it also has some important shortcomings. Most of these stem from the belief that description is impossible and the task of the historian of philosophy consists exclusively in interpretation and evaluation. One of the most obvious disadvantages of this approach is that the literary critic tends to isolate the work from its author and context. Indeed, some postmodernists consciously disregard any kind of historical connection that texts may have and favor looking at them in isolation, as independent pieces whose significance should be gathered from their features and not from the historical circumstances in which they were produced. But such isolation seems to militate against both a proper historical understanding of a text and the overall aim of historians to provide an account of the past. After all, historians are supposed to be after the historical significance of the work, not what it means independently of what it meant at the time it was composed. To pluck the work from its historical setting, severing its tie to its author and context, subverts the whole historical enterprise. It is not that we should fall back into the intentional fallacy or believe that completely objective descriptions of the past are possible. My point is that a text needs to be seen as a product of an author's attempt to convey certain ideas to a certain audience and not as an isolated, atomic entity to be interpreted at will by the historian. The understanding of the author, the audience for which the text was intended, and the context in which the text was created can give us priceless clues as to the meaning of a text, as already suggested in Chapter Four. Indeed, insofar as literary critics reject or neglect such considerations, they must be classified, together with apologists, as having no proper respect for history.

But this is not all. Although for the interpretation of the meaning and significance of some texts the literary form in which they are presented is most important, and for all texts it is a factor that should be taken into account, many texts in the history of philosophy are sufficiently straightforward and devoid of literary embellishments and complexities that it is possible to understand their main conceptual thrust without much knowledge of literary criticism. Plainly, many philosophers have not been primarily or even distantly concerned with literary style and form. They have let their thought take the form most effective in conveying its import. They have not sought to create an impression on the reader, as the rhetorician or the literary writer does, but rather to present and defend a point of view explicitly with arguments as clear and unambiguous as possible. Of course, they have not always succeeded. Philosophical writing often is abstruse and cumbersome, although that is not generally the result of art, but rather of accident. The whole philosophical enterprise is predicated on the search for truth and understanding, and from its very beginning and for the most part, such search has involved a commitment to simplicity, clarity, and the lack of embellishments. Socrates said it himself when he pointed out that the speech of philosophers lacks the graces to which people are usually accustomed, thus appearing strange and odd to them. The whole idea of using rhetorical devices rather than plain language to express one's ideas implies that the ultimate purpose of speech is to persuade, and no philosophers worth their salt will want to say that, unless they have lost all faith in philosophical objectivity. But if this is correct, then the analysis of the literary form of a text may not be as important for the understanding of the text as the literary critic claims.

3. The Dilettante. The *dilettante's approach* to the history of philosophy is not historical; its aim, as that of the last three approaches discussed, is philosophical, but unlike them it is exclusively so. Thus, accurate description is put aside in favor of interpretation and evaluation. Authors who use this approach are not interested in the historical import, relevance, or meaning of the texts they use, or in the historical views of the authors they study. Their interest is exclusively in the philosophical idea, argument, or problem that they take these texts to reveal or these authors to be concerned with. They have no reason, then, to pay attention to historical context, and they ignore the objections of those historians of philosophy who criticize them for anachronistically distorting history. Their most effective answer is that they are not distorting history for the simple reason that their aim is not historical. They are not concerned with what the texts they quote meant to those who read them at the time they were written or what the authors themselves meant to say through them. After all, whatever the authors meant, they expressed themselves in a certain way, and that certain way appears to say something to *us* which is what is relevant to us *qua* philosophers. Let historians of ideas and scholars worry about the historical meaning of texts; for philosophers the important thing is what these texts say to them. Proponents of this position go to the history of philosophy to pick and choose what fits their own needs. They might be described, in a phrase belonging to Bennett, as "looking for pretty pebbles to arrange in a nice pattern."[48] Thus it makes no sense to criticize them for not doing what they do not consider their task to be.[49]

Passmore's example of someone who uses what I call the dilettante's approach is Plato. And, indeed, this is a good example, for Plato's interest in the philosophers he discusses is hardly historical. He not only treats them as if they were his contemporaries, by placing them in a dialogue with contemporary figures, but he is lax in his quotations, mixes quotations with gloss, and his attitude toward them is irreverent, humorous, and ironical.[50] The historical Protagoras is of no concern to Plato, nor even his actual doctrine. Plato is after the well-formulated view so that he may, through the dialectic, test it and advance his knowledge not of history but of truth. In this the dilettante is not very different from the idealist, whose attitude will be discussed shortly.

A more recent example of this view can be found in Plantinga's well-known article "The Boethian Compromise." There he argues, on the basis of a very short text from Boethius's second edition of the *Commentary on "De interpretatione"* (which he found translated in Castañeda's "Individuation and Non-Identity: A New Look,"[51]) that for

Boethius proper names express essence.[52] But this is inaccurate on several counts. In the first place, Boethius does not propose a theory of proper names in his text. His comments about proper names (the expression 'proper names' does not even appear in the text quoted by Plantinga) are secondary to his purpose, which has to do with individuality. Therefore, it is inappropriate to put too much weight on what he appears to say about language. Second, Boethius does not say that proper names express essence. He says only that they point to a definite substance and property, and this is concordant with the function he assigns to them elsewhere. Third, Boethius could not have held that proper names express essence, for essence for him had to do precisely with those features of a thing that are common to the members of the species. In no case would he have said that there is such a thing as an individual essence, which is the only way in which Plantinga's interpretation would make sense. Plantinga's inaccurate description of Boethius's view does not entail, of course, that his own view (or the view he attributes to Boethius) about proper names is wrong; it means only that the historical dimension of his remarks should not be taken seriously.

Plantinga was misled simply because of his lack of knowledge of Boethius's philosophy, the brevity of the text he considers, and his primary concern with the philosophical problem he aimed to solve. The evaluative thrust of his interpretation was so strong, and his concern with description so weak, that his interpretation suffered as a result.

Given the historical's thrust of the dilettantes' approach, we may ask them, Why bother to refer to historical texts at all? If what is important are philosophical positions and those positions can be expressed in contemporary formulations, why bother with quoting or referring to texts and authors that may have to do with something very different? What purpose do quotations and historical references serve?

Dilettantes do not offer good answers to these questions. Indeed, they do not have good answers, for any answer would force them to recognize the paradoxical situation in which they find themselves. I imagine that in all honesty some of them quote other authors because they wish to give some weight to their own ideas. The argument from authority is by no means dead in philosophy, and footnotes and quotations are a subtle and elegant way of using it. And then, of course, there is a natural desire in all intellectuals to find kindred spirits from among those who went before them; it adds some validity and legitimacy to their quests and reassures them. There is an element of curiosity and pride, too, curiosity in finding out about the past and pride in the display of some knowledge about it; for we live in a society whose intellectuals pride themselves on their historical knowledge and put some emphasis and value on it. Third, a nefarious, if unconscious, motive may also be involved: to display brilliance in finding fault with the positions and arguments of past giants. How many times have I listened in disbelief to contemporary philosophers dismiss the views of Aristotle, Plato, or Augustine on the basis of what they regard as "obvious contradictions," generated usually by the artificial manipulation of texts and ideas without a proper regard for their integrity?

Most likely, however, dilettantes quote other philosophers because they have been taught philosophy by reading them. They come out of an educational system in which philosophy is taught through the criticism of what are regarded as past philosophical masterpieces. They have formed the habit of philosophizing in reaction to texts, and well-established habits die hard. So they refer to the past not because they have an interest in history, not even because they may feel the theoretical need to do so; they quote merely out of habit.

There may be a variety of reasons, therefore, why dilettantes concern themselves with historical texts. Sometimes they use them as points of departure for discussion. At other times they use texts to focus attention on the notoriety of a view. Frequently they employ them to formulate clearly a position. And at other times they use them as props for their own theories. In all cases, however, they use them for a purpose that is ancillary to the main task dilettantes have in mind, whatever that may be.

From a historical point of view it is difficult to find much good to say about the approach of the dilettante. There would seem to be, however, at least one positive element in it that stands out. This approach underlines the continuity of the philosophical enterprise through history. It is, indeed, almost miraculous to see that a contemporary thinker, separated by centuries and enormous cultural differences from other philosophers, can develop without much reflection and study some interest in the past. This would seem to be sufficient to restore one's faith both in the philosophical enterprise and the history of philosophy. On the other hand, for all we know from the dilettante'swork, such interest may be based on a misunderstanding of the past, since the dilettante is not concerned with finding out what the past really thought and has no tools to do so or criteria to determine if success has been achieved. Under those conditions, the bases of the dilettante's interest may not be more than anachronisms and false analogies, in which case the single advantage to this approach seems to disappear.

4. The Idealist. The fundamental and distinguishing characteristic of the *idealistic approach* to the history of philosophy is that it seeks to reconstruct a reality that does not exist and may never have existed. Accordingly, the idealistic approach is guided by evaluative and interpretative considerations that tend to override historical considerations of accurate and objective description. Primarily for these reasons this approach cannot be considered historical strictly speaking, for historical approaches aim to reconstruct and provide an account of the past as it existed, not as it should have existed or as we wished it had existed.[53] Historical accounts that reconstruct the past along the lines of what historians think should have existed are usually called *revisionist*: they consciously change the past to adhere to some view or program they have in mind. Note that the requirement of consciousness is indispensible to revisionism. The unconscious and unintended alteration of the past is not revisionist; it is merely sloppiness or incorrectness. For revisionism to take place there has to be an effort to rearrange what we know to be the case about the past in order to fit some other purpose being pursued explicitly (or, more likely, implicitly). This element of conscious distortion for specific aims establishes similarities between this approach and the ideological one. Indeed, ideologues frequently use a revisionist approach.

The idealistic approach is not frequently revisionist, for those who are out to make an ideal reconstruction of the past are either aware of what they are doing or not. Those who are not cannot be classified as revisionists, since they do not intend to distort the past for their own reasons. And those who are conscious of what they are doing cannot be classified as revisionists because their intention is explicitly ideal; their concern with the past is, as it were, accidental. They use it as a way to help themselves build a particular structure that they find appealing or that, alternatively, they intend to attack. Thus, although they might be concerned with the views of a particular author, their interest in those views extends only insofar as they can help in the understanding of a certain particular philosophical view of which the view of the historical author in question is an example. It is that ideal object, then, in which they are primarily interested. Their interest in the view of the historical author is limited to the degree to which it can lead them to the understanding of the ideal object. This is the kind of approach that Russell describes in the Preface to the first edition of his book on Leibniz:

> there remains always a purely philosophical attitude towards previous philosophers—an attitude in which, without regard to dates or influences, we seek simply to discover what are *the great types of possible philosophies,* and guide ourselves in the search by investigating the systems advocated by the great philosophers of

> the past.... Where we are inquiring into the opinions of a truly eminent philosopher, it is probable that these opinions will form, in the main, a closely connected system, and that, by learning to understand them, we shall ourselves acquire knowledge of important philosophic truths. *And since the philosophies of the past belong to one or other of a few great types—types which in our own day are perpetually recurring*—we may learn, from examining the greatest representative of any type, what are the grounds for such a philosophy.... By what process of development he [i.e., the philosopher under study] came to this opinion, though in itself an important and interesting question, is logically irrelevant to the inquiry how far the opinion itself is correct; and among his opinions, when these have been ascertained, it becomes desirable to prune away such as seem inconsistent with his main doctrines, before those doctrines themselves are subjected to a critical scrutiny. Philosophic truth and falsehood, in short, rather than historical fact, are what primarily demand our attention in this inquiry.[54]

The historical view in many ways occupies in the idealist scheme a place similar to that occupied by the world of sense perception in Plato's ontology, and the ideal view is the counterpart of the Platonic idea. The difference between the Platonic scheme and that of historiographical idealists should not be underestimated, however. Methodologically, Plato disregarded the importance of the world of sense perception, whereas historical views are regarded as important by historiographical idealists for achieving the end they have in mind. Historical views help rather than hinder, as we see Russell noting, in suggesting the kind of views, arguments, etc., with which idealists wish to deal.

This methodological interest in history is what separates in part practitioners of this approach from dilettantes, since the latter have no interest in history *qua* history. For dilettantes, historical accuracy can be an obstacle rather than a help; they use history as an occassion to spin their own philosophical tales. Those who use the idealistic approach, by contrast, have as their aim the reconstruction of an ideal scheme based on a historical situation. Their interest is in what a particular author should have held, even if the textual record does not seem to support it. As Russell points out with respect to what he sees as his task in the book on Leibniz: "What is first of all required in a commentator is to attempt a reconstruction of the system which Leibniz should have written."[55] Thus, it is still the historical author and his views that concern them. Dilettantes, on the other hand, are not interested in what view the historical author should have held; their interest is in a position with which they can interact, regardless of its actual or normative historicity.

Philosophically speaking, the advantages of the idealistic position should be clear; it would seem always better to deal with ideal positions, purged from their incidental imperfections, than to deal with actual imprecise and implicit views. The ideal position, whether in accordance with or opposed to ours, should be extremely helpful to us. If it agrees with ours, it supports and helps us perfect and strengthen our view. If it opposes ours, it forces us to come up with a defense that would truly help to establish our own view on firmer ground. Either way, it would seem that philosophy gains by seeking the ideal.

The advantages of the idealistic approach are not only philosophical. Historically it also makes sense to look for the ideal insofar as the search for it may help us reach the actual position held by the historical figure by allowing us to discard incidental mistakes and confusions present in a corrupt text, for example. Using the principle of charity and trying to think of the best position that one could attribute to an author, one may actually approach the original, but unrealized intent of the author, more than if one were to remain a slave of the historical data at one's disposal. After all, past philosophers were, as we are, trying to uncover truth, and we should think of them as having advanced as far as it is possible to think they could have done so at the time they lived.

In spite of all these advantages, however, the idealistic approach is fundamentally unhistorical and, therefore, may lead to historical inaccuracies. Of course, if it is tightly controlled and used only as a methodological attitude to be employed under specific circumstances, then it can be very useful for the historian. By specific cicumstances I mean those in which we have limited information about the views of a historical figure and thus are forced to reconstruct part of the record. Indeed, as already argued in Chapters One and Four, in those circumstances it is obvious that we need to appeal to what is the best reconstruction possible. And the same is the case when we have two or more possible interpretations of the available evidence, and there seems to be no way in which we can, on the basis of that evidence, decide in favor of one. But that is as far as the idealistic approach will take us. In such a context, the construction of an ideal view is put at the service of history, where the aim of the inquiry is to account for what happened, not for what should have happened.

The attitude that we find expressed in the passage from Russell cited earlier is the reverse: History is put at the service of philosophy. The result, as is indeed the case with Russell's interpretation of Leibniz, can be philosophically enlightening but historically inaccurate.

For example, Russell's idea of presenting Leibniz's philosophy as a complete and finished system goes contrary to Leibniz's *modus operandi,* as Russell himself acknowledges.[56] Leibniz's work is unsystematic and his ideas are scattered throughout many writings, always prompted by incidental circumstances. Thus to attempt to systematize them, presenting them in the way that Wolff, for example, presented his views, is to distort their occasional and fragmentary character, leading to the misplacement of their relative significance. Russell himself falls into this trap, for in order to fulfill his systematic aim he is forced to neglect Leibniz's early views, confining himself to the study of what he regards as Leibniz's "mature views"; namely, those he held between January 1686 and 1716, the year he died.[57] As a result, Russell's account is one-sided, emphasizing only later statements of Leibniz's position and neglecting both a sense of historical development and circumstantial relevance. Moreover, Russell's account neglects to study properly the philosophical ideas that influenced Leibniz in his early years. The picture of Leibniz we get, then, is philosophically enlightening, as already noted, but historically inaccurate.

5. The Problematicist. The approach used by the *problematicist*[58] is characterized by its view of past philosophical positions as answers to philosophical problems of concern to all philosophers and thus as useful in the search for the solution to those problems. This approach does not differ qualitatively from the approach used by the dilettante insofar as both are interested primarily in the development of philosophy and not in the study of its history as such; the history of philosophy is used by both for philosophical purposes, not historical ones. Both are in search of solutions to philosophical problems and thus tend to put emphasis on evaluation and interpretation rather than in description. The difference between the two positions is one of degree and emphasis. The dilettante casually uses historical texts without regard for their exact historical import, whereas the problematicist regards them seriously and takes into account their historical character. Although the problematic attitude is one in which historical context is not the primary aim, nonetheless practitioners of this approach take historical figures seriously and, as a result, pay more attention to context, try to avoid plucking texts out of their setting, and on the whole respect the integrity of texts and their authors.

Paradoxically, the differences between dilettantes and problematicists arise from the fact that problematicists, like dilettantes, want to look at historical figures and their ideas as contemporaries to themselves rather than as pieces in a conceptual museum, something that *prima facie* would lead one to think that they would not respect the historical integrity of those authors and their ideas. They wish to treat them as they would treat their contemporaries, taking issue with their statements and arguing with their positions. Aristotle and Hegel, in the problems approach, become current figures worthy of attention. But precisely for this reason, problematicists believe, unlike dilettantes, that one has to accord to historical figures the same respect one would to a contemporary figure. There has to be an effort to become acquainted with what historical figures actually said rather than with second-hand reports of what they said. And their writings have to be carefully studied and analyzed in order not to distort their intent and import, for it is what authors really thought that is valuable and illuminating, not what we think they thought, as the dilettante holds, nor what they should have thought, as the idealist holds. Bennett makes this point quite clear: "When dealing with a genius, one is more likely to get illuminating ideas by discovering what he really thought than by forcing onto him thoughts that he didn't have; so from the standpoint of my kind of work, there are strong probabilistic reasons for wanting to get the author right, i.e., to find out what he actually meant."[59] It is very important, then, for the problematicist to get historical authors right, because this is more useful for doing philosophy and achieving truth. Indeed, Bennett argues that it is precisely the instrumental value of such knowledge that leads him to pursue it.

Problematicists argue, moreover, that their emphasis on problems is necessary to get historical figures right, for their views were developed in answer to problems. Thus, in order to give a proper account of those views, their genesis and relations, it is essential to identify the problems they were meant to solve. As Collingwood states:

> you cannot find out what a man means by simply studying his spoken or written statements, even though he has spoken or written with perfect command of language and perfectly truthful intention. In order to find out his meaning you must also know what the question was (a question in his own mind, and presumed by him to be in yours) to which the thing he has said or written was meant as an answer.[60]

The identification and understanding of the problems that concerned past philosophers is a necessary condition of understanding their ideas and providing an accurate account of them for problematicists. Still, precisely because the emphasis of problematicists is on the contemporaneity of historical figures, those figures are not treated historically and their cultural and temporal context is often ignored. The aim of problematicists is to provide "a *rational* reconstruction" of their ideas, that is, a reconstruction that makes sense, so that they can then use it to work out their own contemporary point of view.

Those who favor the problems approach argue that it is both inevitable and desirable. It is inevitable because the tasks associated with the scholarly approach are not as disinterested as those who oppose the problems approach to the history of philosophy claim. Take conceptual translation, for example. The claim that one can understand past conceptual frameworks through mere paraphrase expunged of interpretation and evaluation is nonsense. Thus Bennett claims that "we understand Kant only in proportion as we can say, clearly and in contemporary terms, what his problems were, which of them are still problems and what contribution Kant makes to their solution."[61] And Rorty echoes this point: "translating an utterance means fitting it into *our* practices."[62] Conceptual translation without interpretation and even evaluation is impossible. Those who believe in the scholarly approach to the exclusion of the problematic are deluding themselves, thinking they have achieved the kind of objectivity and distance that in fact is impossible in understanding past conceptual frameworks. And just as conceptual translation involves interpretation and evaluation, so does the rearrangement of texts. For to rearrange texts in the way mentioned earlier entails, first, separating them from their original context and using them for purposes alien to the original intent of their authors. It also entails, second, making value judgments that are implicitly embedded in the whole process of selection involved in any rearrangement, since there no doubt are "good" and "bad" ways of putting together these texts.

But this is not all. Those who support this point of view argue that the problems approach is not only inevitable but also desirable, at least for philosophers. For the philosopher is interested in the history of philosophy *qua* philosopher, namely, as an interested party whose aim is the search for truth. The problems approach in the history of philosophy, then, fits well the overall philosophical aim, whereas the scholarly approach, even if it were possible, would be appropriate only for those whose aim is exclusively historical, namely, the establishment of the record.

The problems approach is particularly popular today but it can be found throughout the history of philosophy. Indeed, it may be the most common approach used in dealing with the history of philosophy and certainly it was the standard procedure in Western philosophy before a deeper understanding of history developed in the eighteenth century. An excellent example of this approach is found in Francisco Suárez's *Disputationes metaphysicae*. This monumental work is the first systematic treatise on metaphysics produced since antiquity, and it covers in its fifty-four disputations all the major metaphysical issues known during Suárez's times.

Following scholastic tradition, Suárez discusses the main philosophical positions concerning each of the topics he explores, and he assigns these positions to their authors, quoting or referring to the pertinent texts. In the *Disputationes,* then, we have a compendium of metaphysical historical knowledge of great value, for Suárez is conversant with every major thinker that preceded him. Moreover, Suárez's discussion of various authors and positions is subtle, philosophically interesting, and frequently his interpretations turn out to be historically correct. Still, his aims are not historical and he treats authors and texts unhistorically. The *Disputationes* is not a historical work and whatever historical value it may have is incidental to the philosophical aim of the treatise. Suárez treats Aristotle, Averroes, and Thomas Aquinas as contemporaries, even though he was separated by roughly 2,000 years from the first, half a millennium from the second, and 300 years from the third. And if time were not enough, the cultural differences among the first two authors and Suárez were significant, for the differences between Athenian society at the time of Aristotle and Muslim Spain at the time of Averroes on the one hand and Counter-Reformation Spain at the time of Suárez must have been quite drastic. With Thomas there were probably more common cultural grounds, but still thirteenth-century Paris and sixteenth-century Salamanca could not have had too much in common. Nonetheless, there is no hesitation in Suárez about dealing with these authors; he discusses ancient and medieval writers as if they were his colleagues at Salamanca.

These points may be illustrated with respect to Suárez's discussion of individuation, which occurs in Disputation V of the *Disputationes metaphysicae.* The title of the disputation, "Individual Unity and Its Principle," identifies its topic for us; its division into nine sections dealing respectively with specific subtopics reveals its systematic character. It is only within this overall systematic framework that the views of historical authors are discussed. For example, Thomas's view that the principle of individuation is designated matter is presented in section III. The overriding concern, however, is not the accurate description of Thomas's view, but the merits and demerits of a position attributed to Thomas. The fact that Suárez presents a formulation of the position first and only afterwards identifies its presumed source gives us an indication of his priorities. Moreover, although he gives references to pertinent texts of Thomas, he does not quote him at length, nor does he attempt to check carefully his interpretation with Thomas's texts. Indeed, he gives various interpretations of

Thomas's position and treats them with equal respect. And, although he eventually rejects these positions in the Solution to the Question as not reflecting accurately the thought of Thomas, his reasons have to do exclusively with the inadequacy of the views, and thus the unlikelihood that Thomas would have held them, rather than with historical or textual evidence.[63]

What are the dangers of the problems approach? First is anachronism, namely, the cultural misplacement of individuals and texts, with the result that their ideas become misconstrued. Anachronism results in part from the assumption, shared by the univocal question doxographer, that one set of problems is common throughout the history of philosophy. Second is the neglect of much history of philosophy for two reasons: One, if the history of philosophy is viewed only instrumentally, much of the history of philosophy is of only marginal interest to the philosopher.[64] Two, if attention is paid only to ideas that result from the explicit formulation of philosophical problems, then many ideas that arise as a result of other factors are ignored. Both anachronism and the neglect of aspects of the history of philosophy lead to historical misunderstandings. But if there is historical misunderstanding, then the historian of philosophy has failed in the tasks of description, interpretation, and evaluation that are essential parts of a historical account. The problems approach, then, runs a risk of failure, although that should not entail that it does not have anything to contribute to the historical task.

All the same, the risk of failure in the problems approach should not be overemphasized. Take, for example, the first difficulty. It is by no means necessary for the problematicist to assume, like the univocal question doxographer, that one constant set of philosophical problems is common to the entire history of philosophy. The problematicist need only assume that certain types of questions and problems recur. For example, the epistemological questions that Plato asked may be different in some respects from those we ask today, arising as they did from different concerns and historical matrices, yet they share some features that help us both to understand him and to deepen our awareness of the questions we ourselves have formulated. That the problems of the past and the present are not exactly the same, then, does not undermine the problems approach; indeed, in many ways it strengthens it.

As far as the second difficulty is concerned, again, it need not result in complete disaster. For, although problematicists are interested in problems and their solution, they need not go to the history of philosophy with a preestablished list of issues that they need to solve and a mind set to ignore anything that is not directly relevant to them. The historian who uses a problems approach, on the contrary, may go to the history of philosophy with an open mind coupled to a keen awareness for the sort of problem that attracts philosophical attention. Problematicists are not to be confused with dilettantes nor is their interest necessarily ideological or pernicious. As Passmore has pointed out, the problematicist is essentially a puzzled person: "The first question the problematic historian will ask himself about any philosopher is this: 'What problem was he trying to solve?' And then he will go on to ask himself such further questions as: 'How did this problem arise for him?', 'What new methods of tackling it did he use?'"[65]

On the other hand, an excessive emphasis on problems may lead the problematicist to ignore ideas that do not arise out of the explicit formulations of problems but are nonetheless important, although it is by no means necessary that this should happen. The problematicist may still notice and deal with them because they influenced other ideas that themselves were answers to explicitly formulated problems, or because they can be used to deal with problems that, although not explicit, still can be raised.

The contribution of the problems approach to the study of the history of philosophy lies in the fact that it takes historical figures seriously as philosophers without falling into the dilettante's aberrations. In that light, those who adopt this approach see those figures in the proper perspective, as active and thinking authors grappling with ideas. Moreover, philosophers, because of their own involvement with those ideas, are in a better position to interpret what historical figures were trying to do, as well as to judge their success, than non-philosophers. Because philosophers understand how ideas are related, the problems and issues encountered by philosophers in general, and the philosopher's aim, they are in a better position to understand what other philosophers, even from another age, were trying to say and do as well as the successes and failures they had. Naturally, the weakness of the problems approach springs from a lack of attention to historical context. Moreover, those who adopt this perspective also are in danger if they are not aware of the potential pitfalls of their procedure and the proper method to avoid such pitfalls. Nonetheless, problematicists are on the right track because they understand that knowledge of philosophy is essential for the study of the history of philosophy. Moreover, they are in a position to use philosophy and the philosophical tools they have to judge the merits of past accomplishments as well as to understand how those past accomplishments were viewed by those who achieved them, their contemporaries, and subsequent ages.

6. The Eschatologist. Eschatologists deal with the history of philosophy in a way similar to that of problematicists. They have a genuine interest in what past philosophers had to say, taking it seriously and subjecting it to careful analysis and scrutiny. Like problematicists, their aims are fundamentally philosophical, namely, the pursuit of understanding and truth. Finally, they also take a serious interest in philosophical problems, both past and present, and consider their task to find and offer solutions to those problems. What distinguishes eschatologists from problematicists is that the former see the history of philosophy as leading up to their own thought or the thought of an author they consider the culmination of a process of progressive enlightenment. The eschatological enterprise, then, is self-justificatory, finding its own rationale in the history that precedes it and as a result is eminently evaluative and interpretative.

The most notorious eschatologist of all times is Hegel, although the roots of the eschatological reading of history go as far back as Augustine and his Jewish and Christian sources.[66] Hegel not only thought that all philosophy led to his philosophy but, more than that, he held that his thought was the ultimate culmination of philosophical understanding beyond which no further development would be possible: The Absolute became revealed in Hegel's philosophy. Such an extraordinary claim is difficult to take seriously, particularly more than a century after it was put forth, when we know (1) that Hegel was not aware of many issues, ideas, and discoveries that have become commonplace since then; and (2) that he frequently muddled things in a way that has not been helpful in the advancement of clear thinking. But not all eschatologists adopt this position.[67] Many have been content to show that they have improved on their predecessors and that many of the ideas of those predecessors can be seen as steps in the direction of the view that eschatologists come to defend. This approach is not objectionable as, indeed, it is often the case that later discoveries and ideas can be seen as answers to earlier questions and problems.

A recent defender of this approach describes it as follows:

> The fact is that to compose a schematic history [i.e., one composed following the eschatological approach] is in part to create a sequential structure in which the sequence is conditioned by the final stage. The history aims at making it evident how we got from there to here—how the events between the first and the last chapter constitute a progression that has a rationale. The story as told must make philosophical sense. Thus the schematic history comprises a teleological structure in which the episodes can be viewed as stages in the plot. Consequently it is not simply an accident that

> each episode can appear as a step along the way. The story itself imposes such an order on events. What the schematic historian does then is not simply to ignore the original intentions, but to construct them systematically in terms of the final act of the drama. The story has a logic of its own, a dialectic of development, and relative to that logic the relevant intentions can be postulated.[68]

This passage clearly identifies the main characteristic in the eschatological approach: the teleological element that governs the reading and interpretation of ideas. Every idea is conditioned by the place it occupies in the historical schema.

One of the best-known and earliest examples of the eschatological treatment of the history of philosophy is found in Aristotle's discussion of causality. In the *Metaphysics* he presents us with a historical picture of what the philosophers who preceded him had to say about causality and shows that many of their ideas were early and tentative forerunners of his own fourfold theory. Aristotle sees the history of thought preceding him as leading to his own view and he attempts to show also that none of his predecessors had as complete and as worked-out a theory as he. The general thrust of Aristotle's interpretation of his predecessors ultimately may be correct, but that does not mean that legitimate doubts cannot be raised as to Aristotle's interpretation of particular authors and the truth of his claims about the pre-Socratics. Indeed, considering the meager information we have concerning these authors, it would be absurd to think otherwise. But, given what we have, it does look like Aristotle's predecessors were dealing with questions of causality largely similar to those he raises, and it does look as if Aristotle's ideas in some cases are improvements on earlier ideas, although in other cases they seem to be altogether original. The overtidy character of the Aristotelian description of his predecessors' views, however, is bound to raise suspicion. Whether Aristotle is right and the extent to which he is right is rather a matter for historians of ancient philosophy to settle rather than for us to discuss in detail here. Our concern is with providing an example of the eschatological approach, and its problems, and Aristotle's discussion of the pre-Socratic theories of causality appears to be such.

For a historian to be classified as an eschatologist it is not necessary, however, that the historian see his or her own philosophy at the end of a process of progressive improvement, as Hegel and Aristotle do. Some philosophers see someone else's philosophy as that end. Nor is it necessary that the philosopher whose philosophy is seen as the culmination of an eschatological process be temporally contemporaneous with the historian. For example, for many Thomists, like Étienne Gilson, Thomas's philosophy is the highest philosophical achievement of any age and, thus, they see all philosophy before Thomas as consisting of progressive steps leading up to his thought and all philosophy after Thomas as consisting of regressive steps moving away from Thomas's thought (unless of course subsequent philosophy is committed to the revival and understanding of that thought). And, finally, it is not even necessary that there be progress at all. There are eschatologists who see history as regressing rather than progressing. What is fundamental to the eschatological approach is not the time frame involved in the historical process, the identity of the figure or figures that play a role in it, or the progressive or regressive character of the process, but the teleological direction toward or away from the thought of a historical figure.

The eschatological approach has some definite advantages. In the first place, it has a strong historical sense. Indeed, eschatologists may be said to have an excessive historical sense insofar as they not only describe what takes place and interpret and evaluate it, but also have an overriding sensibility to its development. The problem with this approach is that its emphasis on interpretation and evaluation is so strong that the description of the past may be distorted. That is, it is likely that eschatologists, in their zeal to see progress and development leading to a philosophical position that frequently is their own or at least one with which they identify, impose on the past a structure of development not present in it. The actual problems that historical figures addressed may thus be missed and their ideas may become distorted and misinterpreted. In short, the structure the eschatologist reads into history may not be the one it has; it may be no more than an unwarranted superimposition on it. This superimposition is the result of an excessively interested reading of history. Eschatologists are overly interested parties in the sense of having something personal at stake, rather than being interested simply in the development of a historical account; their interest can reflect the sort of pernicious and ideological attitude described in Chapter One. It is this conflict of interest, if we may call it that, that leads to abuses in this approach, undermining its promise. What the approach gains in conceptual precision, philosophical sophistication, and understanding, it may lose in objectivity.

III. REQUIREMENTS OF A PROPER APPROACH

I have described thirteen common approaches to doing the history of philosophy, yet it has become clear that none of them is fully acceptable if considered by itself. Some indeed are unacceptable under any circumstances, whereas others are acceptable in some aspects but are found wanting in others. Most of the approaches discussed have clear advantages, but all of them have serious weaknesses if taken in isolation. Under these conditions, we may ask ourselves: Is there any approach that can overcome the shortcomings of the approaches listed while sharing in their advantages? And if there is, what kind of approach is it? In short, how should the history of philosophy be written?

A frequent answer to the third question found in the relevant contemporary literature as Rorty puts it, is that "there is...nothing general to be said in answer to it."[69] The reason usually given for this discouraging answer is that the history of philosophy is not a natural kind, and thus we should not expect to find a set of necessary and sufficient conditions for it. Obviously, if no necessary and sufficient conditions for it can be identified, it is a waste of time, indeed senseless, to try to find *the* way to do history of philosophy. There is no *one* approach to the history of philosophy; there are only approach*es* to it, as is clear from the preceding discussion.

Interestingly enough, even those authors who favor this reasoning find that there are "good" and "bad" ways of doing the history of philosophy and have no qualms about rejecting some approaches altogether. For example, Rorty himself has no hesitation about condemming in very strong terms the approach called here *univocal question doxography*.[70] But, of course, if there are degrees of adequacy among the ways of doing the history of philosophy and some are unacceptable, then there always is the logical possibility and the real hope that we may be able to determine the best way of doing history of philosophy among the ways we know. Note that I am not trotting out the old Platonic argument that if there is a better then there must be an absolute best. What I am arguing is that degrees among members of a group entail a highest degree among those members, even if that degree is shared by several of the members of the group or is achieved by them in combination. There is no reason, then, why we cannot aspire to produce a model of doing the history of philosophy that is the best of or better than all the ones listed, even if such a model may eventually be superseded by others about which we know nothing yet.

In short, I believe there is an affirmative answer to the first of the three questions I asked at the beginning of this section, that is, I think there is an approach to the history of philosophy that enjoys the advantages of the approaches discussed earlier while avoiding their difficulties and therefore is better than all the ones described. But in order to answer the second question and determine what this approach is we must turn first to the requirements that need to be imposed on such an approach for it to serve appropriately the historical task.

From our early discussion concerning the nature of the history of philosophy in Chapter One we know that it consists of an account of past philosophical ideas and that such an account involves description, interpretation, and evaluation. A proper approach to the history of philosophy, therefore, should be one that leads to the accurate description, interpretation, and evaluation of past philosophical ideas. In other words, it must yield answers to questions about what those ideas are, how they came to be what they are, why they came to be and to be such, and what their importance is. This would seem to be clear. It would also seem to be clear that in order to provide an accurate description we must be objective and yet in order to provide interpretations and evaluations we must abandon the objectivity required in the description, that is, we must become interested parties. So we not only need to devise a way to come up with accurate descriptions, interpretations, and evaluations, but we must also find a way of resolving the apparent conflict between description on the one hand and interpretation and evaluation on the other.

The conflict to which we are referring is one of the reasons why some historians of philosophy prefer the scholarly approach, in which the job of the historian is supposed to be restricted to description, leaving out of it both interpretation and evaluation. But we saw in Chapter One that the history of philosophy does require interpretation and evaluation and in the present chapter we noted the limitations of the scholarly approach taken by itself. Indeed, in Chapter Four we saw that even the understanding of texts requires additions to those texts without which it would be impossible to produce acts of understanding similar to those of the author and contemporaneous audience and therefore achieve an accurate comprehension of the past. So, a strictly descriptive approach that rejects interpretation and evaluation is closed to us. We must find a way, then, to reconcile the descriptive, interpretative, and evaluative aims of the history of philosophy and thus resolve this difficulty.

The difficulty involved in the reconciliation of these aims is not, however, the only difficulty the historian of philosophy encounters. Perhaps a more serious one is that of understanding and finding a common ground to the diversity present in the history of philosophy. For the history of philosophy confronts us with an incredible variety of languages, concepts, issues, authors, traditions, and cultures. How are historians of philosophy going to bridge the gaps not only between themselves and past philosophers but also among past philosophers themselves? What common ground can be found among differing philosophical traditions and authors? If it is so hard, as any historian knows, to determine the exact conceptual import of a term in a single author's philosophy, what hope can we have of extending such understanding to other terms and philosophies within the period and even to other periods? Take the term 'substance.' Can we be sure we understand the use of its Greek counterparts in Aristotle? And then, what do we make of it in Plotinus, Plato, Thomas, Descartes, and Locke, for example? Yet the history of philosophy must do that and much more if it is going to be what we have said it should be. But this is not all, because historical figures in philosophy themselves borrow terms and ideas from their predecessors. Moreover, they also have opinions about them, their accuracy, what they meant in the philosophy from which they borrow them as well as what they mean in their own philosophy. And, of course, they may be entirely wrong in their historical judgments.

The history of philosophy looks and sounds, indeed, like a tower of Babel. Is there a way to reduce this cacophony of ideas so that we may understand it? Can we find a way of presenting accurate descriptions of the philosophical past accompanied by intelligible interpretations and sensible evaluations? I believe the solution to these problems is to be found in what I call the "framework approach."

IV. THE FRAMEWORK APPROACH

The *framework approach* holds that in order to do history of philosophy it is necessary to begin by laying down a conceptual map of the issues in the history of philosophy the historian proposes to investigate. This conceptual map is composed of five basic elements: first, the analysis and definitions of the main concepts involved in the issues under investigation; second, the precise formulation of those issues, together with a discussion of their interrelationships; third, the exposition of solutions that may be given to those issues; fourth, the presentation of basic arguments for and objections against those solutions; and, finally, the articulation of criteria to be used in the evaluation of the solutions to the problems under investigation and the arguments and objections brought to bear on them. In short, the framework is a set of carefully defined concepts, formulated problems, stated solutions, articulated arguments and objections, and adopted principles of evaluation, all of which are related to the issues the historian proposes to explore in the history of philosophy. In the case, for example, of an investigation into Thomas Aquinas's doctrine of individuation, the framework would consist of the following: (1) the definition and analysis of terms such as 'individuation,' 'individuality,' 'individual,' 'numerical difference,' and so on, which are commonly used or the historian thinks should be used in the discussion of individuation; (2) a formulation of the problem of individuation and a discussion of related problems; (3) the presentation of various types of theories of individuation (formal, material, etc.); (4) the examination of arguments in favor of and against those theories; and (5) a set of criteria to be used to evaluate theories of individuation and the arguments that are employed in favor of or against such theories. In (5) may be included general rules that have to do, for example, with coherence, but most useful are specific rules that the historian thinks apply to individuation in particular, such as the rule that a proper principle of individuation of substances must be substantial, and so on. The way all of this works will become clearer when I present a more detailed example of the application of the framework approach later on.

The function of the framework is to serve as a conceptual map for determining the location and relation of ideas and figures in the history of philosophy relative to each other and to us. It does not seek to eliminate the complexity of the issues, positions, or figures by arbitrarily simplifying them. Nor is the framework governed by the teleological aim of the eschatologist's historical schema, where philosophical developments are described, interpreted, and evaluated only to the extent they fit a developmental scheme leading to a prerecognized aim. Finally, the framework should not ignore or try to eliminate real differences among views, author, and cultures as the doxographer does. The function of the conceptual framework in the approach I am proposing here is rather to help establish the differences and similarities among ideas that otherwise would be very difficult to compare; it is not to confirm a predetermined historical direction or to blur existing distinctions. The conceptual framework makes possible the translation of diverse nomenclatures and traditions to a common denominator that will allow the development of an overall understanding. It reduces the cacophony of ideas to certain parameters according to which positions may be more easily understood, and it lays down the basis for possible evaluations and the determination of development throughout history. In this sense, this approach satisfies the need for objectivity required by the accurate description of history and also provides the foundations for interpretation and evaluation that are essential to a philosophical approach to the history of philosophy.

The explicit framework makes clear, moreover, the way in which ideas and authors are being interpreted by the historian and the criteria according to which they are being judged.[71] Most histories of philosophy consciously or unconsciously engage in surreptitious judgments that are passed on as part of historical description. Since a conceptual framework is always at work in any discourse, it is inevitable that its categories affect any account being proposed in that discourse. Anachronism cannot be completely eradicated from historical accounts, for historians are not *tabulae rasae,* nor should they be. Moreover, the aim of a historical account is more than just the re-creation of the acts of understanding of philosophers from the past. Historians of philosophy go beyond that in order to make explicit relations that could not have been made explicit in the past and to make judgments on the basis of evidence unavailable to the players in the historical drama. On the other hand, historical objectivity requires that interpretation and evaluation be clearly identified as such and distinguished as much as possible from description. What is needed are practical ways of recognizing what is or may be anachronistic. The only way to make some headway in the preservation of objectivity, then, is by making the conceptual map at work in the historian's mind as explicit and clear as possible. This, obviously, makes it easier to disagree with the resulting account. Clarity invites disagreement, whereas obscurity helps consensus. This is the reason why ambiguity is so useful in political and legal documents. Rhetoricians know this fact very well and put it to good practical use. But philosophy and history are by nature opposed to such gimmicks. If the aims pursued are truth and understanding, either in philosophy or in history, then clarity is essential and any hidden assumptions and presuppositions must be exposed. Obviously, it is not possible to lay bare every assumption one holds. But the attempt must be made to do so as far as possible. This is the reason why the uncovering of the interpretative and evaluative conceptual map at work in historical accounts must be made explicit at the outset.

Finally, another advantage of the framework approach should not be overlooked: It considers essential to the historical account the description, interpretation, and evaluation not only of positions, but also of problems and arguments. Some of the approaches described earlier were predisposed to concentrate on certain aspects of the past. The problematic approach, for example, concentrated on problems and sometimes on arguments. In contrast, the scholarly approach seemed to be concerned almost exclusively with positions, to the neglect of arguments and problems. In the framework approach, the very procedure requires paying attention and taking into account problems, positions, and arguments. The preparation of the conceptual framework used for the understanding of the past involves systematically distinguishing the various problems and issues that are pertinent, formulating different alternative solutions, examining the fundamental ideas involved in them, and analyzing the sort of arguments used for and against the solutions in question. And all of this is accompanied by a statement of the criteria used for historical selection, interpretation, and evaluation as well as a clear indication of the historian's own views on the issues under discussion.

The noted characteristics allow the framework approach to capture and integrate the best elements of the most promising approaches discussed earlier: It appropriates the objectivity and care of the scholar making explicit the conceptual framework and presuppositions of the historian; it implements the interpretative precision of the problematicist through the explicit formulation of problems and issues; it makes possible the judgment and detection of eschatological directions through the analysis of alternative solutions and problems; it leaves room for the exegetical techniques of the literary critic; it is sensitive to the ideal formulation of diverse views and arguments; and it makes possible for the historian to cover as much ground as the doxographer by providing a simplified and coherent system of classification. Moreover, it does all this by emphasizing a practical procedure that can be easily adapted and used in diverse circumstances.

There is one limiting consequence of the framework approach that should not be overlooked, however. The framework approach works best when it deals with an idea or problem or a closely knit set of ideas or problems rather than with the large scale and general description of all the philosophical dimensions of a period or periods. The reason for this is that the development and presentation of a conceptual framework of the sort that this approach requires would not be feasible if such a framework were to cover all aspects of the thought of a period. It would end up presenting, as Marenbon has rightly suggested, "a medley of logical, scientific, and theological [Marenbon is speaking particularly of the Middle Ages] discussions which would not, for the modern reader, provide a history of *philosophy*."[72] The framework approach, therefore, faces limitations when it comes to the production of comprehensive histories of philosophy. Such works, I believe, need to rely on specialized studies that themselves use the framework approach, but cannot themselves use it to the fullest. Considering the breadth that comprehensive histories must have, they must of necessity be doxographical. This is an important corollary, for it suggests that comprehensive histories of philosophy cannot be carried out with the method that I argue best suits the history of philosophy. Thus, either they must be done using less philosophically appropriate methods, or they must not be done at all.

Some historiographers have argued that they must not be done at all.[73] I believe there is some merit in them, provided they are themselves based on more probing analyses supported by the framework approach and their aim is informational rather than philosophical. In this way, they are backed up by conclusions reached through a sound methodology and at the same time make modest claims about the data they present.

As far as other genres of the history of philosophy are concerned, the framework approach seems to work well. It is particularly suited for the production of either comprehensive or specialized studies of particular problems and ideas, but it can also be effective in dealing with the thought of individual authors.

The advantages of the framework approach are not the result of the eclectic combination of the methodologies of all the approaches discussed earlier. Indeed, such a combination is not possible insofar as several approaches have irreconcilable differences among them. It would be futile to try to put together an apologist and a scholar, for example. Even if possible, such a combination would be undesirable to the extent that some approaches have little to recommend for themselves. What of good is there in the ideological approach, for example? Finally, even if a combination were possible and desirable, the eclectic result would not necessarily constitute an effective method of procedure in the history of philosophy. To be so it would have to come up with a concrete proposal for guidelines that the historian of philosophy should follow. And that can be achieved only through the sensitivity developed in the consciousness of the need to balance the descriptive, interpretative, and evaluative elements that enter into the historical account, not just by the eclectic bundling up together of various procedures that by themselves have been found wanting.

Perhaps the best way to underscore the virtues of the framework approach is by illustrating its application in a very concrete case. Because I have used this approach myself I shall refer to my use of it as an illustration of how it works.[74] I want to make clear, however, that I do not consider the study to which I shall refer a "model" of the framework approach. Indeed, when I was engaged in it my concerns were not historiographical and thus my awareness of the problems faced by the historian of philosophy was rather intuitive. As a result, now that I look back at the study I find much that is wrong with it from the historiographer's point of view. Still, in spite of all its faults, what I tried to do there adheres roughly to the procedure I am advocating here.

Several years ago, after scanning the medieval literature on the problem of individuation, it became clear to me that very little had been done on the development of the problem in the early Middle Ages. There were no books on it, nor did I find articles written specifically about the development of this problem in the period. Yet, it was obvious that the origin of the problem of individuation was to be found in the early Middle Ages. There was in the first place the abundant literature on it in the thirteenth century and after, and also some well-known texts of the early period discussed individuation indirectly, such as Abailard's *Glosses on Porphyry* and Boethius's *On the Trinity*. But no one had done an extensive study of these texts or of any others for that matter in the period that extends from 500 A.D. to 1200 A.D. And no wonder, for the difficulties of the task were enormous. There were the usual problems: corrupt Latin texts, bad editions, unavailability of sources, and so on. But the most difficult part of the whole project was the existence of different conceptual traditions in the period, the neo-Platonic, the Greek patristic, the Augustinian, and the Aristotelian, among others. All of them spoke different conceptual languages that often were sufficiently similar in appearance to create confusion. Moreover, ideas and technical terms seemed to move from one tradition into the others without much difficulty, even though, underneath, these ideas and terminology underwent significant transformations that not only modified them but influenced other ideas. I found, too, different degrees of awareness concerning individuality, various interpretations of the problem of individuation (some epistemic, some ontological, and so on), and some drastically different approaches to it. In addition I was interested in making whatever conclusions I arrived at accessible to the contemporary reader. I did not want to content myself with translating Latin texts into English, offering a close paraphrase, and leaving it at that. Such procedure would not have satisfied the modern reader and would not have made possible judgments about historical developments and comparisons among authors belonging to different conceptual traditions. In short, it would not have produced a philosophico-historical account of the problem.

Faced with these problems and goals I decided that the only sensible way to proceed was to begin by putting together a general and as far as possible neutral conceptual framework that would map out the various issues and basic positions related to individuation. This was done systematically without regard for the particular details I had found or was yet to find in the texts of the early Middle Ages, although the very development and shape of the framework had been prompted by my readings of those texts and reflected in many ways the views contained in them. I also attempted to use a language neutral with respect to philosophical traditions and clear enough to be understood by the average philosopher. It was to serve as a common vehicle of communication not only between the past and the present, but also as a means of comparison of different views within the early Middle Ages itself. In the framework itself, I first identified a series of philosophical issues that are sometimes ignored, at other times purposefully identified, and frequently confused. I found, for example, that there are at least six issues involved in or closely related to the problem of individuation. The first of these issues has to do with the understanding of individuality. The second concerns the extension of that category, namely, the things that are individual and the things that are not. The third involves the ontological status of individuality; that is, questions as to whether individuality is a property, a substance, or something else, and how individuality is to be distinguished from individuals. Fourth is the problem of individuation properly speaking, concerned with the identification of the causes or principles responsible for the individuality of individuals. The fifth concerns the epistemic issue of how we become aware of individuals as such and the criteria that make such awareness possible. Finally, I also identified some questions concerning the meaning and reference of those linguistic signs that we use to refer to individuals, that is, proper names, indexicals, and definite descriptions.

Having identified some basic issues related to the problem of individuation I then proceeded to present simple formulations of the basic positions that one could take with respect to these issues, indicating the most obvious arguments in their support and objections to which they could be liable. Thus, for example, I established that there are at least five different ways of understanding individuality, depending on whether it is conceived as indivisibility, distinction, specific division, identity, or impredicability. And I pointed out their relative strengths and weaknesses as well as the direction in which I believed the best interpretation was to be found.

Doing this with each of the outlined issues allowed me to make explicit previously undetected relations among solutions to one issue and views concerning some of the others. For example, it became obvious that those philosophers who understood individuality as some kind of difference were often led, first, to formulate the problem of individuation in epistemic terms as the problem of how knowers become aware of individuals considered as such and, second, to identify the principle of such knowledge with spatio-temporal location. Both of these corollaries make sense, for if individuality has to do with what makes something different from something else, the issue of individuation appears to be one of differentiating and the principle of individuation one that makes us differentiate. And spatio-temporal location is the most obvious candidate to count as what makes us differentiate between two things, even if they appear to be alike in most respects. But, as noted, these conclusions rely on a certain understanding of individuality. If, for example, we adopt a view of individuality as noninstantiability, the ontological problem of individuation (what makes things noninstantiable) can be distinguished easily from the epistemic problem of individual discernibility (what makes knowers aware of individuals). Moreover, this move opens the doors for other principles of individuation, since the principle of individuation need not be epistemically efficient.

Once the systematic framework was complete, the historical task of my study took center stage. First, I identified the texts and contexts where the pertinent authors discussed individuation or issues related to individuation and then I subjected those texts to standard exegetical techniques as well as to philosophical analysis, taking care to maintain a perspective on the general philosophical point of view of the authors in question. Slowly a picture of what the authors had said and what they had not said emerged. With the use of the categories worked out in the framework I was able to establish and demarcate with precision the issue or issues that concerned the authors under scrutiny, the approaches they used, the assumptions under which they worked and the value of their respective contributions. For example, it became clear that Gilbert of Poitiers is the first author of the period who explicitly makes a distinction between the ontological problem concerned with the principle of individuation and the epistemic problem posed by the discernibility of individuals. It also was clear that Abailard's approach to individuation is primarily logical and that his solution stems largely from his linguistic understanding of individuality as impredicability. It also became possible to summarize the position of each author on the basis of the framework and to compare the positions and achievements of the various authors with those of other authors who used different terminology, approaches, and assumptions. Even though, for example, some authors spoke of particularity and singularity rather than individuality, I was able to show how in some cases they were dealing with the same concept.

All this resulted in an account of the development of the problem of individuation in the early Middle Ages that is descriptive, interpretative, and evaluative. Its objectivity is protected by the explicit framework applied to the period, and its interpretative and evaluative parameters should become clear to anyone who reads the text. Naturally, I expected that some historians of the period would disagree with my conclusions, but the explicitness of the framework facilitates their understanding of where they disagree with me and why, for they should have no difficulty in separating evaluation, interpretation, and description in my study. So much, then, for the illustration of the framework approach. I do not think it appropriate to expand the illustration further here, lest we should steer too far from our course. Now let me turn to the criticisms that can be brought against it.

Two serious criticisms can be leveled against the framework approach. The first is that it assumes too much. Indeed, it may be argued that this approach assumes that it is possible to develop a general and neutral conceptual framework that can serve as the basis of comparison among widely differing views and ideas. But such an assumption is contradicted by our experience of the wide conceptual chasm that separates the present from the past and one culture from another. There is, therefore, no general framework that could be used to compare views from different periods of history. Moreover, the framework could not be neutral, because it would be the product of a historical figure subject to the same cultural pressures and limitations as other historical individuals. The idea of a general and neutral conceptual framework, therefore, is no more than a projection of a historian's desire for objectivity that can never be implemented as conceived.

This sort of objection is not new. We already encountered it in a slightly different form in Chapter One, when referring to the problem of the recoverability of the past, and there I provided some reasons why I thought it was ineffective in that context. Here I would like to add that endorsement of the framework approach and its implementation do not require the actual existence of a perfectly general and neutral conceptual framework. Indeed, part of the rationale for the framework approach is the realization of the biased and culturally oriented perspective of every historian of philosophy. No historian is a *tabula rasa* that can look back at history from a completely neutral stance. And this is why it is necessary to develop procedures that will promote, if not ensure, as much objectivity as possible. The function of the framework in the framework approach is to make explicit, as far as possible, both the historian's understanding of the issues, arguments, and views with which he or she is dealing and his or her own views about how those issues are to be understood, as well as the relative value of contending arguments and views with respect to them. The generality and neutrality of the framework, then, are not conceived as a *fait accompli* required at the outset of the historical inquiry, but rather as a methodological goal that regulates the process whereby the historian tries to understand and recover the philosophical past.

To this I must add, however, that the framework approach does assume that some disciplinary unity runs through the history of philosophy. Philosophy, I believe, does deal with some basic and fundamental issues and procedures. These issues and procedures may surface at different times under different garbs and may even be difficult to recognize in certain circumstances. Moreover, the issues may be posed from sometimes significantly different perspectives. Still, there are threads that run through the history of philosophical thought, and these threads give credence to the notion of a methodological conceptual framework that is sufficiently general and neutral to serve as a basis for comparison of philosophical views from different times and cultures.

The second serious criticism of the framework approach is that it may become a Procrustean bed in which ideas that do not fit are cut off and discarded, and others are stretched beyond what their proper elasticity allows. In other words, the accusation is of having a predetermined scheme that the historian sets out to see substantiated in history, as did eschatologists such as Hegel and Augustine.

Indeed, this is a danger for such an approach, but those who practice it need not fall into it. First of all, the framework must be broad and general enough to include as many alternatives as possible, and it also should be open to alteration. The framework is not a system, a complete and circular set of ideas, but rather an open-ended set of guidelines. There has to be a reciprocal relationship between the conceptual framework and the textual study. Developments in the textual study should prompt modifications in the framework and developments in the framework should heighten the awareness about possible interpretations of texts. Moreover, if the historical context is kept ever-present, the danger of extravagant interpretations and wild evaluations should be substantially reduced. Finally, the explicitness of the framework should help guard against the implicit and surreptitious interpretations and evaluations that permeate most historical accounts.

All in all, then, I see the framework approach as the best way to study the history of philosophy. The synchronic and diachronic integration of ideas that it makes possible cannot be found in any other approach. But even the framework approach can be misapplied. There are many obstacles that the historian needs to overcome to provide an accurate account of past philosophical ideas. Some of these arise precisely from the way those ideas surface and develop. In the next chapter I take up some of these problems.

NOTES

1. Recent studies on identical twins have already tried to pinpoint similarities in such areas as vocation, character, tastes, and habits.

2. Émile Bréhier, *Histoire de la philosophie* (Paris: F. Alcan, 1948–1951), vol. 1, p. 24. I am grateful to Michael Gorman for polishing the translations of this and the other two passages corresponding to notes 5 and 6.

3. Roger Chartier, "Intellectual History or Sociocultural History? The French Trajectories," in LaCapra and Kaplan, eds., *Modern European Intellectual History,* p. 22.

4. Ibid., p. 28.

5. Lucien Febvre, "Leur histoire et la nôtre," originally published in *Annales d'Histoire Economique et Sociale,* and reprinted in *Combats pour l'histoire,* 2d ed.(Paris: Librairie Armand Colin, 1953), p. 278.

6. Lucien Febvre, "Doctrines et sociétés. Étienne Gilson et la philosophie du XIVe siécle," originally published in *Annales d'Histoire Economique et Sociale,* and reprinted in *Combats pour l'histoire,* p. 288.

7. José Ortega y Gasset, "Ideas para una historia de la filosofía," in Émile Bréhier's *Historia de la filosofía* (Buenos Aires: Sudamericana, 1942); in *Obras completas,* vol. 6 (Madrid: Revista de Occidente, 1947), pp. 379–419.

8. John A. Passmore, "The Idea of a History of Philosophy," *History and Theory* Beiheft 5 (1965): 14.

9. I say the implications of his procedure because Bartley is careful not to claim explicitly that the details of Wittgenstein's life do indeed enlighten us about his philosophy; his explicit claim is only that they help us understand the man better. See W. W. Bartley, III, *Wittgenstein* 2d rev. and enlarged ed. (LaSalle, Ill.: Open Court, 1985), p. 13. Bartley explicitly discusses and clarifies his claim only in an Afterword added to the book in 1985, in which he calls "epistemological expressionism" the view that a person's work is the expression of his or her inner states or personality. This claim, however, is made explicitly by Arthur W. Levi in "The Biographical Sources of Wittgenstein's Ethics," *Telos* 38 (1978–1979), 63–76.

10. Bartley claims that it was explicitly raised by George Steiner in *New York Times* (July 23, 1973), p. 77; and in *The Listener,* with Anthony Quinton (March 28, 1974), pp. 399–401.

11. See Levi, "The Biographical Sources."

12. For other examples, see the texts by the Marxist M. N. Pokrovsky and the Nazis Walter Frank and Alexander von Müller, in Fritz Stern, ed., *The Varieties of History: From Voltaire to the Present* (New York: World Publishing, 1956), pp. 330–346. It is no surprise that most practitioners of this approach flourish under totalitarian regimes.

13. For a discussion of Latin American positivism, the classic source is Leopoldo Zea, *Positivism in Mexico,* trans. Josephine H. Schulte (Austin: University of Texas Press, 1974).

14. The most compelling portrait of the humanist I know appears in George Eliot's *Romola*.

15. Jonathan Rée, "History, Philosophy, and Interpretation," p. 44. The romantic approach appears to be a version of hero worship found in general history. Cf. Thomas Carlyle, *On Heroes, Hero-Worship, and the Heroic in History* (London: Everyman's Library, 1940), pp. 239 ff. Behind most romantic approaches lurks the figure of Friedrich Nietzsche, who was convinced both of the impossibility of achieving historical objectivity and of the artistic character of history. See *The Use and Abuse of History*, in *The Complete Works of Friedrich Nietzsche*, ed. Oscar Levy, vol. 5 (New York: Russell & Russell, 1964), p. 51.

16. Rée, "History, Philosophy, and Interpretation," p. 56.

17. Ibid., p. 58.

18. Rorty, "The Historiography of Philosophy," p. 49.

19. Daniel Garber, "Does History Have a Future?" p. 33.

20. Ibid., p. 15.

21. An excellent, relatively recent example of this approach is found in Donald W. Sherburne's *A Key to Whitehead's "Process and Reality"*, where he rearranges the text according to what he calls a "linear" pattern (in contrast with Whitehead's own "weblike" pattern) of topics and adds brief comments from time to time. The purpose of the rearrangement is to make Whitehead's thought accessible, not to defend or criticize Whitehead, and thus the author refrains from critical evaluation. See the mentioned book (Chicago: University of Chicago Press, 1966), pp. 2–3.

22. Borges, "Pierre Menard, Author of the *Quixote*," pp. 36–44.

23. Daniel W. Graham, "Anachronism in the History of Philosophy," p. 140. Even in such cases, as suggested by Borges, there is an element of interpretation since the "reproduction" occurs at a different time than the original. This is why, as pointed out in Chapter Four, reproductions are historically inaccurate renditions of the past; interpretations are essential for the accurate understanding of the past.

24. Passmore, "The Idea of a History of Philosophy," pp. 19–22.

25. Rorty, "The Historiography of Philosophy," pp. 61–67.

26. Paul Oskar Kristeller excludes biographical information from doxography. Such information, according to him, belongs to a different historiographical tradition, which he labels "biographical." See "Philosophy and Its Historiography," p. 620. Kristeller's understanding of doxography is in line with the etymology of the word, which literally means the description of concepts and views, but at odds with much doxographical practice and historiographical opinion.

27. Diogenes Laertius, *The Lives and Opinions of Eminent Philosophers*, Bk. 5, ch. 1, trans. R. D. Hicks, The Loeb Classical Library, 2 vols (London and New York: W. Heinemann and G. P. Putnam's Sons, 1925), vol. 1, p. 477.

28. Passmore, "The Idea of a History of Philosophy," p. 22.

29. Rorty, "The Historiography of Philosophy," p. 62.

30. Robin George Collingwood, *An Autobiography*, (London: Oxford University Press, 1939), pp. 59 ff.

31. Cf. Passmore, "The Idea of a History of Philosophy," pp. 11 ff.

32. Philip P. Wiener, ed., *Dictionary of the History of Ideas*, vol. 1 (New York: Charles Scribner's Sons, 1973), p. vii. For an updated statement of the aim of the history of ideas, as well as its history, see Donald R. Kelley, "What Is Happening to the History of Ideas?" *Journal of the History of Ideas* 51, no. 1 (1990): 3–25.

33. Wiener, ibid., vol. 1, p. viii.

34. Ibid., p. vii.

35. This point is evident in the following passage from Lovejoy: "There are, I have suggested, many 'unit-ideas'—types of categories, thoughts concerning particular aspects of common experience, implicit or explicit presuppositions, sacred formulas and catchwords, specific philosophic theorems, or the larger hypotheses, generalizations or methodological assumptions of various sciences—which have long life-histories of their own, are to be found at work in the most various regions of the history of human thinking and feeling, and upon which the intellectual and effective reactions of men—individuals and masses—have been highly diverse.... Until these units are first discriminated, until each of them which has played any large role in history is separately pursued through all the regions into which it has entered and in which it has exercised influence, any manifestations of it in a single region of intellectual history, or in an individual writer or writing, will, as a rule, be imperfectly understood—and will sometimes go unrecognized altogether." Arthur O. Lovejoy, "The Historiography of Ideas," *Essays in the History of Ideas* (Baltimore: Johns Hopkins University Press, 1948), p. 9. Note that the ideas, although playing roles in history, themselves seem to be unchanging. This resistance to change suggests the Platonic model.

36. Johan Huizinga discusses historical anthropomorphism in "Die Historische Idee," in *Verzamelde Werken*, vol. 7 (Haarlem: H. D. Tjeenk Willink, 1950), pp. 136 ff.

37. As Russell pointed out in the Preface to the first edition of *The Philosophy of Leibniz*, 2d ed. (London: George Allen & Unwin, 1937), p. xi: "There is a tendency...to pay so much attention to the *relations* of philosophies that the philosophies themselves are neglected. Successive philosophies may be compared, as we compare successive forms of a pattern or design, with little

or no regard to their meaning, an influence may be established by documentary evidence, or by identity of phrase, without any comprehension of the systems whose causal relations are under discussion."

38. I am borrowing Passmore's terminology here, but what Passmore means by *polemical* is not exactly what I mean when I use the term. For his view, see "The Idea of a History of Philosophy," pp. 5 ff.

39. Some go so far as to deny any development in an author's thought over a period of time. This attitude is rare. More frequent is the view that the author could not have changed his or her mind.

40. Karl Marx, of course, is another. The case with Marx is similar to that of Thomas in that he has become an institutionalized authority, in this case for the Communist Party and those countries that have adopted communism as their official philosophy.

41. John of St. Thomas, *Cursus theologicus, Tractatus de approbatione et auctoritate doctrinae d. Thomae,* Disp. II, a. 5 (Paris: Desclée, 1931), vol. 1, pp. 297–301.

42. Cf. Jorge J. E. Gracia and John Kronen, "John of St. Thomas," in Jorge J. E. Gracia, ed., *Individuation in Scholasticism: The Later Middle Ages and the Counter Reformation* (Munich and Vienna: Philosophia Verlag, forthcoming).

43. John of St. Thomas, *Cursus philosophicus thomisticus secundum exactam, veram, genuinam Aristotelis et Doctoris Angelici mentem,* ed. B. Reiser, 3 vols. (Turin: Marietti, 1933), vol 2, p. 784.

44. See Umberto Degl'Innocenti, "Il principio d'individuazione dei corpi e Giovanni di S. Tommaso," *Aquinas* 12 (1969): 59–99; and Gracia and Kronen, "John of St. Thomas."

45. The understanding of philosophical texts as literary has received considerable attention in the recent past. See Arthur C. Danto's "Philosophy as/and/of Literature," in Anthony J. Cascardi, ed., *Literature and the Question of Philosophy* (Baltimore and London: Johns Hopkins University Press, 1987, pp. 3–23.

46. See, for example, Michel Foucault, "What Is an Author?" pp. 116 ff.

47. See Stanley Rosen's Introduction to his *Plato's "Symposium"*, 2d. ed. (New Haven and London: Yale University Press, 1987), p. xlviii.

48. Bennett, "Response to Garber and Rée," p. 64.

49. Passmore, "The Idea of a History of Philosophy," p. 7.

50. G. S. Kirk and J. E. Raven, *The Presocratic Philosophers* (Cambridge: Cambridge University Press, 1957), p. 1.

51. Plantinga's article appeared in the *American Philosophical Quarterly* 15 (1978), 129–138; Castañeda's article in the same journal 12 (1975): 131–145;

and Boethius's text may be consulted in *Patrologia latina* 64, 462–464. For a discussion of this text, see my *Introduction to the Problem of Individuation in the Early Middle Ages*, 2d rev. ed. (Munich and Vienna: Philosophia Verlag, 1988), pp. 90 ff.

52. Plantinga, ibid., p. 132b.

53. This is the sort of view that Morgan's "actual author" would have. See Michael L. Morgan, "Authorship and the History of Philosophy," p. 331.

54. Russell, *The Philosophy of Leibniz*, pp. xi–xii. My emphasis.

55. Ibid., p. 2.

56. Ibid., p. 1.

57. Ibid., p. 3.

58. I am adapting one of Passmore's categories here. See Passmore, "The Idea of a History of Philosophy," pp. 27–32.

59. Bennett, "Response to Garber and Rée," p. 9.

60. Collingwood, *An Autobiography*, p. 31.

61. Bennett, *Kant's Analytic* (Cambridge, 1966), back cover. Cited by Michael Ayers, "Analytical Philosophy and the History of Philosophy," p. 54.

62. Rorty, "The Historiography of Philosophy," p. 52.

63. The "Disputatio metaphysica V" is printed in *Opera omnia*, ed. Carolo Berton (Paris: Vivès, 1861), vol. 25, pp. 145b–201a. For the English translation of section III, see my *Suárez on Individuation* (Milwaukee: Marquette University Press, 1982), pp. 74–101, particularly pp. 99–100.

64. Garber, "Does History Have a Future?" p. 4.

65. Passmore, "The Idea of a History of Philosophy," p. 29.

66. These two thinkers in fact represent two different types of eschatology. Both have the sense that history is moving toward a final point of resolution, but the point differs in each case. For Augustine it is the end of the world, whereas for Hegel it is his own thought. Marxism favors the Augustinian type of eschatology, although for Marxism there is no end of the world but instead the establishment of a perfect society. Aristotle's discussion of the pre-Socratics, as we shall see shortly, is another example of the Hegelian variety of eschatology. It should be noted that the Augustinian type of eschatology usually is applied to history as a whole, rather than to the history of philosophy or ideas. The Hegelian variety, on the other hand, is generally adapted to ideas. This is the reason why my description reflects the Hegelian rather than the Augustinian variety. I also should make clear that I do not claim that Augustine provided or thought he could provide a detailed blueprint or timetable of the development of history. His view is not eschatological in that apocalyptic sense.

67. Indeed, some argue that not even Hegel himself held this view. A more moderate and reasonable interpretation holds his thesis is that the thought of each generation, or age, is the culmination of previous thought and thus the philosophy of a period should be seen as a product of the past, which leads to it inexorably.

68. Graham, "Anachronism in the History of Philosophy," pp. 142–143.

69. Rorty, "The Historiography of Philosophy," p. 38.

70. Ibid., p. 62.

71. This statement should be sufficient to make clear that the framework to which I refer is not limited by the conceptual boundaries within which the historian believes the author he or she studies is working, but extends beyond that to include what the historian holds. The more restricted framework has been discussed by Richard A. Watson in "A Short Discourse on Method in the History of Philosophy," *Southwestern Journal of Philosophy* 11, no. 2 (1980): 11–12.

72. John Marenbon, *Later Medieval Philosophy (1150–1350): An Introduction* (London and New York: Routledge & Kegan Paul, 1987), p. 90. Marenbon is describing with these words what he calls "the historical analysis" approach. This approach has much in common with the framework approach presented here.

73. Rorty, "The Historiography of Philosophy," p. 65.

74. Gracia, *Introduction to the Problem of Individuation in the Early Middle Ages.*

Chapter Six

The Development of Philosophical Ideas: Stages, Interpretation, and Progress

Many of the factors that create considerable misunderstanding concerning historical claims about what has occurred in the history of philosophy arise from a lack of a proper understanding of the way philosophical ideas and issues surface and develop. It is quite common, for example, to find historians of philosophy claiming that a historical figure such as Plato actually anticipated the solution of some other philosopher with respect to a particular issue or problem. It seems that every age wants to read back into history its own discoveries and accomplishments. Indeed, it is as if the argument from authority, so well regarded by scholastics in matters of faith and so frequently criticized by philosophers, were not really to be dispensed with in philosophical matters, becoming *de facto* a kind of prop without which new theories cannot stand. That seems to be one kind of motivation for this sort of claim, and, indeed, one of the motivations for the study of the history of philosophy, as we saw in Chapter Three, is based precisely on this attitude.

Another motivation for the claim that the past has anticipated the future comes from a different source and is found among those who suffer from what I call the *Ecclesiastes syndrome*. According to this malady, there is nothing philosophically new under the sun. All that is present in philosophy at any period in its history can be traced back to the thought of some other period. This is a frequent view among practitioners of history of ideas doxography in particular, who seem to see their task as tracing back the ideas of the authors they study to some prior source. But it is also frequently coupled with the nostalgic approach.

Those who favor the nostalgic approach and suffer from the Ecclesiastes syndrome spend their efforts in tracing back all that is philosophically good and useful to the thought of one or more figures who, according to them, achieved the highest philosophical sophistication possible. The most notorious examples of this phenomenon in philosophical circles are the followers of Thomas Aquinas and Karl Marx. But even a superficial examination of the current philosophical scene will reveal the breadth and depth of the Ecclesiastes syndrome. There are Kantians, Heideggerians, Russellians, Peirceans, Wittgensteinians, Aristotelians, and perhaps the most recalcitrant of them all, Platonists. The nostalgics who share the syndrome spend their time showing how their preferred author or age has anticipated everything of value that subsequent philosophers or ages have claimed to have discovered. Errors, of course, are not generally to be traced back to the past. Since most of those who suffer from the Ecclesiastes syndrome adhere also to the principle of infallibility, errors are the only things for which subsequent philosophers can claim originality. Nevertheless, there are some nostalgics who suffer from the syndrome and try to trace back errors to past philosophers, but only to the philosophical enemies of the author whom they regard as anticipatory of all or most truth. This procedure lends support to the view that the authors in question in fact were concerned with the issue at hand and that their answers are not contrivances of historians but historical fact.

The results of the Ecclesiastes syndrome are quite unsatisfactory not just because they distort historical fact by attributing to some author views and ideas the author did not have, but also because it produces considerable anachronism. The anachronism results from thinking of an age in terms of issues and categories that do not apply to it. We saw already in Chapter Five the unfortunate consequences of similar approaches to the study of the history of philosophy, so there is no need to dwell on this syndrome any further.

Almost as widespread as the Ecclesiastes syndrome is its reverse, the view that current ideas are new and what appear to be similar ideas that preceded them are only incomplete and incipient anticipations. This malady, which I call the *primitive syndrome* is more characteristic of polemical approaches to the history of philosophy than of historical ones. Historians often are predisposed to see similarities rather than differences between the past and the present, thus being attracted particularly to the Ecclesiastes syndrome rather than its reverse. The emphasis of some dilettantes and problematicists on the present, on the other hand, leads them to overlook the antecedents of contemporary views.

These kinds of mistakes are the result of a lack of sensitivity to the way philosophical ideas and issues surface and develop.[1] Its remedy consists in making clear how ideas and issues unfold, bringing into the historical discourse the proper sensitivity to the various stages of development through which those ideas and issues pass. The purpose of this chapter, then, is to present a tentative structure that makes explicit such stages. It is tentative because we are dealing with a subject that requires much more reflection and research than I have been able to give it. It should also be clear that the stages to which I call attention here are seldom clearly and sequentially delineated in the history of philosophy. Historical categories are not facts in the world, but rather conceptually interpretative distinctions that help us organize our thoughts about the world, and so it is not always possible to find exact correspondence between them and historical phenomena.

The discussion is divided into four parts. The first presents an outline of the most fundamental stages in the development of philosophical ideas and issues. The second illustrates those stages by referring to the development of the idea of a "principle of individuation" in the Middle Ages. Third, I show very briefly how historical interpretations need to take account of the stages of philosophical development of ideas lest they fall into historical inaccuracies and distortions. And, finally, I raise the question of so-called philosophical progress, which naturally comes up in any discussion dealing with the development of ideas. Let me begin, then, with the stages of development.

I. THE FIVE STAGES

I consider five stages in the development of philosophical ideas and issues fundamental: preanalytical, definitional, problematic, textually independent, and central.[2] The preanalytical stage is further subdivided into a functionally nonexplicit stage and a functionally explicit stage.

A. Preanalytical Stage

Perhaps the most misunderstood stage of the philosophical development of ideas is the first, the *preanalytical stage.* At this stage philosophers use ideas borrowed from ordinary discourse without being aware of, or concerned with, either their exact conceptual import or the problems they pose. They pay no attention to them because at the center of their attention are other ideas or issues that they have already identified and to whose clarification or solution their efforts are explicitly directed. They consider the latter ideas and problems *central* to their concerns. Thus, for example, if they are concerned with establishing whether a certain form of government is good, they might simply use a commonsense idea of goodness without asking themselves exactly what it is and what it implies. At this stage of philosophical development no attempt is made to define the commonsense ideas being used, and philosophers show no awareness of the problems that could be associated with the ideas in question, nor are they concerned with exploring the ideas themselves. Simply, they do not see them as having any philosophical interest. Their concerns are centered on other questions and ideas that they believe require their immediate attention.

The reasons behind their concerns sometimes have to do with philosophical issues themselves, or they may have nothing to do with philosophy. Political, social, theological, or scientific considerations may lead philosophers to concentrate their attention on some issues and ideas and neglect others. Philosophy, as the cliché points out so well, does not develop in a vacuum; it arises in a cultural context and in a historical setting. What philosophers discuss is influenced, if not always determined, by their times and circumstances. This is quite evident, for example, when one contrasts the concerns of Greek, medieval, and modern philosophers. For Plato, ethical and political questions provided his themes and lead him in the directions he took. The death of Socrates, the chaotic state of Athenian democracy, and the rise of sophistry clearly set his agenda to a great extent. On the other hand, the agenda for the medievals was determined by the questions raised when Christian faith met pagan philosophy. The program changed from one motivated by ethical and political considerations in the ancient classical world to one in which theological and apologetic considerations became dominant. In turn, when we get to early modern philosophy, the development of science, the growing consciousness of the role of experience in the acquisition of knowledge, and the increasing application of mathematics to the world prompted the meditation on methodology and the growth of epistemology.

The preanalytical stage of philosophical development is more complex than it appears at first, however, and can be subdivided into two stages of development. The first, which I call the *functionally nonexplicit stage,* occurs when the idea in question has not yet been singled out. There is a sense in which the idea is functionally operative—that is, one could argue that a particular conceptual framework implies or presupposes such an idea—but there are no explicit signs in what philosophers who adhere to it say or write that they are actually conscious of it. A necessary condition for a idea to be classified as belonging to this stage of development is that no term or expression in the language refer to it. Let us take, for example, the idea of contradiction, namely, that two claims cannot have the same truth value.

This idea can be operative in philosophical discourse before anyone pays attention to it or even has a term or expression with which to refer to it. For example, one can imagine a situation of someone arguing: "It is not true that P and ~P" (It is not true that you are both Claudius's child and not his child"), while not having any clear concept of contradiction. This is obvious when the claim in question is compared to two other claims. Let me number them and set them separately to make their contrast obvious:

1. It is not true that P and ~P.
2. Propositions of the sort "P and ~P" cannot be true.
3. P and ~P are contradictory.

Claim 1 uses the idea of contradiction but does not reveal an explicit awareness of the exact nature of contradiction. Claim 2 not only uses the idea of contradiction but also reveals an explicit awareness of that idea, although it does not use a sign to refer to the idea. Finally, in claim 3 we have a case in which a linguistic sign is used to refer to contradiction, clearly isolating the idea from others and making it fully explicit in discourse. What I call the *functionally nonexplicit stage* of development of an idea occurs in cases like 1, where the idea plays an implicit role in discourse but is not explicitly used. It does not occur in cases like 2, where the idea is explicitly used, or in cases like 3, where it is explicitly identified by a term or expression.

In the second substage of the preanalytical stage, which I call the *functionally explicit stage*, the idea becomes explicit. Authors are actually aware of it in the senses illustrated by either 2 or 3. They have a rough understanding of the idea sufficient to allow them to refer to it through some kind of circumlocution or through a specific term. In some cases we find actual statements as to what is involved, but these statements do not attempt to present criteria for the use of the term or aim to develop a rigorous definition of it. Nor is there any indication of an awareness of potential problems related to the implications of diverse understandings of the term. The concept in question is explicit, but that is as far as it goes; it is not subjected to analysis.

B. Definitional Stage

A second stage, which may be called *definitional*, goes beyond the preanalytical insofar as in it there is an awareness of the need to present a clear understanding of the idea being used. Thus the philosophers involved in the evaluation of a particular form of government, for example, might ask for, or try to develop, a definition of goodness that will allow them to discuss with more precision the subject matter that concerns them. But there is not yet at this stage any awareness of the problems that the adopted definition might create or the other issues that might be involved in the idea. The concern at this stage is still primarily with some other issues and ideas, and thus any problem not perceived as directly associated with them is not raised. The immediate need is to develop a more precise and technical concept than that found in ordinary discourse. At this stage we go beyond cases 1, 2, and 3, reaching a higher level of awareness in

4. A contradiction is a logical relation between two propositions that cannot have the same truth value.

But note that the function of the definition at this stage is to avoid ambiguity and unclarity when the *definiendum* is used to solve some other problem. No awareness of possible problems with the definition is contemplated, nor is there an attempt to deal with possibly conflicting definitions. The discussion has other goals unrelated to those that have to do with the clarification and understanding of the idea being defined.

C. Problematic Stage

At the third stage, which I call *problematic,* a consciousness develops with respect to problems related to the idea in question. These problems might have to do with the implications of the definition of that idea, or they might have to do with other issues that have come to the surface as a result of the attention paid to the idea. In the example of good mentioned earlier, at this stage philosophers raise questions as to how one becomes aware of what is good, the causes of goodness in good things, and so on. Still, the issue or issues that surface are dealt with in the context of the original issue that prompted the use of the commonsense idea and are considered propaedeutic to it. The investigation of the causes of goodness, for instance, serves only to clarify what type of government is good. At this stage, we should find statements of a different sort from 1–4. We may find such statements as

5. The definition of *X* as *m* is inconsistent with the definition of *Y* as *n*.
6. If *X* is defined as *m*, then *Y* must be defined as *r*.
7. *X* is *m* because *Y* is *n*.

And so on. In short, what we have is a series of propositions that reflect an awareness of issues specifically related to the idea in question rather than to the original concerns that led to its use in the first place. Yet, these new questions and concerns are still raised and dealt with in the original thematic context and still viewed as somewhat propaedeutic to and as part of the background of the main business at hand—say, settling the question of the most appropriate form of government or the truth value of certain claims about the world, in the examples with which we have been working.

D. Textually Independent Stage

At the fourth stage, however, we have another important development that is revealed not only in the content of the discussion, but becomes established in the very textual structure of philosophical works. Now we find that the discussion of the idea and issues surrounding it that previously surfaced only in the context of another issue, becomes textually separate from the discussion of that original issue. That is, we see in the text a separation that was not present earlier. The issues associated with the originally propaedeutic idea are raised and settled independently of the context, although the issues that provided the context in the first place are still considered central. We might find, thus, a chapter or a clearly separate section of a chapter dealing with what was originally only dealt with marginally. I call this stage the *textually independent stage.* This is actually the stage at which the problematic stage becomes as it were "institutionalized." Now there is not just a conceptual distance between the treatment of the originally propaedeutic idea and the one in the context of which it was formerly discussed, rather textual boundaries are established between them, as revealed in the very headings of the work in which the discussion occurs. Thus, we may find in a treatise on government a chapter dealing with the definition of goodness.

E. Central Stage

Finally, we reach the stage in which there is full development, when the ideas and issues originally considered propaedeutic take on a life of their own and become the subject of discussion outside the context of any other philosophical issue. Textually, this is the stage at which we find separate treatises, books, articles, and monographs on the subject. At this point the ideas and issues originally considered propaedeutic cease to be instrumental and begin to play a central role in philosophical development. Indeed, at this stage they begin to function in such a way that their consideration leads to the use of other commonsense ideas, to the definition of those ideas, and to the formulation of related issues. In some cases, in fact, the order of subservience between these ideas and those that originally introduced them is reversed, so that the originally central ideas are discussed in the context of what were propaedeutic ones. Thus, for example, types of government might be discussed in the context of a treatise whose primary subject matter is the nature of goodness. To reach this stage of development is to become *central* in philosophical discourse.

Note that to say that an issue or problem is central is much more than to say that it is merely important. There are important problems and ideas, actually considered to be central, that are not such. The differences between what is important and what is central can be illustrated easily with references to issues.

At least three differences distinguish a central from an important issue. The first is that the solution to a central issue is a necessary condition for the solution to other issues, whereas the solution to an important issue need not be necessary for the solution of other issues. The second is that a central issue functions as a seminal source for the development and creation of other hitherto unknown issues. Merely important issues may not further philosophical inquiry in this way. The third and final difference is that a central issue either functions as an umbrella under which other issues are discussed or is an issue whose discussion comes first in the logical organization of a philosophical system. An important issue may occupy a prominent place in the system, but its discussion may not have to come first in the logical organization of the system and it may not function as an umbrella under which other issues are raised. Moreover, what has been said concerning philosophical issues applies *mutatis mutandis* to philosophical ideas.

Before we turn to the historical illustration of these stages, I must repeat my earlier warning about taking the stages to which I have referred too rigidly. Indeed, these stages often coexist in the same author who quickly moves from one to another in a steady progression. Nor is the order of progression as neatly ordered or defined as I have described. Sometimes ideas that have become central to an author's thought at a certain point later move to a secondary position. Still, it is also true that one can find authors who deal with certain ideas at just one or two of the stages of development I have described even if others skip some altogether. In particular, it is often possible to determine whether an idea has become central and when it is still in a preanalytical stage for a particular author. Likewise, it is also possible, within limits, to identify times at which the stage of development of a particular philosophical idea never went beyond a preanalytical level of development and when it reached a problematic one. Of course, the existence of many philosophers at any particular historical period complicates matters, for different philosophers might be working at different stages of development with respect to the same idea or they might be working at the same stage with respect to different ideas. This is why it is easier to determine the stage at which individual philosophers work with a specific idea than the stage of a particular historical period with respect to a specific idea.

I would like to add also that not all philosophical ideas reach the central stage of development I have identified as the last stage in the development of philosophical ideas. There is no inexorable movement here. Many ideas remain at various levels of development, offering in this way an opportunity to future generations of philosophers to reflect on and develop them. Moreover, it also should be noted that the development of philosophical ideas does not end with the central stage. Even those ideas that reach that stage experience change afterward. Some are forgotten and others are relegated to a secondary role by subsequent philosophers.[3] Indeed, future generations might have to retravel the roads already traveled by previous generations. The development and progress of philosophy, as I argue later in this chapter, is not linear. Philosophy goes back and forth, retracing its steps and moving forward only in a hesitant and often unclear manner. Thus, the central stage of development is not the end of the history of philosophical ideas; the process continues. Here, however, I shall not try to characterize the process of change that follows the achievement of centrality. Nor will I discuss the fate of ideas that, after reaching one of the stages mentioned, go back to an earlier stage. The possibilities are many and do not affect the thrust of my argument. For my limited purpose, the characterization of the stages followed by ideas until they reach the central stage is sufficient.

Next I would like to illustrate the various stages of development of philosophical ideas, but I would like to do so in terms of historical periods rather than individual authors in spite of the difficulties that such procedure entails. The reason is that my own historical work lends itself handily to such an illustration of some of the points I wish to make.

Those who know my work will by now have guessed that I am going to deal with the principle of individuation and its history in the Middle Ages. My claim is that when one examines discussions of the principle of individuation in the medieval period, it becomes clear that by the end of the thirteenth and the beginning of the fourteenth centuries, this idea had reached the level of centrality represented by the fifth stage just described. Moreover, this level of development contrasts with that of earlier periods, when it was discussed only propaedeutically or marginally.

II. AN ILLUSTRATION: THE PRINCIPLE OF INDIVIDUATION IN THE MIDDLE AGES

Let me begin by pointing out that the idea of a "principle of individuation" is related to the ideas of "individual" and "individuation" as well as to other ideas such as "distinction," "difference," "number," "numerical difference," and "identity." But I shall restrict the discussion to the principle of individuation primarily, although occasionally I shall refer to other ideas in passing. In particular, I do not propose to discuss the idea of "individual," which itself has a long and complicated history in the Middle Ages.[4]

The second point that needs to be made clear at the start is that the principle of individuation is generally taken to mean that in virtue of which individual things are individual. Thus the principle of individuation of Socrates (or of the sheet of paper on which I am now writing) is that in virtue of which Socrates (or the sheet of paper) is individual. I believe it is not necessary to provide further clarifications of this idea in order to understand the discussion that follows.

I shall illustrate the two preanalytical stages, the functionally nonexplicit and the functionally explicit, with reference to the work of two authors: Porphyry (b. ca. 232) and Boethius (ca. 480–524). Moreover, I shall restrict my discussion to those texts of Porphyry in the *Isagoge* that were translated by Boethius into Latin and, therefore, had an impact on later medieval thinking concerning the principle of individuation.

There is only one text of Porphyry in the whole *Isagoge* that has to do with the principle of individuation. It reads:

> Socrates, this white, and...the son of Sophroniscus...are called individual...because each of them is composed of a collection of properties which can never be the same for another.[5]

It seems clear in this text that Porphyry has something like a principle of individuation in mind; that is, that in virtue of which individuals such as Socrates are—he says "are called," which raises the question of whether he has an epistemic or linguistic principle in mind, rather than a metaphysical one—individual. Note, however, that the passage also could be interpreted as providing an understanding of individuality rather than as identifying its principles. Nonetheless, the passage is ambiguous enough to allow for an interpretation that holds that something like a principle of individuation is at work here. But there is no term or phrase whereby we may identify it. Porphyry is too concerned with his topic of discussion, namely, the nature of species, and how predication works between the species and the individual, to think about the principle of individuation. Yet, because he deals with universals and individuals in the text, he indirectly touches on what looks like a principle of individuation. All this indicates that Porphyry's thinking with respect to the principle of individuation is preanalytical and that, although it looks as if the idea of a principle of individuation is at work in his thought, its function is far from explicit.

Boethius says much more about individuality than Porphyry and in the process makes explicit the idea of what makes individuals to be such, although he still does not use a term to refer to it. Thus, his discussion may be considered an example of the functionally explicit preanalytical stage.

Three sorts of passages are found in Boethius that are closely related to individuation. Most of them suffer from the ambiguity we observed in Porphyry's text and, therefore, could not lead us to believe that he is more aware of the principle of individuation than Porphyry. For example, he writes:

> Individual is said in many ways. That is said to be individual which cannot be cut in any way, for example, unity or mind; that is said to be individual which cannot be divided because of its solidity, for example, a diamond; that is said to be individual which cannot be predicated of other things similar to itself, for example, Socrates.[6]

This passage seems to be dealing primarily with the way the term 'individual' is used and with various concepts associated with it. And other texts of Boethius seem to be making the same type of point, dealing with the way 'individual' is used or with its intension. On the other hand, some texts clearly establish a relation between the individual and what makes the individual to be such, so that the idea of a principle of individuation seems to be explicitly at work in them even though the term 'principle of individuation' is not used. One such text reads as follows:

> For this [white] which is in this snow cannot be predicated of any other white, because it is *forced* to singularity and it is *constrained* to an individual form by the participation in an individual...the humanity which is in the individual. Socrates is *made* individual because Socrates is itself individual and singular.[7]

Note the references in this text to what "forces" and "constrains" something to be individual and what "makes" it individual. These are more explicit references to a principle of individuation even though Boethius does not use the expression 'principle of individuation' and has no technical term for that principle. However, we are far from any attempt at trying to define what a principle of individuation is, although instances of it are actually identified in the examples: for humanity it is Socrates, and for the white of the snow it is the snow. Obviously, Boethius's interest is taken up with other matters; he is still working in a preanalytical stage with respect to the idea of a principle of individuation, even though the idea of such principle has an explicit function in his philosophy.

We find examples of the next stage of development, the definitional, in the early twelfth century, in texts from Thierry of Chartres (d. *ante* 1155) and Gilbert of Poitiers (b. ca. 1076, d. 1154). In Thierry of Chartres we find for the first time the use of the term 'cause' in connection with individuation. One point of clarification: Thierry usually speaks about *plurality* and *number* where one would have expected *individuality*, but those terms are used to refer to the fact that something is individual. This terminological difference may be attributed to Thierry's limited awareness of the idea of individuality, its conceptual relatives, and the various problems and issues involved in individuation. He states:

> Those things that differ numerically, differ by accidents. For only accidents, i.e., the variety of accidents, produce number in substances or subjects...the number and plurality in things subject to number comes from accidents.[8]

And more explicitly elsewhere:

> For matter is a cause of plurality, that is, a cause without which it cannot be produced. And form also is a cause of plurality.[9]

In Gilbert of Poitiers we lose the use of a term such as 'cause,' indicating clearly a still early stage of development of the idea of a principle of individuation. But we see a different development that indicates a deepening of awareness and the intention to delimit and define the problem for which the principle of individuation is supposed to provide a solution. This development is revealed in two factors. First, Gilbert tries to distinguish the ideas of individual, singular, and person, which most previous authors had either regarded as equivalent or at least had not bothered to distinguish. Thus Gilbert tells us:

> The property [of a person] is called "singular" for one reason, "individual" for another, and "personal" for another. For, although whatever is individual is also a singular—and whatever is a person is also singular and individual, not every singular is an individual. Nor is every singular or individual a person.[10]

Second, elsewhere Gilbert distinguishes what *makes* something numerically diverse from what *proves to us* that something is numerically diverse. That is, he explicitly distinguishes between two different problems as well as between their solutions, further emphasizing the attempt at defining the boundaries of the issues at stake in individuation and the answers to them.

> For Cato would not be a man similar to Cicero unless the subsistences by which each of them is something were also numerically diverse. And their numerical diversity makes [Cato and Cicero] to be numerically diverse. Moreover, among natural beings the dissimilarity of accidents does not *produce*, but rather *proves* numerical diversity.[11]

Both Thierry and Gilbert are aware of principles or causes of individuation and their awareness goes beyond that of Boethius. Thierry's terminology is more explicit and Gilbert already is working on formulating the problem concerned with the principle of individuation, not just by identifying what the principle is—there were many prior views about that—but by pointing out the unique role it was supposed to play. He does it by distinguishing what *produces* numerical diversity from what *proves* numerical diversity; that is, he distinguishes between an ontological issue and an epistemic one. Neither Thierry nor Gilbert, however, is fully conscious of the kind of issues that particular views of the principle of individuation would raise. But we find that consciousness and, therefore, the next stage of development, in Peter Abailard (b. 1079; d. 1142).

Abailard first presents unambiguously the theory of individuation with which he disagrees, namely, that accidents are the source of individuality:

> Some show that individuals are produced by accidents...accidents produce both individuals and also those things they wish to be understood in the individual name.[12]

Then he proceeds to criticize the position in various ways, of which I reproduce one:

> But if we were to say that individual men, such as Socrates or this man, are caused by accidental properties, then the accidents which complete individuals are naturally prior to the individuals to which they give being [which position is unacceptable].[13]

The actual substance of Abailard's argument as well as the view he criticizes is of no concern to us here.[14] What is noteworthy for us is that Abailard is aware of certain problems inherent in the view that individuation is caused by accidents. It is this awareness of the problematic nature of certain views concerning the principle of individuation that is largely lacking in earlier writers and that Abailard brings out explicitly. His awareness of the idea of a principle of individuation, even though he does not use a technical term to refer to it, is much greater than that of most other writers who preceded him. It should be noted, however, that the context where the discussion of individuation occurs in Abailard is the problem of universals. His concerns are still with universals, and the principle of individuation is dealt with only propaedeutically. Indeed, the very reason why he brings up the question of individuation is that it provides further ammunition against a realist view of universals he is intent on debunking. The principle of individuation and the issues and problems it raises are still, therefore, very much dependent on other, more pressing matters, and remain contextually integrated with them. We see evidence of independence only later, in the thirteenth century; Abailard is still working within the problematic stage.

A good example of a text in which the principle of individuation is treated in a somewhat independent fashion, revealing the author's interest in it as a philosophical subject matter, is Thomas Aquinas's (b. ca. 1225, d. 1274) questions in his *Commentary on Boethius' On the Trinity*. There are also many other texts where Thomas refers in passing to a "principle of individuation." For example, in *On Being and Essence* 2, 4, he writes:

> Because matter is the principle of individuation, it might seem to follow that an essence, which embraces in itself both matter and form, is only particular and not universal. If this were true,

> it would follow that universals could not be defined, granted that essence is what is signified by the definition. What we must realize is that the matter which is the principle of individuation is not just any matter, but only designated matter.[15]

This text has all the marks of the stage I call *problematic*. In the first place, there is an explicit use of the expression 'principle of individuation.' Second, an awareness of possible problems and issues involved in what is identified as the principle of individuation is evident to such a degree that there is a short self-contained discussion of them. Indeed, the discussion continues beyond the quoted passage and reappears later in the work in a different context, in Chapter Five. However, there is no textual separation between the discussion of the principle of individuation and the discussion of the issues that prompted it. In that sense this text cannot be classified under the textually independent stage.

The situation is quite different, however, with the text of the *Commentary on Boethius' "On the Trinity"*. Here we find much more than in *On Being and Essence*, for here there is a textual break between the issue that deals with the principle of individuation and other issues raised by the Christian doctrine of the Trinity, which is indeed Boethius's overall theme and is reflected in Thomas's commentary. The commentary is divided into six questions that deal respectively with the following topics:

I. On the Knowledge of Divine Realities

II. On Making Divine Knowledge Known

III. On Topics Relating to the Praise of Faith

IV. On Factors Relating to the Cause of Plurality

V. On the Division of Speculative Science

VI. On the Methods of Speculative Science According to Boethius

Question IV is the one that deals with the principle of individuation. Note that the term used in the title of the question is not *principle of individuation* (*principium individuationis*), but rather *cause of plurality* (*causa pluralitatis*). The reason for this is that Thomas is following closely Boethius's text insofar as the general identification of topics as well as the terminology is concerned. Nonetheless, it is clear on closer examination that for Thomas the issues raised in this question have to do with the principle of individuation. Indeed, in the body of the question itself he freely exchanges 'cause' with 'principle' and 'plurality' with 'individuation.'[16]

Thomas examines the issues related to the principle of individuation in depth in question IV. First, he subdivides the question into four different articles:

Article 1. Is Otherness the Cause of Plurality?

Article 2. Does a Difference of Accidents Cause a Diversity in Number?

Article 3. Can Two Bodies Exist, or Be Thought to Exist, in the Same Place?

Article 4. Does a Difference in Place Have Some Bearing on a Difference in Number?

The translation of these articles takes up over twenty pages, and the specific discussion of the principle of individuation, continued in Article 2, takes up a third of the whole text. The concluding paragraph of the main body of Article 2 reads:

> It is clear, then, that matter taken in itself is the principle of neither specific nor numerical diversity. But it is the principle of generic diversity inasmuch as it underlies a common form, and so likewise it is the principle of numerical diversity as underlying indeterminate dimensions. Because these dimensions belong to the genus of accidents, diversity in number is sometimes reduced to the diversity of matter and sometimes to the diversity of accidents, and this because of the dimensions mentioned above. But other accidents are not the principle of individuation, though they are the cause of our knowing the distinction between individuals. In this sense individuation can also be ascribed to the other accidents.[17]

What we see here, *inter alia*, is a careful distinction between the principle of individuation, namely, what makes something individual, and the principle of discernibility, that is, that whereby we are able to know something as individual. It is the same sort of distinction that we saw in Gilbert, but now we are presented with a fuller discussion, in which the reasons for the distinction are given and where distinct terminology helps us keep the issues separate.

There is no need for us to dwell on the philosophical content of this passage, since our task is neither the elucidation of the principle of individuation nor the determination of Thomas's views on it. What is important for us to note is that Thomas's discussion demonstrates that the principle of individuation had become an independent topic of discussion *within* larger treatises during Thomas's lifetime. It had become not only a problematic idea, but its independence was revealed by the textual ground that it claimed in Thomas's *Commentary on Boethius' "On the Trinity"*. Nevertheless, it was not yet a central idea in Thomas's thought, for it was still dealt with within the context of other issues. Thomas's *Commentary* is concerned primarily with the central issue raised by Boethius, that is, the Christian doctrine of the Trinity. The principle of individuation is discussed in it only insofar as its elucidation is helpful in the understanding of that doctrine. It was not until the latter part of the thirteenth century and the early part of the fourteenth that we find self-contained, independent treatises, within other works or outside them, dealing with the principle of individuation. These took the form of totally independent tracts and major subsections of very large treatises and mark the stage of centrality for this idea.

Two very well-known instances should serve to establish the point. One is the little treatise entitled *De principio individuationis,* often attributed to Thomas Aquinas; the seven questions devoted to the principle of individuation found in John Duns Scotus's (b. ca. 1265, d. 1308) *Opus oxoniense* is the other.[18]

The significance of the *De principio individuationis* in this context is independent of its authenticity as a work by Thomas.[19] Indeed, its significance for us increases if it is not in fact a work by Thomas, for in such a case whoever wrote it clearly thought that there was an important gap in Thomas's writings about individuation and the topic merited independent and detailed consideration. If we look at the inauthentic works written in the medieval period and passed as authentic, we will notice that they generally deal with what were considered topics of particular importance at the time. On the other hand, if the tract is authentic, then we know that Thomas himself thought the topic important enough and controversial enough to merit separate attention. When one considers that Thomas published independent discussions only of topics that were particularly controversial at the time, such as the eternity of the world or the unity of the intellect, we receive further confirmation of the special place that the principle of individuation had achieved.

We receive further substantiation of the centrality of individuation from the second example cited: John Duns Scotus's seven questions devoted to the principle of individuation in the *Opus oxoniense.*

In this case we do not have a separately published treatise. The seven questions are presented as Part I of Distinction III of Book II of Scotus's lectures on the *Sentences* of Peter Lombard. Two points stand out. First of all, the seven questions make up a complete and rather substantial treatise within the book. The discussion is self-contained and does not indicate that Scotus considered it simply propaedeutic to anything else. On the contrary, the way of presenting it suggests that he considered it a subject worthy of discussion in itself.[20] Moreover, although the overall topic of the question is the principle of individuation, within that general topic Scotus presents some of his most important statements on the ontological status of the common nature, making this text important also for the solution to the problem of universals. This is an extraordinary development, because earlier in the Middle Ages the order of discussion between universals and individuals was just the reverse: universals were the central topic of discussion and the principle of individuation was discussed only in that context and to the extent required to settle the issue or issues concerning universals. This is quite clear in Boethius and Peter Abailard, for example, and the practice continued well into the thirteenth century. But in Scotus's text we have a reversal of this tradition, indicating clearly that the principle of individuation had become at least as fundamental or perhaps more fundamental than universals in his eyes. This trend continued throughout the later Middle Ages culminating with Francisco Suárez (1548–1617), who, in the *Metaphysical Disputations,* dealt with the principle of individuation first, in Disputation V, before he discussed universals in Disputation VI.

One last point concerning the date of the two texts mentioned. If *De principio individuationis* is authentic, then it was written before Thomas's death in 1274, indicating that the principle of individuation had achieved considerable philosophical notoriety before the fourth quarter of the thirteenth century. And, indeed, there is some evidence that this was in fact the case, for Roger Bacon, for example, discussed it in various places, including the *Opus maius*, published in 1267, and in the *Communia naturalium* indirectly complained of the excessive attention given to this problem by calling it a "foolish question."[21] Now, even if the degree of notoriety that the problem had acquired before the end of the thirteenth century were still to be a matter of doubt, what cannot be in doubt is that by the beginning of the fourteenth it had become established as a fundamental philosophical issue, as Scotus's text, among others, demonstrates. Moreover, the status it achieved with Scotus and later writers was such that it not only became the subject of separate attention, but, as I have shown elsewhere, opened up the doors to new philosophical issues and concerns.[22]

Having illustrated the various stages of development most philosophical ideas go through, I now turn to historical interpretation to illustrate the importance of an awareness of those stages in not distorting the account of the development of philosophical ideas.

III. HISTORICAL INTERPRETATIONS

The task of historians of philosophy imposes on them at least three requirements: first, the accurate account and description of the views of the authors they study; second, the understanding of the historical development of ideas; and third, the avoidance of anachronism. Now, I claim that the violation of these requirements often is the result of a lack of awareness of the nature of the historical development of philosophical ideas, which I have illustrated by reference to the five stages previously identified. Errors occur in particular when historians unconsciously mistake one stage for another, that is, when historians misunderstand the level of historical development of an idea or issue. This in many ways is an expected, although unwelcome, by-product of the historians' task and their attitude. Their job, as many of them see it and as I argued in Chapters One and Five, consists to some extent in making explicit the undetected connections between ideas and thinkers, thus bringing out what had gone unobserved before. Naturally, this tends to lead them to see connections where there are none and to emphasize the presence and awareness of ideas that were absent and unknown. Let me make this point more specific by casting it in the context of the stages to which I referred earlier.

One of the most frequent mistakes in this regard occurs when historians mistake the definitional or the preanalytical functionally explicit stages for the preanalytical functionally nonexplicit stage. In this situation the historians in question attribute to the historical author an awareness of an issue or idea that the author never really had. It is true, for example, that something the author might have said may imply a certain view or a certain idea. But it is quite different to hold a view and to be aware of the implications of the view. Few of us are aware of all the implications of most of our views. Indeed, part of the job of philosophy is to help make us aware of them and bring some order and consistency to the views that we consciously hold and their implications. To attribute to authors, therefore, an understanding of the implications of their views, when there is no evidence that they were aware of such implications, is historically inaccurate.

For example, it would be a serious mistake for a historian to say,

(A) Porphyry holds that the principle of individuation is the collection of properties belonging to the individual.

And the reasons become clear when we look at the only text, already cited, on the basis of which such statement might be made:

> Socrates, this white and...the son of Sophroniscus are called individual...because each of them is composed of a collection of properties which can never be the same for another.[23]

Note that Porphyry never uses the terms 'principle,' 'cause,' or 'individuation.' Moreover, he speaks of Socrates, this white, and the son of Sophroniscus, "being called individual," not of them "being individual." Careful historians, then, at least would qualify their claim by saying something like,

(B) Porphyry's text could be interpreted as suggesting that the cause or principle of individuation is the collection of properties belonging to the individual, provided 'are called' is understood to reflect a real state of affairs, and so on.

In summary, (A) represents a historian who reads too much into a text, and (B) represents a more careful scholar.

But historians make the opposite mistake as well, that is, they may confuse earlier stages of development for later ones and thus read too little into a text. This can be easily illustrated with reference to the ideas of individual, singular, and particular. Most historical studies of the thought of the early Middle Ages do not make any distinctions between the ideas of "individual," "singular," and "particular." Indeed, translators pick and choose whatever term better fits the context stylistically to translate occurrences of *individuum, singulare,* and *particulare.* This is quite evident even in translations and studies by such well-known scholars as Richard McKeon.[24] The result, of course, is the general view that these ideas were regarded as equivalent in the early Middle Ages, and only in contemporary philosophical discourse have some attempts been made to distinguish them. However, when one pays careful attention to the pertinent texts, clearly several early medieval authors attempted to introduce distinctions among these ideas and in fact provided definitional analyses of some of the mentioned terms. Indeed, we already saw in one of the texts from Gilbert cited earlier that what he meant by *singular* and *singularity* was something quite different from what he meant by *individual* and *individuality.*[25] And all this resulted in his having different views concerning what made something singular and what made something individual. Gilbert, then, is working within the stage of definition at least, and possibly the problematic stage, with respect to the ideas of individual and singular. Yet many translators and commentators, themselves unaware of the complexity of the ideas of individual and singular and of the issues they raise, have treated his texts as well as other early medieval texts as if their authors were unaware of these distinctions and issues. Based on their own functionally non-explicit preanalytical stage of development with respect to certain ideas, such historians provide an inaccurate picture of the authors they are examining. All of this, by the way, adds support for the use of the framework approach I proposed in the previous chapter.

What has been said concerning the definitional and preanalytical stages of development vis-à-vis historical interpretation applies also to the other stages, but I do not think it is necessary to illustrate such applications further. It should be quite clear from what has been said that whoever neglects to pay attention to the stages in which philosophical ideas and issues develop runs the risk of historical inaccuracy by distorting historical views, misunderstanding their stages of development, and introducing anachronisms into historical accounts.

The discussion of the stages of development of philosophical issues and ideas leads naturally to the controversial issue involved in the notion of philosophical progress. I do not want to pass up the opportunity to raise this issue, so I turn to it next.

V. PHILOSOPHICAL PROGRESS

The English word 'progress' goes back to the Latin *progressus*, a term that meant among other things a going forward, advancement, growth, and increase. The term always has had a strong spatial connotation and often was used in connection with an actual journey or expedition. In all cases the common thread of its usage is headway toward the achievement of a desirable end or goal. This entails that a subsequent stage of development adds something good that was not present in an earlier stage, superseding it. The term is also frequently understood to entail the rejection or leaving behind of something bad or at least less good than the results of subsequent developments.[26]

As noted in Chapter One, the notions of progress, development, and change should be kept separate. Change involves the introduction of a difference, regardless of the type of difference involved. Thus, there can be changes of color, life-style, attitude, and situation. Nor does change imply any direction or end. When we say that the weather changed, that does not imply that it changed in a particular way; the change could be for the better or the worse, for example. For change it is only necessary that there be a difference between one situation and another that follows it. Development, on the other hand, is change with a direction, either toward or away from a goal or end. If we say that there were some developments in the weather, that usually implies that some changes in a certain direction took place. We might not be sure what the direction is, or imply that it is one or another, but the use of the term 'development' indicates a context where a direction is implicit. The direction does not necessarily involve a change for the better, however. Indeed, we often speak of "unfortunate developments" and of developments that bring about death, stagnation, and other such undesirable phenomena. With progress, however, the direction implicit in development generally takes on an optimistic turn; progress usually entails change and development for the better.[27] This is evident in Lovejoy's well-known view of progress as "a tendency inherent in nature or man to pass through a regular sequence of stages of development in past, present, or future, the later stages being—with perhaps occasional retardations or minor regressions—superior to the earlier."[28]

The belief in progress became widespread in the eighteenth century, and in the nineteenth century it became a favorite doctrine of positivists who liberally applied it to science and society. The extraordinary scientific and social achievements of the preceding and present centuries have made the word a commonplace in discourse about the various aspects of human development.[29] Under these conditions it should be no surprise that philosophers also began to speak and discuss the notion of philosophical progress.[30]

On this issue, however, there has been wide disagreement. Not that everyone, and particularly philosophers, accepts the notion of scientific and social progress.[31] There are in fact many scientists and social scientists themselves who have rejected or at least questioned the whole notion of progress. And even among those who accept the notion of progress there is plenty of disagreement as to precisely what progress entails, some emphasizing the negative rejection of the past and others concentrating on a more positive emphasis on the future. Be that as it may in the case of scientists in general and social scientists in particular, when we move to philosophy the limited skepticism of scientists and social scientists becomes accentuated.

Philosophers are a contentious lot and have wasted no time in taking sides on this issue and in presenting arguments on opposite sides of it. The case against philosophical progress is strengthened by some aspects of the history of philosophy.[32] Indeed, those who wish to adopt the antiprogress view can easily point to the fact that most of the fundamental problems in philosophy remain unsolved. Can we say, for example, that we have solved the question Plato raised at the beginning of the *Republic* concerning the nature of justice? Do we have a solution to the problems of universals and individuation? Can we point to a definition of good that is indisputable? Indeed, a quick glance at the current philosophical literature seems to indicate that there are no issues about which the philosophical community is convinced it has reached the solution, and most of the issues that concern that community have a long history, going back sometimes for hundreds and thousands of years. Where is the so-called philosophical progress, then? The study of the history of philosophy does not seem to show any kind of linear advancement toward a goal. We are today as far from, or as near to, that goal as we ever were. So-called progress is an illusion brought about by historical change. This change creates the mirage that we are on the way somewhere and that, having traveled so much, we have only so much more to go. In reality, however, there is no such movement forward but only a cyclical process in which the philosophical past is repeated and ideas come into and go out of fashion periodically.

The reason for this "running in place" of philosophy is to be traced back to the nature of the discipline itself, so the argument goes. Philosophy is not like science. Empirical science can document and experience progress because it depends on gathering data from technological developments. The higher the technology the more empirical data we can gather and the more encompassing, precise, and accurate our theories about their organization can be. A fine microscope, for example, makes all the difference in the study of biology. Before we could observe cells we had no idea of the complex nature of microorganisms. And likewise with chemistry, physics, and the other sciences that depend on empirical observation. But philosophy does not depend on empirical data. The data necessary for philosophy were already available to Plato and even to Thales. Indeed, they are available to every thinking human being. So philosophy cannot, like science, gain access to new facts that could make a difference in the way it organizes its conceptual frameworks. This is the reason why philosophy cannot make progress.[33] Yes, some philosophers are more perceptive than others, and some views make more sense than others. Indeed, one might go even so far as to say that some views are true and others are false. But that does not mean that we have in fact made any progress, for those views were not the result of a process that sustains advancement. In the historical development of philosophy falsehood is as likely to follow truth as the reverse.

The situation is not so simple as has been just painted, however. One easily can find support in the history of philosophy for the view that there is philosophical progress. Granted, in many areas, some of them fundamental, there seems to be no progress, but in many others there are plenty of breakthroughs that can be interpreted only as indicating progress, and substantial progress at that. Two areas that may be cited as examples are logic and the philosophy of language. Even a summary look at the history of logic will reveal, so the argument might go, that the last hundred years of logical speculation have produced momentous discoveries. The connection between logic and mathematics, the formulation of ideal languages, and the development of sophisticated systems of symbols are but three areas in which recent logic has made enormous gains over traditional, namely, Aristotelian and scholastic logic. And the same can be said concerning the philosophy of language. Indeed, the very notion of a philosophy of language, that is, of exploring philosophical issues raised by language, is new and must be considered an important advance in the history of philosophy. These examples could be multiplied, but this is not necessary to show that progress is not impossible in philosophy. Indeed, we can expect further progress, and with the implementation of proper methodologies we can expect reasonable advancement in the discipline. For, although philosophy is not an empirical science like chemistry or physics, it can advance in two respects. On the one hand, it can develop techniques and methods that will allow it to clarify concepts in such a way that will avoid past mistakes and confusions. And, on the other hand, it can advance in a course parallel to the advancement of science, because one of its primary functions is the integration of the new information developed by the sciences into a coherent world-view.

As usual with extreme positions, there is something right and something wrong in the positions that oppose and favor progress. The concrete historical examples that can be given in support of the two positions make the point clear. There are examples of rather obvious advancement in the history of philosophy, but at the same time there seems to be no advancement in most fundamental issues and in some cases one could even speak of regress. So, can we make any sense of this situation and come to some kind of determination as to whether there is philosophical progress and, if there is, in what respect?

One way of trying to solve this problem is to go back to the notion of progress and see whether that notion is applicable to philosophy. Clearly, on the basis of concrete historical examples, we cannot very easily settle the question, so perhaps the only way to do so is to deal with it philosophically, that is, by analyzing the concepts involved in the notion of philosophical progress.

We saw earlier that progress involved movement toward a goal or end, and I believe this general understanding of progress will be sufficient for our discussion. Now, if the notion of progress involves in the movement toward a goal, the notion of philosophical progress should involve in the notion of movement toward a philosophical goal. But what is a philosophical goal? I imagine that the answer is any goal that is instrumental in bringing about the fundamental goal (or goals if there are more than one) of philosophy. So we have to determine the fundamental goal of philosophy. Of course, there are many views concerning the fundamental goal of philosophy, and disagreement on that goal will fuel the disagreement concerning philosophical progress. I do not wish, however, to pose the problem of the fundamental goal or goals of philosophy in this context. Rather I propose four goals of the discipline that seem to me should be acceptable to the majority of philosophers and should help us settle the issue at hand. The four goals in question are the discovery of truth, the rejection of falsehood, the clarification of concepts, and the greater awareness of the complexity of philosophical problems.

I am quite aware that the view that holds that one of the goals of philosophy is to discover and arrive at truth is not popular these days. If truth is understood as narrowly empirical (the correspondence between sense data and our judgments about them) and philosophy is not regarded as an empirical science, then clearly the goal of philosophy could not be the discovery of truth. Still, I want to allow for the traditional understanding of philosophy as a search for truth and thus for a broader notion of both truth and philosophy.

Something similar can be said about the rejection of false views. One of the goals of philosophy is critical, namely, the evaluation and rejection of inadequate (inconsistent or false) views to clear the way for truth. Even many of those who reject the possibility of verifiability, and thus of knowing truth, are willing to accept the notion of falsifiability. We may not be able to know the truth, but we can know what is false.

The understanding of philosophy as therapy and its goal as the clarification of concepts is quite popular today and should pose no difficulties. According to this position one of the goals of philosophy is to produce a clear map of our concepts, dissolving confusions and restoring us to good intellectual health.

Finally, I wish to maintain also that one of the goals of philosophy is to increase our awareness of the complexity of philosophical problems. Philosophy's goal, then, goes beyond a mere clarification of the concepts that we already have and beyond the mere increase in the number of truths and falsehoods of which we are aware. One of its functions is to develop a greater awareness of new areas of concern, new problems and issues, and new perspectives that may change our conceptual map of the world.

Perhaps a story will help us see the distinctions among these three goals of philosophy. The philosopher is like a man asked to climb a mountain located next to a valley so that he can verify a written description of the valley made several years before.[34] After the man climbs the mountain, he proceeds to read the description he had been given and check whether what it says is confirmed by what he sees. For a moment or two things seem to be in order. The text says that the valley is surrounded by mountains on all sides but one, that a river runs through it, and that there is a town in the middle of the valley. All this is corroborated by what he sees. But then the man notices a discrepancy between the description and what he sees. The description says that there is a large building in the center of the town and that the building has two towers. The discrepancy occurs because the man can see clearly that there is not one but two large buildings separated by a narrow street and completely unconnected and that each of the towers mentioned in the description belongs to a different building. The observer is prepared to make the correction in the description, but then he notices another discrepancy. The two buildings he sees are not exactly in the center of the town but slightly to one side. Could it be that the person who wrote the description was so careless? Or could there have been some kind of obstacle that prevented her from seeing what he sees? After more thought, the observer reaches the tentative conclusion that perhaps the position of the previous observer had been different from his, perhaps she had been looking from the top of another mountain. He decides to climb the mountain to his left and see if the view from there adheres more to the description of the valley he has to check. And indeed it does as far as the building in the village and its location are concerned. The observer understands why the description says what it says, but he also knows that the description is wrong insofar as it claims that there is one building, that the building has two towers and is located in the center of the village. Because he observes the village from a different angle he now knows something the previous observer did not know. Moreover, the picture of the village he has been able to acquire allows him to have not only more information but also a clearer view as to what the valley looks like, preventing him from falling into the confusion into which the writer of the description had fallen. Finally, he is also aware of some difficulties involved in describing the valley about which neither he originally nor the person who wrote the description he has been checking were aware. One of these difficulties is that the view from different mountains affect substantially what one sees. So in order to get a completely accurate picture of the valley one would need to look at it from all the mountains that surround it. But this is not possible, since there are no mountains on one side. Moreover, a perspicacious thinker might also surmise that a completely accurate picture would require aerial views as well, that is, looking at the valley from above, whether that is technically possible or not. And so on.

Philosophers are like the observer who has been asked to check the accuracy of the written description of a valley. Their job is to check the accuracy of our philosophical views about the world. So they check those views with their experience and often find reason to add to and clarify them. But not only that, they become aware of the difficulties of the task and of new problems that they need to address.

Now, if as I have indicated, philosophical progress should entail movement toward the discovery and understanding of truth and falsity, the clarification of our concepts, and the realization of the complexities involved in the first two tasks, can we say that there is philosophical progress? Well, yes and no.

There is, I believe, no question that Western philosophy has seen philosophical progress in at least two of the senses mentioned. Indeed, the discussion of the principle of individuation given earlier shows quite clearly, for example, that between 500 A.D. and 1600 A.D. there was a progressive awareness of the complexity of the issues involved in and related to the idea of a principle of individuation. It is also clear that parallel to the progressive awareness of complexity was a progressive sophistication in the clarification and analysis of the various issues and ideas in question. The very separation of the epistemic problem of the discernibility of individuals from the metaphysical one of the cause of individuation substantiates the point. What may not be entirely clear is whether at 1600 A.D. philosophy had achieved a greater number of truths that it had at 500 A.D. This, of course, is a question on which it will be difficult to achieve consensus in the philosophical community, but perhaps such consensus is not necessary for two reasons. First of all, the achievement of a greater sophistication in the awareness of the issues and ideas involved in individuation already indicates not only the achievement of some truth, but also the opening up of areas that had not been discussed before and in which there is potential for discovery. So we might say that there indeed is an increase in both what we might call "methodological truths" and in the potential for substantive truths.[35] At any rate, even if this conclusion were to be denied, we still have two areas where progress was achieved.

Let us assume for the sake of argument, then, that there was philosophical progress with respect to the idea of a principle of individuation from 500 A.D. to 1600 A.D. Does this mean that there is overall philosophical progress? For one can still argue that there really is no overall progress but only cycles that repeat themselves. So that, although there might be progress with respect to an issue or an idea during a particular period of time, philosophy does not show any overall progress to speak of because there may be other areas in which there was regress. And, indeed, one can point to the very history of the idea of the principle of individuation to illustrate the fact that overall progress does not occur. For the gains made in the understanding of that idea in the Middle Ages seem to have been lost in subsequent philosophy and rediscovered only in the twentieth century. The history of philosophy from 1600 until the present is filled with discussions of the principle of individuation that show extraordinary conceptual confusions and insensitivity to the dimensions of the philosophical issues related to that idea.[36] Can we speak of philosophical progress after all, then?

The temptation to give a negative answer to this question and go back to a cyclical view of the development of philosophy is very strong. But such an answer does not really take into account that, even with respect to the principle of individuation, the contemporary discussions by authors who are acquainted with the medieval history of that idea have advantages over the medieval discussions and thus are not retraveling exactly the same road. Nor does that answer do justice to the numerous elements of novelty brought into play in the discussion derived from the recent increased awareness of logic and the philosophy of language. True, in many ways, the recent history of the principle of individuation mirrors in some very substantial ways the medieval discussions, but there are also important differences between the two periods of development, some new elements in the discussions, and an awareness of new complexities. These are sufficient to show that we do not have a repetition of the medieval dialectic.

This does not mean, of course, that regress is impossible and thus that all subsequent philosophical developments constitute an improvement over previous developments. But when one considers the cumulative development of philosophy as a whole over a long period of time, it would seem that there is some improvement.

One way to illustrate what I mean is by referring to the metaphors of the spiral and the line. It seems to me that both those who reject all philosophical progress and those who accept it unqualifiedly look at it in linear terms.[37] They see philosophical progress very much in a linear pattern, as a one-directional vector, where there are no partial returns or detours. Those who oppose progress can easily find detours and returns that seem to invalidate progress, whereas those who are in favor of progress look only at gains and discount the detours and returns. Both mistake the way philosophy actually develops. Philosophy is not a neat and tidy discipline. What philosophers think tends to be closely related to their lives, their beliefs, and what they do. Moreover, philosophers do not work in a vacuum; they are part of a cultural and social matrix that influences them in many ways. Their work, therefore, is not linear. They do move forward on the whole, but their advances are accompanied by hesitations, detours, and regressions. No particular age, therefore, need be unambiguously better, as far as philosophy is concerned, than all the ages that preceded it, nor need every philosopher's thought be clearly an improvement over previous philosophies. And one of the reasons for this is that the course of philosophy is not independent from the course of the rest of history. Politics, religion, natural disasters, society, science, and so forth influence the development of philosophical ideas, introducing changes in them that modify their history.

I like to think about philosophical progress, then, as a spiral rather than a linear process and not a neat spiral at that, but a rather crooked and messy one. On the whole and in the long run I think philosophy advances, even if in doing so it often looks as if it is actually regressing. If one does away with the model of linear progress, I believe it is possible to see progress in the overall history of philosophy, although that progress is not neat and linear but involves motions that appear circular and regressive at times. And, naturally, it is essential for the historian to take into account this character of the history of philosophy. Indeed, the success of the enterprise in which historians of philosophy are engaged depends to a great extent on how well they understand the way philosophy develops.

NOTES

1. This is perhaps part of what Husserl was trying to get at in *Ideas: General Introduction to Pure Phenomenology*, trans. by W. R. Boyce Gibson (New York: Collier Books, 1962), p. 225, where he notes: "Thus it is not until a very highly developed stage of science has been reached that we can count on terminologies being definitely fixed. It is misleading and radically perverse to apply the formal and external standards of a logic of terminology to scientific works in the first stages of progressive effort, and in their first beginning to exact from them terminologies of the kind first used to render stable the concluding results of great scientific developments."

2. Almost thirty years ago, William A. Christian suggested three categories of development as necessary to understand the past within a Whiteheadian framework. He called them *presystematic, postsystematic,* and *systematic.* These categories have some, although not many, elements in common with the first three I have suggested. For Christian's views, see "Whitehead's Explanation of the Past," in George L. Kline, ed., *Alfred North Whitehead: Essays on His Philosophy* (Englewood Cliffs, N.J.: Prentice-Hall, Inc., 1963), p. 97.

3. Newton Garver shows quite clearly, in "Wittgenstein's Reception in America," *Modern Austrian Literature* 20, nos. 3–4 (1987): 207–219, for example, how several of the ideas and issues that were important to Wittgenstein have been largely ignored by the American philosophical community.

4. See Gracia, *Introduction to the Problem of Individuation in the Early Middle Ages; Suárez on Individuation;* and *Individuation in Scholasticism: The Later Middle Ages and the Counter Reformation.*

5. In Boethius, *"Isagoge" Porphyrii commentorum editio secunda,* ed. Samuel Brandt, in *Corpus scriptorum ecclesiasticorum latinorum* vol. 48 (Vienna: Tempsky, 1905; reprinted New York: Johnson Rep. Corp., 1966), pp. 231 and 234–235. The translation of this passage and those given later is mine.

6. Ibid., p. 195.

7. Ibid., p. 183. My emphasis.

8. Thierry of Chartres, *Lectiones in Boethii librum de Trinitate,* in Nikolaus M. Häring, ed., *Commentaries on Boethius by Thierry of Chartres and His School* (Toronto: Pontifical Institute of Mediaeval Studies, 1971), p. 150.

9. Thierry of Chartres, *Commentum super Boethii librum de Trinitate,* in ibid., p. 82.

10. Gilbert of Poitiers, *De Trinitate,* in Nikolaus M. Häring, ed., *The Commentaries on Boethius by Gilbert of Poitiers* (Toronto: Pontifical Institute of Mediaeval Studies, 1966), p. 144.

11. Ibid., p. 77. My emphasis.

12. Peter Abailard, *Incipiunt Glossae secundum magistrum Petrum Abaelardum super Porphyrium (Logica ingredientibus),* ed. B. Geyer, in *Beiträge zur Geschichte der Philosophie des Mittelalters,* Band 20, Heft 1, p. 63.

13. Ibid., p. 64.

14. For a discussion of this, see my *Introduction to the Problem of Individuation,* Ch. 4.

15. Thomas Aquinas, *On Being and Essence,* trans. Armand Maurer, 2d. ed. (Toronto: Pontifical Institute of Mediaeval Studies, 1968), p. 36.

16. Thomas Aquinas, *Faith, Reason and Theology: Questions I–IV of His "Commentary on the 'De Trinitate' of Boethius,"* q. 4, art. 2, trans. Armand Maur-

er (Toronto: Pontifical Institute of Mediaeval Studies, 1987), p. 98. Something similar happens in Chapter 5 of *On Being and Essence,* par. 5, p. 63.

17. Thomas Aquinas, *Faith, Reason, and Theology,* ibid., question 4, article 2, p. 98.

18. *De principio individuationis* is published together with other short works in the *Opuscula philosophica.* It appears both in the Parma and Vivès editions of Thomas's works and more recently has been edited by R. Spiazzi in *Opuscula philosophica* (Rome: Marietti, 1954), pp. 147–151. For Scotus's *Opus oxoniense,* see *Opera omnia,* ed. C. Balić et al., vol. 7 (Civitas Vaticana: Typis Polyglottis Vaticanis, 1973), pp. 391–494, the *Lectura,* ed. Luca Modrić in *Opera omnia,* vol. 18 (1982), pp. 229–293.

19. For details about the controversy concerning the authorship of this tract, see I. T. Eschmann, "A Catalogue of St. Thomas' Works: Bibliographical Notes," in E. Gilson, *The Christian Philosophy of St. Thomas Aquinas* (New York: Random House, 1956).

20. It should be kept in mind, however, that Part I consists of seven questions, of which only the first six deal with the individuation of material substances. The seventh question concerns the individuation of angels and ties the treatise on individuation to the section of the *Opus oxoniense* where it occurs, which is concerned with angels.

21. For the text of Roger Bacon's *Communia,* see *Opera hactenus inedita Rogeri Baconi,* fasc. 2, *Liber primus Communium naturalium fratris Rogeri,* ed. Robert Steele (Oxford: Clarendon Press, 1905 [?]), p. 100.

22. See my "The Centrality of the Individual in the Philosophy of the Fourteenth Century," *History of Philosophy Quarterly* 8 (1991).

23. See note 5.

24. See Richard McKeon's translation of Abailard, for example, in *Selections from Medieval Philosophers,* 2 vols. (New York: Charles Scribner's Sons, 1957), vol. 1, pp. 208–258.

25. See text corresponding to note 10.

26. For classic discussions of the idea of progress, see J. B. Bury, *The Idea of Progress* (New York: Macmillan, 1932), and F. J. Teggart, ed., *The Idea of Progress,* rev. ed. (Berkeley: University of California Press, 1949). A key work in the development of the idea of progress is Antoine-Nicolas Marie Jean de Condorcet's *Esquisse d'un tableau historique des progrès de l'esprit humain* [1793] (Paris: Librairie Philosophique J. Vrin, 1970). Among more recent works, see J. Baillie, *The Belief in Progress* (London: Oxford University Press, 1950); Edward Hallett Carr, *What Is History?* (New York: Alfred A. Knopf, 1962); and Robert E. Wood, ed., *The Future of Metaphysics* (Chicago: Quadrangle Books, 1970).

27. We speak of "the progress of a disease" and of "a crime in progress," however. So there are instances where we use the term 'progress'

to refer to a development that may affect us adversely. In these cases 'progress' is being used as a synonym for 'development.' For other issues involved in the notion of development, see Walter Ehrlich, "Principles of a Philosophy of the History of Philosophy," *The Monist* 53, no. 4 (1969): 533 ff.

28. Arthur O. Lovejoy and G. Boas, *Primitivism and Related Ideas in Antiquity* (Baltimore: Johns Hopkins University Press, 1935), vol. 1, p. 6.

29. As noted earlier, it is one of the two nouns (the other being 'order') that graces the Brazilian flag, indicating the popularity of the notion of progress in nineteenth-century Brazil. For a discussion of the overall influence of this idea, see Morris Ginsberg, "Progress in the Modern Era," in Philip P. Wiener, ed., *Dictionary of the History of Ideas*, vol. 3, pp. 633–650.

30. See Émile Bréhier, "The Formation of Our History of Philosophy," in Raymond Klibansky and Herbert James Paton, eds., *Philosophy and History* (New York: Harper Torchbooks, 1963), pp. 166 ff.

31. Cf. Kuhn's *The Structure of Scientific Revolutions.* Indeed, some, like Ortega y Gasset, see the idea as pernicious. Cf. "History as a System," trans. William C. Atkinson, in Klibansky and Paton, ibid., pp. 292–93.

32. Among those who reject progress in philosophy is Heidegger. See the discussion of his views by J. L. Mehta in *Martin Heidegger: The Way and the Vision* (Honolulu: University Press of Hawaii, 1976), p. 364.

33. Some have argued, in a similar vein, that philosophy is more akin to the arts and humanities, where appreciation rather than progress is expected. Mandelbaum puts the point well in "On the Historiography of Philosophy," *Philosophy Research Archives* 2 (1976): 743–744, where he says: "we do not demand that there should be progress in the drama from Sophocles to our own day, nor progress in sculpture or music. In these fields the chance of appreciating and enjoying that cummulative but non-progressive heritage is sufficient, and why should it not also be so in philosophy?" The answer, of course, is simply that philosophy is not like the arts because it is concerned with truth and cognitive understanding, not just with appreciation and enjoyment.

34. It is assumed for the sake of simplicity throughout this story that, although several years have elapsed between the time when the valley was described and the time when the description is being checked, no changes have occurred in the valley.

35. By methodological truths I do not mean anything more than truths that have to do with methodology and procedure. All other truths I consider "substantive."

36. For a discussion of individuation in a contemporary context see my book, *Individuality;* for a discussion of it in modern philosophy, see Kenneth Barber and Jorge J. E. Gracia, eds., *Individuation and Identity in Early Modern Philosophy: Descartes to Kant* (Munich and Vienna: Philosophia Verlag, forthcoming). In the article on Christian Wolff in the latter I show, for example,

that Wolff's view is a step backward in the development of theories of individuation.

37. This linear model is common in most historical enterprises. Cf. Maurice H. Mandelbaum, "Some Forms and Uses of Comparative History," in *Philosophy, History and the Sciences*, p. 140.

Conclusion

The purpose I had in mind when I set out to write this book was twofold. First and foremost the book was meant to deal with a series of historiographical issues related to the history of philosophy with which I had been concerned over several years. It seemed to me that these issues had to be discussed together in order to come up with a reasonable formulation and solution. However, there also was a second, indirect purpose in writing the book, namely, to find some way of bridging the gap that has developed between the two major philosophical traditions that dominate Western philosophy today. The major theses I defend in response to these aims are also two. The first is presented as an overall answer to the various historiographical issues raised in the volume and proposes that the history of philosophy must be done philosophically. The second thesis is a response to the other aim of the book and claims that the foundation for dialogue and communication between the Anglo-American and Continental traditions is to be found in the study of the history of philosophy and the historiographical issues such a study involves. The aim of this Conclusion is to recount briefly how I have tried to carry out the purposes of the book and how I have defended its theses in the preceding chapters.

Let me begin by going back to the thesis I proposed in the Introduction concerning the role of the history of philosophy and its historiography in the rapprochement between Anglo-American and Continental philosophers. There I pointed out that prior to Kant, Western philosophy had been divided roughly into three major traditions. The *mainstream* tradition, as its name indicates, held sway over the philosophical world and was characterized by the view that the function of philosophy is to know what there is, by a trust in the human faculties of knowledge, and by an argumentative methodology. A second tradition, which I called *poetic,* shared with the mainstream the view that the function of philosophy is to know what there is, but distrusted the natural epistemic powers of human beings to do so and preferred a nonargumentative methodology based on intuition. Finally, the third, which I called *critical*, was characterized by the belief that philosophy cannot yield knowledge of reality. This tradition breaks further into two subgroups, the *skeptics*, who believed that knowledge is impossible in any human enterprise, including what we call today *empirical sciences*, and the *positivists*, who restricted their skepticism to philosophy, allowing the possibility of knowledge in the empirical realm. Both subgroups shared with the mainstream tradition the use of an argumentative methodology.

I argued further that Kant's attack on human reason in the *Critique of Pure Reason* had the effect of undermining the mainstream tradition, pushing it to the sidelines and giving the place of prominence to the two other traditions that prior to Kant had occupied only marginal positions. Kant's effect on the history of philosophy was to divide the philosophical establishment into two groups that maintain their dominance and remain opposed to this day: the poets in Continental Europe and the critics in the Anglo-American world.

The relative unity and continuity of philosophy before Kant can be explained because most philosophers shared some common ground that made possible dialogue and communication, even though individual philosophers might disagree with each other with respect to the positions they adopted and even some of the problems they addressed. Members of the mainstream, of course, shared a common conception of the function of philosophy, an object of investigation, and certain assumptions concerning philosophical methodology. The poets, although distrustful of human faculties and employing a different philosophical methodology, shared with members of the mainstream a view of the function of philosophy. And critics rejected the mainstream conception of the function of philosophy as well as its confidence in its capacity to gain knowledge of reality, but shared with that tradition an argumentative methodology. The common elements that poets and critics, on the one hand, shared with the mainstream, on the other, made possible communication and dialogue among the three groups, even when communication between poets and critics was not always possible or direct. In this sense, the mainstream tradition functioned not only as the preserver of the grounds for philosophical discourse among its own members, but also as a mediator between poets and critics. After Kant, however, due to the ascendancy of poets and critics and the displacement of the pre-Kantian mainstream to the sidelines, the grounds for communication within the philosophical community have been largely eliminated, resulting in the split that characterizes contemporary philosophy.

Nearly everyone seems to agree that the situation has gotten out of hand and requires a remedy. But what remedy? It would be naive to expect poets to change their philosophical assumptions in order to communicate with critics and vice versa. So the solution must lie elsewhere and not require the abandonment of any of the fundamental presuppositions about the function of philosophy, the object of knowledge, or philosophical methodology that poets and critics hold dear.

The solution I have suggested in this book is a return to the study of the history of philosophy and to the historiographical problems that it poses. Both the history of philosophy and philosophical historiography should be able to provide the common ground between poets and critics that will allow them to restore some measure of dialogue and communication. It is easy to see how the history of philosophy can provide a common object of study, since both poets and critics view that history as *their* history and as such maintain an interest in it. But where are we to find the common aim and the common methodological grounds that they can share? It is here I believe that we must turn to philosophical historiography for two reasons: First, philosophical historiography identifies certain fundamental issues whose solution can become a common aim for both poets and critics, taking the place of the pre-Kantian mainstream conception of the function of philosophy as the knowledge of reality; second, philosophical historiography provides us with certain methodological principles that take the place of the methodological assumptions shared by members of the pre-Kantian mainstream.

In order to carry out the task of bringing together poets and critics I have tried to lay the groundwork for such rapprochement, first, by identifying some fundamental issues I believe should be of concern to anyone who takes an interest in the history of philosophy. Not that I claim to have provided an exhaustive list or even to have identified the most important or fundamental of those issues. For my argument I need only to single out some issues that, being fundamental, require the attention of those concerned with doing history of philosophy. In particular, I have tried to raise methodological questions that would provide an opportunity to show some of the procedural rules that are indispensible for historians of philosophy. Second, I have tried to show how the study of the history of philosophy has intrinsic value for philosophers and thus that its study should be given a high priority in philosophical speculation. By these means I have sought to build a bridge between poets and critics, pointing to an object of study they can share, uncovering a common aim for their efforts, and providing some of the methodological principles they need to pursue their inquiry.

Note that I have not attempted or claimed to show that the study of the history of philosophy and of philosophical historiography do in fact bring about a rapprochement between the two main philosophical traditions in vogue today. To carry out that task would involve, as noted in the Preface, much more. It would require the investigation of historiographical discussions of both analytic and Continental philosophers in order to illustrate how their concern with the history of philosophy and philosophical historiography establish common bonds between them. But that kind of detailed investigation would have taken us far from the main historiographical task of this book. In lieu of that, then, I have to content myself with an indirect defense of my thesis. By presenting and dealing with a series of historiographical issues, I have aimed to entice both analysts and Continentalists to a common field of discussion.

Whether I have succeeded or not is for the reader to say, but so long as the issues raised in this book about the history of philosophy and philosophical historiography prove of interest to some poets and critics I consider myself satisfied. Not that I require agreement. Pre-Kantian philosophers seldom agreed with each other and yet they enjoyed lively dialogue and communication. What I seek is to take some steps toward the restoration of the kind of interaction within the contemporary philosophical community that was commonplace before Kant.

Having reviewed my claims, now I would like to present a brief summary of the issues I have raised in this book and the solutions to them that I have suggested in order to illustrate how they substantiate those claims. In short, I intend to recount in a schematic fashion my philosophy of the historiography of philosophy and how that philosophy and the issues it raises serve as a bridge between poets and critics.

Let me begin by pointing out that the overall thrust of the discussions contained in this book is to show that the history of philosophy must be done philosophically and that when done in that way the history of philosophy is intrinsically helpful to the philosopher. It was necessary for me to adopt and defend this thesis, for otherwise the attempt to bring together poets and critics would have been doomed to failure from the start. For my undertaking involves trying to convince both parties that there are fundamental philosophical issues that they need to address and that when they address them, they must do it in certain definite ways. Now, it certainly would not do to try to present the parties in question with issues that are not philosophical. Indeed, one of the points of contention between poets and critics is that they cannot agree on even the most basic aims and methodological principles for philosophy. So if anything is to bring them together effectively it must not only be something common to both, but must be regarded as intrinsically philosophical by them. For these reasons I have tried to show that the study of the history of philosophy is a philosophical enterprise, and I have tried to lay down some guidelines as to how it should be carried out, the dangers to which it is subject, and the problems that various approaches to it encounter.

I began the task of defending the philosophical nature of the history of philosophy by explaining the notions of history, philosophy, and the history of philosophy. History was understood as an account of a series of past events. Philosophy was taken to be a view of the world, or any of its parts, that seeks to be accurate, consistent and comprehensive. And the history of philosophy was understood as an account of a series of past philosophical ideas.

Having established provisional understandings of history, philosophy, and the history of philosophy, I argued that history, when considered as a set of propositions that express an account of a series of past events, is composed of propositions that are descriptive, interpretative, and evaluative. The main function of descriptive propositions is to present accurately those events and their relations for which there can be direct empirical evidence. Interpretative propositions (1) reconstruct the fabric of unstated motives, intangible factors, and implicit circumstances within which events take place and for which there can be no direct empirical evidence; (2) contain broad generalizations based on limited evidence; and (3) include inferences concerning events for which there is no empirical evidence. Finally, evaluative propositions involve evaluations of both historical events and the views of historians concerning those events. Philosophy, like history, contains interpretative and evaluative propositions, but, unlike history, it does not include purely descriptive propositions. Moreover, philosophy also contains some propositions that make explicit the logical relations among ideas that are missing from history. Finally, the history of philosophy, being a historical discipline concerned with philosophical ideas, involves descriptions, interpretations, and evaluations. Indeed, the interpretative and evaluative character of the history of philosophy make it philosophical, for the criteria used in those interpretations and evaluations are philosophical. Contrary to the views of many philosophers, who consider the history of philosophy to be a purely descriptive enterprise, devoid of any philosophical element, I argued that to do history of philosophy nonphilosophically is not only impossible, but also undesirable. The history of philosophy must contain both philosophical interpretations and evaluations, and thus involves an indispensable element of interest.

This does not mean, of course, that the history of philosophy is indistinguishable from philosophy and vice versa. I argued against such a historicist position explicitly. My view is that the history of philosophy must be done philosophically, even though to do history of philosophy is not to do philosophy. Indeed, I also pointed out that to do history of philosophy is not even a requirement of doing philosophy. The history of philosophy needs philosophy, but philosophy does not need its history. To misunderstand this relation, indeed, is the cause of many errors both in philosophy and in the accounts of its history.

But then, one might ask, If philosophy does not need its history, why should philosophers bother with it? In fact, many authors have maintained that the history of philosophy, even though not incompatible with philosophy, has little to do with it and might as well be ignored.

If I were to let this argument stand, then there would be little hope of success for my plan of bringing together poets and critics on the basis of the study of the history of philosophy and its historiography. So I addressed it and tried to show that the history of philosophy, although not necessary for philosophy, has intrinsic value for it. To do philosophy historically, that is, using and relying on the history of philosophy, is justified by the very nature of philosophy and particularly by the nature of the instruments it uses. It is not just that the history of philosophy can serve as a source of inspiration for and lend support and respectability to philosophy, as some have argued. Or that the history of philosophy can be used as a practicum in reasoning, as a rich source of information and truth, or even as a kind of therapeutic tool for the historian, as others have correctly pointed out. The justification for the study of the history of philosophy goes beyond these rhetorical and pragmatic reasons, resting on the close ties that philosophy has to culture.

My argument is not that philosophy is culturally determined and, therefore, historically bound, however. That would lead us into the kind of inflexible historicism according to which philosophers are mere mechanical mouthpieces of the age in which they live. My argument is rather that, although philosophy can transcend a particular culture, it always originates in a specific historico-cultural matrix and depends on cultural phenomena for its function. To achieve the kind of liberation from particular historical circumstances for which philosophers have craved, we must know the matrix from which ideas arise, and in order to surmount our prejudices and biases we must flesh them out. But for that fleshing out to occur it is necessary both to contrast the ideas of our age and culture with those of other cultures and to understand the origin of our ideas in the past, as well as to grasp the way they have come to have the form they have for us. For these reasons, the study of the history of philosophy is of immense value to philosophers and should become a center of discussion and interest for all those interested in philosophy, whether poets or critics. Indeed, the study of the history of philosophy, as I argued in the Introduction, provides a meeting place for poets and critics.

This brings me to another issue of great importance to the historian of philosophy that also can bridge the gap between poets and critics. If we accept the view I have defended here, that there is intrinsic value in the study of the philosophical past by philosophers, we must raise the question as to how we can have access to that past. For historians of philosophy do not encounter past ideas directly; they have access to those ideas only through texts. So we must understand the nature of texts and how they reveal to us past philosophical ideas.

I conceive texts as groups of signs (whether written, spoken, or mental) selected, arranged, and intended by an author to convey some specific meaning to an audience in a particular context. Therefore, the meaning of texts is closely related to their authors and audiences. It is the job of the historian of philosophy, then, to get at the meaning of the text by considering all the factors that may play a role in it. The result of this historical work is a textual interpretation, which is nothing but another text composed of the text whose interpretation it is supposed to be plus other textual elements. The "other textual elements" are added by interpreters to the original text in order to help re-create in their own minds and in those of their contemporary audiences acts of understanding similar to those created by the original text in the audience that had access to it at the time of its composition. In short, an interpretation is meant to bridge the historical gap between a text on the one hand and the historians and their contemporary audiences on the other.

The need for an interpretation to bridge the historical gap between a text and a contemporary audience brings out again the fundamentally philosophical character of the task of the historian of philosophy. For textual interpretations require judgments founded on evaluations and those judgments can be made only on the basis of philosophical criteria in cases where philosophical texts are involved. It also helps us see how the issue we have raised is of fundamental importance, not only for those who see the history of philosophy as their primary vocation, but also for all philosophers, because philosophers depend on texts for communication. The historiographical question concerned with the interpretation of past texts should be one for which both poets and critics seek an answer, even if their answers turn out to be different.

From the consideration of texts and their interpretation, then, we come to the same conclusion reached earlier, namely, that the history of philosophy must be done philosophically, and this means that it must be interpretative and evaluative. But the history of philosophy must also be objective, since its aim is the understanding of past philosophical ideas as they were understood, both by those who proposed them and by their contemporaneous audiences, and not as we may capriciously wish to understand them. So we may ask, How can these two seemingly conflicting aims be reconciled?

I have already argued that the aim of textual interpretation is not, as many think, the understanding of a text as separate from its historical locus. It is rather the understanding of the meaning of a text as understood by its author and its contemporaneous audience. Our task is to determine how this can be achieved and the kind of method the historian should follow that will balance interpretation and objectivity. And if this seems difficult, more difficult still seems the reconciling of objectivity with evaluation. In short, the problem boils down to the question of how to do philosophical history of philosophy without sacrificing historical objectivity and accuracy.

I tried to carry out this task by providing detailed analyses of what I see as the major approaches used by historians to study the history of philosophy. In keeping with the overall thrust of this work, I rejected those approaches that are not philosophical. Among these were the *cultural*, the *psychological*, and the *ideological*. They all share the attempt to account for past philosophical ideas in terms of nonphilosophical factors. For the culturalist, they are cultural factors; for the psychologist, they are factors related to the mental makeup of the individuals in question; and the ideologue simply uses the history of philosophy to achieve his or her own priorities, which usually have nothing to do with philosophy.

I also rejected approaches that provide philosophical accounts of the philosophical past but put too much emphasis on description to the detriment of interpretation and evaluation. This is the case with what I called the *Golden Age nostalgic*, the *romantic*, the *scholarly*, and various *doxographical* approaches. These fail not only because they do not recognize sufficiently the evaluative and interpretative elements that play a role in the production of historical accounts; the first three fail also because they engage in surreptitious evaluative behavior, while seemingly following absolutely objective methodological procedures. And the main problem of doxographers, in addition to their neglect of interpretation and evaluation, is the superficiality of their analyses, again a result of their neglect of interpretation and evaluation in the history of philosophical ideas.

Even those approaches I called *polemical*, which adopt a fundamentally philosophical attitude in the study of the history of philosophy, often are inadequate. They are inadequate because, in contrast to the other approaches mentioned, they emphasize evaluation and interpretation excessively, losing sight of historical objectivity. *Apologists* seem interested only in the defense of a set of beliefs to which they are committed; *literary critics* emphasize too much the role of literary form and interpretation in the understanding of the past; *dilettantes* have no patience or interest in accurate historical detail; *idealists* seek the formulation of ideal systems of thought they can evaluate and see their exemplification in history as accidental; *problematicists*, interested as they are primarily in philosophical problems, tend to neglect philosophical ideas that are not the result of explicitly formulated philosophical problems; finally, *eschatologists* are too concerned with showing how history verifies their developmental schemes to pay attention to historical data that do not fit them.

As we have seen, none of these approaches, if pursued by itself, can yield a satisfactory historiographical methodology for the study of the philosophical past. Nor can we develop a proper method by simply combining all of them into one big eclectic procedure. In the first place, such a combination is not possible, for there are incompatible features in many of these approaches. The scholarly emphasis on faithfulness to the historical record would certainly clash with the revisionist tendencies of some of the other methods, for example. Second, even if possible, the combination of all these approaches is not desirable because some approaches have no redeeming quality to them whatsoever. It is hard to think, for example, of any use that the dilettante or ideological approaches may have. Third, even if a combination of all, or at least of some, of these approaches were possible and desirable, such a combination would not yield an appropriate historiographical methodology for the study of the history of philosophy. The problem with it would rest on two factors: first, a lack of methodological awareness and, second, a lack of a clear procedural blueprint to be followed. The first factor is important because it keeps historians alert, making them sensitive to the need to maintain a balance among description, interpretation, and evaluation. The second factor is important because without some clear guidelines as to how to proceed, it would be difficult, if not impossible, to balance all the elements that play a role in the production of a historical account.

My proposal for a balanced methodology is what I call the *framework approach*. In keeping with my overall claim that the history of philosophy must be done philosophically, it is a fundamentally philosophical approach, but one geared to the accurate and objective understanding of the philosophical past. Its backbone is the development of a conceptual framework founded on an analysis of the problems and ideas under investigation. The framework aims to separate the different issues involved in the problems and ideas in question, the possible answers to those issues, the various ideas that play a role in them and, finally, the types of arguments and objections that can be used both in support of or against the possible solutions to the issues that have been distinguished. The framework and its language should be as neutral as possible in order not to bias the discussion in any way. Moreover, any philosophical preferences and commitments contained in it should be made as explicit as possible in order not to poison the well at the start. Finally, the framework should be held only as a heuristic and instrumental aid and, therefore, should have the kind of flexibility and openness that would allow change, whether superficial or fundamental.

With this framework in mind, then, the historian can proceed to look back into the history of philosophy, applying standard scholarly procedures. The framework provides an explicit basis for interpretation and judgment in cases where doubts arise, while at the same time making as evident as possible the historian's interpretations and evaluations and the principles used to reach them. By making explicit the historian's assumptions and commitments, the framework safeguards historical objectivity, while maintaining the philosophical character of the history of philosophy without which such history would be not only useless to philosophers, but also impossible to accomplish.

The rationale for the use of a conceptual framework is founded on the very mission of the history of philosophy. The study of the history of philosophy seeks an understanding of the philosophical past and such an understanding is not possible without a conceptual framework. It is therefore inevitable that the historian of philosophy have such a framework. The only choice the historian has is whether to make it coherent, clear, and explicit or leave it incoherent, murky, and implicit. Many historians of philosophy think that to do the first is to bias the account and therefore they do the second by default. My argument is that only the first alternative can give us hope of achieving some kind of historical objectivity. The second is doubly perverse, for it not only biases the account, but does so imperceptibly.

In spite of the advantages of the framework approach, it should not stand alone. Historians of philosophy also need an understanding of how the development of philosophical ideas takes place in order to avoid misreading the history of philosophy. The development of such an understanding belongs, however, to the philosophy of the history of philosophical ideas, not to the historiography of philosophy. Now, although this book is primarily historiographical in character—there are some metaphysical and logical asides in it—I had to say something about how philosophical ideas develop in order to complete the methodological picture I have presented and to warn against possible misunderstandings contingent on my philosophical views concerning the history of philosophy.

Of the many problems that arise from a misunderstanding of how philosophical ideas develop two stand out. The first, which I called the *Ecclesiastes syndrome,* occurs when historians read into the past ideas that were not present in the past except perhaps in very seminal and inchoate forms. The second, which I called the *primitive syndrome,* occurs when historians take certain ideas as original and innovative when in fact they already were present and well formed in the past. Both of these problems arise from a misunderstanding of how ideas develop in history and the failure to take into account that they go through various stages marked by diverse degrees of explicitness and awareness. At least five stages are crucial in this development of philosophical ideas: preanalytical, definitional, problematic, textually independent, and central.

In the *preanalytical stage* a philosopher uses ideas borrowed from ordinary discourse without being aware of, or concerned with, either their exact conceptual import or the problems they pose. In the *definitional stage,* philosophers become aware of the need to present a clear understanding of the idea and thus introduce a definition of it, but are still unaware of the problems that such definition might pose. It is in the *problematic stage* that philosophers become concerned with possible problems involved in the idea or its definition and try to solve them through various means. When the concern with these problems reaches such a degree that their discussion takes up separate and distinct parts of a text, then ideas have reached the *textually independent stage.* In all these cases the idea is still discussed in the context of some other idea or problem that is deemed more important and to the solution of which the discussion of the idea in question seems to help. However, it frequently happens that an idea whose discussion always was subservient to some other idea or problem acquires sufficient importance that it comes to be treated and discussed by itself, subordinating the discussion of other ideas and problems to itself. When this happens to an idea, it has reached what I called the *central stage* of development.

From all this, it should be clear that it is terribly important for historians to be aware of these stages of development. For, when they confuse one stage of development with another and treat an idea as if it were at a different stage than it is at a particular time, they distort history.

The discussion of the stages of development of ideas naturally raises questions concerning philosophical progress. Is there such a thing? Has philosophy advanced in its more than 2,500 years of history? Again, like the question of the development of philosophical ideas, this question belongs in the philosophy of the history of philosophy, a branch of the philosophy of history. I take it up only because it naturally arises in the context of historical development.

I maintain a somewhat optimistic view of the development of philosophy based on the progress it has made in its discovery of truth, the rejection of falsehoods, the clarification of concepts, and the awareness of the complexity of philosophical problems. We know now at least some philosophical truths that Thales did not know, and we know that some things that were thought to be true before are false. Likewise, we are clearer about certain concepts at present than our ancestors were. And, finally, we have a greater awareness of some philosophical problems today than our philosophical predecessors had.

One may wish to ask, however, how there is so much disagreement about the question of philosophical progress in the philosophical community if its solution is as simple as I have pretended. My answer is that the matter looks complicated in part because of two misconceptions widely shared by those concerned with it. In the first place, both proponents and opponents of philosophical progress, following in the footsteps of many general historians, interpret progress in linear terms. But philosophical progress is not like that; philosophical development does not occur in a straight pattern, but rather goes back and forth and around. Thus my suggestion is that philosophical progress should be interpreted spirally rather than linearly.

In the second place, most of those who discuss this issue want to see evidence of philosophical progress in the short run, whereas philosophical progress is detectable only in the long run. In the short term, the philosophical picture one finds in history is inconclusive, at times showing progress but at other times regress or stagnation. Only when one looks at the overall and cumulative history of philosophy is evidence of progress detectable.

The issues concerned with the development of philosophical ideas and philosophical progress illustrate once more the inevitability of the philosophical character of the history of philosophy. For at least the rudiments of a philosophy of the history of philosophy seem to be necessary to do a good job in the history of philosophy. I have claimed that the view I hold of the development of philosophical ideas is important for avoiding errors in doing history of philosophy. And whether one adopts my particular view of that development or not, it is clear, first, that one needs some view of that development and, second, that such a view, whatever it is, will affect how one goes about doing history of philosophy. Moreover, the same can be said about the question of progress or the questions concerned with the methodological procedures and other historiographical matters discussed in this book. The history of philosophy cannot avoid being philosophical, but it can, through the methods I advocate, achieve a reasonable degree of objectivity.

It should also be clear that the philosophical issues in philosophical historiography raised in this book are faced by poets and critics alike, as long as they understand the philosophical importance of the study of the history of philosophy. As such, these issues could become the basis of a beginning dialogue between them. Note that I do not say that those issues *have* to become the basis of such a dialogue. Human will is free and seems to be constrained by neither logic nor brute force, and philosophers are particularly fond of exercizing it in unexpected ways. Moreover, I do not claim that the direction to which I have pointed here is the only one that can achieve the desired rapprochement between the Anglo-American and Continental traditions; indeed, there may be others. My claim is only that the direction I have indicated is an effective method of beginning such rapprochement.

There are two objections to this thesis, however, which I must take up very briefly before I finish. The first argues that my thesis rests on a conception of philosophy that goes back to the pre-Kantian mainstream, where philosophy was understood as knowledge of reality or what there is. But such a view is acceptable to neither all Anglo-American nor all Continental philosophers and, therefore, cannot be used to bring them together.

My response to this objection is that the view of philosophy I have presented need not be interpreted as a return to the pre-Kantian mainstream view of the discipline. I should mention at the outset that the understanding of philosophy as a "view of the world" should not be considered necessarily as a return to the view of philosophy as "knowledge of reality." I have avoided on purpose the use of terms such as 'reality' or 'what there is,' which I used to describe the mainstream position, in the description of philosophy. The term 'world' should not be taken to refer to any of those notions. In this context I intend it as a kind of neutral sign that each philosopher may appropriate and use as he or she wishes. Thus some may want to understand "consciousness" or "experience" by it, and others may think of it in terms of "physical reality" or what have you. These various interpretations of 'world' do not affect my thesis; one may understand the term in different ways and still agree with my views concerning the history of philosophy and philosophical historiography and how they can bring about the desired effect of rapprochement and dialogue.

A second objection argues that rapprochement between Anglo-American and Continental philosophers is impossible because they work with such different assumptions about the nature of philosophy and philosophical methodology that no matter what objects or issues they deal with, be they history of philosophy or philosophical historiography, they cannot find a common ground on which to communicate. One might say that Anglo-American and Continental philosophers belong to different philosophical cultures and, since I have granted that philosophy has a cultural dimension, I cannot claim that these cultures can be transcended.

I believe that I have answered this objection already in the body of the book, but let me just summarize again a couple of important points against it. In the first place, although I have granted a cultural dimension to philosophy, I have indicated in various places that such a dimension of philosophy does not permeate the enterprise to such a degree that escape from it is impossible. I argued explicitly against the culturalist position and for a modified version of culturalism that preserves both the cultural and transcultural intentional force of discourse. Second, it has been precisely the aim of this book to show how the history of philosophy and its historiography impose on historians certain limits, both about their object of study and about the methodology with which to study it, that help to bring philosophers together in spite of the presuppositions they may carry into the practice of history.

Let me finish, then, by going back to the beginning of this Conclusion, where I indicated the twofold aim of this book: first, to present an overall theory concerning philosophical historiography; and, second, to show that the issues the theory is meant to solve can form the basis of a new dialogue between Anglo-American and Continental philosophers. The first task I have accomplished, although the reader will have to be the ultimate arbiter of how successfully. As to the second purpose, my hopes are limited. More than likely, poets will regard this work as analytic and critics will regard it as another Continental outburst. So I am prepared for the worst, namely, neglect. But perhaps there are still a few sensible philosophers who see the need for communication and dialogue and, regardless of whether they agree with my views or not or how well they think of my efforts, will endeavor to continue where I have left off and to succeed where I have failed.

Select Bibliography

This bibliography is primarily a guide to recent works that I consider particularly pertinent to the topics discussed in this study. It also contains, however, some works to which reference has been made in the study that are not historiographical in nature. For a more complete list of historiographical sources up to 1977, see Craig Walton, "Bibliography of the Historiography and Philosophy of the History of Philosophy," *International Studies in Philosophy* 19 (1977): 135–166.

Abailard, Peter. *Incipiunt Glossae secundum magistrum Petrum Abaelardum super Porphyrium (Logica ingredientibus)*, ed. B. Geyer. In *Beiträge zur Geschichte der Philosophie des Mittelalters*, Band 20, Heft 1.

Alexander, Peter. "History of Philosophy: The Analytical Ideal." *The Aristotelian Society, Supplementary Volume* 62 (1988): 191–208.

Allaire, Edwin B. "Berkeley's Idealism Revisited." In Colin M. Turbayne, ed., *Berkeley: Critical Interpretative Essays*. Minneapolis: University of Minnesota Press, 1982.

Alquié, Ferdinand. "Structure logiques et structures mentales en histoire de la philosophie." *Société Française de la Philosophie, Bulletin* 46–47, no. 3 (1952–1953): 89–107. Discussion by Mm. Bachelard, Ullmo, Wahl, Schuhl, Berger, Salzi, Bénichou, Burgelin, Wolff, Mesnage, Bénézé, pp. 107–132.

APA Newsletter on Teaching Philosophy 2, no. 3 (1981). See articles by D. O'Connor, Hubert L. Dreyfus, and John Haugeland.

Aquinas, Thomas. See Thomas Aquinas.

Aristotle. *Analytica posteriora*, trans. G. R. G. Mure. In W. D. Ross, ed., *The Works of Aristotle*, vol. 1. London: Oxford University Press, 1928, pp. 71a1–100b17.

———. *Metaphysics*, trans. W. D. Ross. In Richard McKeon, ed., *The Basic Works of Aristotle*. New York: Random House, 1941.

Armstrong, A. M. "Philosophy and Its History." *Philosophy and Phenomenological Research* 19 (1958): 447–65.

Augustine. *The City of God*, trans. G. E. MacCracken and W. C. Greene, The Loeb Classical Library. Cambridge, Mass.: Harvard University Press, 1957–1963.

———. *On the Teacher*, trans. J. H. S. Burleigh. In John Baillie et al., eds., *Augustine: Earlier Writings*, vol. 6 of The Library of Christian Classics. Philadelphia: Westminster Press, 1953, pp. 69–101.

Averroes. *On the Harmony of Religion and Philosophy*, trans. G. F. Hourani. London: Luzac & Company, 1961.

Ayers, Michael. "Analytical Philosophy and the History of Philosophy." In Jonathan Rée, Michael Ayers, and Adam Westoby, *Philosophy and Its Past*. Hassocks, Sussex: Harvester Press, 1978, pp. 41–66.

———. "Substance, Reality and the Great, Dead Philosophers." *American Philosophical Quarterly* 7, no. 1 (1970): 38–49.

Bacon, Francis. *"The New Organon" and Related Writings*, ed. Fulton H. Anderson. New York: The Liberal Arts Press, 1960.

Bacon, Roger. See Roger Bacon.

Baillie, John. *The Belief in Progress*. London: Oxford University Press, 1950.

Bambrough, Renford. "Universals and Family Resemblances." *Proceedings of the Aristotelian Society* 61 (1960–1961): 207–222. Reprinted in Michael J. Loux, ed., *Universals and Particulars: Readings in Ontology*, rev. ed. Notre Dame, Ind., and London: University of Notre Dame Press, 1970, pp. 106–124.

Bann, Stephen. "Towards a Critical Historiography: Recent Work in Philosophy." *Philosophy* 56 (1981): 365–386.

Banu, Ion. "A propos de la méthode structurale dans l'historiographie de la philosophie." *Philosophie et Logique* 28 (1984): 337–345.

Barber, Kenneth, and Jorge J. E. Gracia, eds. *Individuation and Identity in Early Modern Philosophy*, Analytica Series. Munich, Hamden, and Vienna: Philosophia Verlag, forthcoming.

Bartley, W. W., III. *Wittgenstein*, 2d rev. and enlarged ed. La Salle, Illinois: Open Court, 1985.

Barzun, Jacques. "Cultural History: A Synthesis." In Fritz Stern, ed., *The Varieties of History: From Voltaire to the Present*. New York: World Publishing, 1956, pp. 387–402.

Baumer, Franklin L. "Intellectual History and Its Problems." *Journal of Modern History* 21, no. 3 (1949): 191–203.

Baynes, Kenneth, James Bohman, and Thomas McCarthy, eds. *After Philosophy: End or Transformation?* Cambridge, Mass., and London: The MIT Press, 1988.

Beard, Charles. "That Noble Dream." *American Historical Review* 41, no. 1 (1935): 74–87. Reprinted in Fritz Stern, ed., *The Varieties of History*. Cleveland and New York: Meridian Books, 1956, pp. 315–328.

———. "Written History as an Act of Faith." *American Historical Review* 39, no. 2 (1934): 219–229. Reprinted in Hans Meyerhoff, ed., *The Philosophy of History in Our Time*. Garden City, N.Y.: Doubleday Books, 1959, pp. 14–51.

Beardsley, Monroe C. *Aesthetics: Problems in the Philosophy of Criticism*, rev. ed. New York: Macmillan, 1980.

———. "Intentions and Interpretations: A Fallacy Revived." In Michael J.

Wreen and Donald M. Callen, eds., *The Aesthetic Point of View*. Ithaca, N.Y.: Cornell University Press, 1982, pp. 188–207.

———. *The Possibility of Criticism*. Detroit: Wayne State University Press, 1970.

———. "Some Problems of Critical Interpretation: A Commentary." *Journal of Aesthetics and Art Criticism* 36, no. 3 (1978): 351–360.

Beck, Lewis White. "Introduction and Bibliography." *The Monist* 53, no. 4 (1969): 523–531.

Bénézé, G. "Valeur philosophique de l'histoire de la philosophie." In *L'homme et l'histoire*. Paris: Presses Universitaires de France, 1952, pp. 355–358.

Bennett, Jonathan. "Response to Garber and Rée." In Peter H. Hare, ed., *Doing Philosophy Historically*. Buffalo, N.Y.: Prometheus Books, 1988, pp. 62–69.

Berstein, Richard. "Philosophical Rift: A Tale of Two Approaches." *New York Times* (Dec. 29, 1987), pp. A–1 and A–15.

Beuchot, Mauricio. "Hacia una metodología de la historia de la filosofía en el México colonial." In *Memorias del Primer Congreso Mexicano de Historia de la Ciencia y la Tecnología*. Mexico: Sociedad Mexicana de Historia de la Ciencia y la Tecnología, 1989, vol. 1, pp. 132–138.

Blake, Christopher. "Can History Be Objective?" In Patrick Gardiner, ed., *Theories of History*. Glencoe: Free Press, 1959, pp. 329–343.

Blau, J. L. "The Philosopher as Historian of Philosophy: Herbert Wallace Schneider." *Journal of the History of Philosophy* 10, no. 2 (1972): 212–215.

Boas, George. "A. O. Lovejoy as Historian of Philosophy," *Journal of the History of Ideas* 9 (1948): 404–411.

———. "The History of Philosophy." In Y. H. Krikorian, ed., *Naturalism and the Human Spirit*. New York: Columbia University Press, 1944, pp. 133–153.

———, Harold Cherniss, et al. *Studies in Intellectual History*. Baltimore: Johns Hopkins University Press, 1953.

Bodéüs, Richard. "Contre-propos sur le theme 'philosophie et histoire de la philosophie.'" *Carrefour* 10 (1988): 43–61.

Boethius. *De Trinitate* I, in *The Theological Tractates*, trans. H. F. Stewart and E. K. Rand, The Loeb Classical Library. Cambridge, Mass.: Harvard University Press, 1968.

———. *In librum Aristotelis "De interpretatione"*, 2 editions, ed. J. P. Migne. In *Patrologiae cursus completus; Series latina*, vol. 64. Paris, 1891.

Bonaventure. *Collationes in Hexaëmeron*, ed. R. Delorme. Florence: Ad Claras Aquas, 1934.

———. *Retracing the Arts to Theology*. In Sister Emma Thérèse Healy, *St. Bonaventure's De reductione artium ad theologiam, A Commentary with an Introduction and Translation*. St. Bonaventure, N.Y.: Saint Bonaventure College, 1939.

Borges, Jorge Luis. "Pierre Menard, Author of the *Quixote*," trans. James E. Irby. In *Labyrinths*, eds. Donald A. Yates and James E. Irby. Norfold, Conn.: New Directions, 1962, pp. 36–44.

Boss, Gilbert. "Philosophie et histoire des philosophies." *Carrefour* 10 (1988): 28–42.

Boutroux, E. "Role de l'histoire de la philosophie dans l'etude de la philosophie." In *Deuxième Congrès Internationale de Philosophie.* Geneva, 1904.

Braun, Lucien. "Exigences théoriques en histoire de la philosophie." In *La storiografia filosofica e la sua storia.* Padova: Editrice Antenore, 1982, pp. 53–66.

———. *Histoire de l'histoire de la philosophie.* Paris: Edition Ophrys, 1973.

Bréhier, Émile. "Comment je comprends l'histoire de la philosophie." In *Études de philosophie antique.* Paris: Presses Universitaires de France, 1955, pp. 1–9.

———. "The Formation of Our History of Philosophy." In Raymond Klibansky and Herbert James Paton, eds., *Philosophy and History.* New York, Evanston, Ill., and London: Harper & Row, 1963, pp. 159–172.

———. *Histoire de la philosophie,* vol. 1. Paris: F. Alcan, 1948–1951. Introduction and pp. 523–787.

———. "Méthodes et problèmes de l'histoire de la philosophie." In *Études de philosophie moderne.* Paris: Presses Universitaires de France, 1965, pp. 1–45.

———. *La philosophie et son passé.* Paris: Presses Universitaires de France, 1940.

Brodbeck, May. "Explanation, Prediction and 'Imperfect' Knowledge." In Herbert Feigl and Grover Maxwell, eds., *Minnesota Studies in the Philosophy of Science* 3. Minneapolis: University of Minnesota Press, 1962, pp. 231–272.

Brunner, M. Fernand. "Histoire de la philosophie et philosophie." In *Études sur l'histoire de la philosophie en hommage à M. Guéroult.* Paris: Éditions Fischbacher, 1964, pp. 179–204.

———. "Histoire et théorie des philosophies selon Martial Guéroult." *Société Française de la Philosophie, Bulletin* 76 (1982): 3–73.

Brunschvicg, Léon. "History and Philosophy." In Raymond Klibansky and Herbert James Paton, eds., *Philosophy and History.* New York, Evanston, Ill., and London: Harper & Row, 1963, pp. 27–34.

Brunschwig, Jacques. "Faire de l'histoire de la philosophie, aujord'hui." *Société Française de la Philosophie, Bulletin* 70 (1976): 125–149.

Buckle, Henry Thomas. *History of Civilization in England,* 3d ed. London: Longmans, Green & Co., 1866.

Bury, H. T. "The Science of History." In H. Temperley, ed., *Selected Essays of J. B. Bury.* Cambridge: Cambridge University Press, 1930, pp. 3–22.

Bury, J. B. *The Idea of Progress.* New York: Macmillan Co., 1932.

Butler, J. F. "Some Epistemological Problems about the History of Philosophy." *Philosophical Quarterly* (Amalner, India) 22 (1949–1950): 125–135.

Cain, William E. "Authors and Authority in Interpretation." *Georgia Review* 34 (1980): 617–634.

Carlyle, Thomas. *On Heroes, Hero-Worship, and the Heroic in History.* London: Everyman's Library, 1940.

Carr, Edward Hallet. *What is History?* New York: Alfred A. Knopf, 1962.

Cascardi, Anthony J., ed. *Literature and the Question of Philosophy.* Baltimore and London: Johns Hopkins University Press, 1987.

Cassirer, Ernst. *The Problem of Knowledge: Philosophy, Science, and History since Hegel,* trans. by William H. Woglom and Charles W. Hendel. New Haven, Conn.: Yale University Press, 1950.

Castañeda, Héctor-Neri. "Individuation and Non-Identity: A New Look." *American Philosophical Quarterly* 12 (1975), 131–140.

———. "Philosophy as a Science and as a Worldview." In A. Cohen and M. Dascal, eds., *The Institution of Philosophy: A Discipline in Crisis.* LaSalle, Ill.: Open Court, 1989, pp. 35–59.

Castelli, Enrico, ed. *La philosophie de l'histoire de la philosophie.* Paris: J. Vrin, 1956. Trans. of *La filosofia della storia della filosofia.* Milano: Bocca, 1954.

———. "La philosophie de l'histoire de la philosophie." In Enrico Castelli, ed., *La philosophie de l'histoire de la philosophie.* Paris: J. Vrin, 1956, pp. 9–18.

Cerutti Guldberg, Horacio. *Hacia una metodología de la historia de las ideas (filosóficas) en América Latina.* Guadalajara: Universidad de Guadalajara, 1986.

Chartier, Roger. "Intellectual History or Sociocultural History? The French Trajectories." In Dominick La Capra and Steven L. Kaplan, eds., *Modern European Intellectual History: Reappraisals and New Perspectives.* Ithaca, N.Y., and London: Cornell University Press, 1982, pp. 13–26.

Christian, William A. "Whitehead's Explanation of the Past." In George L. Kline, ed., *Alfred North Whitehead: Essays on His Philosophy.* Englewood Cliffs, N.J.: Prentice-Hall, 1963, pp. 93–101.

Cohen, Avner, and Marcelo Dascal, eds. *The Institution of Philosophy: A Discipline in Crisis.* La Salle, Ill.: Open Court, 1990.

Cohen, Howard. "Keeping the History of Philosophy." *Journal of the History of Philosophy* 14 (1976): 383–390.

Cohen, Lesley. "Doing Philosophy Is Doing Its History," *Synthese* 67, no. 1 (1986): 51–55.

Cohen, Sande. "Structuralism and the Writing of Intellectual History," *History and Theory* 17 (1978): 175–206.

Collingwood, Robin George. *An Autobiography.* London: Oxford University Press, 1939.

———. *The Idea of History.* Oxford: Clarendon Press, 1946.

Condorcet, Antoine-Nicholas Marie Jean de. *Esquisse d'un tableau historique des progrès de l'esprit humain* [1793]. Paris: Librairie Philosophique J. Vrin, 1970.

Copleston, Frederick. *On the History of Philosophy and Other Essays.* Totowa, N.J.: Barnes & Noble, 1979.

Corcoran, John. "Future Research on Ancient Theories of Communication and Reasoning." In John Corcoran, ed., *Ancient Logic and Its Modern Interpretations.* Dordrecht and Boston: D. Reidel, 1974, pp. 185–187.

Croce, Benedetto. "Il concetto filosofico della storia della filosofia." In *Il carattere della filosofia moderna.* Bari: G. Laterza, 1941, pp. 52–71.

———. *The Theory and History of Historiography,* trans. Douglas Ainslie. London: G. G. Harrap and Co., 1921.

Curley, Edwin. "Dialogues with the Dead." *Synthese* 67, no. 1 (1986): 33–49.

D'Amico, Robert. *Historicism and Knowledge.* New York and London: Routledge, 1989.

Dal Pra, Mario. "Storia della filosofia e storia della storiografia filosofica." In *La storiografia filosofica e la sua storia.* Padova: Editrice Antenore, 1982, pp. 13–38.

Daniel, Stephen H. "Metaphor in the Historiography of Philosophy," *Clio* 15, no. 2 (1986): 191–210.

Danto, Arthur C. *Analytical Philosophy of History.* Cambridge: Cambridge University Press, 1965.

———. *Narrative and Historical Knowledge.* New York: Columbia University Press, 1985.

———. "Philosophy as/and/of Literature." In Anthony J. Cascardi, ed., *Literature and the Question of Philosophy.* Baltimore and London: Johns Hopkins University Press, 1987, pp. 1–23.

Dauenhauer, Bernard P., ed. *At the Nexus of Philosophy and History.* Athens and London: University of Georgia Press, 1987.

Davidson, Donald. *Inquiries into Truth and Interpretation.* Oxford: Clarendon Press, 1984.

Davis, Walter A. *The Act of Interpretation: A Critique of Literary Reason.* Chicago: Chicago University Press, 1978.

Degl'Innocenti, Umberto. "Il principio d'individuazione dei corpi e Giovanni di S. Tommaso." *Aquinas* 12 (1969), 59–99.

Delbos, Victor. "Les conceptions de l'histoire de la philosophie" (I). *Revue de Métaphysique et de Morale* 24, no. 2 (1917): 135–147.

Dempf, Alois. "Philosophie de l'histoire de la philosophie." In Enrico Castelli, ed., *La philosophie de l'histoire de la philosophie.* Paris: J. Vrin, 1956, pp. 69–80.

Descartes, René. *A Discourse on Method,* trans. John Veitch. New York and London: Everyman's Library, 1951.

———. *Philosophical Letters,* ed. and trans. Anthony Kenny. Oxford: Clarendon Press, 1970.

Devivaise, C. "Réflexions sur le caractère philosophique de l'histoire de la philosophie." In *L'homme et l'histoire.* Paris: Presses Universitaires de France, 1952, pp. 337–341.

Dewey, John. "Historical Judgments." In Hans Meyerhoff, ed., *The Philosophy of History in Our Time.* Garden City, N.Y.: Anchor Books, 1959, pp. 163–172.

Dilthey, Wilhelm. "Archive der Literatur in Ihrer Bedeutung für das Studium der Geschichte der Philosophie" [1889]. In *Gesammelte Schriften* 4. Leipzig and Berlin: B. G. Teubner, 1921, pp. 555–575.

———. "Der Aufbau der geschichtlichen Welt in den Geisteswissenschaften." In *Gesammelte Schriften* 7. Leibzig and Berlin: B. G. Teubner, 1927, pp. 77–188.

Diogenes Laertius. *The Lives and Opinions of Eminent Philosophers,* trans. R. D. Hicks, 2 vols. The Loeb Classical Library. London and New York: W. Heinemann and G. P. Putnam's Sons, 1925.

Dray, William H. "The Historian's Problem of Selection." In Ernest Nagel, Patrick Suppes, and Alfred Tarski, eds., *Logic, Methodology and Philosophy of Science: Proceedings of the 1960 International Congress.* Stanford, Calif.: Stanford University Press, 1962, pp. 595–603.

———. *Laws and Explanation in History.* London: Oxford University Press, 1957.

———, ed. *Philosophical Analysis and History.* New York and London: Harper & Row, 1966.

———. *Philosophy of History.* Englewood Cliffs, N.J.: Prentice-Hall, 1964.

———. "Philosophy of History." In Paul Edwards, ed., *Encyclopedia of Philosophy* 6. New York, London: Macmillan, 1967, pp. 247–254.

———. *On History and Philosophy of History.* Leiden: E. J. Brill, 1989.

Dumont, Fernand. "Une contribution a l'histoire de la philosophie au Québec." *Philosophiques* 10 (1983): 119–126.

Dunn, John. "The Identity of the History of Ideas." *Philosophy* 43, no. 164 (1968): 85–104. Reprinted in Peter Laslett et al., eds. *Philosophy, Politics and Society: Fourth Series.* Oxford: Basil Blackwell, 1972.

Dupré, Louis. "Is the History of Philosophy Philosophy?" *Review of Metaphysics* 42, no. 3 (1989): 463–482.

Edley, Roy. Editorial Foreword. In Jonathan Rée, Michael Ayers, and Adam Westoby, *Philosophy and Its Past.* Hassocks, Sussex: Harvester Press, 1978.

Ehrlich, Walter. "Principles of a Philosophy of the History of Philosophy," *The Monist* 53, no. 4 (1969): 532–562.

Eliot, T. S. "Tradition and the Individual Talent." In *Selected Essays.* New York: Harcourt, Brace & World, 1960, pp. 3–11.

Ellis, John M. "Critical Interpretation, Stylistic Analysis, and the Logic of Inquiry." *Journal of Aesthetics and Art Criticism* 36, no. 3 (1978): 253–262.

Engels, Friedrich. *Dialectics of Nature,* trans. and ed. C. Dutt. New York: International Publishers, 1940.

Eschmann, I. T. "A Catalogue of St. Thomas's Works: Bibliographical Notes." In Étienne Gilson, *The Christian Philosophy of St. Thomas Aquinas.* New York: Random House, 1956, pp. 381–383.

Fain, H. "History as Science." *History and Theory* 9 (1970): 154–173.

Faurot, J. H. "What Is History of Philosophy?" *The Monist* 53, no. 4 (1969): 642–655.

Fazio Allmayer, V. "La storicità della filosofia." In *Annali della Scuola Normale Superiore di Pisa* 21 (1952): 1–12.

Febvre, Lucien. "Doctrines et sociétés. Étienne Gilson et la philosophie du XIVe siècle." Originally published in *Annales d'Histoire Economique et Sociale*. Reprinted in *Combats pour l'histoire*, 2d ed. Paris: Librairie Armand Colin, 1965, pp. 284–288.

———. "Leur histoire et la nôtre." Originally published in *Annales d'Histoire Economique et Sociale*. Reprinted in *Combats pour l'histoire*, 2d ed. Paris: Librairie Armand Colin, 1965, pp. 276–283.

Feibleman, James K. "The History of Philosophy as a Philosophy of History." *Southern Journal of Philosophy* 5, no. 4 (1967): 275–283.

Ferrater Mora, José. "Filosofía, Historia de la." In *Diccionario de la filosofía*, vol. 2. Madrid: Alianza Editorial, 1980, pp. 1216–1223.

Fish, Stanley. *Is There a Text in This Class?* Cambridge, Mass.: Harvard University Press, 1980.

Foucault, Michel. *The Order of Things: An Archaeology of the Human Sciences.* New York: Random House, 1970.

———. "What Is an Author?" In Donald F. Bouchard, ed.; Donald F. Bouchard and Sherry Simon, trans., *Language, Countermemory, Practice: Selected Essays and Interviews.* Ithaca, N.Y.: Cornell University Press, 1977, pp. 113–138.

———. *Language, Countermemory, Practice: Selected Essays and Interviews,* ed. with Introduction Donald F. Bouchard, trans. Donald F. Bouchard and Sherry Simon. Ithaca, N.Y.: Cornell University Press, 1977.

Fraile, G. *Historia de la filosofía.* Madrid: Biblioteca de Autores Cristianos, 1956.

Franchini, Raffaello. "Teoria e storia della storiografia di B. Croce." *Rivista di Studi Crociani* 14 (1977): 288–297.

Frede, Michael. "The History of Philosophy as a Discipline." *Journal of Philosophy* 85, no. 11 (1988): 666–672.

Gadamer, H. G. *Truth and Method,* trans. by G. Barden and J. Cumming. London: Sheed & Ward, 1975.

Gadamer, H. G., E. K. Specht, and W. Stegmüller. *Hermeneutics Versus Science? Three German Views,* trans. and ed., John M. Connolly and Thomas Keutner. Notre Dame, Ind.: University of Notre Dame Press, 1988.

Galgan, Gerald J. "What's Special about the History of Philosophy?" *American Philosophical Quarterly* 24, no. 1 (1987): 91–96.

Gallie, W. B. *Philosophy and the Historical Understanding.* New York: Schocken Books, 1964.

Gaos, J. *Filosofía de la filosofía e historia de la filosofía.* Mexico: Stylo, 1947.

Garber, Daniel. "Does History Have a Future? Some Reflections on Bennett and Doing Philosophy Historically." In Peter H. Hare, ed., *Doing Philosophy Historically.* Buffalo, N.Y.: Prometheus Books, 1988, pp. 27–43.

Gardiner, Patrick. *The Nature of Historical Explanation.* London: Oxford University Press, 1952.

Garin, Eugenio. "Filosofia e storia della storiografia filosofica." In *La storiografia filosofica e la sua storia.* Padova: Editrice Antenore, 1982, pp. 39–52.

———. "L'unità nella storiografia filosofica." *Rivista Critica della Storia della Filosofia* 11 (1956): 206–217.

Garver, Newton. "Wittgenstein's Reception in America." *Modern Austrian Literature* 20, no. 3–4 (1987): 207–219.

Geldsetzer, Lutz. "Fragen der Hermeneutik der Philosophiegeschictsschreibung." In *La storiografia filosofica e la sua storia.* Padua: Editrice Antenore, 1982, pp. 67–102.

———. *Die Philosophie der Philosophiegeschichte im 19, Jahrhundert-Zur Wissenschaftstheorie der Philosophiegeschichteschreibung und-betrachtung.* Meisenheim am Glan: A. Hain, 1968.

———. *Was Heisst Philosophiegeschichte?* Düsseldorf: Philosophia Verlag, 1968.

Gentile, Giovanni. "Il concetto della storia della filosofia." In *La riforma della dialettica hegeliana.* In *Opere* t. 27. Florence: Sansoni, 1954, pp. 97–138.

———. "La storicità della filosofia." *Giornale Critico della Filosofia Italiana* 17, no. 42 (1963): 1–21.

Gentile, Marino. *Se e come é possibile la storia della filosofia.* Padua: Liviana, 1963.

Gerber, William. "Is there Progress in Philosophy?" *Journal of the History of Ideas* 34, no. 4 (1973): 699–673.

Ghent, Henry of. See Henry of Ghent.

Gilbert of Poitiers. *De Trinitate.* In Nikolaus M. Häring, ed., *The Commentaries on Boethius by Gilbert of Poitiers.* Toronto: Pontifical Institute of Mediaeval Studies, 1966, pp. 62–180.

Gilson, Étienne. *History of Christian Philosophy in the Middle Ages.* New York: Random House, 1955.

———. *History of Philosophy and Philosophical Education.* Milwaukee: Marquette University Press, 1948.

———. "Introduction to *A History of Philosophy.*" In Armand A. Maurer, *Medieval Philosophy.* New York: Random House, 1962, pp. vii–x.

Ginsberg, Morris. "Progress in the Modern Era." In Philip P. Wiener, ed., *Dictionary of the History of Ideas,* vol. 3, pp. 633–650.

Goodman, Nelson and Catherine Elgin. *Reconceptions on Philosophy and Other Arts and Sciences.* Indianapolis and Cambridge: Hackett Publishing Co., 1988.

Gouhier, Henri Gaston. "Note sur le progrès et la philosophie." In *Études sur l'histoire de la philosophie en hommage à M. Guéroult.* Paris: Éditions Fischbacher, 1964, pp. 111–114.

———. *La philosophie et son histoire,* 2d ed. Paris: J. Vrin, 1947.

Gould, Josiah B. "A Response to Graham's 'Anachronism in the History of Philosophy.'" In Peter H. Hare, ed., *Doing Philosophy Historically.* Buffalo, N.Y.: Prometheus Books, 1988, pp. 149–152.

Gracia, Jorge J. E. "The Centrality of the Individual in the Philosophy of the Fourteenth Century." *History of Philosophy Quarterly* 8 (1991).

———. "Filosofía e historia de la filosofía." *Crisis* 19 (1972): 63–72.

———. "Filosofía y su historia." *Revista Latinoamericana de Filosofía* 13 (1987): 259–278.

———. *Individuality: An Essay on the Foundations of Metaphysics.* Albany: SUNY Press, 1988.

———, ed. *Individuation in Scholasticism: The Later Middle Ages and the Counter-Reformation,* Analytica Series. Munich and Vienna: Philosophia Verlag, forthcoming.

———. *Introduction to the Problem of Individuation in the Early Middle Ages,* 2d rev. ed. Munich and Vienna: Philosophia Verlag, 1988.

———. "Philosophy and Its History: Veatch's *Aristotle.*" In Peter H. Hare, ed., *Doing Philosophy Historically.* Buffalo, N.Y.: Prometheus Books, 1988, pp. 92–116.

———. "Texts and Their Interpretation." *Review of Metaphysics,* 43 (1990): 495–542.

———. *Suárez on Individuation.* Milwaukee: Marquette University Press, 1982.

———. and Iván Jaksić, eds. *Filosofía e identidad cultural en América Latina.* Caracas: Monte Avila, 1987.

———. and John Kronen. "John of St. Thomas." In Jorge J. E. Gracia, ed., *Individuation in Scholasticism.* Munich and Vienna: Philosophia Verlag, forthcoming.

Graham, Daniel W. "Anachronism in the History of Philosophy." In Peter H. Hare, ed., *Doing Philosophy Historically.* Buffalo, N.Y.: Prometheus Books, 1988, pp. 137–148.

Graham, Daniel W. "The Structure of Explanation in the History of Philosophy." *Metaphilosophy* 19, no. 2 (1988): 158–170.

Graham, Gordon. "Can There Be History of Philosophy?" *History and Theory* 21 (1982): 37–52.

Greenlee, D. *Peirce's Concept of Sign.* The Hague and Paris: Mouton, 1973.

Groethuysen, Bernard. "Les paradoxes de l'histoire de la philosophie." *Theoria* 5 (1939): 235–264.

Grube, G. M. A. *Plato's Thought.* Boston: Beacon Press, 1958.

Guéroult, Martial. *Histoire et technologie des systémes philosophiques.* Leçon inaugurale du 4 déc. 1951. Paris: Collège de France, Leçons inaugurales, 1952.

———. "The History of Philosophy as a Philosophical Problem." *The Monist* 53, no. 4 (1969): 563–587.

———. "Méthode en histoire de la philosophie." *Philosophiques* 1, no. 1 (1974): 7–19.

———. "Le problème de la légitimité de l'histoire de la philosophie." In Enrico Castelli, ed., *La philosophie de l'histoire de la philosophie.* Paris: J. Vrin, 1956, pp. 45–68.

Guthrie, H. *Introduction au problème de l'histoire de la philosophie. La métaphysique de l'individualité à priori de la pensée.* Paris: Alcan, 1937.

Guthrie, W. K. C. "Aristotle as Historian." In David J. Furley and R. E. Allen, eds., *Studies in Presocratic Philosophy,* 1. London: Routledge & Kegan Paul, 1970, pp. 239–254.

Hacking, Ian. "Five Parables." In Richard Rorty, J. B. Schneewind, and Quentin Skinner, eds., *Philosophy in History: Essays on the Historiography of Philosophy*. Cambridge: Cambridge University Press, 1984, pp. 103–124.

Haeckel, Ernst. *The Riddle of the Universe*, trans. Joseph MacCabe. N.Y.: Harper & Brothers, 1900.

Hancher, Michael. "The Science of Interpretation and the Art of Interpretation," *MLN* 85 (1970): 791–802.

Harari, Josué V., ed. *Textual Strategies: Perspectives in Post-Structuralist Criticism*. Ithaca, N.Y.: Cornell University Press, 1979.

Hare, Peter H., ed. *Doing Philosophy Historically*. Buffalo, N.Y.: Prometheus Books, 1988.

Hartman, Geoffrey, ed. *Deconstruction and Criticism*. New York: Seabury Press, 1979.

Hegel, G. W. F. *Lectures on the History of Philosophy*, trans. E. S. Haldane and Frances H. Simson, 3 vols. London: Routledge & Kegan Paul, and N.Y.: The Humanities Press, 1974.

———. *Logic* (Encyclopedia), trans. William Wallace, 2d ed. Oxford: University Press, 1892.

Heidegger, Martin. *Kant and the Problem of Metaphysics*, trans. J. S. Churchill. Bloomington, Ind.: Indiana University Press, 1962.

Hempel, C. G. "The Function of General Laws in History." Reprinted in Patrick Gardiner, ed., *Theories of History*. Glencoe: Free Press, 1959, pp. 344–356.

Henning, E. M. "Archaeology, Deconstruction, and Intellectual History." In Dominick LaCapra and Steven L. Kaplan, eds., *Modern European Intellectual History: Reappraisals and New Perspectives*. Ithaca, N.Y., and London: Cornell University Press, 1982, pp. 153–196.

Henry of Ghent. *Summae quaestionum ordinariarum*, ed. Eligius M. Buytaert, O. F. M. St. Bonaventure, N.Y.: The Franciscan Institute, 1953.

Hertzberg, Lars, and Juhani Pietarinen. *Philosophy of History and Culture*. Leiden: E. J. Brill, 1990.

Hirsch, Eric Donald, Jr. *The Aims of Interpretation*. Chicago: Chicago University Press, 1976.

———. *Validity in Interpretation*. New Haven, Conn.: Yale University Press, 1967.

Hoffman, Paul. "Über die Problematik der philosophiegeschichtlichen Methode." *Theoria* 3, Part 1 (1937): 3–37. Discussion by Julius Kraft, pp. 306–313; by T. T. Segerstedt, pp. 313–320; by Ake Petzäll, pp. 321–330.

Holland, A. J., ed. *Philosophy, Its History and Historiography*. Dordrecht: D. Reidel, 1985.

Hook, Sidney, ed. *Philosophy and History: A Symposium*. N.Y.: New York University Press, 1963.

Horowitz, Maryanne Cline. "Complementary Methodologies in the History of Ideas," *Journal of the History of Philosophy* 12, no. 4 (1974): 501–509.

Huizinga, Johan. "Die Historische Idee." In *Verzamelde Werken*, vol. 7. Haarlem: H. D. Tjeenk Willink, 1950, pp. 134–150.

Hume, David. *A Treatise of Human Nature*, ed. L. A. Selby-Bigge. Oxford: Clarendon Press, 1965.

Hungerland, Isabel Payson. *Poetic Discourse*. Berkeley: University of California Press, 1958.

Husserl, Edmund. "Formale und transzendentale Logik: Versuch einer Kritik der logischen Vernunft." *Jahrbuch* 10 (1929): 1–298. English trans. Dorion Cairns, *Formal and Transcendental Logic*. The Hague: Nijhoff, 1969.

———. *Ideas: General Introduction to Pure Phenomenology*, trans. W. R. Boyce Gibson. N.Y.: Collier Books, 1962.

Iggers, Georg G. *The German Conception of History: The National Tradition of Historical Thought from Herder to the Present*, rev. ed. Middletown, Conn.: Wesleyan University Press, 1983.

Ingarden, Roman. *Ontology of the Work of Art: The Musical Work, the Picture, the Architectural Work, the Film*, trans. R. Meyer and J. T. Goldthwait. Athens: Ohio University Press, 1989.

———. "Reflections on the Subject Matter of the History of Philosophy." *Diogenes*, no. 29 (1960), 111–121.

Iser, Wolfgang. *Prospecting: From Reader-Response to Literary Anthropology*. Baltimore: Johns Hopkins University Press, 1989.

Janaway, Christopher. "History of Philosophy: The Analytical Ideal." *Aristotelian Society, Supplementary Volume* 62 (1988): 169–189.

Jay, Martin. "Should Intellectual Hitory Take a Linguistic Turn? Reflections on the Habermas-Gadamer Debate." In Dominick LaCapra and Steven L. Kaplan, eds., *Modern European Intellectual History: Reappraisals and New Perspectives*. Ithaca, N.Y., and London: Cornell University Press, 1982, pp. 86–110.

John Duns Scotus. *Lectura*. In Luca Modrić, ed., *Opera omnia*, vol. 18. Civitas Vaticana: Typis Polyglottis Vaticanis, 1982, pp. 229–293.

———. *Opus oxoniense*. In C. Balić et al., eds., *Opera omnia*, vol. 7. Civitas Vaticana: Typis Polyglottis Vaticanis, 1973, pp. 391–494.

John of St. Thomas. *Cursus theologicus. Tractatus de approbatione et auctoritate doctrinae d. Thomae*, Disp. II, vol. 1. Paris: Desclée, 1931.

———. *Cursus philosophicus thomisticus secundum exactam, veram, genuinam Aristotelis et Doctoris Angelici mentem*, ed. B. Reiser, 3 vols. Turin: Marietti, 1933.

Jordan, Mark. "History in the Language of Metaphysics." *Review of Metaphysics* 36, no. 4 (1983): 849–866.

Joynt, Carey B., and Nicholas Rescher. "The Problem of Uniqueness in History." *History and Theory* 1 (1961): 150–162.

Juárez, Agustín Uña. *Herméneusis: Estudios y textos de historia de la filosofía*. Madrid: EDES, 1987.

Juhl, P. J. "The Appeal to the Text: What Are We Appealing To?" *Journal of Aesthetics and Art Criticism* 36, no. 3 (1978): 277–287.

Kant, Immanuel. *Critique of Pure Reason*, trans. Norman Kemp Smith. London: Macmillan, 1963.

Kaufmann, Fritz. "The Phenomenological Approach to History." *Philosophy and Phenomenological Research* 2 (1941–1942): 159–172.

Kaufman, Walter, ed. *Existentialism from Dostoevsky to Sartre*. Cleveland and N.Y.: World Publishing Company, 1956.

Kelley, Donald R. "Horizons of Intellectual History: Retrospect, Circumspect, Prospect." *Journal of the History of Ideas* 48, no. 1 (1987): 143–169.

———. "What Is Happening to the History of Ideas?" *Journal of the History of Ideas* 51 (1990): 3–25.

Kellner, Hans. "Triangular Anxieties: The Present State of European Intellectual History." In Dominick LaCapra and Steven L. Kaplan, eds., *Modern European Intellectual History: Reappraisals and New Perspectives*. Ithaca, N.Y., and London: Cornell University Press, 1982, pp. 111–136.

Kirk, G. S., and J. E. Raven. *The Presocratic Philosophers*. Cambridge: Cambridge University Press, 1957.

King, Preston, ed. *The History of Ideas: An Introduction to Method*. Totowa, N.J.: Barnes and Noble, 1983.

Klibansky, Raymond, and Herbert James Paton, eds. *Philosophy and History*. Oxford: Clarendon Press, 1936. Reprinted New York, Evanston, and London: Harper & Row, 1963.

Krämer, Hans. "Funktions-und Reflectionsmöglichkeiten der Philosophiehistorie. Vorschläge zu ihrer wissenschaftstheoretischen Ortsbestimmung." *Zeitschrift für allgemeine Wissenschaftstheorie* 16, no. 1 (1985): 67–95.

Kristeller, Paul Oskar. "History of Philosophy and History of Ideas." *Journal of the History of Philosophy* 2, no. 1 (1964): 1–14.

———. "The Philosophical Significance of the History of Thought." *Journal of the History of Ideas* 7, no. 3 (1946): 360–366.

———. "Philosophy and Its Historiography." *Journal of Philosophy* 82, no. 11 (1985): 618–625.

Krüger, Lorenz. "Why Do We Study the History of Philosophy?" In Richard Rorty, J. B. Schneewind, and Quentin Skinner, eds., *Philosophy in History: Essays on the Historiography of Philosophy*. Cambridge: Cambridge University Press, 1984, pp. 77–101.

Kuderowicz, Zbigniew. "Wladyslaw Tatarkiewicz as Historian of Philosophy." *Reports on Philosophy* 5 (1981): 3–8.

Kuhn, Thomas S. "Objectivity, Value Judgment, and Theory Choice." In *Scientific Knowledge*, ed. Jamet Kourany. Belmont, Calif.: Wadsworth Publishing Company, 1987.

———. *The Structure of Scientific Revolutions*, 2d ed. Chicago: University of Chicago Press, 1970.

Kuklick, Bruce. "Seven Thinkers and How They Grew: Descartes, Spinoza, Leibniz; Locke, Berkeley, Hume; Kant." In Richard Rorty, J. B. Schneewind, and Quentin Skinner, eds., *Philosophy in History: Essays on the Historiography of Philosophy*. Cambridge: Cambridge University Press, 1984, pp. 125–139.

———. "Studying the History of American Philosophy." *Transactions of the Charles S. Peirce Society: A Quarterly Journal in American Philosophy* 18, no. 1 (1982): 18–33.

Kuntz, Paul G. "The Dialectic of Historicism and Anti-Historicism." *The Monist* 53, no. 4 (1969): 656–669.

Kupperman, Joel J. "Precision in History." *Mind* 84 (1975): 374–389.

LaCapra, Dominick. "Rethinking Intellectual History and Reading Texts." In Dominick LaCapra and Steven L. Kaplan, eds., *Modern European Intellectual History: Reappraisals and New Perspectives.* Ithaca, N.Y., and London: Cornell University Press, 1982, pp. 47–85.

———, and Steven L. Kaplan, eds. *Modern European Intellectual History: Reappraisals and New Perspectives.* Ithaca, N.Y., and London: Cornell University Press, 1982.

Lafrance, Yvon. "La méthode positive en histoire de la philosophie: Résponse à MM. Leroux, Boss et Bodéüs." *Carrefour* 10 (1988): 62–84.

———. *Méthode et exégèse en histoire de la philosophie.* Montréal: Les Éditions Bellarmin, 1983.

Lakatos, Imre. *Proofs and Refutations: The Logic of Mathematical Discovery,* ed. J. Warrall and E. Zahar. Cambridge: Cambridge University Press, 1976.

Lamprecht, Sterling P. "Historiography of Philosophy." *Journal of Philosophy* 36 (1939): 449–460.

Lang, Helen S. "Philosophy as Text and Context," *Philosophy and Rhetoric* 18 (1985): 158–170.

Lange, Erchard, and F. Lindner. "Tasks and Findings of the Investigation into the History of Philosophy." *Deutsche Zeitschrift für Philosophie* 29 (1981): 944–950.

Lavine, T. Z., and V. Tejera, eds. *History and Anti-History in Philosophy.* Dordrecht: Kluwer Academic Publishers, 1989.

LePore, Ernest, ed. *Truth and Interpretation.* London: Basil Blackwell, 1986.

Leroux, Georges. "Questions de méthode en histoire de la philosophie." *Carrefour* 10 (1988): 11–27.

Levi, Arthur W. "The Biographical Sources of Wittgenstein's Ethics." *Telos* 38 (1978–1979): 63–76.

Levinson, Jerrold. "What a Musical Work Is." *Journal of Philosophy* 77, no. 1 (1980): 5–28.

Lewis, C. S. "On the Reading of Old Books." In *First and Second Things: Essays on Theology and Ethics,* ed. Walter Hooper. Glasgow: Collins, 1985, pp. 25–33.

Leyden, W. von. "Philosophy and Its History." *Proceedings of the Aristotelian Society* 54 (1953–1954): 187–208.

Ligoto, C. R., and Robert Strassfeld. "Bibliography of Works in the Philosophy of History 1973–1977." *History and Theory,* Beiheft 18 (1979): 1–111.

Lovejoy, Arthur O. *Essays in the History of Ideas.* Baltimore: Johns Hopkins University Press, 1948.

———. "The Historiography of Ideas." *Proceedings of the American Philosophical Society* 78 (1938): 529–543. Reprinted in Arthur O. Lovejoy, *Essays in the History of Ideas*. Baltimore: The Johns Hopkins University Press, 1948, pp. 1–13.

———. "Introduction: The Study of the History of Ideas." In *The Great Chain of Being*. Cambridge, Mass.: Harvard University Press, 1936, pp. 3–23.

———. "Present Standpoints and Past History." Reprinted in Hans Meyerhoff, ed., *The Philosophy of History in Our Time*. Garden City, N.Y.: Anchor Books, 1959, pp. 173–187.

———. "On Some Conditions of Progress in Philosophical Inquiry," *Philosophical Review* 26 (1917): 123–63.

———. "Reflections on the History of Ideas." *Journal of the History of Ideas* 1, no. 1 (1940): 3–23. Reprinted in Philip P. Wiener and Aaron Noland, eds., *Ideas in Cultural Perspective*. New Brunswick, N.J.: Rutgers University Press, 1962, pp. 3–23.

———, and George Boas. *Primitivism and Related Ideas in Antiquity*. Baltimore: Johns Hopkins Unitversity Press, 1935.

McCormick, Peter. "Philosophical Discourses and Fictional Texts." In Anthony J. Cascardi, ed., *Literature and the Question of Philosophy*. Baltimore and London: Johns Hopkins University Press, 1987, pp. 52–73.

MacIntyre, Alasdair. "The Relationship of Philosophy to Its Past." In Richard Rorty, J. B. Schneewind, and Quentin Skinner, eds., *Philosophy in History: Essays on the Historiography of Philosophy*. Cambridge: Cambridge University Press, 1984, pp. 31–48.

Madden, Edward H. "Myers and James: A Philosophical Dialogue." In Peter H. Hare, ed., *Doing Philosophy Historically*. Buffalo, N.Y.: Prometheus Books, 1988, pp. 299–319.

Major, John S. "Myth, Cosmology, and the Origins of Chinese Science." *Journal of Chinese Philosophy* 5, no. 1 (1978): 1–20.

Makin, Stephen. "How Can We Find Out What Ancient Philosophers Said?" *Phronesis* 33, no. 2 (1988): 121–132.

Malusa, Luciano. "Le ricerche di storia della storiografia filosofica nel momento presente," *Rivista di Filosofia Neo-Scolastica* 71 (1979): 213–220.

Mandelbaum, Maurice H. "Causal Analysis in History." *Journal of the History of Ideas* 3, no. 1 (1942): 30–50.

———. "Historical Explanation: The Problem of 'Covering Laws'." *History and Theory* 1 (1961): 229–242.

———. "The History of Ideas, Intellectual History, and the History of Philosophy." *History and Theory*, Beiheft 5 (1965): 33–66.

———. "On the Historiography of Philosophy." *Philosophy Research Archives* 2. Bowling Green, Ohio: Philosophy Documentation Center, Bowling Green State University Press, 1976, pp. 708–744.

———. "The History of Philosophy: Some Methodological Issues." In *Philoso-*

phy, History, and the Sciences: Selected Critical Essays. Baltimore: Johns Hopkins University Press, 1984, pp. 120–130.

———. *Philosophy, History, and the Sciences: Selected Critical Essays*. Baltimore: Johns Hopkins University Press, 1984.

———. "The Presuppositions of Hayden White's *Metahistory*." In *Philosophy, History, and the Sciences: Selected Critical Essays*. Baltimore: Johns Hopkins University Press, 1984, pp. 97–111.

———. "Some Forms and Uses of Comparative History." In *Philosophy, History, and the Sciences: Selected Critical Essays*. Baltimore: Johns Hopkins University Press, 1984, pp. 131–144.

———. *The Problem of Historical Knowledge*. New York, Evanston, and London: Harper & Row, 1967.

Mandt, A. J. "The Inevitability of Pluralism: Philosophical Practice and Philosophical Excellence." In A. Cohen and M. Dascal, eds., *The Institution of Philosophy: A Discipline in Crisis*. LaSalle, Ill.: Open Court, 1989, pp. 77–101.

Marenbon, John. *Later Medieval Philosophy (1150–1350): An Introduction*. London and N.Y.: Routledge & Kegan Paul, 1987.

Margolis, Joseph. *The Language of Art and Art Criticism*. Detroit: Wayne State University Press, 1965.

———. "The Ontological Peculiarity of Works of Art." *Journal of Aesthetics and Art Criticism* 36, no. 1 (1977): 45–50.

———. "Reinterpreting Interpretation." *Journal of Aesthetics and Art Criticism* 47, no. 3 (1989): 237–251.

———. "Works of Art as Physically Embodied and Culturally Emergent Entities." *British Journal of Aesthetics* 14, no. 3 (1974): 187–196.

Marías, J. "Introducción." In *Historia de la Filosofía*. Madrid: Revista de Occidente, 1941. Reprinted in *Obras*, vol. 1 (Madrid: Revista de Occidente, 1958).

———. *Introducción a la Filosofía*. Madrid: Revista de Occidente, 1947. Reprinted in *Obras*, vol. 2 (Madrid: Revista de Occidente, 1958).

Mash, Roy. "How Important for Philosophers Is the History of Philosophy?" *History and Theory* 26, no. 3 (1987): 287–299.

Matthews, Robert J. "Describing and Interpreting a Work of Art." *Journal of Aesthetics and Art Criticism* 36, no. 1 (1977): 5–14.

McKeon, Richard. *Selections from Medieval Philosophers*, vol. 1. N.Y.: Charles Scribner's Sons, 1957.

———. "Plato and Aristotle as Historians: A Study of Method in the History of Ideas." *Ethics* 51 (1940): 66–101. Rev. and republished as Chapter 2, "Truth and the History of Ideas." In *Thought, Action and Passion*. Chicago: University of Chicago Press, 1954, pp. 54–88.

Meiland, Jack W. "Interpretation as a Cognitive Discipline." *Philosophy and Literature* 2, no. 1 (1978): 23–45.

———. *Scepticism and Historical Knowledge*. N.Y.: Random House, 1965.

Mehta, J. L. *Martin Heidegger: The Way and the Vision*. Honolulu: University Press of Hawaii, 1976.

Michelfelder, Diane P., and Richard E. Palmer, eds. *Dialogue and Deconstruction: The Gadamer-Derrida Encounter*. Albany: SUNY Press, 1989.

Mill, John Stuart. *Dissertations and Discussions*. N.Y.: Henry Holt, 1882.

Milligan, John D. "The Treatment of an Historical Source." *History and Theory* 18 (1979): 177–196.

Minnis, A. J. *Medieval Theory of Authorship: Scholastic Literary Attitudes in the Later Middle Ages*. London: Scholar Press, 1984.

———, and A. B. Scott, eds., with the assistance of David Wallace. *Medieval Literary Theory and Criticism c.1100–c.1375: The Commentary-Tradition*. Oxford: Clarendon Press, 1988.

Mittelstrass, Jürgen. "Das Interesse der Philosophie an Ihrer Geschichte." *Studia Philosophica* 36 (1976): 3–15.

Mondolfo, Rodolfo. *Problemas y métodos de la investigación en historia de la filosofía*. Tucuman: Universidad de Tucumán, 1949.

Moreau, J. "L'histoire de la philosophie, l'historien et le philosophe." In *L'homme et l'histoire*. Paris: Presses Universitaires de France, 1952, p. 373–379.

Morgan, Michael L. "Authorship and the History of Philosophy," *Review of Metaphysics* 42, no. 2 (1988): 327–355.

———. "The Goals and Methods of the History of Philosophy" *Review of Metaphysics* 40 (1987): 717–732.

Morton, Bruce N. "Beardsley's Conception of the Aesthetic Object." *Journal of Aesthetics and Art Criticism* 32, no. 3 (1974): 385–396.

Mulhern, J. J. "Treatises, Dialogues, and Interpretation." *The Monist* 53, no. 4 (1969): 631–641.

Murphey, Murray G. "Toward an Historicist History of American Philosophy." *Transactions of the Charles S. Peirce Society: A Quarterly Journal in American Philosophy* 15, no. 1 (1979): 3–18.

Nadel, S. F. *The Foundations of Social Anthropology*. London: Cohen & West, 1951.

Nagel, Ernest. *The Structure of Science: Problems in the Logic of Scientific Explanation*. N.Y.: Harcourt, Brace and World, 1961.

Nehamas, Alexander. "The Postulated Author: Critical Monism as a Regulative Ideal." *Critical Inquiry* 8, no. 1 (1981): 133–149.

———. "What an Author Is." *Journal of Philosophy* 83, no. 11 (1986): 685–691.

———. "Word, Text, Work, Author." In Anthony J. Cascardi, ed., *Literature and the Question of Philosophy*. Baltimore: Johns Hopkins Press, 1987, pp. 267–291.

Nelson, Leonard. "What Is the History of Philosophy?" *Ratio* 4, no. 1 (1962): 22–35.

Nietzsche, Friedrich. *The Use and Abuse of History*, trans. Adrian Collins. In Oscar Levy, ed., *The Complete Works of Friedrich Nietzsche*, vol. 5, part 2. N.Y.: Russell and Russell, Inc., 1964, pp. 1–100.

Nordin, Svante. *Interpretation and Method: Studies in the Explication of Literature*. Lund: Akademisk Avhandling, 1978.

Oehler, Klaus. "Der Entwicklungsgedanke als heuristisches Prinzip der Philosophiegeschicte." *Zeitschrift für philosophische Forschung* 17 (1963): 604–613.

O'Hear, Anthony. "The History that Is in Philosophy." *Inquiry* 28, no. 4 (1985): 455–466.

Oja, Matt F. "Fictional History and Historical Fiction: Solzhenitsyn and Kis as Exemplars." *History and Theory* 27, no. 2 (1988): 111–124.

Olafson, Frederick A. *The Dialectic of Action: A Philosophical Interpretation of History and the Humanities.* Chicago: University of Chicago Press, 1979.

Olsen, Stein Haugom. "Interpretation and Intention." *British Journal of Aesthetics* 17, no. 3 (1977): 210–218.

Ortega y Gasset, José. "History as a System," trans. William C. Atkinson. In Raymond Klibansky and Herbert James Paton, eds., *Philosophy and History.* New York, Evanston, and London: Harper & Row, 1963, pp. 283–322.

———. *El hombre y la gente.* In *Obras Completas,* vol. 7. Madrid: Revista de Occidente, 1964.

———. "A dos ensayos de historiografía." In *Obras Completas,* vol. 6. Madrid: Revista de Occidente, 1947, pp. 357–359.

———. "Ideas para una historia de la filosofía," Preface to Émile Bréhier's *Historia de la filosofía.* Buenos Aires: Sudamericana, 1942. Reprinted in *Obras Completas,* vol. 6. Madrid: Revista de Occidente, 1947, pp. 379–419.

———. "A 'Historia de la filosofía,' de Karl Vorländer." In *Obras Completas,* vol. 6. Madrid: Revista de Occidente, 1947, pp. 292–300.

Parkinson, George Henry Radcliffe. *Logic and Reality in Leibniz's Metaphysics.* Oxford: Clarendon Press, 1965.

Passmore, John Arthur. "The Idea of a History of Philosophy," *History and Theory,* Beiheft 5 (1965): 1–32.

———. "Philosophy, Historiography of." In P. Edwards, ed., *Encyclopedia of Philosophy* 6. New York, London: Macmillan 1967, pp. 226–230.

Peperzak, A. "On the Unity of Systematic Philosophy and History of Philosophy." In T. Z. Lavine and V. Tejera, eds., *History and Anti-History in Philosophy.* Dordrecht: Kluwer Academic Pubs., 1989, pp. 19–31.

Pereyra, Carlos. "Objeto teórico de la historia de la filosofía," *Diánoia* 31 (1985): 143–153.

Plantinga, Alvin. "The Boethian Compromise." *American Philosophical Quarterly* 15 (1978): 129–138.

Plotinus. *The Essential Plotinus: Representative Treatises from the Enneads,* ed. and trans. Elmer O'Brien. Indianapolis: Hackett Publishing Co., 1975.

Poincaré, H. *Science et Méthode.* Paris: Flammarion, 1908.

Pólya, G. "The Teaching of Mathematics and the Biogenetic Law." In I. J. Good, ed., *The Scientist Speculates.* London: Heinemann, 1962.

Popkin, Richard H. "Philosophy and the History of Philosophy." *Journal of Philosophy* 82, no. 11 (1985): 625–632.

Popper, Karl Raimund. *The Poverty of Historicism.* London: Routledge & Kegan Paul, 1957.

Porter, Dale H. *The Emergence of the Past: A Theory of Historical Explanation.* Chicago: University of Chicago Press, 1981.

Poster, Mark. "The Future According to Foucault: *The Archaeology of Knowledge* and Intellectual History." In Dominick LaCapra and Steven L. Kaplan, eds., *Modern European Intellectual History: Reappraisals and New Perspectives.* Ithaca, N.Y., and London: Cornell University Press, 1982, pp. 137–152.

Power, Lawrence H. "On Philosophy and Its History." *Philosophical Studies* 50, no. 1 (1986): 1–38.

Putnam, Hilary. "Why Is a Philosopher?" In A. Cohen and M. Dascal, eds., *The Institution of Philosophy: A Discipline in Crisis.* LaSalle, Ill.: Open Court, 1989, pp. 61–75.

Randall, John Herman, Jr. *How Philosophy Uses Its Past.* N.Y.: Columbia University Press, 1963.

———. *Nature and Historical Experience.* N.Y.: Columbia University Press, 1958.

———. "On Understanding the History of Philosophy." *Journal of Philosophy* 36 (1939): 460–474.

Ranke, Leopold von. *Geschichten der romanischen und germanischen Völker von 1494 bis 1514,* 3d. ed. Leipzig: Duncker and Humblot, 1885.

Rauche, G. A. "Systematic Aspects of the History of Philosophy." *Man and World* 6 (1973): 63–78.

Rée, Jonathan. "History, Philosophy, and Interpretation: Some Reactions to Jonathan Bennett's *Study of Spinoza's 'Ethics'.*" In Peter H. Hare, ed., *Doing Philosophy Historically.* Buffalo, N.Y.: Prometheus Books, 1988, pp. 44–61.

———. "Philosophy and the History of Philosophy." In Jonathan Rée, Michael Ayers, and Adam Westoby, *Philosophy and Its Past.* Hassocks, Sussex: Harvester Press, 1978, pp. 1–39.

———, Michael Ayers, and Adam Westoby. *Philosophy and Its Past.* Hassocks, Sussex: Harvester Press, 1978.

Ricoeur, Paul. "Explanation and Understanding: On Some Remarkable Connections among the Theory of the Text, Theory of Action, and Theory of History." In Charles E. Reagan and David Stewart, eds., *The Philosophy of Paul Ricoeur: An Anthology of His Work.* Boston: Beacon Press, 1978, pp. 149–166.

———. "L'histoire de la philosophie et l'unité du vrai." In *Histoire et vérité.* 2d ed. Paris: Éditions du Seuil, 1964, pp. 581–613.

———. *Interpretation Theory: Discourse and the Surplus of Meaning.* Austin: University of Texas Press, 1976.

———. "On Interpretation." In Kenneth Baynes et al., eds. *After Philosophy: End or Transformation?* Cambridge and London: The MIT Press, 1988, pp. 357–380.

———. "The Model of the Text: Meaningful Action Considered as a Text." In Paul Rabinow and William M. Sullivan, eds., *Interpretive Social Science: A Reader.* Berkeley: University of California Press, 1979, pp. 73–101.

———. "Narrative Time." *Critical Inquiry* 7, no. 1 (1980): 169–190.
———. "Structure, Word, Event." In Charles E. Reagan and David Stewart, eds. *The Philosophy of Paul Ricoeur: An Anthology of His Work.* Boston: Beacon Press, 1978), pp. 109–133.
———. *Time and Narrative,* trans. Kathleen McLaughlin and David Pellauer. Chicago: University of Chicago Press, 1984–1988.
———. "What Is a Text? Explanation and Interpretation." In *Mythic-Symbolic Language and Philosophical Anthropology,* trans. D. M. Rasmussen. Dordrecht: Martinus Nijhoff, 1971.
Ritchie, Robert W., ed. *New Directions in Mathematics.* Englewood Cliffs, N.J.: Prentice-Hall, 1964. See panel discussion on "New Directions in College Mathematics."
Robin, Leon. "L'histoire et la légende de la philosophie." *Revue Philosophique de la France et de l'Étranger* 120 (1935): 161–175.
———. "Sur la notion d'histoire de la philosophie." *Société Française de la Philosophie, Bulletin* 36 (1936): 103–106. Discussion by M. M. Baruzi, Brunschvieg, Berre, Ducassé, Etard, Koyré, Levy, Parodi, Schrecker, and Wahl, pp. 106–140.
Robinet, André. "De l'histoire comme technique presupposée a toute activité créatrice en philosophie." *Études Philosophiques* 12, no. 3 (1957): 405–409.
Robinson, John Mansley. *An Introduction to Early Greek Philosophy.* Boston: Houghton Mifflin Co., 1968.
Robinson, Richard. *Plato's Earlier Dialectic,* 2d ed. Oxford: Oxford University Press, 1962.
Roger Bacon. *Communia.* In *Opera haetenus inedita Rogeri Baconi,* fasc. 2, *Liber primus Communium naturalium fratris Rogeri,* ed. Robert Steele. Oxford: Clarendon Press, 1905?
Romero, Francisco. *La estructura de la historia de la filosofía.* Buenos Aires: Losada, 1967.
———. *Sobre la historia de la filosofía.* Tucuman, Argentina: Universidad de Tucumán, 1943.
Rorty, Richard. "The Historiography of Philosophy: Four Genres." In Richard Rorty, J. B. Schneewind and Quentin Skinner, eds., *Philosophy in History: Essays on the Historiography of Philosophy.* Cambridge: Cambridge University Press, 1984, pp. 49–75.
———. *Philosophy and the Mirror of Nature.* Princeton, N.J.: Princeton University Press, 1979.
———. "Philosophy as Science, as Metaphor, and as Politics." In A. Cohen and M. Dascal, eds., *The Institution of Philosophy: A Discipline in Crisis.* LaSalle, Ill.: Open Court, 1989, pp. 13–33.
Rorty, Richard, J. B. Schneewind, and Quentin Skinner, eds. *Philosophy in History: Essays on the Historiography of Philosophy.* Cambridge: Cambridge University Press, 1984.
Rosen, Stanley. *Plato's "Symposium"*, 2d. ed. New Haven, Conn., and London: Yale University Press, 1987.
———. "The Limits of Interpretation." In Anthony J. Cascardi, ed., *Literature*

and the Question of Philosophy. Baltimore and London: Johns Hopkins University Press, 1987, pp. 210–410.

Rosenblatt, Louise M. *The Reader, the Text, the Poem: The Transactional Theory of the Literary Work.* Carbondale and Edwardsville: Southern Illinois University Press, 1978.

Russell, Bertrand. "Preface to the First Edition." *The Philosophy of Leibniz,* 2d ed. London: George Allen and Unwin, Ltd., 1937, pp. xi–xv.

Saksena, S. K. "Is There a History of Philosophy?" *Philosophical Quarterly* (Amalner, India) 22 (1949–1950): 1–13.

Santinello, Giovanni. "Note sulla storiografia filosofica nell'età moderna." In *La storiografia filosofica e la sua storia.* Padua: Editrice Antenore, 1982, pp. 103–128.

Sass, Hans-Martin. "Philosophische Positionen in der Philosophiegeschichtsschreibung. Ein Forschungsbericht." *Deutsche Vierteljahresschrift für Literaturwissenschaft und Geistesgeschichte* 46, no. 3 (1972): 539–567.

Schmidt, Alfred. *History and Structure. An Essay on Hegelian-Marxist and Structuralist Theories of History.* Cambridge: MIT Press, 1981.

Schmitz, Kenneth L. "The History of Philosophy as Actual Philosophy." *Journal of Philosophy* 85, no. 11 (1988): 673–674.

Schneewind, J. B. "The Divine Corporation and the History of Ethics." In Richard Rorty, J. B. Schneewind, and Quentin Skinner, eds., *Philosophy in History: Essays on the Historiography of Philosophy.* Cambridge: Cambridge University Press, 1984, pp. 173–191.

Sclafani, Richard J. "The Logical Primitiveness of the Concept of a Work of Art." *British Journal of Aesthetics* 15, no. 1 (1975): 14–28.

Scriven, Michael. "Increasing Philosophy Enrollments and Appointments through Better Philosophy Teaching." *Proceedings and Addresses of the American Philosophical Association* 50, no. 3 (1977): 232–234, and continued in 50, no. 4 (1977): 326–328.

———. "Truisms as the Grounds for Historical Explanations." In Patrick Gardiner, ed., *Theories of History.* Glencoe: Free Press, 1959, pp. 443–475.

Sebba, G. "What Is 'History of Philosophy'? I. Doctrinal and Historical Analysis." *Journal of the History of Philosophy* 8, no. 3 (1970): 251–262.

Sellars, Wilfrid. "Abstract Entities." In *Philosophical Perspectives.* Springfield, Ill.: Charles C Thomas, 1967

Shapiro, Gary. "Canons, Careers, and Campfollowers: Randall and the Historiography of Philosophy." *Transactions of the Charles S. Peirce Society: A Quarterly Journal in American Philosophy* 23, no. 1 (1987): 31–43.

Sherburne, Donald W., ed. *A Key to Whitehead's "Process and Reality."* Chicago: University of Chicago Press, 1966.

Shorey, Paul. *What Plato Said.* Chicago: University of Chicago Press, 1933.

Sindoni, Paola Ricci. "Teleology and Philosophical Historiography: Husserl and Jaspers." In Anna-Teresa Tymieniecka, ed., *Analecta Husserliana* 9. Dordrecht: Reidel, 1979, pp. 281–300.

Skinner, Quentin. "Conventions and the Understanding of Speech Acts." *Philosophical Quarterly* 20, no. 79 (1970): 118–138.

———. "Hermeneutics and the Role of History." *New Literary History* 7, 1 (1975): 209–232.

———. "Meaning and Understanding in the History of Ideas." *History and Theory* 8, no. 1 (1969): 3–53.

———. "Motives, Intentions and the Interpretation of Texts." *New Literary History* 3, no. 2 (1972): 393–408.

———. "On Performing and Explaining Linguistic Actions." *Philosophical Quarterly* 21, no. 82 (1971): 1–21.

Slinn, E. Warwick. "Deconstruction and Meaning: The Textuality Game." *Philosophy and Literature* 12 (1988): 80–87.

Smart, Harold Robert. *Philosophy and Its History*. La Salle, Ill.: Open Court, 1962.

Smith, Barry. "Austrian Origins of Logical Positivism." In B. Gower, ed., *Logical Positivism in Perspective*. London and Sydney: Croom, 1987; and Totowa: Barnes and Noble, 1988, pp. 35–68.

———. "On the Origins of Analytic Philosophy." *Grazer Philosophische Studien* 35 (1989): 153–173.

Spengler, Oswald. *The Decline of the West*. N.Y.: Alfred A. Knopf, special ed., 1939.

Stambovsky, Phillip. "Metaphor and Historical Understanding." *History and Theory* 27, no. 2 (1988): 125–134.

Stecker, Robert. "Apparent, Implied, and Postulated Authors." *Philosophy and Literature* 11, no. 2 (1987): 258–271.

Steig, Michael. "The Intentional Phallus: Determining Verbal Meaning in Literature." *Journal of Aesthetics and Art Criticism* 36, no. 1 (1977): 51–61.

Stern, Fritz. *The Varieties of History: From Voltaire to the Present*. N.Y.: World Publishing, 1956.

Stevenson, Charles L. "On the Reasons that Can Be Given for the Interpretation of a Poem." In Joseph Zalman Margolis, ed., *Philosophy Looks at the Arts*. N.Y.: Charles Scribner's Sons, 1962, pp. 121–139.

Stone, I. F. *The Trial of Socrates*. Boston: Little, Brown and Co., 1988.

Strawson, P. F. *Individuals*. Garden City, N.Y.: Doubleday and Company, 1963.

Suárez, Francisco. *Disputationes metaphysicae*. In *Opera omnia*, vols. 25 and 26, ed. Carolo Berton. Paris: Vivès, 1861.

Tanselle, Thomas. "Greg's Theory of the Copy-Text and the Editing of American Literature." *Studies in Bibliography* 28 (1975): 167–229.

Tatarkiewicz, Ladislas. "The History of Philosophy and the Art of Writing It." *Diogenes* 20 (1957): 52–67.

Taylor, Charles. "Philosophy and Its History." In Richard Rorty, J. B. Schneewind, and Quentin Skinner, eds., *Philosophy in History: Essays on the Historiography of Philosophy*. Cambridge: Cambridge University Press, 1984, pp. 17–30.

Teggart, F. J., ed. *The Idea of Progress*, rev. ed. Berkeley: University of California Press, 1949.

Tejera, Victor. "Introduction: On the Nature of Philosophic Historiography." In T. Z. Lavine and V. Tejera, eds., *History and Anti-History in Philosophy*. Dordrecht: Kluwer Academic Pubs., 1989, pp. 1–18.

Tennessen, Herman. "History Is Science: Preliminary Remarks toward an Empirical, Experimentally Oriented, Behavioural Science of History." *The Monist* 53, no. 1 (1969): 116–133.

Thayer, H. S. "The Philosophy of History and the History of Philosophy: Some Reflections on the Thought of John Herman Randall, Jr." *Transactions of the Charles S. Peirce Society: A Quarterly Journal in American Philosophy* 23, 1 (1987): 1–15.

Thierry of Chartres. *Commentum super Boethii librum de Trinitate*. In Nikolaus M. Häring, S. A. C., ed., *Commentaries on Boethius by Thierry of Chartres and His School*. Toronto: Pontifical Institute of Mediaeval Studies, 1971, pp. 55–116.

———. *Lectiones in Boethii librum de Trinitate*. In N. M. Häring, ed., *Commentaries on Boethius by Thierry of Chartres and His School*. Toronto: Pontifical Institute of Mediaeval Studies, 1971, pp. 123–230.

Thomas Aquinas. *On Being and Essence*, trans. Armand Maurer, 2d ed. Toronto: Pontifical Institute of Mediaeval Studies, 1968.

———. *De ente et essentia*, ed. M. D. Roland-Gosselin. Paris: J. Vrin, 1948.

———. *Expositio super librum Boethii de Trinitate*, ed. B. Decker. Leiden: Brill, 1959.

———. *Faith, Reason and Theology: Questions I–IV of His "Commentary on the 'de Trinitate' of Boethius,"* question 4, article 2, trans. Armand Maurer. Toronto: Pontifical Institute of Mediaeval Studies, 1987.

———. *De principio individuationis*. In R. Spiazzi, ed., *Opuscula philosophica*. Rome: Marietti, 1954, pp. 147–151.

———. *Summa theologiae*, ed. B. De Rubeis et al. Turin: Marietti, 1932.

Tolhurst, William E. "On What a Text Is and How It Means." *British Journal of Aesthetics* 19, no. 1 (1979): 3–14.

Tompfins, Jane P. *Reader-Response Criticism: From Formalism to Post-Structuralism*. Baltimore: Johns Hopkins University Press, 1980.

Tonelli, Giorgio. "A Contribution towards a Bibliography on the Methodology of the History of Philosophy." *Journal of the History of Philosophy* 10, no. 4 (1972): 456–458.

———. "Qu'est-ce que l'histoire de la philosophie?" *Revue Philosophique de la France et de l'Étranger* 152 (1962): 290–306.

Toynbee, Arnold Joseph. *A Study of History*. London: Oxford University Press, 1935–1961.

Veatch, Henry B. *Aristotle: A Contemporary Appreciation*. Bloomington and London: Indiana University Press, 1974.

———. "Response to Commentators." In Peter H. Hare, ed., *Doing Philosophy Historically*. Buffalo, N.Y.: Prometheus Books, 1988, pp. 127–136.

———. "Introduction: On Trying to Be an Aristotelian or a Thomist in

Today's World." In *Swimming Against the Current in Contemporary Philosophy: Occasional Essays and Papers.* Washington, D.C.: Catholic University of America Press, 1990, pp. 1–20.

Vegas González, Serafín. "Un papel para la historia de la filosofía." *Pensamiento* 37 (1981): 257–286.

Vico, Giovanni Battista. *The New Science,* trans. from the 3d ed. [1744] Thomas Goddard Bergin and Max Harold Fisch. Garden City, N.Y.: Anchor Books, 1961.

Voltaire. "Conseils à un journaliste." In M. Adrien Jean Quentin Beuchot, ed., *Ouvres de Voltaire,* vol. 37. Paris: Lefèvre, 1829–1840, pp. 362–367.

———. "Da l'utilité de l'histoire." In *Dictionnaire philosophique.* In M. Adrien Jean Quentin Beuchot, ed., *Ouvres de Voltaire,* vol. 30. Paris: Lefèvre, 1829–1840, pp. 207–209.

Wachterhauser, Brice R. "Interpreting Texts: Objectivity or Participation?" *Man and World* 19 (1986): 439–457.

Walsh, W. H. *An Introduction to Philosophy of History.* London: Hutchinson's University Library, 1951.

Walton, Craig. "Bibliography of the Historiography and Philosophy of the History of Philosophy." *International Studies in Philosophy* 19 (1977): 135–166.

Warnke, Georgia. *Gadamer: Hermeneutics, Tradition and Reason.* Stanford, Calif.: Stanford University Press, 1987.

Watson, Richard A. "Method in the History of Philosophy." Ch. 1 of *The Breakdown of Cartesian Metaphysics.* Atlantic Highlands, N.J.: Humanities Press International, 1987, pp. 3–17.

———. "A Short Discourse on Method in the History of Philosophy." *Southwestern Journal of Philosophy* 11, no. 2 (1980): 7–24.

Weisheipl, James A. *Friar Thomas D'Aquino: His Life, Thought and Work.* Garden City, N.Y.: Doubleday and Co., 1974.

Weitz, Morris D. *Hamlet and the Philosophy of Literary Criticism.* Chicago: University of Chicago Press, 1964.

———. *Philosophy of the Arts.* Cambridge, Mass.: Harvard University Press, 1950.

White, Hayden V. *Metahistory: The Historical Imagination in Nineteenth-Century Europe.* Baltimore: Johns Hopkins University Press, 1973.

———. "Method and Ideology in Intellectual History: The Case of Henry Adams." In Dominick LaCapra and Steven L. Kaplan, eds., *Modern European Intellectual History: Reappraisals and New Perspectives.* Ithaca, N.Y., and London: Cornell University Press, 1982, pp. 280–310.

———. "The Question of Narrativity in Contemporary Historical Theory." *History and Theory* 23, 1 (1984): 1–33.

———. "Rhetoric and History." In Hayden V. White and Frank E. Manuel, *Theories of History.* Los Angeles: William Andrews Clark Memorial Library, 1978, pp. 3–25.

———. "The Tasks of Intellectual History." *The Monist* 53, no. 4 (1969): 606–630.

———. *Tropics of Discourse; Essays in Cultural Criticism.* Baltimore: Johns Hopkins University Press, 1978.

White, M. G. *Foundations of Historical Knowledge.* N.Y.: Harper & Row, 1965.

Whitehead, Alfred North. *Process and Reality,* ed. D. R. Griffin and D. W. Sherburne. New York: Free Press, 1979.

Wiener, Philip P., ed. *Dictionary of the History of Ideas.* New York: Charles Scribner's Sons, 1973.

———. "Logical Significance of the History of Thought." *Journal of the History of Ideas* 7, no. 3 (1946): 366–373.

———. "Some Problems and Methods in the History of Ideas." *Journal of the History of Ideas* 22, no. 4 (1961): 531–548. Reprinted in Philip P. Wiener and Aaron Noland, eds., *Ideas in Cultural Perspective.* New Brunswick, N.J.: Rutgers University Press, 1962, pp. 24–41.

Williams, W. H. "Comment on John Yolton's 'Is There a History of Philosophy? Some Difficulties and Suggestions.'" *Synthese* 67, no. 1 (1986): 23–32.

Wilsmore, Susan. "The Literary Work Is Not Its Text." *Philosophy and Literature* 11 (1987): 307–316.

Wimsatt, William K., Jr., and Monroe C. Beardsley. "The Intentional Fallacy." In Joseph Zalman Margolis, ed., *Philosophy Looks at the Arts.* New York: Charles Scribner's Sons, 1962, pp. 91–105.

Winch, Peter. *The Idea of a Social Science and Its Relation to Philosophy.* London: Routledge and Kegan Paul, 1958.

———. "Understanding a Primitive Society." *American Philosophical Quarterly* 1 (1964): 307–324.

Windelband, Wilhelm. *A History of Philosophy,* trans. James H. Tufts. New York: Harper and Brothers, 1958.

Wittgenstein, Ludwig. *Notebooks, 1914–16,* ed. G. H. von Wright and G. E. M. Anscombe, trans. G. E. M. Anscombe. Oxford: Basil Blackwell, 1961.

Wolff, Christian. *Preliminary Discourse on Philosophy in General,* trans. Richard J. Blackwell. Indianapolis and New York: Bobbs-Merrill Co., 1963.

Wollheim, Richard. *Art and Its Objects.* New York: Harper & Row, 1968.

Wolterstorff, Nicholas. "Toward an Ontology of Art Works." *Nous* 9, no. 2 (1975): 115–142.

Wood, Alan. "Russell's Philosophy: A Study of Its Development." In Bertrand Russell, *My Philosophical Development.* London: George Allen & Unwin Ltd., 1959, pp. 190–205.

Wood, Robert E., ed. *The Future of Metaphysics.* Chicago: Quadrangle Books, 1970.

Yolton, John W. "Is There a History of Philosophy? Some Difficulties and Suggestions." *Synthese* 67, no. 1 (1986): 3–21.

———. "Some Remarks on the Historiography of Philosophy." *Journal of the History of Philosophy* 23, no. 4 (1985): 571–578.

Zea, Leopoldo. *Positivism in Mexico,* trans. Josephine H. Schulte. Austin: University of Texas Press, 1974.

Zubiri, Xavier. "El saber filosófico y su historia." *Cruz y Raya* (Madrid). Reprinted in *Naturaleza, historia, Dios.* Madrid: Revista de Occidente, 1944.

Index of Authors

Only the names of authors, editors, and translators of texts have been recorded in this index. Authors of works in the arts have not been included. The bibliography has not been indexed.

Index of Subjects